NEW PROCLAMATION

YEAR B, 2006

EASTER THROUGH PENTECOST

BERNARD BRANDON SCOTT
MATTHEW L. SKINNER
ADELE STILES RESMER
RONALD J. ALLEN

DAVID B. LOTT, EDITOR

FORTRESS PRESS
MINNEAPOLIS

NEW PROCLAMATION
Year B, 2006
Easter through Pentecost

Since the different lectionary traditions often provide several alternative texts, for space con-siderations, authors have chosen in some cases to comment only on one option. We encour-age the reader to consult earlier editions of *New Proclamation* or to visit the Web site www.FortressPress.com for additional commentary.

The Library of Congress has catalogued this series as follows.
New proclamation year A, 2001–2002: Advent through Holy Week / Francis J. Moloney . . . [et al.].

      p. cm.
  Includes bibliographical references.
  ISBN 0-8006-4245-7 (alk. paper)
      1. Church year. I. Moloney, Francis J.
  BV30 .N48 2001
  251'.6—dc21   2001023746

New Proclamation, Year B, 2006, Easter through Pentecost
ISBN 0-8006-4254-6

The paper used in this publication meets the minimum requirements of American National Standard for Information Sciences—Permanence of Paper for Printed Library Materials, ANSI Z329.48-1984.

Manufactured in the U.S.A.
10   09   08   07   06   1   2   3   4   5   6   7   8   9   10

CONTENTS

THE SEASON OF PENTECOST
ADELE STILES RESMER

THE SEASON OF PENTECOST
RONALD J. ALLEN

PREFACE

New Proclamation continues the time-honored Fortress Press practice of offering a lectionary preaching resource that provides first-rate biblical exegetical aids for a variety of lectionary traditions. This present volume covers the lections for the second half of the church year, Easter Morning through Pentecost, which culminates with the Sunday of Christ the King/Sovereign Ruler, and also includes comments on texts assigned for the Ascension of Our Lord, the Episcopal and Roman Catholic celebrations of the Transfiguration, Reformation Day, All Saints Day, and Thanksgiving Day.

Thoroughly ecumenical and built around the three-year lectionary cycle, *New Proclamation* focuses on the biblical texts, based on the conviction that acquiring a deeper understanding of the pericopes in both their historical and liturgical contexts is the best means for preachers to be informed and inspired to deliver engaging and effective sermons. For this reason, the most capable North American biblical scholars and homileticians are invited to contribute to *New Proclamation*.

Although we provide contributors with common instructions and a general "template" for their writing, each is given the freedom to alter and improve that pattern in ways they think will be most helpful to the user. What is most important is that the biblical texts themselves, set in their liturgical context, provide the basis on which each writer determines the format they choose to follow. So, for example, you will note that some authors split their comments into sections on "Interpreting the Text" and "Responding to the Text." In other instances, some authors have chosen to combine those two dimensions into a single section. Since the different lectionary traditions often provide several alternative texts, for space considerations, authors have chosen in some cases to comment only on one option. We encourage the reader to consult earlier editions of *New Proclamation* or to visit the Web site www.FortressPress.com for additional commentary.

In general, *New Proclamation* is planned and designed to be user-friendly in the following ways:

- *New Proclamation* is published in two volumes per year, with a lay-flat binding, a large, workbook-style page, and space for making notes.

- Each season of the church year is prefaced by an introduction that provides insights into the background and spiritual significance of the period, as well as ideas for planning one's preaching during the season.

- The application of biblical texts to contemporary situations is an important concern of each contributor. Exegetical work is concise, and thoughts on how the texts address today's world, congregational issues, and personal situations have a prominent role.

- Although the assigned psalms ("Responsive Reading") are infrequently used as preaching texts, brief comments on each are included so that the preacher can incorporate reflections also on these in the sermon. The psalms, for the most part, represent the congregation's response to the first reading and are not intended as another reading.

- Boxed quotations in the margins help signal important themes in the texts for the day.

- The material for Year B is here dated specifically for 2006 for easy coordination with other dated lectionary materials. However, we hope the text itself has a timeless quality so that preachers can keep these volumes on their shelves and refer to them in future years for preaching inspiration.

- These materials can be adapted for uses other than for corporate worship on the day indicated. They are well suited for adult discussion groups or personal meditation and reflection.

The contributors to this latest volume of New Proclamation represent both established and newer scholars in the fields of New Testament and homiletics, as well as a variety of Protestant faith traditions. Bernard Brandon Scott and Ronald Allen will undoubtedly be familiar to many readers for their many acclaimed writings in biblical studies and preaching. They each tackle some of the lectionaries' most difficult texts with uncommon, and sometimes provocative, insight, as well as extraordinary sensitivity to the anti-Semitic traditions that have attached themselves to certain texts. Matthew Skinner and Adele Stiles Resmer, though likely less well known, represent the sort of exciting "new" voices that we are continuing to seek out for *New Proclamation*. Their solid and thoughtful aids stand in line with the very best this series has to offer and preachers will surely appreciate their invigorating dedication to the Word and its proclamation. We are grateful to each of these contributors for their insights and their commitment to effective Christian preaching, and we are confident that you will find in this volume ideas, stimulation, and encouragement for your ministry of proclamation.

David B. Lott

THE SEASON OF EASTER

BERNARD
BRANDON
SCOTT

I n these weeks of Easter we confront the central mystery of our faith, the death
and resurrection of Jesus. This is not an easy task, since what resurrection means
is not always obvious. That is to be expected, because resurrection is a mystery.
Like us, early Christian communities were trying to bring to language something
that is beyond language, yet language is all we have.

Resurrection is about God, Jesus, and us. About what God has done and is
doing in Jesus. About the conviction that Jesus yet lives. About our experience that
convicts us of Jesus' continuing presence.

Many of the important texts for indicating how various New Testament writings understand resurrection are in the lectionary. Unfortunately, the lectionary
is not a particularly helpful vehicle in this task. The ordering of the texts is not
helpful, and some important texts are missing, for instance, most of 1 Corinthians
15, the earliest discussion of resurrection. The majority of the lectionary Gospel
readings for Easter come from the Third and Fourth Gospels, the latest New Testament texts. A preacher should attend to all these issues.

Pericope reading often disembodies the scriptures so that we fail to see how
readings fit into the whole from which they have been ripped. Often they serve
liturgical needs that are at odds with their evangelical context. This gives the
readings an ahistorical, disembodied character. A preacher must restore a reading to its original context so that an audience can engage it as a real community

I

struggling with real issues. To facilitate that, I have emphasized understanding the text in context. You are in the best position to translate it to the actual experience of your community.

None of the Gospel texts are eyewitness reports, so they must be situated in their historical contexts. They are not windows into the events of 30 or 33 C.E., the first Easter morning, but illuminate and reflect the communities that gave them birth. To ignore this is to create a fantasy text that takes us back to an imagined Easter morning. Thus, I attempt to interpret the texts as about the community experience contemporary to the text, not about Easter Day. Only in this way can we begin to see that the New Testament texts are always struggling to make sense of their continuing experience of the risen Jesus. Easter did not happen on the third day. It happens every day. The task of preaching is to rediscover and announce that ongoing Easter.

New Testament views of resurrection are more fluid and diverse than ours. We basically use one term, resurrection, to stand for the church's experience and conviction of Jesus' being alive. But early Christians used a variety of models. Resurrection is based on the metaphor of rising from sleep or standing up. Another model was exaltation, for instance, Phil. 2:6-11, or in the Gospel of John. Others employed the notion of God vindicating God's martyrs (Q and Mark), and still others thought in terms of translation or assumption (the empty tomb). These models are not contradictory, and a single author can use more than one model. They represent different ways to use the available cultural models within Judaism to express and understand what the early communities were experiencing. The experience precedes its designation or naming. Preaching should help overcome our impoverished view of resurrection.

> EASTER DID NOT HAPPEN ON THE THIRD DAY. IT HAPPENS EVERY DAY. THE TASK OF PREACHING IS TO REDISCOVER AND ANNOUNCE THAT ONGOING EASTER.

Given the problems with understanding resurrection, I have put the major emphasis on those New Testament texts that explicitly deal with the topic. As I mentioned above, the order in the lectionary makes it difficult to understand the unfolding and at times contrary views of resurrection in the New Testament. For your own guidance I suggest reading the texts and my commentary in the following order as a way of grasping what the New Testament has to say about resurrection. This arranges the important texts in chronological order.

1 Corinthians 15
    Second reading, Easter Morning
Luke 24:36-48
    Gospel, Third Sunday of Easter, "Flesh and Bones"

Mark 16
    Gospel, Easter Morning
John 20
    Gospel, Easter Morning
    Gospel, Second Sunday of Easter
Luke 24:13-49
    Gospel, Easter Evening
Luke 24:36-48
    Gospel, Third Sunday of Easter
Luke 24:44-53
    Gospel, the Ascension of Our Lord

Since the Hebrew Bible did not envision the resurrection of its Messiah, we must first understand these readings within their context in Israel's life. Christian usurpation of Hebrew history has had a disastrous outcome. We who live after the Holocaust need to take seriously the role supersessionism has played in anti-Semitism. We can interpret these texts in a Christian sense, but only after acknowledging their primary Hebrew sense.[1]

Note

1. Two helpful books on avoiding supersessionism or anti-Semitism in preaching are Ronald J. Allen and Clark M. Williamson, *Preaching the Gospels without Blaming the Jews: A Lectionary Commentary* (Louisville: Westminster John Knox, 2004), and Marilyn J. Salmon, *Preaching without Contempt: Overcoming Unintended Anti-Judaism* (Minneapolis: Fortress Press, 2006 [forthcoming]).

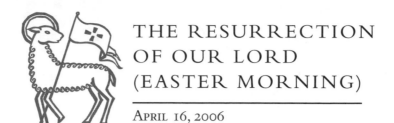

THE RESURRECTION OF OUR LORD (EASTER MORNING)

APRIL 16, 2006

REVISED COMMON	EPISCOPAL (BCP)	ROMAN CATHOLIC
Acts 10:34-43	Acts 10:34-43	Acts 10:34a, 37-43
or Is. 25:6-9	or Isa. 25:6-9	
Ps. 118:1-2, 14-24	Ps. 118:14-29	Ps. 118:1-2, 16-17,
	or 118:14-17,	22-33
	22-24	
1 Cor. 15:1-11	Col. 3:1-4	Col. 3:1-4
or Acts 10:34-43	or Acts 10:34-43	or 1 Cor. 5:6b-8
John 20:1-18	Mark 16:1-8	John 20:1-9
or Mark 16:1-8		or Mark 16:1-7

FIRST READING
ACTS 10:34-43 (RCL, BCP)
ACTS 10:34a, 37-43 (RC)

Traditionally throughout Eastertide, readings from the Acts of the Apostles replace the first reading from the Hebrew Bible. These readings from Acts focus our attention on the spread of the gospel from the tiny circle in Jerusalem to an ever-wider world.

This first reading comes from Peter's speech following his vision on his way to Joppa, to Cornelius's house. The Peter and Cornelius episode is central to the plot of Acts since it marks the early community's shift from Jerusalem to beyond Jerusalem and, more important, the expansion of the mission from Jews alone to Gentiles. It signals the ongoing emergence of an inclusive community. Peter reiterates this inclusive direction in his address before the Jerusalem council (11:1-18). The emphasis on Peter's action keeps this major shift in the church's mission under apostolic control.

This reading falls into three parts. The introduction (10:34-36) stresses God's impartiality based on Jesus' lordship. The middle section (10:37-43) briefly summarizes Christian preaching and the witness of the apostles. Following this preaching the Holy Spirit descends upon the Gentiles, and the witnesses who came with Peter are amazed (10:44-48). This three-part structure is, of course, the basic structure of the entire Acts of the Apostles here presented in miniature. This three-part structure—God shows no partiality, the preaching and witness, the coming of the Spirit—is repeated over and over again in Acts and should never be lost sight of when reading Acts.

The translation "God shows no partiality" (10:34) is accurate, although it renders abstractly what is a much more concrete image in the Greek. The word (*prosopolemptes*) translated "partiality" is, literally, "taker or welcomer of face," and "face" is often used as a word for a person—that is, the face *is* the person, where the part stands for the whole. So the phrase means "a respecter of persons." This is apparently a peculiarly Christian word. Paul uses another form of the word in Rom. 2:10-11 to make a similar point to the one here: "but glory and honor and peace for everyone who does good, the Jew first and also the Greek. For God shows no partiality." To respect a person's face or to respect a person is a primary value in the Mediterranean world. Loss of face or respect equals a loss of honor, a most important value in such a culture. The movie *The Godfather* has several great examples of the importance of face and honor in Mediterranean cultures. For example, when the mortician approaches Don Corleone for a favor, the Don reminds him of the time he dishonored the don and of the importance of honor.

To insist as Paul and Acts do that God is no respecter of persons, that God is impartial, creates a fundamental challenge to an honor/shame culture's notion of God, whether that be for Jews or pagans. A god in the ancient world was a god of the god's own people. Gods were quite localized. There were gods of Rome, of each city and tribe, and of powerful families. A family or a city was powerful because its god was powerful; thus, when a city or country was defeated, this meant either its gods were defeated or they had bestowed favor on another people.

Israel had wrestled with this localized notion of God for some time. Was Yahweh just the God of Israel or of all the nations? A broadening sense of God was one of the great achievements of Second Isaiah during the period of the Babylonian exile.

The first reading of Easter reminds us that the resurrection makes a universal claim on God's part. By the resurrection Jesus is made Lord of all, or as Paul has it, "In Christ God was reconciling the world to himself" (2 Cor. 5:19). God's impartiality does not mean a special favor upon

GOD'S IMPARTIALITY DOES NOT MEAN A SPECIAL FAVOR UPON US BUT A DEMAND THAT WE PROCLAIM WHAT HAS HAPPENED IN CHRIST AND BEAR WITNESS TO THE ACTIVITY OF THE HOLY SPIRIT.

6

THE SEASON
OF EASTER
──────
BERNARD
BRANDON
SCOTT

us but a demand that we proclaim what has happened in Christ and bear witness to the activity of the Holy Spirit.

The importance of the Cornelius story in Acts cannot be overestimated. It marks a major shift in early Christianity. Nothing had prepared Peter and the apostles for this shift to the Gentiles, not even Pentecost. Now Peter comes to terms with what God has done in the resurrection: God shows no partiality, is no respecter of persons; God is a God for all. That is what we are called to witness. In Acts, the Spirit leads the community into a new future, a future that we are still discovering.

ISAIAH 25:6-9 (RCL ALT., BCP ALT.)

See the first reading for Easter Evening, below.

RESPONSIVE READING
PSALM 118:1-2, 14-24 (RCL)
PSALM 118:14-29 or 118:14-17, 22-24 (BCP)
PSALM 118:1-2, 16-17, 22-23 (RC)

This psalm accompanies the fourth cup of wine at the Passover celebration and, along with Psalms 113–17, was sung during pilgrimages to the Jerusalem temple. Verse 22, "The stone that the builders rejected has become the chief cornerstone," became important to early Christianity's effort to understand the significance of Jesus' death. This powerful hymn gives thanks for what the Lord has done.

SECOND READING
1 CORINTHIANS 15:1-11 (RCL)

1 Corinthians 15 is the most important chapter in the New Testament on the topic of resurrection because it is the earliest extended discussion of the resurrection. Written in the mid 50s C.E., the letter predates all the Gospels. We know who wrote 1 Corinthians, while all the Gospels are anonymous. Finally, Paul was known to Jesus' original disciples, and they accepted his apostleship, his experience of the risen Lord. Thus, we should assume that his *kerygma*, preaching, corresponds to theirs. It may not be identical, but it should not be drastically different.

The RCL presents only a short section of this chapter, while the other lectionaries do not have it as an option. Were it up to me, I would make the whole of chapter 15 the topic for all the sermons of the Easter season. This chapter will reward our coming to terms with it, because it is the only window into a pre-70 C.E. view of resurrection.

Paul begins his discussion with a formula indicating that he is handing on tradition. This is Paul's good news, his gospel. This summary statement required his readers to fill in the blanks. He hands on a proto-creed, not set in the form of what he believes, but what he terms "the first things."

"Christ died for our sins in accordance with the scriptures" (15:3). Unsurprisingly, Paul begins with the death of Jesus, as he earlier in this letter stresses that he preaches Christ crucified (1:23). The phrase contains two formulaic phrases. "For our sins" stands for the Greek *hyper*, which means on our behalf, for our sake, in our place. This represents the efforts of early communities to develop a model for Jesus' death. As such, it is not the complete model but a summary of the effort to develop models from the language of ransom (slavery) and sacrifice. In Paul's formula, this is

> EARLY CHRISTIANS APPEAR TO BE MUCH MORE INTER-
> ESTED IN SEEING THE PATTERNS REVEALED IN SCRIP-
> TURE BY THE DEATH AND RESURRECTION RATHER THAN
> PROOF-TEXTING SPECIFIC SCRIPTURE PASSAGES.

"in accordance with the scriptures," without denoting which scriptures. *Scriptures* here means the scriptures of Israel. It indicates that the scriptures are the hermeneutical tool by which to understand Jesus' death. Early Christians appear to be much more interested in seeing the patterns revealed in scripture by the death and resurrection rather than proof-texting specific scripture passages.

"And that he was buried" (15:4). This bald, simple statement comes with no commentary. Its simplicity surely accents the reality of Jesus' death. He really died; he was buried.

"He was raised on the third day in accordance with the scriptures" (15:4). This phrase parallels the first one, and the threefold patterning creates a strong rhythm. "The third day" may well be a reference to Hosea 6:2: "After two days he will revive us; on the third day he will raise us up." Paul may be exposing here the origin of the tradition that the resurrection occurred on the third day.

Then Paul outlines a list of Jesus' appearances. Like the threefold proto-creed, this list has a structure:

- Cephas and the Twelve
- Five hundred of the brothers
- James and the apostles
- Finally Paul

The parallelism of the first three lines is obvious, while Paul appears to be a tag on to the list. This list identifies Cephas with the Twelve and James with the apostles. This separation of the Twelve from the apostles reminds us that Paul predates the Acts of the Apostles. Luke-Acts combines the two groups and creates the fiction of twelve apostles. Paul represents the earlier tradition in which they are two different groups. Paul provides us little information about the Twelve, nor does either group appear in Q, the Synoptic sayings source. The apostles are for Paul an important group because he is one, and he expended a great deal of energy in defense of his apostleship, especially in Corinth and Galatia. The apostles are for Paul those who have seen the resurrected Jesus and have been called to preach the gospel. In Romans 16:7 he sends greetings to Andronicus and Junia, whom he says "are prominent among the apostles." Neither of these names is on any list of the Twelve in the Synoptics, and Junia is almost certainly a woman.

Paul's list is difficult to reconcile with the later appearance stories in the Gospels, especially those of Luke and John. For example, no women occur in Paul's list and he has appearances of Jesus to folks of whom we have no stories at all. What happened to the five hundred all at one time? This is a very large group, and its size would imply that it took place outdoors. How could such an event drop out of Christian memory? I raise these questions not to cast doubt on Paul's list; I accept its historical veracity. Paul is as close as we get to an eyewitness. He knows many of the people on this list, so we should accept it. But this list does cause severe problems for the appearance stories in the Gospels.

Paul's inclusion on this list reminds us that in the early tradition, the appearances of the resurrected Jesus were not limited to forty days, as in the Acts of the Apostles, but extended over a much longer period of time, perhaps several years. Acts, written toward the end of the first century, has artificially cut short and restricted the appearances. That is a construct of Acts; Paul's list implies a different story.

Paul's list reminds us of how little we know about these important events. The pre-70 c.e. period remains, and probably always will remain, shrouded in mystery. What is important about Paul's list is its ongoing nature. It witnesses to the continuing activity of the risen Jesus, a list in which we stand.

COLOSSIANS 3:1–4 (BCP, RC)

Colossians and Ephesians are two letters that are ascribed to Paul, but most scholars believe they both come from the generation after Paul and were written by "students" of Paul. Pseudonymous writings were common in the ancient world as a way of honoring the name of a school's founder. Questions of authorship are much more important in a capitalist society because of copyright issues.

This reading is the introduction to the last section of the letter, which addresses how a Christian is to live—what is technically referred to as a *paranesis*, a Greek rhetorical term for moral advice or exhortation. The initial phrase, "So if you have been raised with Christ," balances the phrase in 2:20, "If with Christ you died to the elemental spirits of the universe." Colossians puts a strong emphasis on the Christian's already-risen standing. Such an understanding is at odds with Paul, who views the believer's resurrection as a future reality (for instance, 1 Cor. 15:51).

For Colossians the raised status of the Christian forms the basis for Christian ethics. We are to set our minds on the things that are above, where Christ is, and not on the earth, where the elemental spirits rule. But this dualistic division of heaven and earth is not a mandate for an escape from this world. In the ethical exhortation that continues after this introduction, the emphasis is on life here on earth.

> FOR COLOSSIANS THE RAISED STATUS OF THE CHRISTIAN FORMS THE BASIS FOR CHRISTIAN ETHICS.

THE GOSPEL

The Revised Common Lectionary offers two texts, John 20:1-18 and Mark 16:1-8. Both present real challenges for a preacher. John's images are firmly imprinted on the Western consciousness in art and films. A preacher will have to bear these in mind and at times struggle against them. On the other hand, Mark's empty-tomb text does not correspond with the image most folks have in mind when they think of resurrection. Furthermore, the John text is the first part of a complete unit of which the second part is the Gospel reading for the Second Sunday of Easter.

Finally, these two Gospel readings come from very different parts of the tradition. Mark's empty tomb may be the very first resurrection narrative, while John 20 is among the latest of canonical Gospel resurrection narratives. The very earliness and strangeness of Mark's text commend it, as it will force most folks to rethink their ideas of resurrection.

JOHN 20:1-18 (RCL)
JOHN 20:1-9 (RC)

Chapter 20 in the Fourth Gospel is a long and complete unit divided into four parts. It most likely served as the Gospel's original ending. Chapter 21 is clearly an add-on; its themes and setting are different. The lectionary selection for today presents the first two parts of this unit, while the last two parts of the unit comprise the Gospel for the Second Sunday of Easter. Part one of the reading (20:1-10) concerns the discovery of the tomb, while the second part (20:11-18) concerns the appearance to Mary Magdalene.

Given the date of the Gospel of John (sometime between 85 and 100 C.E.), we should not assume that stories of resurrection events are unknown to John's audience. Three parts of the story appear to be traditional: the discovery of the empty tomb by the women, Peter's visit to the tomb, and an appearance to the disciples. John has elaborated each of these traditional stories by focusing on an individual to bring out the story's significance.

The Empty Tomb (20:1-10)

The two male characters in this section have played central roles in the Gospel: Peter since the very beginning, and the mysterious beloved disciple who first appears in 13:23. Despite efforts to solve the puzzle of this disciple's identity, the beloved disciple remains a mystery. Mary Magdalene, on the other hand, was mentioned only once before with Mary, the mother of Jesus, at the foot of the cross (John 19:25). This double presence of Mary Magdalene is no accident. For John, Jesus' death is essential to his exaltation.

> JESUS' BODY DOES NOT REQUIRE CLOTHES. UNLIKE LAZARUS, WHO HAS TO BE FREED FROM HIS BURIAL CLOTHES AS BONDAGE, JESUS IS FREE.

"'And I, when I am lifted up from the earth, will draw all people to myself.' He said this to indicate the kind of death he was to die" (John 12:32-33). Mary Magdalene, a witness to Jesus' death/exaltation, will also be the first witness to hear the risen Jesus' voice. Like Nicodemus (3:1-2), Mary comes while it is still dark. The audience thus anticipates a parallel between Nicodemus and Mary Magdalene, and darkness in John (8:12; 12:35, 46) indicates something negative. Mary's report to Peter and "the other disciple" reveals that she believes that "they" have taken the body of Jesus. Hers becomes the first response to the evidence of the missing body.

While Mary's report initially seems to confirm the rumor in Matthew's Gospel (27:64) that the body of Jesus was stolen, John's Gospel decidedly rejects this rumor by the recurring phrase "linen wrappings lying there," which implies that the body is missing but not stolen; otherwise the burial garments also would be missing. Jesus' body does not require clothes. Unlike Lazarus, who has to be freed from his burial clothes as bondage, Jesus is free.

Mary does not see this evidence, but only Peter and the other disciple. The verb "he ran in front" (*pro-*) and "he came first" (*protos*) accents this unknown one's priority. The one whom Jesus loved is the first to the tomb and the first to believe, thus setting up a decided contrast with Peter.

He came, he saw, he believed—this describes the activity of the beloved disciple. This is the way he is: he believes. Coming, seeing, believing define his character. He needs no more. In contrast to Peter, his narration is strongly focused. The narrator does not say what the disciple believes or why he believes. But he presents an image of belief. As biblical scholar John Ashton has so forcibly argued, "He [John] is able to record the response the beloved disciple makes, not to the voice of an intermediary, but to a vision of emptiness."[1] This vision of emptiness is not far from Mark's empty tomb (see below). The beloved disciple becomes the first example of faith in the resurrection. As the beloved disciple, the model for the community that claims his heritage, he exhibits a faith that is the archetype or the standard by which to judge the others. That faith is not based on hearing, seeing, or touching the resurrected Jesus.

This first section presents three points of view on the empty tomb: Peter draws no conclusion; Mary Magdalene assumes that someone has stolen the body; only the beloved disciple comes, sees, and has faith.

A Voice in the Garden (20:11-18)

The introduction of Mary Magdalene sounds like that of both the other disciple and Peter. Like the other disciple, she was first to reach the tomb, and both bend down to look into the tomb. But whereas Peter observes linens, she observes two angels. She contacts heavenly realities; he contacts leftover artifacts. Yet the angels have no portentous message. While an audience could draw from their appearance a sign that Jesus has risen, Mary draws the same conclusion as when she had seen the stone rolled away. Mary's response to the angels is to repeat her report to the disciples, reinforcing the insight that not even the sight of angels produces faith.

Mary is described four times as weeping. Twice in rapid succession at the section's very beginning, the narrator notes Mary's weeping, and both the angels and Jesus ask why she is weeping. Mary sees but does not know that it is Jesus. Physical seeing does not produce recognition or faith.

Jesus repeats the angels's question with a significant addition. He asks, "Who are you looking for?" which echoes the question he earlier asked the two unnamed disciples of John the Baptist (1:38). Significantly, their address of Jesus as "Rabbi" parallels Mary's.

The exchange between Jesus and Mary, consisting of a single word for each, constitutes the heart of the section and subtly draws the audience into the story's creative performance. Two words are exchanged, and the audience must fill in a great gap. There is strong irony in the passage since an audience knows more than Mary and keeps waiting for her to find out what is happening. Yet there are traps for an audience, such as the angels. An audience can overanticipate. When Jesus says Mary's name and she responds, the audience must supply her joy or emotion. While weeping is expressed, its opposite is only implied in her voice. Her recognition of Jesus when he says her name recalls Jesus' saying, "I

> THERE IS STRONG IRONY IN THE PASSAGE SINCE AN AUDIENCE KNOWS MORE THAN MARY AND KEEPS WAITING FOR HER TO FIND OUT WHAT IS HAPPENING.

know my own and my own know me" (10:3, 14). This voice which she recognizes draws attention to the risen Jesus as the earthly Jesus. She may not recognize the physical body, but she does recognize the voice. Here the narrator drops a clue for the audience: this is Jesus, but not the physical Jesus. Voice, like breath, is a perfect model for the Spirit. It has body, but it is not physical (John 3:8).

At Jesus' pronouncing of Mary's name, she responds, "Rabboni." Its foreignness draws attention to her response. The Hebrew produces verisimilitude. Mary's "turning around" focuses the audience's attention on her action and may perhaps have a double meaning. She turns around physically, but "turning around" is, in Hebrew, a metaphor for conversion, a change of perspective or commitment.

Jesus' response to Mary has often been mistranslated. The Vulgate phrase, *noli tangere*, has been fixed in art and the Western imagination.[2] Danker/Bauer's *Greek-English Lexicon* collects the evidence to show that the sense is not "Don't touch me," as though Jesus were forbidding Mary to touch him. Given the Thomas story that follows, such a position would involve either an awful contradiction (over which exegetes have strained) or a terrible sexism. As Bauer shows, the sense is "Stop clinging to me!"[3]

Jesus gives as his reason for demanding that Mary let go of him that he has not yet ascended to his Father. In John the ascent to the Father refers to Jesus' death, something to which Mary Magdalene was a witness. The classic references are John 3:13 ("No one has ascended into heaven except the one who descended from heaven, the Son of Man") and 6:62 ("Then what if you were to see the Son of Man ascending to where he was before?"). Ashton has pointed out that the author is here caught trying to reconcile two different and originally separate ways of trying to envision the resurrection faith. The form of Mary's story is a recognition scene, while the language of ascent is drawn from the exaltation motif (compare Phil. 2:6-11). "Now this procedure means combining two ideas of resurrection that are conceptually very difficult to reconcile, one [recognition] temporal (before/after), the other [ascent] spatial (below/above)."[4] This conflict of models warns an audience of the impossibility of explaining fully the resurrection in terms of physical reality and of separating the cross from the resurrection.

> THOSE WHO BELIEVE IN THE RESURRECTION ARE A NEW FAMILY, THE FAMILY OF THE DIVINE FELLOWSHIP.

Jesus' reference to the disciples as "brothers" recalls the early Christian address. But as Jesus had proclaimed in his final address, "I do not call you servants any longer, because the servant does not know what the master is doing; but I have called you friends, because I have made known to you everything that I have heard from my Father" (15:15). Those who believe in the resurrection are a new family. Jesus acknowledges this by solemnly proclaiming, "My Father and your Father, my God and your God." It is the family of the divine fellowship.

MARK 16:1-8 (BCP, RCL ALT.)
MARK 16:1-7 (RC ALT.)

13

EASTER
MORNING

BERNARD
BRANDON
SCOTT

If one were to set the New Testament writings on a timeline, the earliest treatment of the resurrection in the New Testament is 1 Corinthians 15. The earliest narrative of resurrection appearances is Mark 16:1-8, and it narrates not an appearance of Jesus, but an empty tomb. There is no narration of resurrection appearances prior to the destruction of the temple. The Gospel of Mark, written in the aftermath of the temple's destruction, is the first such narration. Furthermore, Matthew and Luke derive the initial part of their resurrection stories from Mark. Here the two-source theory works perfectly. A simple glance at Gospel parallels will confirm that Matthew and Luke are following Mark's narrative until 16:8, at which point they go their own ways.

Mark 16 serves as the conclusion of Mark's Gospel and is the first resurrection narrative; that is, it is the first text in the New Testament to narrate the resurrection. In 1 Corinthians 15 Paul supports a resurrection body (*soma*) that is "spiritual" (*pneumatikos*). He makes clear that it is not physical (*psychikos*). We find this distinction contradictory, but for Paul it is important. I would assume that whoever wrote the Gospel of Mark agrees with this Pauline distinction, that it is not unique to Paul and was in general agreement among early Christians. So he has to narrate something that is bodily and spiritual but not physical—a very tall order, since narration takes place in physical space.

We should ask how the author of this Gospel envisioned or imagined the narration of Jesus' resurrection as the conclusion of his writing. He did not know he was writing a "Gospel," nor should we view this as an eyewitness report. It is an author in the post-70 C.E. period trying to narrate Jesus' resurrection

The Young Man

The young man has plagued commentators, but one should note that the presence of the young man sets a tone for the story. Compared to the other Gospel stories, Mark's story has a decidedly less otherworldly character. This is surely ironic given the topic of resurrection.

In the tomb is a young man, dressed in a white robe. The last mention in Mark's Gospel of a young man is 14:51-52: "A certain young man was following him, wearing nothing but a linen cloth. They caught hold of him, but he left the linen cloth and ran off naked."

Who is the young man? The tradition has an answer: the young man in 14:51 was Mark, the Gospel's author, while the young man in 16:5 was really an angel! Here we see the power of Matthew's Gospel on the tradition. Since

Matthew had angels, then Mark's young man must really be an angel. Tradition-ally, Gospel texts were harmonized rather than appreciated for their distinctive points of view.

Once the Gospels were no longer seen as eyewitness reports, the young man became a problem. But there are clues to his identity. A young man flees naked, and a young man dressed in white is present in the empty tomb. In between these two appearances, Jesus is crucified. In early Christianity this outlines the rite of baptism. As the Pauline formula has it: "Do you not know that all of us who have been baptized into Christ Jesus were baptized into his death? Therefore we have been buried with him by baptism into death, so that, just as Christ was raised from the dead by the glory of the Father, so we too might walk in newness of life" (Rom. 6:3-4).

Although the evidence for the rite of baptism is later than the Gospel, still it seems likely that early Christians were baptized naked and when they came out of the water were robed in white. Thus, the young man represents the newly baptized Christian, who has died and risen with Christ. As a representative of the newly baptized Christian, he stands in for the reader. This might strike us modern readers as far-fetched, but we should remem-ber that Mark is an allegorical thinker. His interpretations of the parables in Mark 4 and 12:1-12 demonstrate clearly this way of thinking. So the young man is an allegorical stand-in for the reader.

> IT SEEMS LIKELY THAT EARLY CHRISTIANS WERE BAP-TIZED NAKED AND WHEN THEY CAME OUT OF THE WATER WERE ROBED IN WHITE.

Confession

If one considers the young man as a stand-in for the reader, then his announce-ment to the women is very interesting. The English translation loses a little of its parallelism and nobility. The following translation, while literal, preserves the Greek sense:

> You seek Jesus
>> the Nazareth one
>> the crucified one.

What one expects in this announcement is a christological title, for example, "You seek Jesus, Son of God, the Lord." Instead, the young man uses Jesus' name, modified by two title-like phrases—"the Nazareth one" and "the crucified one." It is almost as though he identifies Jesus by his address and legal execution. Both of these, like the young man instead of an angel, draw a reader toward seeing the resurrection as in continuity with the earthly Jesus and keep our attention on the here and now.

We should read texts not backwards but forwards. We all carry in our minds an idealized, homogenized, even mythological view of the resurrection. In that model following the resurrection, Jesus appears for forty days, then the ascension. This model comes from Acts, a document of the late first century. The young man indicates that Jesus "has risen" and that "he goes before you to Galilee." What is missing, and should not be read into Mark, is a view of resurrection that ends with Jesus' ascension into heaven. Mark indicates that the resurrected Jesus is among us and not departed.

Address to the Disciples and Peter

The young man instructs the women to give his message to the disciples and Peter. Throughout Mark's Gospel the status of the disciples has been most problematic. In the first part of the Gospel, the demons know who Jesus is, the Pharisees get the significance of Jesus and reject him, but the disciples wander around lost and confused. He even calls them "hard-hearted" when they fail to understand the meaning of the feeding of the crowds (8:14-21). Peter and the disciples reject Jesus' mission as the suffering Son of Man, and Jesus even goes so far as to curse Peter: "Get behind me, Satan!" (8:33).

> WE ALL CARRY IN OUR MINDS AN IDEALIZED, HOMOGENIZED, EVEN MYTHOLOGICAL VIEW OF THE RESURRECTION.

Throughout the Gospel's second part, the status of the disciples does not improve. At the Last Supper, when Jesus prophesizes that "one of you will betray me," they all began to ask, "Surely, not I?" (14:18-19). Even here, nearing the Gospel's climax, the disciples are unclear about their devotion and loyalty to Jesus. When Jesus is arrested, they all flee, and in the garden of the high priest, three times Peter denies or betrays Jesus. At the story's conclusion we have no idea of Peter's status. Now the young man tells us that the women are to go and tell the disciples and Peter that Jesus will meet them in Galilee. Status apparently resolved.

The Women

The naming of the women reminds the reader of the last mention of the women at the foot of Jesus' cross (15:40-41). They are the witnesses to Jesus' death, and their loyalty and fidelity to Jesus stand in stark contrast to that of the disciples and Peter. This indicates their fitness to carry the young man's message to the disciples and Peter.

The story's ending is most confounding. Following the young man's confession/announcement, the women flee in fear and say nothing to anyone. This ending has disturbed readers from a very early date. Both Matthew and Luke shift this ending of Mark's Gospel. Other endings of Mark were constructed (see the

Ascension of Our Lord, the Gospel for the Episcopal (alternative) and Roman Catholic lectionaries). If the women told no one, how did Peter and the disciples come to learn of the resurrection? Even more, if they told no one, where did this story come from?

One obvious way around this conundrum is to argue that of course they did tell and then go with one of the later Gospel stories, for example, Matthew or Luke. (The Roman Catholic lectionary solves this problem by simply cutting v. 8 out of the reading.) But this ignores what Mark's text actually says: they told no one.

If this is Mark's ending, how then is it a conclusion?

The relation between signs and faith signals a major theme in Mark's Gospel. The first half of the Gospel elaborates the signs of Jesus' messiahship. In the first three chapters, Jesus goes about Galilee healing and casting out demons, and beginning in chapter 4, the nature of the signs escalates—he walks on water, calms the storm, and feeds the multitudes. He truly exhibits the signs of a messiah.

> IF THE WOMEN TOLD NO ONE, HOW DID PETER AND THE DISCIPLES COME TO LEARN OF THE RESURRECTION?

But then, just before the confession at Caesarea Philippi (which in Mark might more adequately be called Peter's exorcism), the Pharisees request a sign from heaven (8:11). This really has to be a silly request. What do they think he has been doing since the story's beginning? He has performed sign after sign. But Jesus' answer is even more astounding: "No sign will be given to this generation" (8:12).

Toward the Gospel's climax, the question of signs once more appears when the disciples ask Jesus, "Tell us, when will this be, and what will be the sign that all these things are about to be accomplished?" (13:4). Jesus launches into an apocalyptic discourse concerning the signs for the end. Now the reader thinks we will be given the answer and the signs will come, or so it appears. But near the discourse's end, Jesus announces, "But about that day or hour no one knows, neither the angels in heaven, nor the Son, but only the Father" (13:32). This statement of Jesus jerks the rug out from under the reader. What then is the status of these "signs" that Jesus has just given if he now claims he does not know the hour, but only the Father? The author has set a trap for the reader. Having warned the reader that no sign will be given, in chapter 13 the disciples, like the Pharisees in chapter 8, ask for a sign. Both have proven to be unreliable characters in Mark's Gospel, so the reader should be on guard. Yet we fall into the trap and seek a sign. For Mark there is no sign, only faith.

Even in the crucifixion scene, Mark constructs yet another test for the reader. The chief priests taunt, "Let the Messiah, the King of Israel, come down from the cross now, so that we may see and believe" (15:32). Here they ask for a messianic sign. The reader should be forewarned that a request from the chief priests is probably a bad one, but we probably fall for the trap. As biblical scholar Eugene Boring has noted, if Jesus came down from the cross, would he be the Messiah?[5] Those of us impressed by signs will agree with the chief priests; Mark offers a different answer.

When Jesus cries out, "My God, my God, why have you forsaken me?" (15:34), the bystanders think he is calling for Elijah and wait to see if Elijah will come. Once again they expect a sign. But none is coming. Instead, the centurion, the man who put Jesus to death, says, "Truly this man was God's Son!" (15:39). As the NRSV footnote indicates, this statement is ambiguous. Does he say Jesus is God's Son or a son of God? Even more, should it be interpreted as a confession or as sarcasm? Both are possible. It is more likely that a Roman centurion would mean it sarcastically. But Mark means the reader to understand it as the Christian's confession. "Son of God" is a title that has

> FOR MARK THE PROOF, THE SIGN OF JESUS' MESSIAH-SHIP, IS NOT THE MIGHTY MESSIANIC SIGNS BUT HIS DEATH ON THE CROSS.

appeared at the Gospel's opening (1:1, although there is a textual problem here), in the baptism as the voice of God (1:11), and in the transfiguration (9:7). For Mark the proof, the sign of Jesus' messiahship, is not the mighty messianic signs but his death on the cross. And Jesus' last words in this Gospel are despairing.

Mark creates in his resurrection narrative both an ending for his Gospel and a test for the reader. The young man recalls for the reader that faith is in "Jesus, the Nazareth one, the crucified one, who has risen." Mark has stripped away every sign and leaves the reader alone in faith. The reader must look at the brutality of Jesus' death and see there the act of God. The tomb offers no proof, no angel, and the women go away afraid.

What is Mark's good news? We have heard the story. The signs are gone. We have the crucified and risen one. We must find him in Galilee. He goes before us.

Notes

1. John Ashton, *Understanding the Fourth Gospel* (Oxford: Clarendon Press, 1991), 506.

2. The Web site www.textweek.com has an excellent collection of such examples; go to http://www.textweek.com/art/noli_me_tangere.htm.

3. Walter Bauer, *A Greek-English Lexicon of the New Testament and Other Early Christian Literature*, edited by Frederick William Danker, 3rd ed. (Chicago: University of Chicago Press, 2000), 126.

4. Ashton, *Understanding the Fourth Gospel*, 507; see pp. 507–8 for additional very insightful remarks about this problem.

5. Eugene Boring, *Truly Human/Truly Divine: Christological Language and the Gospel Form* (St. Louis: CBP Press, 1984), 93.

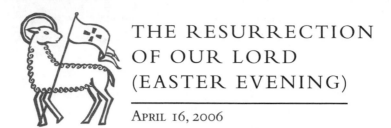

THE RESURRECTION OF OUR LORD (EASTER EVENING)

APRIL 16, 2006

REVISED COMMON	EPISCOPAL (BCP)	ROMAN CATHOLIC
Isa. 25:6-9	Acts 5:29a, 30-32 or Dan. 12:1-3	
Psalm 114	Psalm 114 or Psalm 136 or Ps. 118:14-17, 22-24	
1 Cor. 5:6b-8	1 Cor. 5:6b-8 or Acts 5:29a, 30-32	
Luke 24:13-49	Luke 24:13-35	Luke 24:13-35

FIRST READING
ISAIAH 25:6-9 (RCL)

The composition of Isaiah is extremely complex. Today's reading comes from a section usually referred to as "First Isaiah." It is an edited collection of the prophet Isaiah's sayings. This editing gives the book an almost "timeless" character and at times has shifted the context from the specific to the general.

Today's reading is part of a small fragment that celebrates what God will do for God's people. The blessing of God is pictured as a banquet on the holy mountain. Fine aged wines and choicest pieces of meat, the bone marrow, will be served up. The passage has a strong universalist tone. All peoples and all nations will come to this banquet of the Lord. The great sign of this banquet is that "he will swallow up death forever" (25:8). We will *eat* fine foods, and God will *swallow* up death. The image is nicely balanced.

Although not part of today's reading, the passage in Isaiah concludes with a strong condemnation of Moab (25:11-12). In this pattern, God's blessing is a two-edged sword. Blessing also brings condemnation for those who have opposed God's people. "The high fortifications of his walls will be brought down, laid low, cast to the ground, even to the dust" (25:12).

ACTS 5:29A, 30–32 (BCP)

This reading comes from Peter's hearing before the high priest's council. The high priest's question unfortunately has been omitted from the reading, so that we have no context in which to understand his response. Therefore, Peter's response takes on an abstract, ahistorical sense. The high priest accuses Peter of being "determined to bring this man's blood on us" (5:28). Since the Acts of the Apostles was written at the end of the first century, this charge represents the conflict between the synagogue and early Christianity, not the situation in Jerusalem in the 30s C.E. While this passage does not go as far as Matt. 27:25 in blaming the Jews for Jesus' death, this whole passage needs to be handled with care and sensitivity, as we know the outcome of this blaming of the Jews for Jesus' death.

> THIS WHOLE PASSAGE NEEDS TO BE HANDLED WITH CARE AND SENSITIVITY, AS WE KNOW THE OUTCOME OF THIS BLAMING OF THE JEWS FOR JESUS' DEATH.

Peter's actual response is a summary of the *kerygma* of Acts—Jesus died at the hands of the Jews and was raised up by God, and we are his witnesses (see the first reading for Easter Morning, Acts 10:34–35, above). The title "leader" (NRSV) is unusual. The word also appears in another speech by Peter in 3:15, where the NRSV translates it as "author of life." The usage in this passage, which follows Peter's speech in Acts 3, probably carries the same sense. Jesus is the leader or predecessor of us all into a new life.

DANIEL 12:1–3 (BCP ALT.)

The last part of the book of Daniel turns to the future and the first part of chapter 12 to the distant future of its first readers. This is probably the first mention of resurrection in the Hebrew scriptures, unless Isa. 26:19 is a reference to resurrection (although most commentators think not). At this stage the ideas about resurrection are understandably inchoate. A time of anguish precedes the resurrection. Many, but not all, will awake. The play on words of those who *sleep* in the dust will *awake* points out how important the metaphor of sleeping/awaking is in understanding the image of resurrection. It may be that the text understands those who have awakened to enter the realm of the angels or to become angel-like since they will shine like the stars.

RESPONSIVE READING
PSALM 114 (RCL, BCP)

This is one of the earliest psalms since it still envisions Israel and Judah as unified. This hymn of praise employs imaginative and fantastic metaphors to rephrase the escape from Egypt and the parting of the Red Sea. The seas flee and mountains become animals who skip away. The final stanza of the hymn calls on the earth to tremble before God, "who turns the rock into a pool of water, the flint into a spring of water." In a desert country surrounded by rock and short of water, this double image of rock and flint turning into water creates a powerful impact.

PSALM 136 (BCP ALT.)

A great hymn of thanksgiving and praise, this psalm was meant originally to be sung antiphonally, with the second voices announcing the response, "for his steadfast love endures forever." The first voice gives thanks by reviewing God's mighty works for God's people. It might prove effective to perform it antiphonally with a solo voice singing the first part and the congregation answering with the repetitive phrase.

PSALM 118:14-17, 22-44 (BCP ALT.)

See the responsive reading for Easter Morning, above.

SECOND READING
1 CORINTHIANS 5:6b-8 (RCL, BCP)

This section of 1 Corinthians comes from a long section (chapters 5–7) dealing with ethical issues that have arisen in the Corinthian community. These two verses are the conclusion to a discussion about a man who had an incestuous relationship with his father's wife (5:1). You might ask, Why would the Corinthians and Paul have to argue about this? Why is it not obvious that such behavior is wrong? From the Corinthian perspective, after baptism the soul is resurrected or separated from the body. So the body can go about its sinful way (incest), while the resurrected soul speaks in tongues. This dualist anthropol-

A DUALIST ANTHROPOLOGY BEDEVILS PAUL'S EFFORTS AT EVERY TURN TO COMMUNICATE WITH HIS CORINTHIAN CORRESPONDENTS.

ogy bedevils Paul's efforts at every turn to communicate with his Corinthian correspondents.

Paul calls for the man to be excluded, cut off from the community. He employs the analogy of the yeast/leaven to support his argument. In the view of the ancients, the leaven corrupted the dough on the analogy of a corpse swelling up after death and exposure. For this reason leaven was associated with evil (Mark 8:15) and unleavened with the holy (Exod. 12:15). The analogy is very similar to the American aphorism, "One rotten apple spoils the whole barrel."

Paul's use of this analogy assumes an understanding of the Passover celebration (see Exod. 12:15-19). The implied reference to the Passover feast suggests that Jesus is the Paschal Lamb, who is sacrificed for us. So Paul weaves a tight web from argument by analogy, implied reference to Passover, and Jesus as Paschal Lamb. In Exodus, the leaven had to be cleansed out before the sacrifice of the lamb, whereas God in Jesus' death has made us holy, so the cleansing comes after the sacrifice.

THE GOSPEL
LUKE 24:13-49 (RCL)
LUKE 24:13-35 (BCP, RC)

The Gospel reading from the RCL falls into two narrative parts (vv. 13-35 and vv. 36-49), and since the second part is also the Gospel for the Third Sunday of Easter, my discussion of that section will be found there.

Chapter 24 of Luke's Gospel serves as both a conclusion to the Gospel and a bridge to the Acts of the Apostles. The Emmaus story is an integral part of that concluding and bridging. The scene dominates the Lukan resurrection account, and it is so well conceived that it often has been part of the artistic tradition in the West, especially the final recognition scene of the breaking of the bread (for example, Caravaggio's famous painting).[1]

This scene is of Luke's own construction. The passage is replete with vocabulary frequently found in Luke. The endings of the Gospels of Matthew and Luke are much like their beginnings. If you compare their outlines to Mark, who is the source of their narrative outline, evidently both Matthew and Luke add birth narratives to Mark's narrative, which begins with Jesus' baptism, and at the end of Mark's narrative they add resurrection and ascension stories to round off his abrupt ending with an empty tomb (Mark 16:8; see above, the Gospel for Easter Morning). While both Matthew and Luke have birth narratives, it has proven impossible to reconcile them. The same is true of their resurrection accounts. They follow Mark to its ending, and then each goes his own way. So we must deal with these stories as the evangelists' own efforts to understand what the resurrection means in their own communities and time and not as a historical report of what happened. As Lukan scholar Robert Tannehill notes, Luke uses chapter 24 as "a major commentary on the significance of Jesus' death and resurrection."[2]

The scene is carefully set. Two people are on the road to Emmaus, and one of them, Cleopas, is even named. While the artistic tradition has imagined these two travelers as males, it may be otherwise. When a male is named and the other character remains unnamed, ancient convention normally dictates that the unnamed character is a female. Such are the assumptions of patriarchy. So maybe that is the situation that Luke imagines.

The couple is discussing the just-narrated events—Jesus' crucifixion and the report of the women who had gone to the tomb. Their identification of Jesus as "a prophet mighty in deed and word before God and all the people" is a standard and proper for Luke (Luke 4:24; 13:33; Acts 3:22; 7:37; 2:22). Further, they had thought that Jesus was the one to redeem Israel, another correct description for Luke of Jesus' mission (Luke 1:68; 2:38; Acts 2:30-36; 13:32-34). And they are sad, what we call "down" or depressed. The women's story does not suggest to them that Jesus is raised, but they seem to agree with the eleven that the women's story is an "idle tale" (24:11), that is, gossip.

Luke's narrative underlines three important themes—the necessity of Jesus' death and resurrection; the status of the appearances; and the meal as recognition. We will examine each of these in turn.

The Necessity

After Cleopas's summary of the events they had been discussing, the unrecognized Jesus turns on them and accuses them (and by implication all the disciples and probably the readers as well) of being foolish and slow of heart, that is, failing in understanding since the heart is the organ of thinking. "Was it not necessary that the Messiah should suffer these things and then enter into his glory?" Well, that is precisely the problem. Why was it necessary? Was not the Messiah supposed to defeat his enemies, not be defeated by them? The solving of this enigma is a key issue in Luke-Acts—to see Jesus' death, resurrection, and rising into glory as part of God's plan, the fulfillment of scripture. Jesus' predictions of his passion (9:22; 17:25) foretell its necessity, and Peter's speech in Acts will make the same point (2:30-36). The angels in the tomb (24:7), the Emmaus story, and the immediately following appearance of Jesus to the disciples all stress this necessity (24:26, 44-45). So *why* the necessity?

A KEY ISSUE IN LUKE-ACTS IS TO SEE JESUS' DEATH, RESURRECTION, AND RISING INTO GLORY AS PART OF GOD'S PLAN, THE FULFILLMENT OF SCRIPTURE.

Jesus explained the scriptures to them, but no explicit texts are quoted. The same is true in 24:45, where "he opened their [the disciples'] minds to understand the scriptures," but no specific scriptures are denoted. Is Luke thinking of proof texts, the use of specific texts to prove the point? That does not seem to be the case, since in general the author of Luke-Acts does not employ scripture in that fashion. In both 24:27 and 44 the reference is to "Moses and all the prophets," not to individual texts. Luke has in view a grand, sweeping view of the biblical story. Stephen's speech in Acts 7 makes exactly this type of move: "You stiff-necked people, uncircumcised in heart and ears, you are forever opposing the Holy Spirit, just as your ancestors used to do. Which of the prophets did your ancestors not persecute? They killed those who foretold the coming of the Righteous One, and now you have become his betrayers and murderers" (Acts 7:51-52). And Jesus has made a similar claim in the Gospel: "Yet today, tomorrow, and the next day I must be on my way, because it is impossible for a prophet to be killed outside of Jerusalem. Jerusalem, Jerusalem, the city that kills the prophets and stones those who are sent to it! How often have I desired to gather your children together as a hen gathers her brood under her wings, and you were not willing!" (Luke 13:33-34).

For Luke the destiny of prophets is that of the Messiah, and for Luke Jesus is the prophet par excellence. The prophet/Messiah proclaims God's word and is always rejected, persecuted, and killed, and yet God still affirms the prophet. Such is the pattern of divine necessity. It is also the pattern for the disciples. In the Gospel, when Jesus for the first time prophesies his own death, he immediately makes his fate

> THE PROPHET/MESSIAH PROCLAIMS GOD'S WORD AND IS ALWAYS REJECTED, PERSECUTED, AND KILLED, AND YET GOD STILL AFFIRMS THE PROPHET. SUCH IS THE PATTERN OF DIVINE NECESSITY.

the disciples' fate: "If any want to become my followers, let them deny themselves and take up their cross daily and follow me" (9:23). Only in Luke is this made a *daily* part of being a follower of Jesus. In Acts 9:16 the risen Lord charges Ananias that Paul is to go to the Gentiles, and "I myself will show him how much he must suffer for the sake of my name." Suffering marks Paul's mission at every turn.

Luke wants the reader to understand that the divine plan, illuminated by scripture, is not what we humans expect. The proclamation of God's word, rejection, suffering, and finally resurrection are how God operates. It is all a matter of point of view. As Tannehill notes, "Jesus' death is seen from two perspectives at the same time: it is the rejection of Jesus and God's purpose in him; it is also the means by which God's purpose is achieved."[3] The resurrection is not for Luke something that banishes the suffering of Jesus' death, but it is the acknowledgment that this is how God operates. Luke's understanding is especially important today when we tend to use resurrection as a Hollywood dream to banish our sorrows—almost as a promised narcotic that all will be well. The resurrection is not the plot of the *Wizard of Oz*. God's plan meets rejection and crucifixion because it overturns our plans, the plans of empire to dominate the world. The difficulty in understanding God's plan is reinforced in the text by the couple's failure to understand Jesus' explanation.

Nonrecognition and Recognition

If we could see the risen Lord, everything would be okay. That would prove everything. The resurrection accounts of Luke argue against this notion. The apostles (24:11) and the couple on the road to Emmaus reject the women's witness. When Jesus walks beside them, they do not recognize him, and his strangeness is emphasized in the story when Cleopas addresses him as "stranger" (24:18). Likewise, in the immediately following story of the disciples, when Jesus first appears they are frightened and think they have seen a ghost or spirit (24:37). Luke argues strongly against the notion that an appearance of the resurrected Lord would answer all questions, would be the definitive proof of the resurrection.

When Jesus is reclining ("at the table," NRSV), he "took bread, blessed and broke it, and gave it to them." This fourfold pattern recalls a ritual gesture. It closely parallels the feeding story, "And taking the five loaves and the two fish, he looked up to heaven, and blessed and broke them, and gave them to the disciples to set before the crowd" (9:16), and the Last Supper, "Then he took a loaf of bread, and when he had given thanks, he broke it and gave it to them" (22:19). It also looks forward to the meals in Acts (2:42, 46; 20:7, 11). As the references to Acts makes clear, "breaking bread" becomes a summary of this ritual formula. The Emmaus story concludes with the couple reporting, how "he had been made known to them in the breaking of the bread" (24:35).

Besides looking back to the meals of the Gospel narrative and forward to those in Acts, the formula of the breaking of the bread also points outside the text to the actual practice of Luke's community. The author points to the breaking of the bread as the community's recognition of the resurrected Jesus. Where is the resurrected Jesus? Luke answers, "Where he

THE AUTHOR POINTS TO THE BREAKING OF THE BREAD AS THE COMMUNITY'S RECOGNITION OF THE RESURRECTED JESUS.

has always been, in the breaking of the bread." What was true for the original followers—in the feeding and last supper, at Emmaus—was true in Luke's own day, late in the first century, and in our day, early in the twenty-first century. For Luke, the breaking of the bread is where God's plan, as foretold in scripture, becomes evident. That is how God redeems Israel, heals the world.

Notes

1. The Web site www.textweek.com has an excellent collection of images; go to http://www.textweek.com/art/Emmaus.htm.

2. Robert C. Tannehill, *The Narrative Unity of Luke-Acts, a Literary Interpretation: Vol. 1, The Gospel According to Luke*, Foundations and Facets (Philadelphia: Fortress Press, 1986), 277.

3. Ibid., 288.

SECOND SUNDAY
OF EASTER

REVISED COMMON	EPISCOPAL (BCP)	ROMAN CATHOLIC
Acts 4:32-35	Acts 3:12a, 13-15, 17-26 or Isa. 26:2-9, 19	Acts 4:32-35
Psalm 133	Psalm 111 or Ps. 118:19-24	Ps. 118:2-4, 13-15, 22-24
1 John 1:1—2:2	1 John 5:1-6 or Acts 3:12a, 13-15, 17-26	1 John 5:1-6
John 20:19-31	John 20:19-31	John 20:19-31

FIRST READING
ACTS 4:32-35 (RCL, RC)

These verses are a summary statement that leads into the story of Ananias and Sapphira and looks back on the early period of the apostles as an ideal time. The description of all being held in common is a theme repeated from 2:44. Many commentators point to the saying in Aristotle, "Among friends everything is common" (*Nicomachean Ethics*, 9.8). In Hellenistic culture such a practice would be understood to indicate that this is the perfect community, a community of friends (see John 15:15). In a hierarchical society like the Mediterranean, such a community of friends, with everything in common, points to a strong egalitarianism. The note "There was not a needy person among them" (4:34) reinforces this theme.

IN A HIERARCHICAL SOCIETY LIKE THE MEDITERRANEAN, SUCH A COMMUNITY OF FRIENDS, WITH EVERYTHING IN COMMON, POINTS TO A STRONG EGALITARIANISM.

Deuteronomy notes that when Israel comes into the promised land, "there will, however, be no one in need among you, because the LORD is sure to bless you in the land that the LORD your God is giving you as a possession to occupy, if only you will obey the LORD your God by diligently observing this entire commandment that I command you today" (15:4-5). So this becomes another sign that the new community is fulfillment of Israel's promise.

ACTS 3:12a, 13-15, 17-26 (BCP)

See the first reading for the Third Sunday of Easter, below.

ISAIAH 26:2-9, 19 (BCP ALT.)

This reading is made up of verses from two different hymns (see the first reading for Easter Evening, above, for notes about this section of Isaiah). The first hymn, 26:1-6, is a song in celebration of Zion. As dwellers in a city of victory and peace, the poor and needy will trample upon those who formerly dwelt on the heights. This is part of the main message of First Isaiah.

The second hymn, 26:7-21, is a lament that the righteous do not yet rule the land, but the time will come when God will restore all.

RESPONSIVE READING
PSALM 133 (RCL)

This song celebrates the joy of Jerusalem pilgrims and employs two images for joy. The first is the oil running down the beard of Aaron the high priest onto his collar and robes. Anointing in the ancient world is a sign of luxury and celebration. Bathers anoint themselves, while those in mourning do not.

The second image is the dew of Mount Hermon, which is in the extreme northeast part of Israel (the Golan Heights). It is the tallest mountain range in Israel and normally is snowcapped. In a dry region an image of water is always a blessing.

PSALM 111 (BCP)

This psalm dates from the postexilic period. Its context appears to be the schoolroom, as the psalmist celebrates how good it is to be "in the company of the upright, in the congregation" (111:1). The upright study the works of the Lord. The Hebrew word for "studied" (111:2) has the same root as "midrash," which was a standard form of rabbinic interpretation. The psalm has close ties to the wisdom tradition.

PSALM 118:19-24 (BCP ALT.)
PSALM 118:2-4, 13-15, 22-24 (RC)

See the responsive reading for Easter Morning, above.

SECOND READING
1 JOHN 1:1—2:2 (RCL)

For most of the weeks of Easter, the second reading will come from 1 John. The style and vocabulary of the three letters of John are similar to that of the Fourth Gospel. It is not clear whether the Gospel and the letters have the same author, but they do belong to the same community or school. The letters were written either after the completion of the Gospel or during the final editing of the Gospel's second edition, sometime toward the end of the first century.

The situation the letters are addressing is clear: the community has experienced a serious split. "Children, it is the last hour! As you have heard that antichrist is coming, so now many antichrists have come. From this we know that it is the last hour. They went out from us, but they did not belong to us; for if they had belonged to us, they would have remained with us. But by going out they made it plain that none of them belongs to us" (1 John 2:18-19). The situation facing the community is dire, so dire that the author identifies it as the apocalyptic end. He apparently sees no hope of unity with this group and is appealing to those who are left to stay. This situation of community schism must be kept in mind in dealing with these letters.

> THE SITUATION FACING THE COMMUNITY IS DIRE, SO DIRE THAT THE AUTHOR IDENTIFIES IT AS THE APOCALYPTIC END.

Today's reading is from the opening of 1 John. In many ways it echoes the opening of the Fourth Gospel—for example, "from the beginning," "the word of life." The purpose of the letter is made clear: fellowship. The Greek *koinonia* is a notoriously difficult word to translate. Danker/Bauer suggests a definition of "close association involving mutual interests and sharing, *association, communion, fellowship, close relationship*."[1] This fellowship/communion/unity is between author and reader, and then between the Father and Son.

Three times in the letter the author offers definitions of God. First, "This is the message we have heard from him and proclaim to you, that God is light and in him there is no darkness at all" (1:5). In the second instance the author states that God "is righteous" (2:29), and finally that "God is love" (4:8). In each case the author draws a conclusion about how we are to behave. In this first instance, the fact that God is light means that we should walk in the truth. The light makes evident what is true, while darkness conceals the lie.[2]

1 JOHN 5:1-6 (BCP, RC)

See the second reading for the Sixth Sunday of Easter, below.

ACTS 3:12a, 13-15, 17-26 (BCP ALT.)

See the first reading for the Third Sunday of Easter, below.

The Gospel
JOHN 20:19-31 (RCL, BCP, RC)

Today's Gospel reading continues the reading from Easter Sunday and only makes full sense when we see it as part of that story. The four scenes of John 20 represent a scale of responses to the risen Lord. Lectionary preaching unfortunately encourages us to disembody texts from their evangelical context. The first part of the chapter presents two responses: The beloved disciple, the community's hero, sees the empty tomb and believes. Peter sees the linens in the empty tomb and is confused. Mary Magdalene, when she first sees Jesus, thinks he is the gardener, but when he speaks her name, she recognizes the Master. In a Gospel that begins with a hymn to the *Logos*—word in the sense of sound or speech (not written)—to believe by hearing is only slightly less than to believe by just looking at the empty tomb. So Mary becomes the second hero, behind the first hero, the beloved disciple. To ignore this development in the chapter in preaching today's Gospel is to miss the point of the author of the Fourth Gospel.

Today's Gospel reading has three distinct parts: appearance to the disciples (20:19-23), appearance to Thomas (20:24-29), and conclusion (20:30-31).

Behind Closed Doors

Verse 19 exhibits multiple signs of a major shift, so the stories of the beloved disciple and Mary Magdalene form unit one and those of the disciples unit two. The reference to the "first day of the week" repeats the similar time notice from v. 1. A time shift has occurred, however. Although it is now evening, rather than morning, both episodes begin in the dark. The locked doors and the disciples' fear reinforce the darkness theme.

Jesus' "Peace be with you" (*shalom*) is a normal Jewish greeting. One should be careful about over-reading this phrase. While obviously contrasting with the disciples' fear, it is still a normal greeting.

In the NRSV the doors were locked for "fear of the Jews." The Greek *Ioudaioi* has become a difficult word to translate. It literally means "Judeans," much in the way that we use a place name, America, to represent the people who live there, Americans. John frequently employs the term in such a way to mean "the Jerusalem leaders" (for instance, 5:10), and that most likely is its meaning here. What it does *not* mean is the Jewish people as a whole or the Jewish religion. I suggest translating this word for the congregation as "the Jewish or Jerusalem leaders" or "the Judeans." Too much horror has resulted from anti-Semitism associated with the death of Jesus. We need to put a stop to it, and making translations more accurate and responsible is a small first step.

Jesus came and stood. Coming and standing is the way of describing Jesus' resurrection experience to the disciples. John's does not use appearance language, as Paul does in 1 Corinthians 15: "He was seen." Rather, he uses very physical terms—he came and he stood.

Furthermore, he shows them his hands and his side. The reference to the hands and side involves on an audience's part the formation of a complex gestalt. First, the hands and the side show that the risen Jesus is the crucified Jesus, a theme implied before, now forcibly proclaimed. *Side* also refers back to the Passion's conclusion (19:31-37). The truth of what was reported is sworn to by the witness of the beloved disciple, "that you also may believe" (19:35). Then a part of the verse from Zech. 12:10 is quoted: "They shall look on the one whom they have pierced" (19:37). Finally in this section the first part of the quote from Zechariah will be fulfilled in the disciples' commission: "And I will pour out a spirit of compassion and supplication on the house of David and the inhabitants of Jerusalem so that, when they look on him whom they have pierced, they shall mourn for him, as one mourns for an only child, and weep bitterly over him, as one weeps over a firstborn."

COMING AND STANDING IS JOHN'S WAY OF DESCRIBING JESUS' RESURRECTION EXPERIENCE TO THE DISCIPLES.

The description of the disciples draws a strong contrast with Mary Magdalene. Their fear while hiding behind locked doors contrasts with her boldness of action; their joy contrasts with her weeping. They see and are filled with joy. She sees and does not recognize, but believes at the sound of his voice. An audience begins to notice a progression in the points of view. The beloved disciple saw only an empty tomb and believed; Mary heard Jesus' voice and believed. Now the disciples see the hands and side of Jesus and believe. The images are becoming progressively more physical.

The translation of Jesus' commission to the disciples is difficult. The NRSV is not so much incorrect as misleading. His own sending by the Father is in Greek in the present perfect tense, indicating its past point of origin but its continuing validity, while Jesus' sending of the disciples is in the present tense, the audience's immediate foreground. So it might make more sense to translate it, "As the Father has sent me and still does, so I am sending you." Jesus' sending is not over as the English past tense implies but continues on and is the basis for the disciples' sending.

Jesus' breathing on the disciples alludes to Gen. 2:7, where God "formed man from the dust of the ground, and breathed into his nostrils the breath of life." The LXX uses the same Greek word as in John. Thus, the commissioning is a creation story.

The actual commission refers back to Jesus' promise in the farewell discourse: "As you [the Father] have sent me into the world, so I have sent them into the world" (17:18). The attentive listener would pick up many strong echoes of the farewell discourse—peace, joy, mission, and Spirit.

Holy Spirit is rare in John (normally John uses *Spirit*) and the *the* should be omitted. This is not a trinitarian reference, but in connection with the allusion to Genesis refers to God's creating, life-giving spirit or breath. The saying about forgiveness has to do with preaching and being sent, as the context makes clear. The community preaches to the world and offers forgiveness. John the Baptist introduced Jesus in 1:29 as "the Lamb of God who takes away the sin of the world." In this commission, that announcement finds its fulfillment. This section began with a reference to the disciples' fear of the Judeans and Jesus' showing them his side. The audience now begins to put the pieces together. The Zechariah quote, the creation story in Genesis, and the announcement of John the Baptist form the context in which this commission is understood.

Touching and Feeling

The indications for this new section invoke a minimal shift. Thomas, the Twin, and the Twelve identify the main characters. The foreign Aramaic name Thomas is translated for the benefit of a Greek-speaking audience.

Thomas has appeared twice before in the Gospel. In his first appearance (11:16) the translation "Twin" was also given. The phrase "Thomas, the one called the Twin" may well function as a way to recall to the audience's mind a whole series of extratextual references. With the discovery of the *Gospel of Thomas*, we may well be in a position to speculate about those extratextual references triggered by "Thomas the Twin." In that Gospel, Thomas is referred to as "Didymos Judas Thomas." Thomas is the great mystic seer, in contrast to his function in the Fourth Gospel. His commissioning scene in the *Gospel of Thomas* brings out the difference.

Jesus said to his disciples, "Compare me to something and tell me what I am like."

Simon Peter said to him, "You are like a just angel."

Matthew said to him, "You are like a wise philosopher."

Thomas said to him, "Teacher, my mouth is utterly unable to say what you are like."

Jesus said, "I am not your teacher. Because you have drunk, you have become intoxicated from the bubbling spring that I have tended."

And he took him and withdrew, and spoke three sayings to him.

When Thomas came back to his friends, they asked him, "What did Jesus say to you?"

Thomas said to them, "If I tell you one of the sayings he spoke to me, you will pick up rocks and stone me, and fire will come from the rocks and devour you." (*Gospel of Thomas*, 13)

In the *Gospel of Thomas*, Thomas is the hero while the other disciples play the role of buffoons. But in the Gospel of John, Thomas does not understand. He takes a very literal position. In 11:16, when Jesus goes to Bethany to raise Lazarus, Thomas tells the other disciples he will go with Jesus to Jerusalem to die. And in the farewell discourse Thomas complains, "Lord, we do not know where you are going. How can we know the way?" (14:5).

> IN THE *GOSPEL OF THOMAS*, THOMAS IS THE HERO WHILE THE OTHER DISCIPLES PLAY THE ROLE OF BUFFOONS. BUT IN THE GOSPEL OF JOHN, THOMAS DOES NOT UNDERSTAND.

It is not hard to imagine that among the community of the beloved disciple, the claims of Thomas's followers, as represented in the tradition of the *Gospel of Thomas,* are viewed with a certain skepticism and scorn.

Thomas's response to the disciples' declaration, "We have seen the Lord," is harsh and negative. The repetition of "mark of the nails" and the escalation from sticking in his finger to his whole hand create an exaggerated physical sense of the need for proof. "I will not believe" is, in the Greek, an aorist subjunctive, a classical form, that emphasizes an emphatic negative in the future, more like "Never will I." Jesus' command to Thomas, on the other hand, is constructed very differently. Where Thomas is harsh and negative, Jesus is elegant and pleading: "Put your finger here and see my hands." So magnificently composed is this scene, so strong is the contrast, that it has inspired magnificent art (for instance, Caravaggio).[3]

Jesus' commands end in Greek with an aphoristic saying: *apistos alla pistos,* which the NRSV renders, "Do not doubt but believe." The RSV was closer with "Do not be faithless but believing." "Doubting" is pandering to a much later tradition. John's sense is more "Be not faithless but faithful."

Commentators often take Thomas's response to Jesus' command as the climax to the Gospel. Rarely in the New Testament is Jesus called God. The closest parallel to Thomas's confession is the title of the emperor Domitian, who ruled during the Gospel's time frame (81–96 C.E.). He required that he should be addressed as "our Lord and God" (*dominus et deus noster*; Suetonius, *Domitian*, 13). John has used imperial titles before. At the end of the Samaritan woman's narrative, Jesus is proclaimed as Savior of the world (4:42), clearly an ironic usage. Here, too, Thomas's confession exposes the pretensions of the Roman emperor. Thomas's confession acknowledges what Jesus has already told Mary: Jesus is God's agent, the bridge between my God and your God, creating the new family of God. "Whoever has seen me has seen the Father" (14:9).

Jesus responds to Thomas's confession with a question and a beatitude. The question, "Have you believed?" is slightly ironical, challenging Thomas to examine his belief. The beatitude contrasts seeing and believing. Truly blessed are those who believe without seeing, like the beloved disciple and Mary Magdalene. In the end, the narrative comes back to its first example of faith. Johannine scholar Barnabas Lindars has observed, "Being absent when Jesus appeared to the disciples on Easter night, Thomas was virtually in the position of the Christian who has not seen the risen Jesus, and he should not have needed a further appearance in order to come to faith."[1] The text has quietly drawn attention to another alternative to seeing in the description of Jesus' presence as "coming." Jesus is not absent; he abides forever, always coming to his disciples.

> TRULY BLESSED ARE THOSE WHO BELIEVE WITHOUT SEEING, LIKE THE BELOVED DISCIPLE AND MARY MAGDALENE.

The Ending

Verses 30–31 conclude the whole chapter and originally the whole Gospel. The writing of the book (that is, the Gospel of John) employs the Greek perfect tense ("are written," NRSV), indicating the book's continuing validity. The book is center stage. Writing in the ancient world was strongly connected with auditory activity. One writes so that others may hear. Silent reading was almost unknown (see Acts 8:26–40, the first reading for the Fifth Sunday of Easter, below). The purpose of writing/hearing is to bring one to faith in Jesus the Messiah, the Son of God, so that "you may have life in his name." The very writing/hearing of the book is the voice of the risen Jesus. We have no need to see or touch and feel, only to hear.

This concludes the argument of the chapter. Faith now comes through hearing, not seeing. The audience who hears the book confronts in its reading/hearing the conditions for believing. They have experienced the risen Lord. They fulfill the beatitude: "Blessed are those who have not seen and yet have come to believe."

Notes

1. Walter Bauer, *A Greek-English Lexicon of the New Testament and Other Early Christian Literature*, ed. Frederick William Danker, 3rd ed. (Chicago: University of Chicago Press, 2000), 552.

2. In dealing with 1 John, I highly recommend the magisterial commentary of Raymond Brown, *The Epistles of John*, Anchor Bible (Garden City, N.Y.: Doubleday, 1982.

3. The Website www.textweek.com has an excellent collection of art associated with this scene; go to http://www.textweek.com/art/thomas.htm.

4. Barnabas Lindars, *The Gospel of John*, New Century Bible (London: Oliphants, 1972), 616.

THIRD SUNDAY OF EASTER

APRIL 30, 2006

REVISED COMMON	EPISCOPAL (BCP)	ROMAN CATHOLIC
Acts 3:12-19	Acts 4:5-12	Acts 3:13-15, 17-19
	or Micah 4:1-5	
Psalm 4	Psalm 98 or 98:1-5	Ps. 4:2, 4, 7-8, 9
1 John 3:1-7	1 John 1:1—2:2	1 John 2:1-5a
	or Acts 4:5-12	
Luke 24:36b-48	Luke 24:36b-48	Luke 24:35-48

FIRST READING

ACTS 3:12-19 (RCL)
ACTS 3:13-15, 17-19 (RC)

Peter's speech arises because of his healing of a lame beggar. When the beggar requests alms, Peter replies that he has no gold or silver, "but what I have I give you; in the name of Jesus Christ of Nazareth, stand up and walk" (Acts 3:6).

Peter's speech takes place in Solomon's portico. The Greek refers to a *stoa,* which is a colonnade where one could walk and be protected from the sun. To date its location has not been found.

This speech follows the pattern found in the other early speeches in Acts that involve Jesus' death at the hands of the Jews, his resurrection, and the apostles as witnesses, but it contains some interesting variations. Peter begins by acknowledging that the cure is not by his power or piety. *Eusebeia,* piety, might also have in English the sense of religiosity. It is not because of his goodness that the cure has taken place.

Three verbs describe the activity of the Jews—hand over, reject, and killed. These indicate an escalating violence. The killing of Jesus is contrasted with their request to have a murderer released. At the same time Pilate is let off the hook, "he had decided to release him" (3:13). Three times in Luke's Passion account, Pilate pronounces Jesus innocent (Luke 23:4, 14-15, 22). This theme recurs throughout Acts. The author does mitigate this charge in v. 17 when Peter states, "I know that you acted in ignorance, as did also your rulers." This seems to put the blame more on the rulers than on the nation or people themselves.

Luke's Gospel and Acts were written at the end of the first century and reflect that situation, and not the historical situation at the time of the death of Jesus. Following the destruction of the Temple, an increasingly Gentile Christianity began to shift the blame for the death of Jesus from Rome to the Jews. Historically, Pilate was responsible for the death of Jesus, as the form of his death makes clear: crucifixion. If you read the Gospels in chronological order, you will see a growing tendency to exculpate Rome and blame the Jews. As Christians who come after the Holocaust, we can no longer take these texts at face value. We have seen their effect. Not that the authors intended this effect; but this has been the tragic outcome of the narrative. We must learn to proclaim the gospel without blaming the Jews.

> IF YOU READ THE GOSPELS IN CHRONOLOGICAL ORDER, YOU WILL SEE A GROWING TENDENCY TO EXCULPATE ROME AND BLAME THE JEWS.

Peter's speech employs a number of interesting christological titles. "The God of our ancestors has glorified his servant Jesus" (3:13). "Servant" here does not represent the Greek *doulos*, which means servant in the sense of slave, but *pais*, which means a young servant, even one's own child. In the Septuagint, this term is used to describe the servant in Isaiah 52, the suffering servant. The early church used the servant passages in Isaiah as a way to understand Jesus' death. Peter's speech may well be referring to Isa. 52:13, where "servant" and "glorified" occur together: "My servant shall prosper; he shall be exalted [literally, *glorified*] and lifted up, and shall be very high."

"Holy and Righteous" (3:14) are both titles from the Hebrew Bible. Psalm 106:16 calls Aaron holy, and Genesis 6:9 names Noah as righteous. "Author of life" (3:15) is problematic. It also appears without the modifier "of life" in Acts 5:31 (see the Episcopal lectionary's first reading for Easter Evening, above). The Greek root *arch* indicates a ruler or the beginner, as in the first words of the Gospel of John, "In the beginning [*arche*]." It has the sense of the originator, founder, or source of life.

Finally, Peter uses "Messiah" or "Christ" (v. 18). *Christos* is a Greek translation of the Hebrew *mashiah*. Both are words that indicate one has been anointed with oil, so "Anointed" is an appropriate translation for both. "Anointed" in this instance comes from the anointing of the high priest and especially the king. So calling Jesus Messiah indicates that one thinks he is like David.

What these titles indicate is how difficult it is to classify Jesus. These titles hint at what God has accomplished in Jesus, but they do not adequately comprehend it. They are both right and wrong. They both lead and mislead. This is an important lesson to learn from Peter's speech.

ACTS 4:5-12 (BCP)

See the first reading for the Fourth Sunday of Easter, below.

MICAH 4:1-5 (BCP ALT.)

Micah was a Judean prophet during an expansive phrase of the Assyrian Empire (eighth century B.C.E.). Today's alternative reading in the Episcopal lectionary is a marvelous vision of universal peace centered around Jerusalem because the Lord will establish it as the highest of all mountains. The symbol of this peace is that the nations "shall beat their swords into plowshares, and their spears into pruning hooks; nation shall not lift up sword against nation, neither shall they learn war any more" (4:3).

RESPONSIVE READING
PSALM 4 (RCL)
PSALM 4:2, 4, 7-8, 9 (RC)

This psalm is the prayer of an individual, perhaps while offering temple sacrifices (4:5). The psalm begins by thanking God for the room ("wide space," literally) God has given the petitioner when in distress.

The petitioner is beset by enemies who "love vain words" (4:2), yet he remains confident "the LORD has set apart the faithful for himself" (4:3). His enemies taunt him that God is absent; just let us see him, they call out (4:6). This taunt recalls that confidence in God relies not upon the mighty presence of God but upon God's peace: "I will both lie down and sleep in peace; for you alone, O LORD, make me lie down in safety" (4:8).

PSALM 98 or 98:1-5 (BCP)

See the responsive reading for the Sixth Sunday of Easter, below.

SECOND READING

1 JOHN 3:1-7 (RCL)

For the context of 1 John, see the second reading for the Second Sunday of Easter, above. The division of this reading is particularly bad. Most modern printed Bibles indicate that chapter 3 does not begin a new unit or section of the letter. This reading belongs to a section of the letter that extends from 2:28 to 3:10, and the whole unit has as it primary theme righteousness.

To understand this reading it is important to realize that in the Johannine literature sin has little to do with moral wrongdoing and more to do with unbelief. "And when he comes, he will prove the world wrong about sin and righteousness and judgment: about sin, because they do not believe in me; about righteousness, because I am going to the Father and you will see me no longer; about judgment, because the ruler of this world has been condemned" (John 16:8-11). Both sin and righteousness are used in this passage in this distinctive Johannine sense.

> TO UNDERSTAND THIS READING IT IS IMPORTANT TO REALIZE THAT IN THE JOHANNINE LITERATURE SIN HAS LITTLE TO DO WITH MORAL WRONGDOING AND MORE TO DO WITH UNBELIEF.

God's love makes us God's children, and that means we know God's Son because we are God's children. For John, those who know (believe in) Jesus cannot sin. His being revealed so that we may believe takes away sin (that is, unbelief). The contrary is also so: "No one who sins has either seen him or known him" (3:6). This identification of unbelief with sin makes it very difficult for us to hear and understand this argument, conditioned as we are to understand sin as a moral transgression.

1 JOHN 1:1—2:2 (BCP)
1 JOHN 2:1-5a (RC)

See the second reading for the Second Sunday of Easter, above.

ACTS 4:5-12 (BCP ALT.)

See the second reading for the Fourth Sunday of Easter, below.

THE GOSPEL

39

THIRD SUNDAY
OF EASTER

BERNARD
BRANDON
SCOTT

LUKE 24:36b–48 (RCL, BCP)
LUKE 24:35–48 (RC)

Today's Gospel is a continuation of the Easter Evening Gospel, the Road to Emmaus story. You should recall that context in dealing with this story. If you did not employ the Emmaus story on Easter Evening, I encourage you to go back and read it before continuing with this selection and by all means remind your audience of the connection between today's Gospel and the Emmaus story.

Stopping the reading at v. 48 does a certain violence to Luke's narrative. Chapter 24 is both a conclusion to the Gospel as a whole and a bridge to the Acts of the Apostles. Excising the Gospel's concluding verses truncates this bridging activity to Acts. But then, 24:44–53 is the Gospel reading for the Ascension of Our Lord (below).

In Luke's Gospel, the beginning of v. 36 draws a strong connection with the Emmaus story. The scene opens with "they," meaning the eleven and those with them (24:33), discussing the couple's report concerning Jesus' appearance to them on the road to Emmaus and the appearance to Peter, of which, astonishingly, we hear no more.

We have a tendency to harmonize Gospel accounts. Often such harmonizing is unintentional and results from common exposure to the Gospel readings out of their evangelical context. If I were to ask you to imagine the situation Luke has in mind for the scene of today's Gospel, you would probably unreflectively reply, "The upper room." But Luke provides us with no description of the physical situation except to say that it is in Jerusalem. John's Gospel has the upper room. While imagining this scene as taking place in the upper room is probably harmless, it nevertheless unconsciously moves us to harmonize Luke and John and so hides their distinctive points of view.

Flesh and Bones

When Jesus suddenly stands among the disciples, they are "startled and terrified, and thought that they were seeing a ghost" (v. 37). Strangely, the appearance to Simon mentioned in v. 34 has not resolved the issue, but the fear does point to the theme we saw in Luke in the Emmaus story. Appearances of the risen Lord do not in themselves provoke belief in the resurrection. More is needed.

APPEARANCES OF THE RISEN LORD DO NOT IN THEMSELVES PROVOKE BELIEF IN THE RESURRECTION. MORE IS NEEDED.

The NRSV has "ghost," which gets at the correct sense in English, but the Greek reads *pneuma*, which literally means "spirit." This may prove significant in light of Paul's use in 1 Corinthians 15 of *pneumatikos* (spiritual) to describe the resurrected body (*soma*) of Jesus. We will return to this issue below.

Jesus then shows them his hands and feet (not his side, as in John) to prove that it is him. Once again, the resurrected Jesus is the crucified Jesus. The resurrection does not eliminate or overcome the crucifixion, but it indicates that the crucifixion is God's way.

Then Jesus concludes, "Touch me and see; for a ghost [spirit] does not have flesh and bones as you see that I have" (24:39). This reference to the physical character of the risen Jesus is the strongest such reference in the New Testament. John, written around the end of the first century like the Gospel of Luke, does not go quite this far in the physical character of the risen Jesus. Matthew, probably written in the mid-80s C.E., has a very short appearance story and avoids the issue of what kind of body the risen Jesus has. In Mark, written shortly after the destruction of the temple, the tomb is empty, and so the risen Jesus makes no appearance. There is a clear trajectory here—in the earliest Gospel, Mark, there is no mention of the body of the risen Jesus, but by the end of the first century, the physical character of the risen

IN THE EARLIEST GOSPEL, MARK, THERE IS NO MENTION OF THE BODY OF THE RISEN JESUS BUT BY THE END OF THE FIRST CENTURY THE PHYSICAL CHARACTER OF THE RISEN JESUS IS BEING EMPHASIZED.

Jesus is being emphasized. Clearly, at the end of the first century, this has become an issue, perhaps as a result of the debate with emerging Gnosticism or docetism.

When we turn to Paul the contrast could not be stronger. In 1 Corinthians 15 Paul draws a clear distinction between the physical body and the spiritual body: "It is sown a physical [*psychikon*] body, it is raised a spiritual [*pneumatikon*] body" (1 Cor. 15:44). The issue dividing the Corinthians and Paul is not resurrection itself. They both agree that Jesus rose from the dead. But Paul insists upon resurrection from the dead, which for him means the body (*soma*) will rise. For the Corinthians, the body (*soma*) is the problem. In baptism their soul separates from the body, and so the soul can speak in tongues and the body can curse the Lord (1 Cor. 12:3; or 1 Cor. 5:6b–8, the second reading for Easter Evening, above). The soul, the divine spark, was entrapped in the body, and baptism has released it. The last thing they want to hear is that the body will rise. Yet that is precisely what Paul affirms. The body will rise, but it will be not a physical body but a spiritual body. Paul drives his argument home with the conclusion, "Flesh and blood cannot inherit the kingdom of God" (1 Cor. 15:50).

Paul and Luke are at opposite ends of the pole. Nor is there any easy way to reconcile them. When we add in the evidence discussed above, a clear trajectory emerges. Paul in the 50s C.E., the earliest discussion of the resurrection, argues for a spiritual body. Luke at the end of the first century argues for a physical understanding of the resurrection. Even for Luke the physical body of the risen Jesus is not like an ordinary physical body since it is not recognizable to the couple on the road to Emmaus and Jesus suddenly appears among them. So it is not a normal physical body.

There is no biblical position on the resurrected body—there are differing positions. Perhaps that is where we should leave it. What the two extremes have in common is their attempts to affirm the reality of the resurrection. Both Paul and Luke would agree that it is not a ghost or a phantom. What both lack is an anthropology to explain resurrection, so they operate within the anthropological models they have. We, too, are probably in the same situation when dealing with the mystery.

It Was Necessary

After establishing the reality of his resurrection, "he opened their minds to understand the scriptures" (24:45). This returns to the major theme of the angel in the tomb and the Emmaus story, pointing to its importance and centrality in Luke's resurrection narratives. The Son of Man sayings prophesying his death and resurrection are rephrased as a Messiah saying: "Thus it is written, that the Messiah is to suffer and to rise from the dead on the third day" (24:45; see 9:22; 17:25; 18:32). Jesus is not appealing to specific texts to prove his messiahship; he is not proof-texting. He is appealing to the pattern of scripture as indicated in the stories of Moses and the prophets. The prophets and the Messiah proclaim God's word and are always rejected, persecuted, and killed, and still God affirms them. That is the pattern of divine necessity. (For details, see the Emmaus story, in the Gospel for Easter Evening, above.)

> THE PROPHETS AND THE MESSIAH PROCLAIM GOD'S WORD AND ARE ALWAYS REJECTED, PERSECUTED, AND KILLED, AND STILL GOD AFFIRMS THEM. THAT IS THE PATTERN OF DIVINE NECESSITY.

What is now added is "that repentance and forgiveness of sins is to be proclaimed in his name to all nations, beginning from Jerusalem" (24:47). This moves beyond the angel's announcement and the Emmaus story. The theme of repentance and forgiveness of sins extends back into the Gospel and looks forward to Acts.

John the Baptist had proclaimed repentance: "He went into all the region around the Jordan, proclaiming a baptism of repentance for the forgiveness of sins" (Luke 3:3). In Jesus' inaugural speech in the synagogue in Nazareth, a critical passage for Luke's Gospel, the Isaiah 61 passage summarizes Jesus' ministry. That quote begins, "The spirit of the Lord is upon me," and includes the phrase "He has sent me to proclaim release to the captives" (4:18; Isa. 61:1 LXX). The Greek word translated "release" is the same one used for forgiveness in 3:3 and 24:47. Furthermore, in Nazareth Jesus announces that the spirit of the Lord is upon him, while at the end of today's reading he tells the disciples to remain in Jerusalem until clothed in power (24:49).

Making the tie to Acts, Peter tells those in Jerusalem, "Repent, and be baptized every one of you in the name of Jesus Christ so that your sins may be forgiven; and you will receive the gift of the Holy Spirit" (Acts 2:38). In defending himself before Agrippa, Paul summarizes his ministry: "But [I] declared first to those in Damascus, then in Jerusalem and throughout the countryside of Judea, and also to the Gentiles, that they should repent and turn to God and do deeds consistent with repentance" (Acts 26:20).

Luke pulls together a number of major themes in both the Gospel and Acts. Luke is frequently credited with creating the Christian periodization of history, the period of Israel, Jesus as the Middle of Time, and the period of the church.[1] Yet here at the end of the Gospel, he is making another move. He paints with a broad brush outlining and hinting at a grand sweep of divine history. The fate of

JESUS FULFILLS THE DIVINE PLAN. BUT THAT PLAN LOOKS FORWARD TO REACHING THE WHOLE WORLD.

the prophets is still the fate of Jesus and the disciples. Jesus fulfills the divine plan. But that plan looks forward to reaching the whole world. And its pattern is always the same. God's word meets rejection because it opposes the powers, brings release to the captives. Just as the Gospel ends with Jesus confronting Rome, so Acts will end with Paul awaiting his confrontation with Rome. There is no doubt how the empire will act. Empires always act in the same way. Yet the resurrection announces that this is still the way God acts.

Note

1. Hans Conzelmann, *The Theology of St. Luke* (Philadelphia: Fortress Press, 1960; reprint, 1982).

FOURTH SUNDAY OF EASTER

May 7, 2006

Revised Common	Episcopal (BCP)	Roman Catholic
Acts 4:5-12	Acts 4:(23-31) 32-37 or Ezek. 34:1-10	Acts 4:8-12
Psalm 23	Psalm 23 or Psalm 100	Ps. 118:1, 8-9, 21-23, 26, 28, 29
1 John 3:16-24	1 John 3:1-8 or Acts 4:(23-31) 32-37	1 John 3:1-2
John 10:11-18	John 10:11-16	John 10:11-18

First Reading

ACTS 4:5-12 (RCL)
ACTS 4:8-12 (RC)

Today's first reading forms a complex of stories about the preaching of the apostles after Pentecost. Peter and John have been arrested following the healing of a lame man (3:1-10) and Peter's preaching in Solomon's portico. The setting of the scene before the council draws a sharp contrast between the professionalism of the judges and the lay character of the prisoners. A triad of rulers, elders, and scribes is matched by four names—"Annas the high priest, Caiaphas, John, and Alexander" (4:5). This elaboration of the groups and the names situates the "leaders" against the two apostles. The weight of authority highlights the disciples' smallness.

The authorities ask, "By what power or by what name did you do this?" (4:7). The chief priests, scribes, and elders had asked a similar question about Jesus' authority when he was teaching in the temple (Luke 20:2). What distinguishes the question the authorities asked Jesus from that put to the two apostles is the addition of the phrase "by what name." Jesus acts on his own authority, while the disciples act in the name of Jesus. Jesus had warned that they would be hated for his name (Luke 21:17), and acting in the name of Jesus is a recurring theme in Acts (thirty times).

When Peter responds to the authorities, he is filled with the Holy Spirit. This, too, is a major theme in Luke-Acts (see the Ascension of Our Lord, below, for discussion of Spirit). The Spirit emboldens Peter, who does not cower before the authorities as he did before in the high priest's garden (Luke 22:54-62). Apparently the healed man was arrested with Peter and John, because Peter refers to him as standing before them "in good health by the name of Jesus Christ of Nazareth, whom you crucified, whom God raised from the dead." Another sharp contrast is drawn, this time between the authorities, who crucified Jesus, and God, who raised him from the dead. Thus, the authorities no longer represent God but have become God's enemies.

The healing of the lame man marks the first confrontation between the apostles and the authorities. It was also Jesus' healing activity that led to his first confrontation with the authorities. Luke-Acts reflects the situation of the early Christian communities at the end of the first century. Neither is a historical report about the events of the early 30s C.E. Healing was an important and distinctive early Christian activity. Historian Rodney Stark, in *The Beginnings of Christianity,* has argued that taking care of the sick is one of the primary reasons early Christianity grew.[1] Galen, the great author of medical guides in the ancient world, advised doctors to flee the cities during outbreaks of the plague. Thus, pagans were left without medical care, while Christians cared for the sick and dying. As a result, according to Stark, during the plague Christians had a higher survival rate and better health in general as a result of their care for the sick.

> ANOTHER SHARP CONTRAST IS DRAWN, THIS TIME BETWEEN THE AUTHORITIES, WHO CRUCIFIED JESUS, AND GOD, WHO RAISED HIM FROM THE DEAD.

Healing the sick lays the very foundation of the ministry of Jesus and the apostles. It forms part of the gifts of God for God's people. Healing is resurrection, and part of our fundamental mission is to bring healing to the world. It signals the way God wants the world to be—whole, healed, full of life.

At the end of this story, Peter proclaims, "There is salvation in no one else, for there is no other name under heaven given among mortals by which we must be saved" (v. 12). While a number of New Testament authors use the term "salvation," it is a particularly favorite term in Luke-Acts. "Salvation" is Luke's inclusive term for expressing what God has accomplished in Jesus. Biblical scholar Joseph Fitzmyer has a good summary of the meaning of salvation for Luke: "By it he means deliverance of human beings from evil, whether

> SALVATION IS THE FULFILLMENT OF GOD'S PLAN FOR ISRAEL TO BRING ALL OF HUMANKIND INTO GOD'S GRACE.

physical, political, cataclysmic, moral, or eschatological, and the restoration of them to a state of wholeness."[2] This narrative began by listing the Jewish authorities who are set in opposition and ends with the exclusive claim of salvation in the name of Jesus. The Jewish authorities have rejected Jesus, and God by raising Jesus acknowledges that they have also rejected God. But God has not rejected Israel. Luke-Acts makes no such move. Salvation is the fulfillment of God's plan for Israel to bring all of humankind into God's grace.

This claim to exclusiveness of salvation in the name of Jesus is not really posed against Israel but against the Roman Empire. Salvation is the gift the emperor brings to the empire, and an important imperial title is *savior*. Thus, the claim that salvation is only in the name of Jesus is a direct challenge to the claims of the empire. If Luke-Acts was written in the late 90s C.E., this reflects the growing conflict between empire and church.

It should be pointed out that Luke does not have in mind the modern issue of nonbelievers. That is a context beyond his concerns.

ACTS 4:(23-31) 32-37 (BCP)

See the first reading for the Second Sunday of Easter, above.

EZEKIEL 34:1-10 (BCP ALT.)

Ezekiel 30 collects a number of the prophet's sayings against the leaders of Israel. Today's reading employs the metaphor of the leaders as shepherds. God rages against them, "You have not strengthened the weak, you have not healed the sick, you have not bound up the injured, you have not brought back the strayed, you have not sought the lost, but with force and harshness you have ruled them" (34:4). This reading points out that attacks on the leaders are an ancient tradition and that they do not signal the rejection of the people. This reading nicely reinforces the first reading from Acts. It also offers a strong contrast with Psalm 23, where God is the good shepherd.

RESPONSIVE READING
PSALM 23 (RCL, BCP)

This psalm has long been a favorite, and the resonant and majestic translation of the King James Version has fixed these phrases in the English language. In early

Christianity Psalm 23 was recited as the newly baptized emerged from the font. So this is a very appropriate psalm during this Easter period.

The psalm has three stanzas. In the first two stanzas, the psalm employs the metaphor of God (Yahweh) as the shepherd who provides green pastures and whose shepherd's crook protects the sheep. But in the last stanza, the metaphor shifts to God as a host at a meal.

PSALM 100 (BCP ALT.)

This psalm envisions the pilgrim coming into the temple into God's presence and singing a hymn of thanksgiving while coming through his gates. The final stanza, in celebrating God's steadfast love and faithfulness to all generations of Israel, gives thanks that God will be faithful to God's covenant.

PSALM 118:1, 8-9, 21-23, 26, 28, 29 (RC)

See the responsive reading for Easter Morning, above.

SECOND READING
1 JOHN 3:16-24 (RCL)

For the context of 1 John, see the second reading for the Second Sunday of Easter, above. Today's reading continues the argument of last Sunday's reading. In the Johannine literature sin is unbelief (see above, the second reading for the Third Sunday of Easter). Believing that Jesus was sent by the Father and knowing Jesus create unity with Jesus and the Father, so that we are encompassed in the love of the Father as God's children. The sign of belief is love.

The example of love is Jesus' laying down his life, and since we are unified with Jesus, his example becomes our example. Yet this notion of love is not some idealized model but has a practical outcome: "How does God's love abide in anyone who has the world's goods and sees a brother or sister in need and yet refuses help?" (3:17).

> THE EXAMPLE OF LOVE IS JESUS' LAYING DOWN HIS LIFE, AND SINCE WE ARE UNIFIED WITH JESUS, HIS EXAMPLE BECOMES OUR EXAMPLE.

The passage concludes with a single commandment with a double edge— "We should believe in the name of his Son Jesus Christ and love one another" (3:23). Since belief in John is not *belief about* but *abiding in*, being unified with

Jesus, the sign of this unity is love. So an all-tight web is woven together that fuses our unity with Jesus and the Father and has its outcome in the action of loving one another.

1 JOHN 3:1-8 (BCP)
1 JOHN 3:1-2 (RC)

See the second reading for the Third Sunday of Easter, above.

ACTS 4:(23-31) 32-37 (BCP ALT.)

See the first reading for the Second Sunday of Easter, above.

THE GOSPEL
JOHN 10:11-18 (RCL, RC)
JOHN 10:11-16 (BCP)

Many commentators have noted that Jesus in the Fourth Gospel speaks as the resurrected Lord, quite different from the Jesus of the Synoptics. These speeches are in the form of revelatory discourses. They were developed within the community of the beloved disciple as a distinctive form of the Jesus tradition. There has been endless

> MANY COMMENTATORS HAVE NOTED THAT JESUS IN THE FOURTH GOSPEL SPEAKS AS THE RESURRECTED LORD, QUITE DIFFERENT FROM THE JESUS OF THE SYNOPTICS.

speculation on their background. We can safely conclude that they represent the community working out its unique understanding of Jesus sometime toward the end of the first century.

This passage uses the same shepherd metaphor as Psalm 23 but applies it to Jesus rather than Yahweh. The metaphor is elaborated in some complex and intriguing ways. By beginning with v. 11, we miss the metaphorical comparison with the thief in v. 10. The thief comes "only to steal and kill and destroy," whereas Jesus ("I") comes to give life. This announces the basic Johannine position—a choice between death and life. The preacher should therefore seriously consider beginning the Gospel reading with v. 10.

The shift suggests a comparison. The thief is bad; the shepherd is good. The Greek here is *kalos*, literally "beautiful" or, perhaps better in English, "ideal"—"I am an ideal shepherd."[3] The ideal shepherd "lays down his life for the sheep" (10:11). The language draws on that effort of early Christians to use Isaiah 53 to understand the death of Jesus. This demonstrates the complexity of the metaphor.

Jesus is not a literal shepherd any more than we are literally sheep, and while the life of a shepherd can be dangerous (see the story of David in 1 Sam. 17:34–37), laying down one's life is not the first thing required of an ideal shepherd (see, for example, Psalm 23 above). This metaphor jumps immediately into a theological reflection on Jesus' death (see the second reading above for a similar move in 1 John).

Now another contrast is introduced with the hired hand. The thief represents an extreme, while the hired hand represents a more moderate negative example. The thief kills; the hired hand flees when the wolf attacks. Why does the hired hand flee? Because he does not own the sheep. The image is now within the metaphor, and we are not encouraged by the text to identify allegorically the hired hand or the wolf. The metaphor is explicating the difference.

Verse 14 repeats the initial positive metaphor—"I am the ideal shepherd." And in contrast with the hired hand, the ideal shepherd knows his own sheep and they know him. Now the discourse jumps out of the metaphor into theological reflection: "just as the Father knows me and I know the Father" (10:15). What does "to know" mean? In the metaphor the shepherd "knows" his own sheep and they know him. The discourse does not elaborate on this, but the implication is clear. The sheep know the shepherd's voice. But the comparison between the Father and the Son escalates the image out of the original metaphor into the range of theological revelation. What is not at stake is mystical knowing in which the differences between knower and known dissolve.

> THE FOURTH GOSPEL CONSISTENTLY ARGUES FOR A KNOWING IN WHICH THE FATHER KNOWS AND INITIATES THE KNOWING.

The Fourth Gospel consistently argues for a knowing in which the Father knows and initiates the knowing. To know is to be known by God. And the outcome of being known by God is that "I [Jesus] lay down my life for the sheep" (10:15), reiterating the initial introductory metaphor. The knowing is for us, on our behalf. Jesus gives his life for us. Precisely for this reason John speaks of Jesus' death as a lifting up, an exaltation, because in that death God is "for us," thus making us one with God.

The metaphor now elaborates in a nonmetaphorical fashion with the reference to other sheep. In the context of the discourse, this probably should be understood allegorically to refer to Gentiles or even divisions within early Christianity, a theme that concerns the Fourth Gospel (see John 17:20). The community is founded not upon doctrinal unity but

> THE COMMUNITY IS FOUNDED NOT UPON DOCTRINAL UNITY BUT UPON GOD'S KNOWING US AND BEING FOR US.

upon God's knowing us and being for us. We do not achieve that, but it is the way God is. God is for us.

God's knowing now transmutes, almost like a theme modulates in a piece of music, into "love." The Father loves Jesus because he lays down his life, a demonstration of his and God's love for those who are known by God and therefore know and love God. The two terms become interchangeable.

The final part of the reading concerns Jesus' freedom over his death, an issue that we know was debated between Christians and Jews at the end of the first century. This strong apologetic motif is reinforced in v. 19, which is not included in today's Gospel reading, when it is reported that this discourse creates a division among the Judeans.

The good or ideal shepherd discourse gives us once again an opportunity to reflect on the multiple images early Christians employed to make sense of Jesus' death and resurrection and also asks yet again about the relation between Jesus' death and resurrection. This one draws an intimate image of God the shepherd, of Jesus the shepherd. Both Psalm 23 and John 10 play with this image. But John goes further and argues that through Jesus we are known by God, and we know that God is for us because the shepherd will lay down his life for us so that we may have life more abundantly.

Notes

1. Rodney Stark, *The Beginnings of Christianity: How the Obscure, Marginal Jesus Movement Became the Dominant Religious Force in the Western World in a Few Centuries* (San Francisco: HarperSanFrancisco, 1997).

2. Joseph A. Fitzmyer, *The Acts of the Apostles*, Anchor Bible 31 (New York: Doubleday, 1998), 301.

3. Barnabas Lindars, *The Gospel of John*, New Century Bible (London: Oliphants, 1972), 361.

FIFTH SUNDAY OF EASTER

MAY 14, 2006

REVISED COMMON	EPISCOPAL (BCP)	ROMAN CATHOLIC
Acts 8:26–40	Acts 8:26–40 or Deut. 4:32–40	Acts 9:26–31
Ps. 22:25–31	Ps. 66:1–11 or 66:1–8	Ps. 22:26–27, 28, 30, 31–32
1 John 4:7–21	1 John 3:(14–17) 18–24 or Acts 8:26–40	1 John 3:18–24
John 15:1–8	John 14:15–21	John 15:1–8

FIRST READING
ACTS 8:26–40 (RCL, BCP)

The story of the conversion of the Ethiopian eunuch serves as a transition in Acts between the stoning of Stephen and the conversion of Saul. In the immediately preceding story, Philip has evangelized Samaria; now he turns to Gaza. Thus, the gospel is spreading north of Jerusalem into Samaria and south into Gaza. Geography in the Gospels and Acts frequently has a theological significance. As the geography expands, the preaching will spread beyond Israel. This explains the placing of Saul at the death of Stephen and his conversion following this story. When Ananias is instructed to go to Paul, the Lord says, "For he is an instrument whom I have chosen to bring my name before Gentiles and kings and before the people of Israel" (9:15). In chapter 10 Peter will have his vision of clean and unclean and preach to Cornelius, the real opening of the mission to the Gentiles in Acts.

Many commentators take the Ethiopian as the first Gentile, but there are real problems with this association. That ministry appears to begin more properly with the Peter and Cornelius story and then Paul. This is made clear in Peter's speech at the Jerusalem council: "You know that in the early days God made a choice among you, that I should be the one through whom the Gentiles would hear the message of the good news and become believers" (15:7). It is probably better to understand the Ethiopian as a Jew or proselyte and not as a Gentile/pagan.

The author is presenting a theological sketch of the spread of the good news, not a historical account. The origins of the mission to the Gentiles are shrouded in mystery, like much else in early Christianity. Certainly it did not originate with Paul.

Gaza was an old Philistine city situated on the major caravan route to Egypt. The city gave its name to the Gaza Strip, which is often in the news as a major hot spot in the Palestinian-Israeli conflict. It now is one of the most densely populated regions of the world.

Ancient Ethiopia is not identical with the modern state of Ethiopia. For the ancients the name designated the region south of Egypt. "Ethiopian" is derived from the Greek root *aithos*, "a burning heat," and so *aithops* ("Ethiopian") means "burnt-faced." The term goes back at least to Homer. The language of the Ethiopians was a Semitic language, like Hebrew and Aramaic, so it is not surprising that an Ethiopian would be a Jew.

> THE AUTHOR IS PRESENTING A THEOLOGICAL SKETCH OF THE SPREAD OF THE GOOD NEWS, NOT A HISTORICAL ACCOUNT.

The story's structure has a strong resemblance to the Emmaus story and is probably therefore of Luke's construction. Instead of Jesus' coming alongside the couple and interpreting the scripture, Philip plays this role under the direction of an angel of the Lord. Philip comes alongside the eunuch's chariot and interprets the scripture for him. There are two striking differences from the Emmaus story—the eunuch believes following the interpretation, and the narrative ends in baptism instead of the breaking of the bread.

As Philip runs alongside the eunuch's chariot, he hears him reading the scripture, which reminds us that people in the ancient normally read out loud, not silently as we do (an important point in understanding the conclusion to John 20; see above, the Gospel for the Second Sunday of Easter). He is reading out loud Isa. 53:7-8, a section from the suffering servant passage of Isaiah. This passage was very important in early Christianity's effort to understand the meaning of Jesus' death.

In Isaiah, this passage refers to Israel, not to the Messiah. After centuries of Christian usurpation of the Jewish scriptures, we should be honest with our audience that what is going on in Acts is christological reinterpretation of scripture. The Jewish scripture of Isaiah does not look forward to a suffering Messiah. Rather, Christians look back through the suffering of Jesus and use that suffering to reinterpret

> AFTER CENTURIES OF CHRISTIAN USURPATION OF THE JEWISH SCRIPTURES, WE SHOULD BE HONEST WITH OUR AUDIENCE THAT WHAT IS GOING ON IN ACTS IS CHRISTOLOGICAL REINTERPRETATION OF SCRIPTURE.

the meaning of Isaiah's suffering servant. We can have both interpretations. Texts can and do have multiple meanings. We need not deny, hide, or avoid the Jewish scripture to achieve these multiple interpretations. People who think a text can have only one meaning are like those who think the perfect form of water is ice.

The text is quoted in the Greek Septuagint form, which is significantly different in v. 8 from the Hebrew Bible.

Hebrew	**Greek Septuagint**
By a perversion of justice he was taken away.	In his humiliation justice was denied him.
Who could have imagined his future?	Who can describe his generation?
For he was cut off from the land of the living.	For his life is taken away from the earth.

The Isaiah text stresses the silence of the suffering Lamb, and the Septuagint version adds the note concerning the humiliation of the lamb as it dies. Both fit the Lukan version of Jesus' death.

The story of Philip and the eunuch is an example of the early community searching the scriptures to make sense of the death and suffering of Jesus. That search is ongoing because we are constantly forced to make sense in new situations of what God has accomplished and continues to accomplish in the death and resurrection of Jesus.

ACTS 9:26-31 (RC)

This is a transition following Paul's conversion. Barnabas introduces Paul to the apostles in Jerusalem. Acts emphasizes Paul's close alignment with and subordination to Jerusalem, whereas in Galatians 1–2 Paul underlines his independence, going so far as to say, "I was still unknown by sight to the churches of Judea that are in Christ" (Gal. 1:22).

Paul preaches boldly, a theme we have seen elsewhere in Acts, and because of his preaching the Hellenists seek to kill him. That preaching provokes rejection is likewise a familiar theme in Acts.

DEUTERONOMY 4:32-40 (BCP ALT.)

This passage concludes Moses' speech, which inaugurates Deuteronomy (1:1—4:43). As the conclusion of this long speech, it summarizes the great things God has done for God's people and ends on a note of God's faithfulness: "Keep his statutes and his commandments, which I am commanding you today for your own well-being and that of your descendants after you, so that you may long remain in the land that the LORD your God is giving you for all time" (4:40). The land is the promise of the covenant.

RESPONSIVE READING
PSALM 22:25–31 (RCL)
PSALM 22:26–27, 28, 30, 31–32 (RC)

Psalm 22 was frequently employed in the Passion accounts of the Gospels (nine times), and its opening words are on the dying Jesus' lips in Mark (15:34) and Matthew (27:46). The first part of the psalm (vv. 1–21) describes the distresses, suffering, and abandonment of the psalmist, and in v. 22 the psalmist shifts to a hymn of thanksgiving in confidence that God will answer his prayers. Today's psalm reading comes from this final thanksgiving section. The psalmist, as the rejected and reviled one, identifies in his confidence with the poor and outcast.

This psalm reminds us that true confidence in God is based only upon the deepest suffering and rejection and that rejection and suffering teach us identification with the poor and outcast. Resurrection only follows suffering. If we have not suffered and been rejected, we have no basis for confidence in the resurrection. It is precisely this dynamic of the psalm that made it so intriguing and helpful to early Christians.

> IF WE HAVE NOT SUFFERED AND BEEN REJECTED, WE HAVE NO BASIS FOR CONFIDENCE IN THE RESURRECTION.

PSALM 66:1–11 or 66:1–8 (BCP)

The psalm gives thanks to God for what God has done for God's people, especially during the exodus, a recurring theme in many psalms. But at the end of today's reading, the psalmist sounds a note that God has tried us, has tested us as silver.

SECOND READING
1 JOHN 4:7–21 (RCL)

In this section of the letter, the author returns to the theme of the new commandment that "you love one another just as I [Jesus] loved you" (John 13:34; restated in 1 John 2:9-11). In this passage the elder draws a moral, ethical conclusion: "Since God loved us so much, we also ought to love one another" (4:11). Salvation, in the Johannine literature, is to know God (John 17:3). But this knowledge is never intellectual; rather, it is union with God, an "abiding" or indwelling. Yet that union with God is expressed or seen only in love of another. "No one has ever seen God; if we love one another, God lives in us, and his love is perfected in us" (4:12). This is the passage's logic. It is an utter and complete attack on private piety. Love is not between God and me. It finds expression only in the love of one another.

The author is making a most forceful argument against those who have divided the community and have walked away in the name of truth (see the second reading for the Second Sunday of Easter). "Those who say, 'I love God,' and hate their brothers or sisters, are liars" (4:20). Those who have deserted and divided the community claim to love God whom they cannot see. The author rejects that claim. Love of God, abiding in God, always takes expression in loving one another and abiding (dwelling) together.

> THIS PASSAGE IS AN UTTER AND COMPLETE ATTACK ON PRIVATE PIETY. LOVE IS NOT BETWEEN GOD AND ME. IT FINDS EXPRESSION ONLY IN THE LOVE OF ONE ANOTHER.

1 JOHN 3:(14-17) 18-24 (BCP)
1 JOHN 3:18-24 (RC)

See the second reading for the Fourth Sunday of Easter, above.

THE GOSPEL
JOHN 15:1-8 (RCL, RC)

The Gospel readings for the Fifth and Sixth Sundays come from the same section in the Fourth Gospel and are part of the same argument. The lectionary division is artificial and truncates the passage's logic and rhetoric. You need to keep both this week's and next week's Gospel readings firmly in an audience's mind.

This text comes from Jesus' last discourse, John 13–17. This is a long and extensive discourse (see the Episcopal Lectionary Gospel reading, below, for an introduction to chapters 13–17). Originally it ended at 14:31, where Jesus says, "Rise, let us be on our way," yet the discourse continues for three more chapters. These three chapters were added when the Gospel was edited and expanded into its second edition. Today's reading comes from the second edition.

Viticulture supplies the metaphorical system underlying the text. What is true of growing grapes is true of the relationship between the Father, Son, and believing community. The allegory proceeds in a straightforward way. Jesus is the vine, the Father the vinedresser, and the community the branches. The vinedresser lops off any branch that does not produce and prunes any branch that does. From this allegory the author draws the same conclusion that he did in the 1 John 4 reading. The branch must produce fruit. It has a moral, ethical outcome, which will be made absolutely clear in next week's Gospel reading, the allegory's climax.

Just as the branch is a part of the vine and cannot live apart from vine, so we abide or dwell in Jesus, the true vine or real vine. Again, this is not individual piety but community. *We* are the branches, not "*I* am the branch." And the point of the abiding is to bear fruit.

JOHN 14:15-21 (BCP)

Jesus' last discourse in the Fourth Gospel is a long and extensive speech. Jesus begins by washing his disciples' feet, a ritual act of a slave, quite in contrast with the Synoptic beginning of the Passion account in which Jesus enters triumphantly, although ironically, into Jerusalem. At this last supper

> WHAT IS TRUE OF GROWING GRAPES IS TRUE OF THE RELATIONSHIP BETWEEN THE FATHER, SON, AND BELIEVING COMMUNITY.

there is no Passover meal, since in the Fourth Gospel Jesus dies on Passover. There is also no reference to the words of institution or Eucharist.

In the Gospel's first edition, the discourse ended at 14:31, and so this reading comes from near the end of the original discourse (see immediately above, John 15:1-8, for a short discussion of this issue). Following the washing of the disciples' feet, the original discourse has two main objectives. First, Jesus proclaims a new commandment: "I give you a new commandment, that you love one another. Just as I have loved you, you also should love one another. By this everyone will know that you are my disciples, if you have love for one another" (13:34-35). The second goal is to prepare his disciples for his departure. As the conclusion to the discourse, today's reading deals with both of these topics.

The "Advocate" is a strange image. *Parakletos* literally means "one called to the side of," that is, an advocate. In secular Greek it often appears in a legal context, roughly equivalent to a lawyer. Jerome in the Latin Vulgate transliterated the word as "Paraclete," and that is how the term entered the tradition in the West. The King James Version translated the word as "Comforter" and the RSV as "Counselor." While obviously a term of some importance in the community of the beloved disciple, it appears out of the blue in this passage, and so it is impossible to know exactly how it functioned in that community.

"Advocate" is a metaphorical term applied to the Spirit (14:26) in an effort to understand the Spirit's role in the community. It functions much as christological titles do. They, too, are metaphors that try to bring to language an understanding and experience of the community. The Advocate comes to our side, advocates for us, supports us. Jesus says the Father will send "*another* Advocate" (v. 16). "Another" indicates that there is more than one, and 1 John 2:1 makes evident that the other Advocate is Jesus. The Advocate functions to assure the community that Jesus and God are always present and to explain the community's experience of God's and Jesus' overwhelming presence. "They who have my commandments and keep them are those who love me; and those who love me will be loved by my Father, and I will love them and reveal myself to them" (14:21).

THE ADVOCATE COMES TO OUR SIDE, ADVOCATES FOR US, SUPPORTS US.

SIXTH SUNDAY OF EASTER

REVISED COMMON	EPISCOPAL (BCP)	ROMAN CATHOLIC
Acts 10:44–48	Acts 11:19–30 or Isa. 45:11–13, 18–19	Acts 10:25–26, 34–35, 44–48
Psalm 98	Psalm 33 or 33:1–8, 18–22	Ps. 98:1, 2–3, 3–4
1 John 5:1–6	1 John 4:7–21 or Acts 11:19–30	1 John 4:7–10
John 15:9–17	John 15:9–17	John 15:9–17

FIRST READING
ACTS 10:44–48 (RCL)

This is the conclusion of the Cornelius story from the first reading of Easter Morning; see above for an explanation of the context of this truncated reading.

The NRSV translation of v. 44 is particularly misleading. It is an under-translation. In Greek Peter is speaking *rhemata*, "literal words," while his audience hears *logos*, "the message." The Greek text sets up a difference that clearly anticipates the conclusion. The Revised English Bible does a better, though not adequate, job of translating this verse: "Peter was still speaking when the Holy Spirit came upon all who were listening to the message."

In the plot of the Acts of the Apostles, the conclusion of the Peter and Cornelius story marks a major shift. It is truly a second Pentecost. Pentecost itself had been in Jerusalem and was the Spirit's coming upon Israel. Now, following Peter's preaching, the circumcised witness the coming of the Spirit upon the uncircumcised. They "were astounded that the gift of the Holy Spirit had been poured out even on the Gentiles" (10:45). We think of *Gentiles* as

> NOW, FOLLOWING PETER'S PREACHING, THE CIRCUMCISED WITNESS THE COMING OF THE SPIRIT UPON THE UNCIRCUMCISED. IT IS TRULY A SECOND PENTECOST.

a positive term, especially since we are the Gentiles. But in this context *Gentiles* is a negative term. *Ethne*, from which the English word "ethnic" derives, means "those folks" as distinguished from *laos*, "our folks." The believers are referred to as "the circumcised" rather than "the Jews" because the author wants to accent the sign of their being God's people, *laos*. The Gentiles (*ethne*), because they are uncircumcised, are inherently unclean. From the point of view of the circumcised, the Gentiles/*ethne* are immoral. This explains the astonishment of the circumcised that the others have now become part of God's people.

The Peter and Cornelius story describes a most momentous moment in the life of the church from the point of view of the end of the first century. When the author looks back, he does not imagine a debate, a reasoned argument. There is no appeal to precedent, to scripture, which has been so important to this author up to this point. The outpouring of the Spirit determines the issue. Those standing with scripture would have been more than amazed. They would have been resistant.

ACTS 11:19–30 (BCP)

In this reading Acts sketches the spread of Christianity to Antioch, the third-largest city in the empire after Rome and Alexandria. Antioch will play a major role in the second part of Acts.

Following the success of the preaching by the Hellenists, Barnabas is sent to Antioch. This reflects Acts' concern to see the Apostles in Jerusalem overseeing the expanding mission. Barnabas then goes to Tarsus to get Paul. This is impossible to reconcile with Paul's own description of his activity in Galatians 2.

"It was in Antioch that the disciples were first called 'Christians'" (11:26). The purpose of this nickname is not explained. It probably came from outsiders as a way of differentiating these folks from other Jews or as a subset of the Jewish community. It probably has the sense of "messianists."

ISAIAH 45:11–13, 18–19 (BCP ALT.)

The introduction to this word of the Lord has been left off so that the term "Maker" in v. 11 is without referent. It refers back to the introductory metaphor of God as a potter. Can the clay argue with the potter? Of course not, so God asks, "Will you question me about my children, or command me concerning the work of my hands?" (45:11). Argument with God's will is futile. Israel must accept God's design. And that plan involves the use of Cyrus, the Persian emperor. Isaiah 45:1 refers to Cyrus as "God's anointed" or messiah. He authorized the return of the Judean exiles from Babylon and the rebuilding of the temple.

PSALM 98 (RCL)
PSALM 98:1, 2-3, 3-4 (RC)

This psalm confidently sings of God's future because God "has remembered his steadfast love and faithfulness to the house of Israel" (98:3). The jumble of images in this psalm creates a joyful noise to the Lord. There are not only the musical instruments but also the roar of the sea, the floods clapping their hands, and the hills singing. People and creation join together to make this new song.

PSALM 33 or 33:1-8, 18-22 (BCP)

This postexilic psalm has strong connections to the wisdom tradition. It celebrates the faithfulness and steadfast love of God for God's people and the covenant that binds the people to God. "Happy is the nation whose God is the LORD, the people whom he has chosen as his heritage" (33:12).

SECOND READING
1 JOHN 5:1-6 (RCL)

For the past several weeks the second readings have come from the First Letter of John. The letter is now drawing to its conclusion. The purpose of his letter was to hold a divided community together. The author employs the metaphor "Everyone who loves the parent loves the child" (5:1). The parent/family metaphor is extremely important and strong in the Johannine literature. God is the Father, Jesus is the Son,

> THE PARENT/FAMILY METAPHOR IS EXTREMELY IMPORTANT AND STRONG IN THE JOHANNINE LITERATURE. GOD IS THE FATHER, JESUS IS THE SON, AND WE ARE THE CHILDREN.

and we are the children. This family metaphor underlies a great deal of the author's thinking. To love the parent (God) is to love the children (the community), and to love the children is to love the parent.

"God's commandments" is a reference not to the Ten Commandments but to the commands to believe and love (3:23-24): "The commandment we have from him is this: those who love God must love their brothers and sisters also" (4:21). The parent metaphor continues with those who are born of God. The author can use interchangeably the terms *born of, abide in, know,* and *love.* In the hands of this author, all these metaphors are trying to say the same thing: God creates unity, not division.

The metaphor now shifts from a parent metaphor to a military one: "Whatever is born of God conquers the world." Why? Because Jesus is the Savior of the world (4:14; John 4:42). "Savior of the world" is an imperial title, applicable to Augustus and his successors because by their military power they delivered the world from chaos. They brought the world salvation. The Gemma Augustea presents a visual image of this view of power.[1] At the top of the image, Augustus is enthroned as Jupiter, while at the bottom his defeated enemies are being crucified.

The author of 1 John moves in a different direction. Military power does not conquer the world, but love, a love that gives its life away. In the context of the first century, this is an ironic statement since it flies in the face of that society's standards.

> TO BELIEVE THAT JESUS IS THE SON OF GOD IS TO LOVE ONE ANOTHER, TO GIVE ONE'S LIFE AWAY, AND SO TO CONQUER THE WORLD.

To believe that Jesus is the Son of God is to love one another, to give one's life away, and so to conquer the world. Come to think of it, this truth is counter to the values of our own society today.

The author points to the death of Jesus as the way this happens. "Water and blood" (v. 6) is a reference to the Johannine Passion narrative: "One of the soldiers pierced his side with a spear, and at once blood and water came out" (John 19:34). As the sign of victory, the author points to the empire's destroying Jesus, thus heightening the irony of the Savior of the world who achieves his victory by giving his life while dying on a cross, the Roman symbol of their domination of the world.

1 JOHN 4:7-21 (BCP)
1 JOHN 4:7-10 (RC)

See the second reading for the Fifth Sunday of Easter, above.

THE GOSPEL
JOHN 15:9-17 (RCL, BCP, RC)

The Gospel reading for the Fifth and Sixth Sundays comes from the same section in the Fourth Gospel and are part of the same argument. The lectionary division is artificial and truncates the logic and rhetoric of the passage. The preacher needs to keep both this week's and last week's Gospel reading firmly in the audience's mind.

This reading draws the conclusion of the allegory of the vine (see above, the Fifth Sunday of Easter, for details). There is a certain fusion of language in this passage. "Love" and "abide" are used interchangeably. To love is to abide in and vice versa. The image of abiding derives from the allegory of the vine, in which Jesus is the vine and the community ("you") is the branch.

There is also a play on the words "commands" (plural) and "command" (singular). To keep Jesus' commandments is to abide in his love. Then the commands are condensed into the command to "love one another as I have loved you" (15:12). And the example of that love is specified: "No one has greater love than this, to lay down one's life for one's friends" (15:13). The crucifixion is the example of love and is the standard by which our love is to be judged.

The laying down of one's life shifts the image of the relationship between Jesus and the community. One does not lay down one's life for a slave but for a friend. This passage subtly questions Christology. One of the traditional christological titles at the end of the first century, when this passage was composed, was *kurios*, "lord" or "master" (Greek uses the same word for two different senses in English).

> THE CRUCIFIXION IS THE EXAMPLE OF LOVE AND IS THE STANDARD BY WHICH OUR LOVE IS TO BE JUDGED.

The Fourth Gospel frequently employs this title. The correlative term for *kurios* is *doulos*, "slave" or "servant." As the NRSV footnote indicates, it makes more sense to translate this passage with "master/slave," rather than "master/servant." Jesus as master/Lord automatically implies Christian as slave. The Fourth Gospel here shifts the image. Jesus' love makes the believer his friend. "Friend" indicates an intimacy that is totally absent from "slave." "Friend" fits better with the images of abiding and loving.

The unity of Jesus and the Father and our unity with Jesus (abiding) bring forth the fruit of love, of laying down one's life for the other, of going to the limit. The Johannine image is not one of quietism but one of ethics and action that knit or prune humanity back together in love.

Note

1. For a picture of the Gemma Augustea, go to the Web page http://ctext.lib .virginia.edu/users/morford/augimage.html.

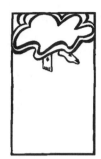

THE ASCENSION OF OUR LORD

MAY 25, 2006

REVISED COMMON	EPISCOPAL (BCP)	ROMAN CATHOLIC
Acts 1:1-11	Acts 1:1-11 or Ezek. 1:3-5a, 15-22, 26-28	Acts 1:1-11
Psalm 47 or Psalm 93	Psalm 47 or Ps. 110:1-5	Ps. 47:2-3, 6-7, 8-9
Eph. 1:15-23	Eph. 1:15-23 or Acts 1:1-11	Eph. 1:17-23 or Eph. 4:1-13 or 4:1-7, 11-13
Luke 24:44-53	Luke 24:49-53 or Mark 16:9-15, 19-20	Mark 16:15-20

The first reading, Acts 1:1-11, and the Gospel, Luke 24:44-53, are closely related, so one will have to decide how to handle the slight differences between them. The theme that holds both together is the worldwide mission of the church. Because these two readings are so close, I will treat them together.

FIRST READING AND THE GOSPEL

ACTS 1:1-11 (RCL, BCP, RC)
LUKE 24:44-53 (RCL)
LUKE 24:49-53 (BCP)

The Ascension

The ascension occurs only in Luke. Mark has no appearance of the risen Jesus. In Matthew the eleven meet Jesus on the mountain in Galilee, where he commissions them to go to the nations, but we are not told what happens to Jesus other than "I am with you always, to the end of the age" (Matt. 28:20). While one might assume an ascension, none is narrated. Likewise in the Fourth Gospel, the scene in chapter 21 ends with Jesus' speaking to the disciples. There may be an indirect reference to an ascension in Jesus' response to Mary Magdalene (John 20:17). Luke alone provides an answer to what happens.

The notion of an ascension may be dependent upon the very early Christian notion of the exaltation of Jesus. The hymn in Phil. 2:6-11 is an excellent example of this model. As early Christians tried to figure out how to make sense of their experience that Jesus was alive, they employed a number of models, among them resurrection and exaltation. We see in Paul the use of both of these models, depending on the point he wishes to make.

It also may be that ascension is related to the notion found in Judaism of the assumption or translation of the body of a holy one. Such stories about Moses, Elijah, and Enoch were popular in Judaism at the time. There is even such a story about Apollonius of Tyana, a popular Greek philosopher of the first century.[1]

> AS EARLY CHRISTIANS TIRED TO FIGURE OUT HOW TO MAKE SENSE OF THEIR EXPERIENCE THAT JESUS WAS ALIVE, THEY EMPLOYED A NUMBER OF MODELS, AMONG THEM RESURRECTION AND EXALTATION.

When does Luke envision the ascension taking place? In the Gospel, after Jesus appears to the disciples, he takes them outside Jerusalem to Bethany and there is carried up to heaven. The whole of chapter 24 clearly takes place on Easter Sunday. While Acts 1:2 seems to imagines the same situation, the events of Acts 1:9-11 take place forty days later (Acts 1:3). As Joseph Fitzmyer remarks: "Why Luke has dated the ascension of Jesus in these two different ways no one will ever know."[2] While supporting this conclusion, I would point out that the mix-up in dates indicates that Luke does not think he is describing strict history.

The ascension is more graphically imagined in Acts than in the Gospel. In the Gospel Jesus blesses them and "was carried up into heaven [or 'the skies']" (24:51). Then the disciples worship Jesus, which is the acknowledgment that they recognize Jesus. In Acts while the disciples are looking into the heavens, two men in white robes (angels) suddenly appear and chide the disciples: "Men of Galilee, why do you stand looking up toward heaven? This Jesus, who has been taken up from you into heaven, will come in the same way as you saw him go into heaven" (1:11). The angels are asking, "Why are you hanging around here? Get on with it." Just as Jesus offered no hint as to when Israel would be redeemed, so the angels offer no hint as to when Jesus will return. Our goal is to be witnesses, not to speculate about the signs of the future.

> JUST AS JESUS OFFERED NO HINT AS TO WHEN ISRAEL WOULD BE REDEEMED, SO THE ANGELS OFFER NO HINT AS TO WHEN JESUS WILL RETURN.

There are clear and deliberate parallels between the end of the Gospel and the beginning of Acts. The following four are the most obvious.

- The command to stay in Jerusalem (Luke 24:49; Acts 1:4)
- You are witnesses (Luke 24:48; Acts 1:8)
- The Spirit's coming (Luke 24:49; Acts 1:5, 8)
- To the nations (Luke 24:47; Acts 1:8)

The close similarity of the Gospel's end and Acts' beginning stresses the continuity of these two books, even though Acts initiates a new phase in salvation history, the period of the church. Yet the ascension functions differently in the two sections. In the Gospel the ascension brings closure, while in Acts it inaugurates a new period.

The Spirit

The Spirit is a dominant theme in Luke-Acts; indeed, hardly a chapter of Acts does not mention the Spirit.

John the Baptist had announced, "I baptize you with water; but one who is more powerful than I is coming; . . . He will baptize you with the Holy Spirit and fire" (Luke 3:16), which is referred to in Acts 1:5. Following Jesus' baptism, twice it is remarked that Jesus is full of the Spirit (4:1, 14). In Jesus' inaugural speech in the synagogue in Nazareth, he reads from the Isaiah scroll, "The Spirit of the Lord is upon me, because he has anointed me to bring good news to the poor" (4:18). So the Spirit marks out the beginning of Jesus' mission.

Likewise, Pentecost marks the coming of the Spirit and inaugurates the period of the church. "All of them were filled with the Holy Spirit and began to speak in other languages, as the Spirit gave them ability" (Acts 2:4). This Spirit's overcoming of these language differences points to the church's worldwide mission. In Peter's vision, where God commands him to kill and eat common and unclean animals, the Spirit commands him to meet with the emissaries from Cornelius the centurion, "for I have sent them" (10:20). Thus, the Spirit commands, "What God has made clean, you must not call profane" (10:15). This prepares the way for the Gentile mission: "While Peter was still speaking, the Holy Spirit fell upon all who heard the word. The circumcised believers who had come with Peter were astounded that the gift of the Holy Spirit had been poured out even on the Gentiles" (10:44-45; see the first reading for the Sixth Sunday of Easter). When Peter reports to Jerusalem on this experience, he ties it in with John the Baptist's prophecy: "And I remembered the word of the Lord, how he had said, 'John baptized with water, but you will be baptized with the Holy Spirit.' If then God gave them the same gift that he gave us when we believed in the Lord

IN PETER'S VISION, THE SPIRIT COMMANDS HIM TO MEET WITH THE EMISSARIES FROM CORNELIUS THE CENTURION. THIS PREPARES THE WAY FOR THE GENTILE MISSION.

Jesus Christ, who was I that I could hinder God?" (11:16-17). At the Council of Jerusalem, Peter appeals to this outpouring of the Spirit as proof of what God wills (15:8-11).

Frequently the narrator of Acts remarks that Paul is led on his various missions by the Spirit (9:17; 13:2, 4; 16:7; 19:21; 21:4). It is the Spirit who is leading Paul on and opening up the universal mission of the church.

From Jerusalem to the Nations

In both the conclusion of the Gospel and the beginning of Acts, the disciples are commanded to stay in Jerusalem. Jerusalem is both the goal of the Gospel and the starting points of Acts. But Jerusalem is not abandoned in Acts. Even though Paul does not die in Acts, the reader can have no doubt that his fate in Rome will be the same as Jesus' in Jerusalem. The fate of Jerusalem raises the fate of Israel in the program of Luke-Acts. Cleopas remarked that they had hoped Jesus was to be "the one to redeem Israel" (Luke 24:21), and the disciples ask Jesus, "Is this the time when you will restore the kingdom to Israel? (Acts 1:6). Jesus rebukes the disciples, saying, "It is not for you to know the times or periods that the Father has set by his own authority" (1:7). In this response Luke banishes the apocalyptic seduction of predicting the outcome. It cannot be known. But there is no note of Israel's rejection or replacement. Acts makes clear that by receiving the Spirit the Gentiles are now part of God's plan. But this does not replace Israel, nor is there any sign of Israel's replacement. Acts ends, as we noted above, not with Paul's death but with his preaching to the Jews of Rome. Jerusalem and Israel are always the starting point of God's plan. Just because Paul died in Rome does not mean God has abandoned the Gentiles.

> ACTS MAKES CLEAR THAT BY RECEIVING THE SPIRIT THE GENTILES ARE NOW PART OF GOD'S PLAN. BUT THIS DOES NOT REPLACE ISRAEL, NOR IS THERE ANY SIGN OF ISRAEL'S REPLACEMENT.

Witnesses

For Luke the ascension shifts ministry from Jesus to us. We are to be his witnesses under the guidance of the Spirit. Moses and the prophets and Jesus lay out the basic pattern. The word of God always meets rejection and death. Resurrection is God's acknowledgment that this is God's way. We are Jesus' witnesses to this. But the Spirit leads us into an unknown future. Just as Peter had to change what he thought God's way was concerning clean and unclean, and just as Paul had to follow the Spirit into Macedonia and beyond, being a witness means to be open to where God's Spirit is working. We cannot predict where that will be, but we can be sure that the world, the empire, will reject God's word.

EZEKIEL 1:3–5a, 15–22, 26–28 (BCP ALT.)

Ezekiel is a prophet of the Babylonian exile (sixth century B.C.E.). The book's superscription, which is omitted from this reading, sets the historical context: "In the thirtieth year, in the fourth month, on the fifth day of the month, as I was among the exiles by the river Chebar, the heavens were opened, and I saw visions of God" (1:1).

The first three chapters of Ezekiel are an elaborate description of his call in the form of a vision of the divine glory.

IMAGES, REGARDLESS OF HOW MAGNIFICENT THEY ARE, ALWAYS FALL SHORT OF THE REALITY OF EXPERIENCE.

Initially the prophet sees a cloud, but then the cloud appears to be on fire; then four beasts appear, and finally a heavenly throne on which sits one in human form. But this form is none other than the glory of God.

While the prophet undoubtedly drew on many sources for his imagery, the fantastic imagery clearly attempts to convey a deep mystical experience of the presence of God. Images, regardless of how magnificent they are, always fall short of the reality of experience.

RESPONSIVE READING
PSALM 47 (RCL, BCP)
PSALM 47:2–3, 6–7, 8–9 (RC)

This psalm celebrates God's victory over Israel's enemies. As such it is a battle hymn, probably celebrating a victory of Israel over its enemies. The "great king" language of the psalm was employed by the Assyrian and Babylonian monarchs (Isa. 36:4; 2 Kings 18:19).

PSALM 93 (RCL ALT.)

The Talmud understands this psalm as celebrating God's enthronement following the creation of the world as God rests on the Sabbath. God's throne is frequently envisioned in the heavens and above the floodwaters (Pss. 11:4; 29:3). The hymn opens with God as king, robed in majesty, and ends with a celebration of God's decrees and holiness that endures forever.

This psalm was part of the enthronement ceremony for the kings. The enthronement took place over many days. The psalm played a large role in developing Christology in early Christianity.

SECOND READING

EPHESIANS 1:15-23 (RCL, BCP)
EPHESIANS 1:17-23 (RC)

This letter was written in Paul's name during the generation after he lived. The reading falls into three parts. In the first part the author gives thanks (1:15-16) for the Ephesians' faith in the Lord Jesus and their love for the saints. The textual evidence for "love" is weak and is probably a later scribal addition.

In the second part of the reading (1:17-19), the author prays for God to give them wisdom and revelation so that "you may know what is the hope to which he has called you" (1:18). This prayer is not a call for esoteric knowledge as in Gnosticism but a call for a deeper understanding of Christian life.

The final part of the reading (1:20-23) is a fragment of a Christian hymn that draws upon Psalm 110. The raised Jesus is exalted "far above all rule and authority and power and dominion" (1:21). This image is much like the "super-exalted" notion of Phil. 2:9. At the hymn's end a curious collapse or fusion of images takes place. No distinction is made between the exaltation and the subjection of the powers and authorities, so the present and future collapse together in the hymn. When all things are put under his feet, Jesus is made the head of the church, which is his body, not the world. So in the image of this hymn, the church and subjected world become one.

> WHEN ALL THINGS ARE PUT UNDER HIS FEET, JESUS IS MADE THE HEAD OF THE CHURCH, WHICH IS HIS BODY, NOT THE WORLD.

The notion of the body of Christ in Ephesians is different from that of Paul in 1 Corinthians 12. The model in this hymn is hierarchical and cosmological. Christ is the head in heaven, the church the body on earth. In Paul the church is the body of Christ, and Christ is the body—there is no notion of a head. In Paul the model functions in an egalitarian mode: "The eye cannot say to the hand, 'I have no need of you'" (1 Cor. 12:21).

EPHESIANS 4:1-13 or 4:1-7, 11-13 (RC ALT.)

The author of Ephesians in this section of the letter appeals for unity in the midst of diversity. The word "one" rings throughout vv. 4-5, accenting the unity, while v. 8 introduces the notion of different gifts, which are then enumerated in v. 11.

THE GOSPEL

MARK 16:9-15, 19-20 (BCP ALT.)
MARK 16:15-20 (RC)

This so-called longer ending of Mark's Gospel is not part of the original Gospel. The Gospel originally ended at 16:8. Affixing a date to this ending is difficult, but it has to be after the composition of the Gospels of Matthew and Luke because they follow Mark's narrative until 16:8 and then go their independent ways.

There are a number of reasons for rejecting this ending as original. It does not occur in the earliest and best manuscripts, and its vocabulary is very different from that of the Gospel of Mark. Furthermore, its understanding of faith departs from that of Mark. It supports the importance of signs, which Mark at every point undermines (see the Gospel for Easter Morning, Mark 16:1-8). This ending appears to be cobbled together from Luke and John's resurrection accounts.

The Episcopal lectionary reading omits the contentious issue of signs, the most famous of which is snake handling, a prominent practice in the churches of Appalachian Kentucky in my youth. Because of these problematic textual issues, I suggest that one use Luke 24:44-53, the lectionary reading from the Revised Common Lectionary, discussed above.

Notes

1. See Joseph Fitzmyer, *The Gospel According to Luke*, Anchor Bible 28A (Garden City, N.Y.: Doubleday, 1985), 1588, for references.

2. Ibid. See also Robert C. Tannehill, *The Narrative Unity of Luke-Acts: A Literary Interpretation,* vol. 2, *The Acts of the Apostles* (Minneapolis: Fortress Press, 1990), 10–11, who has an ingenious explanation that may be right.

SEVENTH SUNDAY OF EASTER

MAY 28, 2006

REVISED COMMON	EPISCOPAL (BCP)	ROMAN CATHOLIC
Acts 1:15-17, 21–26	Acts 1:15–26 or Exod. 28:1-4, 9–10, 29–30	Acts 1:15-17, 20a, 20c-26
Psalm 1	Ps. 68:1-20 or Psalm 47	Ps. 103:1-2, 11–12, 19–20
1 John 5:9 13	1 John 5:9-15 or Acts 1:15-26	1 John 4:11-16
John 17:6-19	John 17:11b-19	John 11b-19

FIRST READING

ACTS 1:15-17, 21–26 (RCL)
ACTS 1:15-26 (BCP)
ACTS 1:15 17, 20a, 20c-26 (RC)

This episode occurs between the ascension of Jesus and the coming of the Spirit at Pentecost. This story deals with the tragedy of Judas and the hole his betrayal has made in the group of the twelve apostles. A major theme of the Acts of the Apostles is the assignment of responsibility for the death of Jesus, usually to the Jerusalem leadership. At the beginning of Acts the Judas story serves to acknowledge that blame lies in the first place with Judas, one of the Twelve, "for he was numbered among us and was allotted his share in this ministry" (1:17). The NRSV translation has Judas as a "guide to those who arrested Jesus" (1:16), but "leader" would be a more accurate translation. Luke often paints an idyllic picture of the early Christian community, but here he acknowledges that at the heart of the first group chosen by Jesus was a traitor, a warning for all Christians.

The selection of Matthias is a curious story. It rounds up the Twelve back to their original number. But this group was not meant to be ongoing or hereditary, as, for example, was the case with priesthoods in the ancient world. After Matthias is selected he disappears from the story, never to be mentioned again in Acts. When Herod Agrippa puts James the son of Zebedee to death, no effort is made to elect a new member to the group of the twelve apostles. After chapter 16, the twelve apostles disappear from Acts and it becomes the story of Paul, who was clearly not one of the twelve apostles. As the Pauline letters made clear, Paul had to fight hard for his own claim to apostleship. While this story of the selection of Matthias would seem to indicate that the twelve apostles are to be an ongoing group, such does not turn out to be the case. They disappear into the mist of history, yet their mission and witness continue to this day.

> AFTER MATTHIAS IS SELECTED HE DISAPPEARS FROM THE STORY, NEVER TO BE MENTIONED AGAIN IN ACTS.

EXODUS 28:1-4, 9-10, 29-30 (BCP ALT.)

The first part of Exodus 28 describes the clothing of the high priest. The ephod is a loincloth with two shoulder straps. On the shoulder straps was a carved lapis stone with the names of the twelve tribes of Israel. The breastplate is not a shield but a garment with a pocket that covers the breast. The pockets contained various items needed for divining. The ephod covered a blue robe or tunic.

RESPONSIVE READING
PSALM 1 (RCL)

Psalm 1 is a beatitude, a description of the happy life, a desperate goal of our consumerist, fast-paced lives. The happy one's "delight is in the law of the LORD [Yahweh]" (1:2). "Law" (*torah*) in this psalm does not mean the legal prescriptions nor the Torah in the sense of the first five books of the Hebrew Bible. Rather, *Torah* means "instruction" or even "story." The happy person delights in God's instruction and "meditate[s] day and night."

The happy person is like a tree "planted by streams of water" (1:3), while the wicked, that is, the unhappy, "are like chaff that the wind drives away" (1:4). The happy person is planted and solid, meditates day and night, while the unhappy person is like wind blown by chaff, rushing here and there, always on the move.

PSALM 68:1-20 (BCP)

The whole sweep of Hebrew history is celebrated in this hymn; from Moses to

David, from the desert to the temple in Jerusalem, thanks is given God for God's mighty deeds. And through it all God remains: "Father of orphans and protector of widows is God in his holy habitation. God gives the desolate a home to live in; he leads out the prisoners to prosperity" (68:5-6).

PSALM 47 (BCP ALT.)

See the responsive reading for the Ascension of Our Lord, above.

PSALM 103:1-2, 11-12, 19-20 (RC)

This psalm calls on Israel to bless God for God's steadfast love, the sign of everlasting covenant.

Second Reading
1 JOHN 5:9-13 (RCL)
1 JOHN 5:9-15 (BCP)

This reading continues the reading from the Sixth Sunday of Easter and comes from the conclusion of the elder's letter to his divided community.

The witness of the three is a reference not to the Trinity but to the Spirit, the water, and the blood. As we saw last Sunday, the water and the blood refer to Jesus' death when, in the Gospel of John, the soldier's spear pierced Jesus' side and water and blood ran out (John 19:34). This is God's witness, and by human standards it falls far short. Yet those who believe that Jesus is God's Son have life, eternal life. In the Johannine literature eternal life refers not to life after death but to the life God gives us (see the Nicodemus story, John

> IN THE JOHANNINE LITERATURE ETERNAL LIFE REFERS NOT TO LIFE AFTER DEATH BUT TO THE LIFE GOD GIVES US.

3:16). For the elder, eternal life is a present reality, a life that cannot be taken away because it is life from God. "I write these things to you who believe in the name of the Son of God, so that you may know that you have eternal life" (5:13).

1 JOHN 4:11-16 (RC)

See the second reading for the Fifth Sunday of Easter, above.

BERNARD
BRANDON
SCOTT

THE GOSPEL
JOHN 17:6-19 (RCL)
JOHN 17:11b-19 (BCP, RC)

This prayer of Jesus to his Father on behalf of his disciples comes from the Gospel's second edition (see 14:31 for the original ending of the supper discourse). Like much in the Fourth Gospel, this prayer is unique in the Jesus tradition. In the Synoptics Jesus also prays before his arrest in the Garden of Gethsemane, but that prayer is full of anguish, while this one is serene. This prayer is a profound meditation by the community of the beloved disciple on the life of a disciple.

In the other readings from the Gospel of John and the First Letter of John, the theme is of the unity of the Father and Son and the corresponding unity of God's children and God's Son. Jesus as God's Son mediates our unity with the Father. His laying down his life brings this about. That is his lifting up, his exaltation, his glorification.

> THIS PRAYER IS A PROFOUND MEDITATION BY THE COMMUNITY OF THE BELOVED DISCIPLE ON THE LIFE OF A DISCIPLE.

Life, eternal life, is life in God, a present gift. "All mine are yours, and yours are mine; and I have been glorified in them" (17:10). The world hates life, chooses death, and lies. It lives in darkness. The coming of Jesus, his death, and his resurrection present a stark reality—a choice for life or death, a choice for love or hate. There is no middle ground in the Johannine view.

What does the author mean by "world"? *Kosmos* in Greek always has a sense of order out of chaos. In John, however, it never has that sense. For John, *kosmos*, "world," is always simply chaos. So in the Johannine writings, "world" is always used ironically from a Greek perspective. By "world" the text does not mean creation, nor does it mean the place where we live. Rather, "world" is the reality created by humans who refuse God, who choose death over God's life. In that sense we are not of this world—not because we do not belong here in creation, but because we have chosen to live by God's light and

> WE ARE NOT OF THIS WORLD—NOT BECAUSE WE DO NOT BELONG HERE IN CREATION, BUT BECAUSE WE HAVE CHOSEN TO LIVE BY GOD'S LIGHT AND LIFE.

life. The Gospel's use of "world" forces us to see that there is creation, which is God's reality for us, and world, which is our self-construction of reality. Creation is from love; world is about power and death.

THE SEASON
OF PENTECOST

MATTHEW L.
SKINNER

The Day of Pentecost, the Seventh Sunday after Easter, formally concludes the fifty-day Easter season. At the same time, because the day celebrates the genesis of the church through the bestowal of the Holy Spirit, Pentecost also emphatically points forward into the time that follows, forging a meaningful connection between the definitive statement of Jesus' resurrection and the sending of the church into the world in the name of Christ.

Background to the Day of Pentecost

Contemporary Christians celebrate Pentecost as a feast marking the events of Acts 2, where the Holy Spirit fills Jesus' followers, resulting in inspired, prophetic speech and the creation of a community characterized by worship and service. The Christian observance of Pentecost derives from a previously existing Jewish pilgrim festival of the same name, which fell on the fiftieth (*pentēcostē* is the Greek word for *fiftieth*) day after Passover. No evidence exists, however, for a distinctively Christian observance of this feast until late in the second century.[1] At that time, Christians typically referred to "Pentecost" as the entire fifty-day period commenced on Easter, an extended and joyful celebration of Christ's resurrection, his appearances to his followers, his ascension, and the descent of the Holy Spirit. Not until the late fourth or early fifth century does Pentecost widely emerge as a distinctive feast *day*, demarcating the end of Easter and focusing especially on the gift of the Spirit. Tertullian, writing during the first years of the third century, commended the Pentecost season as particularly appropriate for baptisms. This tradition has persevered, as seen in some English churches' practice of calling Pentecost by its alternate name of Whitsunday, indicating the white garments worn by those being baptized.

The Pentecost setting explains the large and diverse crowd that Peter and others encounter in Acts 2:5-11. These Jewish visitors were in Jerusalem for Pentecost, the Greek name for the Feast of Weeks, also known as the Day of the First Fruits (Exod. 23:16a; 34:22a; Lev. 23:15-16; Num. 28:26; Deut. 16:9-10; Tob. 2:1) and commonly called *Shavuot*, the Hebrew word meaning "weeks." This feast, one of the three pilgrim festivals (along with Passover and Sukkoth) ordained in the Old Testament, was an agricultural festival in which Jews acknowledged God's provision and rendered thanks for the first fruits of the wheat harvest by bringing an offering to the Jerusalem Temple. Soon after the destruction of the temple in 70 C.E., Jews began to celebrate Shavuot as the anniversary of Moses' reception of the Law on Mount Sinai. This additional significance of Shavuot does not appear to have become common, however, until the second or third century.[2] There is, therefore, good reason to conclude that the earliest generations of Christians who read and listened to Acts would generally not have associated or contrasted God's gift of the Spirit on Pentecost with God's prior gift of the Law on Sinai.

Preaching during the Season after Pentecost

Pentecost and the period that immediately follows offer preachers a wealth of potent themes to pursue over the course of a number of Sundays. The Spirit-filled activity of the Day of Pentecost sets the tone, directing our attention toward numerous horizons. This activity points beyond itself, for within the overarching biblical story it appears as a demonstration of God's fidelity to God's promises. In the narrative landscape of Luke-Acts, the coming of the Spirit is hardly an isolated episode, nor does it surprise readers. Rather, the events of Acts 2 fulfill the explicit promises made by Jesus and the Father in Luke 24:49 and Acts 1:4-8. Likewise, Jesus' description of the coming Advocate or Spirit in John 14:15-29; 15:26—16:15 also prompts us to view the gift of the Spirit as a sign that God is faithful and a very present help.

This God who is proved reliable and powerful through conferring the Spirit also declares on Pentecost to the community of faith something of what its roles will be as a people infused with God's own presence. In the Pentecost story in Acts 2, the Spirit propels Jesus' followers *outside* of the house in which they are gathered to speak prophetically to people representing the whole world of Judaism. The miraculous and bold events remind us that Jesus' final words in Acts 1:8—"You will receive power when the Holy Spirit has come upon you; and you will be my witnesses in Jerusalem, in all Judea and Samaria, and to the ends of the earth"— make an indicative statement about the church's testimony, not an imperative or a proposal for believers to discuss. Through the power of the Spirit, the church throughout the ages exists as the community that collectively bears witness to Christ. In doing so, the church always carries the God-given potential to "turn the world upside down" (according to the accusation of opponents in Acts 17:6) as the gospel upends and defies the world's cherished value systems. Additionally, the events of Acts 2 focus our attention on the work of the Spirit *inside* of the household, within the bounds of the Christian community itself. The Pentecost story does not conclude with Peter's proclamation and the overwhelming response of the repentant crowd; it ends with the Spirit's bringing people into a close-knit community of true fellowship, unity, and charity (Acts 2:41-47).

It would be a mistake for sermons to proclaim Acts 2 with any sense of nostalgia or as an isolated phenomenon confined to an ancient context. We miss the point of the Pentecost story and its aftermath if we limit the inceptive dimensions of the Spirit's work to the past. Many congregations suffer from a limited exposure to the book of Acts and its theological significance. It behooves these communities to discover that Acts imagines Pentecost less as a once-and-for-all sort of occurrence and more as the introduction of a recurring pattern in the experiences of believers.[3] In subsequent passages the Spirit continues to mobilize Jesus' followers, empowering prophecy and inaugurating new directions in ministry and community. The Spirit's role in such passages as Acts 4:23-37; 8:14-17; 10:1—11:18; 13:1-4; 15:1-35; 19:1-7 is crucial for our understanding of these individual accounts and of the theological vision of Acts as a whole. This Spirit still guides churches toward new frontiers of witness and service.

> THE CHURCH ALWAYS CARRIES THE GOD-GIVEN POTENTIAL TO "TURN THE WORLD UPSIDE DOWN" AS THE GOSPEL UPENDS AND DEFIES THE WORLD'S CHERISHED VALUE SYSTEMS.

The Day of Pentecost's attention to the durative faithfulness of God and the prophetic character of Christian witness creates a powerful segue into the church's observance of ordinary time during the season after Pentecost. Just as the account in Acts 2 points backward to prior promises and forward to the ongoing testimony of the church in the world, so also our celebration of Pentecost can launch us into sustained reflection on the nature of Christian communities and the work to which God continues to call them in their corners of the world. The sensitive preacher will recognize that these reflections are not excuses for ecclesiological egotism but occasions for congregations to discern, celebrate, and reaffirm their identity as a people gathered, empowered, and sent by the Spirit of God in their midst.

> OUR CELEBRATION OF PENTECOST CAN LAUNCH US INTO SUSTAINED REFLECTION ON THE NATURE OF CHRISTIAN COMMUNITIES AND THE WORK TO WHICH GOD CONTINUES TO CALL THEM IN THEIR CORNERS OF THE WORLD.

Throughout the next several months, lectionary assignments present worship leaders with many biblical passages and themes that anticipate, recall, and amplify one another. The commentary on these readings regularly emphasizes their implications concerning believers' identities and roles in the world. Those who design worship services can benefit from charting a course through the season, planning ahead by developing a preaching strategy that brings to light certain recurring and complementary ideas.

Notes

1. Martin F. Connell, "From Easter to Pentecost," in *Passover and Easter: The Symbolic Structuring of Sacred Seasons*, ed. Paul F. Bradshaw and Lawrence A. Hoffman, Two Liturgical Traditions 6 (Notre Dame: University of Notre Dame Press, 1999), 94.

2. Louis Jacobs, "Shavuot," *Encyclopaedia Judaica* (Jerusalem: Encyclopaedia Judaica, 1971), 14:1320–21.

3. See Earl Richard, "Pentecost as a Recurrent Theme in Luke-Acts," in *New Views on Luke and Acts*, ed. Earl Richard (Collegeville, Minn.: Liturgical Press, 1990), 133–49.

VIGIL OF PENTECOST

Revised Common	Episcopal (BCP)	Roman Catholic
Exod. 19:1-9 or Acts 2:1-11	Gen. 11:1-9 or Exod. 19:1-9a, 16-20a; 20:18-20 or Ezek. 37:1-14 or Joel 2:28-32	Gen. 11:1-9 or Exod. 19:3-8a, 16-20b or Ezek. 37:1-14 or Joel 3:1-5
Ps. 33:12-22 or Psalm 130	Ps. 33:12-22 or Canticle 2 or Canticle 13 Psalm 130 or Canticle 9 Ps. 104:25-32	Ps. 104:1-2, 24, 35, 27-28, 29, 30
Rom. 8:14-17, 22-27	Acts 2:1-11 or Rom. 8:14-17, 22-27	Rom. 8:22-27
John 7:37-39a	John 7:37-39a	John 7:37-39

Since, as outlined in the introduction, the Day of Pentecost demonstrates God's fidelity to promises, those Christian communities that conduct a Pentecost Vigil discover in the assigned readings statements of hope and descriptions of a Spirit that preserves and vivifies those in whom it dwells. Some texts describe problems—disunity, death, and the travails of life in this world—for the Holy Spirit to address. Focusing on our need for the Spirit's help intensifies the longings that God promises to meet on Pentecost. These readings about promise and renewal thereby fuel our expectations, creating space for the message of Pentecost to speak to us with greater clarity and relevance.

FIRST READING
EXODUS 19:1–9 (RCL)
EXODUS 19:1–9a, 16–20a; 20:18–20
(BCP ALT.)
EXODUS 19:3–8a, 16–20b (RC ALT.)

This passage describes the beginning scenes of God's revelation to Moses and the Israelites at Mount Sinai. The giving of the Law commences with God's reminding Moses of God's power and fidelity manifested in the deliverance of the people from Egypt. Next follows dialogue mediated by Moses that initiates a covenant between God and the people. God promises to be present in visible manifestations to validate the trustworthiness of Moses, who will serve as God's spokesperson and prophet. Later in chapter 19 frightening phenomena attend God's arrival upon the mountain: thunder, lightning, cloud, smoke, fire, earthquake, and explosive trumpet peals make for a terrifying and arresting image of the Lord's visitation. By Exod. 20:19, some Israelites fear that any closer encounter with this God would be deadly.

The appropriateness of this particular text for setting the stage for an observance of Pentecost is dubious. On the positive side, the Sinai narrative introduces stock imagery that signals the unmistakable presence of God, just as visible and audible signs accompany the sudden arrival of the Holy Spirit in Acts 2:2–3. In this regard, Exodus 19 reminds us that God's presence among us is never something that mortals should take lightly. That God comes near to call or empower us means many things, but this is never without its dangers. One of the beavers in C. S. Lewis's *The Lion, the Witch and the Wardrobe* voices this truth when answering Lucy's question about whether the lion Aslan, the story's allegorical representation of Christ, is safe: "Who said anything about safe? 'Course he isn't safe. But he's good."[1]

EXODUS 19 REMINDS US THAT GOD'S PRESENCE AMONG US IS NEVER SOMETHING THAT MORTALS SHOULD TAKE LIGHTLY. THAT GOD COMES NEAR TO CALL OR EMPOWER US MEANS MANY THINGS, BUT THIS IS NEVER WITHOUT ITS DANGERS.

On the negative side, however, the selection of this passage threatens to invite unwarranted associations between the Pentecost setting of Acts 2 and the giving of the Law on the third new moon after the first Passover. As explained above in the introduction, the Jewish practice of celebrating God's revelation at Sinai on Shavuot (Pentecost) did not become established until well after the writing of Acts. The coming of the Holy Spirit on Pentecost does not create a new people, mark a new deliverance, or issue a new covenant in the manner of God's work in Exodus 19–20. The narrative of Acts interprets the meaning of Pentecost from other perspectives (see the comments for the Day of Pentecost, below).[2] Worship leaders who choose this passage for the Vigil of Pentecost should take care to delimit its relevance for the occasion and especially for an understanding of Acts 2.

ACTS 2:1-11 (RCL ALT., BCP SECOND READING)

For a discussion of this passage, see the comments for the Day of Pentecost, below.

GENESIS 11:1-9 (BCP, RC)

The confusion and scattering effected by God in response to the Tower of Babel creates an ideal foil for the Pentecost narrative of Acts 2. The human legacy of alienation, misunderstanding, and discord represented in this passage from Genesis is one of the problems that the phenomena and proclamation of the Day of Pentecost address and begin to dismantle. In addition, while we human beings vainly aspire to "make a name for ourselves" (Gen. 11:4), God's promises take hold of us when we submit to "the name" of the Lord (Acts 2:21, 38).

EZEKIEL 37:1-14 (BCP ALT., RC ALT.)

The bones Ezekiel observes in the valley are not only dry and lifeless; they are also "cut off" and scattered. Their renewal includes a restoration to the land, as well as knowledge of the Lord. The bones' transition from death to life stems from an infusion of God's Spirit (echoing Ezek. 36:26-27), which both causes the revivification and indwells the people. Every occurrence of "breath" and "spirit" in this passage translates the same Hebrew word, rûaḥ.

JOEL 2:28-32 (BCP ALT.)
JOEL 3:1-5 (RC ALT.)

Both the Episcopal and Roman Catholic lectionaries assign the same passage from Joel; varying versification among biblical translations accounts for the differences in chapter and verse. The apostle Peter quotes and modifies this prophecy (Joel 2:28-32a in the NRSV) in his Pentecost address in Acts 2:17-21. Joel addresses the kingdom of Judah in a state of devastation, calling it to repent and promising God's blessings upon the land. As part of this restoration and at a future time before the arrival of the day of the Lord, God's Spirit will come to "all flesh," without distinctions based on sex, age, or social class. Through Joel, God pledges an era of rampant prophecy, complete with cosmic signs, in which the Spirit will not be the exclusive possession of certain people. The prophet therefore anticipates a new direction in God's activity, in which he suggests that the spirit of the Lord's influence will be more permanent and universal than it had been in previous times. Instead of individuals receiving the Spirit for specific, temporary undertakings, one day God will create a society of Spirit-inspired prophets. The ultimate end of this, declares Joel, is that "everyone who calls on the name of the Lord shall be saved."

Responsive Reading
PSALM 33:12–22 (RCL, BCP)

As this psalm praises the providential oversight God exercises over creation and human affairs, its imagery has regrettably reinforced various misunderstandings of God as a master puppeteer and of modern nations as uniquely blessed. While the psalm challenges our scientific and rationalistic assumptions about the universe, that is not its point as much so is its insistence that our ultimate trust must be in God and not in ourselves or our political achievements. The theology of the psalm calls for humility in response to God's loving-kindness, and it opposes both quietism and impudence in our dealings with others.

PSALM 130 (RCL ALT., BCP)

This psalm, known in liturgical and devotional contexts by its Latin title *De profundis,* arises from "out of the depths" that characterize the chaos and destruction of the seas. It professes God as a forgiver, lover, and redeemer who can hear into the deepest torrents of human despair. The psalmist can resolve to wait only because of who God is.

PSALM 104:25–32 (BCP)
PSALM 104:1–2, 24, 35, 27–28, 29, 30 (RC)

This psalmic celebration of God's creative activity also glorifies God's ability to sustain every living thing. Verse 30 assigns creation and renewal to the sending of God's Spirit. The only conceivable response is lavish praise (vv. 31–35).

CANTICLE 2; CANTICLE 13; CANTICLE 9 (BCP)

Canticles 2 and 13 in the BCP are based on vv. 29–34 of the Song of the Three Young Men, a section of a larger apocryphal text sometimes called the Prayer of Azariah and the Song of the Three Jews, which some ancient manuscripts insert between Dan. 3:23 and 3:24. These canticles proclaim the majesty and sovereignty of God. Canticle 9 is based on Isa. 12:2-6; it focuses on God as the source of salvation, and it calls its hearers to extol the great works of God to all people.

SECOND READING

ROMANS 8:14-17, 22-27 (RCL, BCP ALT.)
ROMANS 8:22-27 (RC)

Paul's letters certainly have much to say about Jesus' death and resurrection, but their discussions of what it means to share in Christ's benefits often appeal to the roles of the Holy Spirit. Paul considers the Spirit the definitive mark that one has been claimed by God (see also Gal. 3:2–5; Rom. 8:9-11). To have received the Spirit is to have received adoption papers; God welcomes us as God's own children, which means we also inherit the glorification that belongs to Christ. Not only is God's Spirit

> JUST AS THE SPIRIT INCORPORATES BELIEVERS INTO A FAMILIAL RELATIONSHIP WITH GOD, SO TOO IT CONNECTS US TO ONE ANOTHER AND TO THE WIDER COSMOS THAT AWAITS ITS FULL REDEMPTION.

a pledge of believers' new identity and future benefits, it also actively empowers them to bear witness concerning this new relationship.

Paul's language acknowledges the struggles and sufferings of this life. Indeed, the overarching message of this passage is that the Spirit preserves hope precisely in the midst of present travails. In this regard, the Spirit is not a private possession that boosts one's personal confidence, but a guarantee and sustainer for the whole of creation. Just as the Spirit incorporates believers into a familial relationship with God, so too it connects us to one another and to the wider cosmos that awaits its full redemption. The connections among believers, the world, and the Spirit emerge more clearly through Paul's use of related Greek words (*sustenazō, stenazō, stenagmos*) to name the groaning voiced by the creation, ourselves, and even the Spirit in vv. 22, 23, and 26. As biblical scholar Katherine Grieb observes, "Paul's pattern of argument assumes that the church will be present in the place of the world's deepest need and that God will be present in the midst of the church in the world: God participates in the sufferings of the new creation from within them."[3]

This passage affirms the present benefits of the Spirit, yet much of it orients readers toward the future in an insistence that we still await our complete adoption and the ultimate redemption of our selves and the creation. With regard to this future, the Spirit engenders hope, just as the first fruits from any crop usually bring assurance and excitement concerning the harvest to come. Paul consistently depicts the Spirit not as a passive guarantee but as an active comfort and help to people living in the difficult time of "not yet."

Of all the lections designated for the Vigil of Pentecost, this one offers the most detailed glimpse into the significance of the Holy Spirit in the life of believers. Christian preaching that observes and celebrates God's giving of the Spirit does well to accentuate the Spirit's vital functions in and on behalf of the world. At least three dimensions of the Spirit's significance warrant preachers' attention. First, the Spirit operates in a manner that does not shy away from acknowledging the struggles of living in this world. Paul's metaphors of groaning and labor pains reflect the Spirit's involvement in the troubles that afflict all creation. These images also capture a sense of humanity's longing for completion and deliverance. On one hand, the Spirit's intercessions salve the agonies associated with these yearnings. On the other hand, the mere presence of the Spirit as a persistent assurance of what is yet to come makes our longings more acute. The Spirit nevertheless testifies that God is present in and for the world, that God will continue to engage the world, and that God calls the church to participate in the transformation of a broken world.

A second point of application has particular relevance for contemporary North American culture, which typically despises the need to wait for anything. In contrast to our desires for "high-speed" or "on-demand" products and services, Paul depicts life in the Spirit as a life of patient hope (vv. 22–25). The Spirit provides a basis for this hope, to be sure, but the practices of Christians' patient (yet active) expectation and waiting remain difficult for many of us to cultivate in this place and time.

> IN CONTRAST TO OUR DESIRES FOR "HIGH-SPEED" OR "ON-DEMAND" PRODUCTS AND SERVICES, PAUL DEPICTS LIFE IN THE SPIRIT AS A LIFE OF PATIENT HOPE.

Finally, to claim that the Holy Spirit provides both help for the present and a pledge for the future can be so familiar to some people as to risk becoming trite. An effective sermon on Romans 8 must recover the audacity of the notion that we are adopted as God's own daughters and sons. While the image of a God who claims people as God's children appears frequently in the Old Testament and other ancient literature, Paul's use of this language in this context, precisely after several chapters depicting the problem of sin and humanity's alienation from God, is wonderfully striking.

JOHN 7:37-39a (RCL, BCP)
JOHN 7:37-39 (RC)

Despite its brevity, this passage contains at least three significant exegetical challenges. Explaining all these challenges in a sermon would disorient most congregations, but briefly noting them here will serve to disclose the verses' primary assertions about the source, functions, and identity of the Holy Spirit. First, as the NRSV's footnotes reveal, the Greek syntax is ambiguous, leading to uncertainty about punctuation. This results in a question concerning the source of the rivers (the NRSV supplies the words "the believer's" in place of the Greek word for "his" in v. 38), whether they flow from the believer or from Jesus. Other passages in John lend support to the conviction that Jesus remains the ultimate source of living water (4:14; 6:35), the water that the Gospel identifies as the Spirit in 7:39. Second, the reference to "the scripture" in v. 38 cannot resolve the ambiguity about the flowing water, because no known biblical text reads this way. Instead of fretting about which particular scripture might be in view, we are better off noting that the quenching of thirst is a recognizable biblical motif (Isa. 55:1), as is water as a representation of God's Spirit (Isa. 44:3; Ezek. 36:25-27). These motifs are fully consistent with what Jesus promises here in John. Third, the comment that "as yet there was no Spirit" (v. 39) does not repudiate the Spirit's work in the Old Testament or in John 1:32-33. Instead, the statement claims that the Holy Spirit known to John's audience, the church, had yet to come to believers and had yet to acquire its new significance and character through Jesus' death, resurrection, and return to the Father.

This passage offers a suggestive and powerful image of the Holy Spirit. It is *suggestive* insofar as it includes only a meager amount of detail about the Spirit's nature or role. These verses anticipate a more expansive discussion of the Spirit later in John's Gospel, in passages assigned for the Day of Pentecost. They set the stage for what is to come, while still affirming that the giving of the Spirit is the fulfillment of a promise and connected to the work of the Son.

The *powerful* aspect of this image of the Spirit comes in the reference to "rivers of living water" that slake thirst. When we consider that Jesus utters these words in Palestine, a land frequently prone to drought because of its lack of watersheds and major streams, we recognize that his audience likely has a sharp sense of the fundamental connection between water and life. Furthermore, when we recall that Jesus speaks here at the end of an agricultural festival, the Feast of Booths, or Sukkoth (John 7:2), his water metaphor acquires greater meaning. To commemorate God's provision for the Israelites during the wilderness wanderings, Sukkoth included processions from the pool of Siloam, where priests drew water, to the temple altar, where the water was poured out as a libation. As living water, the Holy Spirit is no small refreshment. It is the indispensable source of our spiritual vitality, a sign of God's care for us during our sojourn in this life.

Notes

1. C. S. Lewis, *The Lion, the Witch and the Wardrobe* (New York: Macmillan, 1950), 75–76.

2. A handful of interpreters still insist, nevertheless, that Acts 2 includes faint allusions to the Sinai narrative. Notable among these is Joseph A. Fitzmyer, *The Acts of the Apostles*, Anchor Bible 31 (New York: Doubleday, 1998), 233–34.

3. A. Katherine Grieb, *The Story of Romans: A Narrative Defense of God's Righteousness* (Louisville: Westminster John Knox, 2002), 80.

THE DAY OF PENTECOST

JUNE 4, 2006

REVISED COMMON	EPISCOPAL (BCP)	ROMAN CATHOLIC
Acts 2:1-21	Acts 2:1-11	Acts 2:1-11
or Ezek. 37:1-14	or Isa. 44:1-8	
Ps. 104:24-34, 35b	Ps. 104:25-37	Ps. 104:1, 24, 29-30,
	or Ps. 104:25-32	31, 34
	or Ps. 33:12-15,	
	18-22	
Rom. 8:22-27	1 Cor. 12:4-13	1 Cor. 12:3b-7, 12-13
or Acts 2:1-21	or Acts 2:1-11	or Gal. 5:16-25
John 15:26-27;	John 20:19-23	John 20:19-23
16:4b-15	or John 14:8-17	or John 15:26-27;
		16:12-15

A rich array of biblical texts speaks powerful words to congregations celebrating the giving and ongoing work of the Holy Spirit. The designated passages for the day complement one another well, although preachers will want to keep in mind the shades of difference among various biblical books' perspectives on the Spirit and its work. When we listen to these texts in concert, it becomes clear that the coming of the Holy Spirit proclaims something about God's fidelity, care, and intentions, as well as something about the church's persistent hope and public witness. In God's gracious act of pouring out the Spirit, Christians learn about their particular identity and vocation—who they are and what God does through and among them.

FIRST READING
ACTS 2:1-21 (RCL)
ACTS 2:1-11 (BCP, RC)

The coming of the Holy Spirit on Pentecost prompts ecstatic speech that baffles onlookers. Although all the speakers are clearly Galilean (an identification inviting stereotypes of ignorant, backwater folk), nevertheless Jewish people from near and far-off regions situated in all directions around Jerusalem hear intelligible proclamation about God in their native languages. Initial responses vary: some jeer, but many are moved to inquire, "What does this mean?" Peter's answer to this question dominates the Pentecost narrative. Other phenomena accompanying the Spirit's arrival receive only minuscule attention in comparison to the primary concern: the event's significance. What does this mean? What is God declaring on this Pentecost?

Peter's sermon (2:14–36) begins with a single sentence to refute the scoffers before turning to interpret the event by borrowing words from the prophet Joel. Faced with a need to explain the present, Peter looks to the past and employs scripture to provide a framework for making sense of things. The scripture he cites (Joel 2:28–32; see the comments for the Vigil of Pentecost, above) promises the coming of God's Spirit and emphasizes the prophecy that the Spirit will inspire. The phrase "and they shall prophesy" in v. 18 is an addition to the text of Joel, repeating the promise in v. 17. The Holy Spirit is a Spirit of prophecy. Prophecy confronts people on the streets of Jerusalem. The remainder of Peter's sermon offers an example of the nature of Christian prophecy. It is truth telling, proclaiming God's intervention in the world and the salvation God offers.

Two other aspects of the citation from Joel shed light on Peter's understanding of the nature of prophetic speech. First, Joel's promise of the Spirit is an inclusive one, encompassing people of all sexes, ages, and social classes.[1] Likewise, later in the sermon Peter recalls that Jesus promised the Holy Spirit (2:33) and restates that this Spirit does not belong to an exclusive group of believers: "The promise is for you, for your children, and for all who are far away" (2:39). Given that his current audience is composed of Jews (2:5), Peter's Pentecost sermon does not necessarily envision the gathering of *all* people into the community of the Holy Spirit.

> PETER REGARDS PENTECOST AS INAUGURATING A NEW ERA. THE CONCLUDING, CULMINATING EPOCH OF WORLD HISTORY HAS BEGUN. GOD'S SALVATION IS NEAR.

Still, the sermon is consistent with the prospect that even Gentiles might receive the Spirit. Readers nevertheless must wait until Acts 10:1—11:18 for the surprising realization that this promise extends to all peoples. Second, Peter alters the Joel text in another significant way that interprets the events of this Pentecost. He changes Joel's introductory clause from "after these things" to "in the last days." This means Peter regards Pentecost as inaugurating a new era. The concluding, culminating epoch of world history has begun. God's salvation is near. The answer, therefore, to "What does this mean?" is weighty. God is fulfilling promises. God is creating a community full of prophets to declare the word. God is offering salvation as the end of history draws near.

Peter's willingness to alter the oracle from Joel can make congregations in some traditions uneasy. Preachers might want to emphasize, in response, that these kinds of interpretive strategies are hardly rare in the Bible and the history of its interpretation. The gist of Peter's exegetical maneuvers is that the living words of the scriptures continue to nurture and guide the people of God, even as they move into new circumstances offering new realities and challenges.

A sermon on the Pentecost narrative can go a long way toward shaping Christians' understandings of the Holy Spirit's work and of their identity as speakers of prophecy. Preachers should note that in Acts the significance of Pentecost is not explained by an omniscient narrator standing outside of the story's action. Instead, a character fully enmeshed in the drama interprets strange and wonderful events as he experiences them.[2] Peter does not perceive in advance what God is doing; he discovers it as he goes along. His resources for making sense of God's activities through believers are his own past and present experiences and the scriptures that record the stories of God from the past. Peter does not interpret scripture so much as he is pressed to interpret the present moment through the defining lens of the scriptural witness. Biblical scholar Loveday Alexander describes this movement nicely: "Peter starts with what is happening now ('this'), and then goes back into Scripture to find a correspondence ('that'). The Scripture, once identified, then provides a revelatory framework for reaching a better understanding of the present."[3] When God's word thus makes sense of the present, hopes for the future (hopes that the word itself promises) are reaffirmed, as connections between present events and those future hopes become more plausible in our imaginations.[4]

In his conviction that the scriptures continue to speak a new, living word to present circumstances, Peter's sermon offers an example of the prophetic work of the Holy Spirit among us. The idea of "prophecy" suffers from a bad reputation, thanks to Nostradamus, Jeane Dixon, and "prophecy seminars." The Acts narrative depicts Peter doing something altogether different, however. This kind of "prophecy" does not wield the Bible as a source of self-justifying "proof texts," nor does it decode ancient texts and their symbols as if they hold hidden predictions that reveal a secret road map detailing current events. Peter's brand of "prophecy" mirrors the task of every preacher and every Christian who believes that God is engaged with this world, namely, the task of identifying our own circumstances as somehow in line with testimony about God from the past and in line with the promises of what God is yet to do. This creative, "prophetic" task requires us to take the Bible seriously as a living word that continues to speak and undergird faith in God when we read it and converse with it as a dialogue partner that shapes our outlooks on

> THE SPIRIT MAKES THE CHURCH A FELLOWSHIP OF VISIONARIES AND DREAMERS, WITH EYES TO PERCEIVE AND IMAGINE GOD'S ALWAYS-ONGOING WORK ON BEHALF OF THE WORLD.

our societies, relationships, and futures. The Spirit makes the church a fellowship of visionaries and dreamers, with eyes to perceive and imagine God's always-ongoing work on behalf of the world.

Many Christian traditions remain less than fully comfortable speaking about the work of the Holy Spirit. Some people react with rational or emotional discomfort to the ineffability and unpredictability of the Bible's depictions of the Spirit. Some find themselves put off by the spiritual excesses of other Christian groups. Wherever a given tradition locates itself, this biblical passage offers an essential statement about what the gift of the Spirit means to Christians as we navigate the terrain of this world. Through the Spirit, God provokes and empowers a view of reality that requires us to make sense of our lives and the happenings of the day in light of God's presence in the world, through the promises God has kept and those yet to be realized. The Spirit equips today's churches for this task in the same way as what we observe at the end of Acts 2, where the Spirit creates not a disparate group of individual believers but a community of faith and practice (2:43-47).

For more discussion of Acts 2 and the importance of the Pentecost narrative for the book of Acts, see the Introduction to Pentecost and the Season after Pentecost, above (pp. 73–76).

EZEKIEL 37:1-14 (RCL ALT.)

For a discussion of this passage, see the comments for the Vigil of Pentecost, above.

ISAIAH 44:1-8 (BCP ALT.)

The first of these two Isaianic oracles (vv. 1-5), which continues but redirects ("But now . . .") the preceding trial discourse of 43:22-28, promises help for the wayward people, accomplished by God's willingness to pour out God's Spirit like water upon the desert. This Spirit gives life, just as water nourishes grateful desert flora such as the tamarisk, a tree or large shrub that can grow quickly (up to a foot in a month) when water is available.[5] As a result, the glad recipients of God's blessings publicly declare their identities as God's own possessions. Even outsiders will "adopt the name of Israel," suggesting a time to come in which previously fixed boundaries between people are obliterated. This prophetic word continues to convey hope,

> THIS PROPHETIC WORD CONTINUES TO CONVEY HOPE, PROMISING THAT GOD CAN BRING LIFE TO THE MOST DESOLATE SOCIAL AND MORAL LANDSCAPES OF OUR WORLD.

promising that God can bring life to the most desolate social and moral landscapes of our world.

In the second oracle (vv. 6-8) God's majesty provides a certain basis for putting away fear and an impetus for giving testimony, even as Judah continues to dwell in the midst of the competing claims of Babylonian religion.

RESPONSIVE READING
PSALM 104:24-34, 35b (RCL)
PSALM 104:25-37 or 104:25-32 (BCP)
PSALM 104:1, 24, 29-30, 31, 34 (RC)

For a discussion of this psalm, see the comments for the Vigil of Pentecost, above.

PSALM 33:12-15, 18-22 (BCP ALT.)

For a discussion of this psalm, see the comments for the Vigil of Pentecost, above.

SECOND READING
1 CORINTHIANS 12:4-13 (BCP)
1 CORINTHIANS 12:3b-7, 12-13 (RC)

This passage highlights the unity and diversity that the Spirit creates as it equips Christians for various yet complementary ministries in the service of the one God. The concluding metaphor of our incorporation into the single body of Christ demonstrates the cohesive work of the Spirit through the interdependence of the community that it calls into existence.

GALATIANS 5:16-25 (RC ALT.)

Paul sets "the desires of the flesh" in opposition to the Spirit's leading, positing an ongoing struggle between two separate ways of life. Although it has been crucified (v. 24), the influence of the believer's former condition remains threatening. The remedy is to "live by the Spirit" (this is, as the NIV captures, the only imperative in v. 16), which will produce its fruit in the lives of Christians and their communities.

ROMANS 8:22-27 (RCL)

For a discussion of this passage, see the comments for the Vigil of Pentecost, above.

THE GOSPEL
JOHN 15:26-27; 16:4b-15 (RCL)
JOHN 15:26-27; 16:12-15 (RC ALT.)

In John 13:31—17:26 Jesus bids farewell to his followers by praying for them, teaching them, and preparing them for life after he departs. A key aspect of his instruction concerns the functions of the coming Holy Spirit, who will comfort, help, and exhort people while also serving as an advocate for them and for the truth revealed in Jesus (all of these roles are encompassed in the term *paraklētos,* which the NRSV renders as "Advocate"). Proclamation of this text can guide congregations toward a deeper grasp of the capacities of the Spirit in their corporate lives and their ministries in the world.

Some editions of the NRSV print the section heading "The World's Hatred" before John 15:18—16:3. This apt summary causes us to keep in mind that 15:26-27 belongs to a discussion of the opposition that Jesus' followers should expect. In the face of conflict, the Holy Spirit serves as a forensic advocate, bearing witness concerning Jesus in partnership with believers. This encourages Jesus' followers to testify boldly to his truth, because the Spirit is present with them. It also encourages them to understand the Spirit at work in their own deeds and claims as Christ's witnesses.

IN THE FACE OF CONFLICT, THE HOLY SPIRIT SERVES AS A FORENSIC ADVOCATE, BEARING WITNESS CONCERNING JESUS IN PARTNERSHIP WITH BELIEVERS.

The Gospel of John's particular perspective on believers' expecting conflict from a hostile world carries the imprint of conflicts that erupted in certain Jewish communities near the end of the first century (see 16:2; 9:22). The Gospel presents promises about the Spirit to give confidence to first-century people facing specific ordeals (see 16:1-4a). Sermons on this text that inordinately dwell on those ancient conflicts risk diverting focus away from the more salient points about the Spirit's work and should be avoided.[6] A preacher's knowledge of the historical context of John's Gospel nevertheless reinforces his or her sense that Jesus here does not describe the Spirit as a helper in an equivocal or sentimental sense, as if the Spirit were a generic good-luck charm. The Spirit, instead, is the necessary and very practical means by which the church speaks a particular truth in any given context.

Beginning in 16:6, Jesus senses the sorrow that greets his declaration that he will leave his followers to return to his Father. In response, he restores confidence and explains why "it is to your advantage that I go away": because then the Holy Spirit will come. His explanation outlines the work of the Spirit around two foci, the environment external to Jesus' followers among those who oppose Jesus (vv. 8-11) and the internal environment of the life of the Christian community (vv. 12-15).

In the first section (vv. 8-11), Jesus says that the Spirit will encounter "the world," indicating people who do not know Jesus (see 1:10; 7:7; 15:18-19; 17:14), by exposing three things: the sin of the world, the righteousness of the Son, and the judgment of Satan.[7] The sin Jesus describes is the failure to believe in him, not specific moral faults. The sheer existence of the Spirit, as the presence of the glorified Christ, attests to Jesus' righteousness by proving that the Father has vindicated the Son against any charges. Such a divine acquittal confirms the ultimate judgment against Satan, "the ruler of this world." The Spirit continues Jesus' work of exposing, through the work of the witnessing community, by shining light into dark places (see 3:19-20). The Spirit does not aim to issue condemnation on any but Satan, suggesting that the purpose of exposing sin is to bring about the world's reconciliation. The Spirit guides believers to expose unbelief not so that they might levy condemnations but so that they might simultaneously extend promises of salvation (compare 3:17; 12:47).

> THE SPIRIT GUIDES BELIEVERS TO EXPOSE UNBELIEF NOT SO THAT THEY MIGHT LEVY CONDEMNATIONS BUT SO THAT THEY MIGHT SIMULTANEOUSLY EXTEND PROMISES OF SALVATION.

The second focus, concerning the life and knowledge of Jesus' followers, includes the promise that the Spirit will bring recognition and apprehension of truths about Jesus that were inaccessible to the disciples and others prior to the cross and resurrection.[8] The intermediary language of vv. 13-15 confirms that the Spirit's primary role is to make Jesus present to the believing community, locating him in its midst.

If it is early June, it must be commencement season. For those participating, the joy and hopes of a graduation also come with sorrow for what must be left behind. Enthusiastic commencement speakers brace graduates for change and try to soothe anxieties. Their speeches typically confirm graduates' credentials and exhort them to make an impact on the world by drawing from the reservoir of knowledge and experience that they take with them. As Jesus says farewell to his followers, he likewise readies them for the difficulties of change, orienting their attention away from the anguish of his departure toward the advantages of life with the Spirit. The difference between Jesus' words and the commencement speaker's lies in the fact that Jesus does not encourage people to build on a foundation they have attained or to go off boldly on their own. Jesus promises that the foundational presence of himself will continue to accompany them and work in their midst through the reality of the Spirit. The coming of the Spirit will commence a new, better era by actively uniting believers to the glorified Jesus, who serves as an altogether different kind of reservoir (see John 4:14) to empower the faithful.

Any sermon on the depiction of the Holy Spirit in John should recognize that this Spirit is thoroughly integrated with the identity and witness of the Word, Jesus Christ. The Spirit is no entirely independent agent; it creates dynamic communion between the risen Jesus and the community of his followers. When the church seeks the guidance and nourishment of the Spirit, it rightly seeks neither a vague sense of "spirituality" nor some privatized experience. To be led by the Holy Spirit, insists the Fourth Gospel, is to be led into the truth and testimony of the Word of God.

> THE SPIRIT IS NO ENTIRELY INDEPENDENT AGENT; IT CREATES DYNAMIC COMMUNION BETWEEN THE RISEN JESUS AND THE COMMUNITY OF HIS FOLLOWERS.

For additional discussion of the Gospel of John's distinctive outlook on the Holy Spirit, see the comments on related Johannine passages, both above (for the Vigil of Pentecost) and immediately below.

JOHN 20:19-23 (BCP, RC)

John locates the advent of the Holy Spirit not on Pentecost but on Easter, when the resurrected Lord appears to and commissions his followers. Describing v. 22, biblical scholar Raymond Brown writes, "For John this is the high point of the post-resurrectional activity of Jesus," because the event initiates new life for those present.[9] The verb indicating Jesus' breathing (*emphysaō*) suggests a kind of re-creation as it recalls God's giving life to Adam in Gen. 2:7 and revivifying the bones in Ezek. 37:9.

JOHN 14:8-17 (BCP ALT.)

This passage introduces John's unique term for the Holy Spirit: *Advocate* or *Paraclete* (meaning "one called to assist another"). The Father sends the Spirit in v. 16 and in 14:26, but elsewhere Jesus does (John 15:26; 16:7). This difference in senders underscores the mutuality between Father and Son that is a hallmark of John's Gospel (see 5:19; 10:30, 37-38; 14:8-11). The Spirit empowers Jesus' followers to continue his work (v. 12) and confirms both the truth and the world's ignorance (v. 17; compare 3:19; 17:25).

Notes

1. The slaves mentioned in Joel 2:29 denote a social class. In Acts 2:18, however, Peter changes the oracle to have God speaking about "my slaves." This diminishes the focus on social standing (Joel puts slaves in contrast to free people) by suggesting that *all* recipients of the Spirit offer their prophecy as people in service to God.

2. Loveday Alexander, "'This Is That': The Authority of Scripture in the Acts of the Apostles," *The Princeton Seminary Bulletin* 25 (2004): 193.

3. Ibid., 192.

4. Paul S. Minear, "Dear Theo: The Kerygmatic Intention and Claim of the Book of Acts," *Interpretation* 27 (1973): 140–41.

5. The Hebrew text of Isa. 44:4 is problematic. Where the NRSV reads, "spring up like a green tamarisk," other viable alternatives include "sprout like grass" (NJPS) and "spring up among the grass" (NJB). In any case, emphasis falls on the lush response to God's pouring Spirit like water.

6. This counsel is against *excessive* preoccupation with the struggles that faced some Jewish Christians in the first century. At the same time, the sharp sectarian tone of John's Gospel requires that Christian leaders find avenues to address these issues in their teaching and preaching in a way that demonstrates that the Gospel does not advocate renunciation of the world or vilification of others. For valuable suggestions, see Gail R. O'Day, "The Gospel of John: Introduction, Commentary, and Reflections," in *The New Interpreter's Bible,* vol. 9 (Nashville: Abingdon, 1995), 766–68.

7. In John 16:8, the verb *elegchō* (rendered by the NRSV as "prove wrong about") can mean "bring to light," "convince," or "convict." In English, *expose* (or *lay bare*) probably best captures all these senses. The verb also appears with a similar usage in John 3:20.

8. The expression "all the truth" in John 16:13 refers to truth about Jesus, thereby depicting the Spirit as a theological teacher and interpreter. See D. Moody Smith, *John*, Abingdon New Testament Commentaries (Nashville: Abingdon, 1999), 296–97.

9. Raymond E. Brown, *The Gospel according to John XIII–XXI,* Anchor Bible 29A (New York: Doubleday, 1970), 1037.

HOLY TRINITY SUNDAY / FIRST SUNDAY AFTER PENTECOST

JUNE 11, 2006

REVISED COMMON	EPISCOPAL (BCP)	ROMAN CATHOLIC
Isa. 6:1-8	Exod. 3:1-6	Deut. 4:32-34, 39-40
Psalm 29	Psalm 93 or Canticle 2 or Canticle 13	Ps. 33:4-5, 6, 9, 18-19, 20, 22
Rom. 8:12-17	Rom. 8:12-17	Rom. 8:14-17
John 3:1-17	John 3:1-16	Matt. 28:16-20

Although Christians regularly recite familiar creeds and produce mountains of books that formulate and fine-tune the dogma of our confessions, Trinity Sunday brings a prime opportunity to praise the God who ultimately lies beyond our comprehension. The mystery of the Trinity reasserts the transcendence, or sheer otherness, of God. At the same time, the relationships and activities of the revealed Persons of the Trinity convince us of God's immanence, that God remains accessible to human experience. Transcendent and immanent: God is both, and our faith *needs* God to be both. Spiritual writer Kathleen Norris calls God's transcendence a "refuge," describing her need for a God greater than herself in this way: "When I read the New Age author Starhawk, although I enjoy her very much as a writer . . . I ultimately grow bored. She is so insistent on living in a world in which holiness is all immanence, without the possibility of transcendence, that I feel flattened out and left without hope."[1]

The lections assigned for today offer images and language that capture the transcendence and immanence of the triune God. Some, such as Isaiah 6 and Psalms 29 and 93, offer glimpses of God's glory in effusive descriptions that possess all the subtlety of a heavy-metal concert. Others, such as Romans 8 and John 3, describe how this same God comes intimately near to us.

ISAIAH 6:1–8 (RCL)

No latent evidence for the Trinity hides in this passage. The triple acclamation of God as "holy" in v. 3 is emphatic, and the mention of "us" in v. 8 refers to God among the whole host of supernatural beings, including the seraphs, who compose the heavenly court. The scene's contribution to our understanding of God lies foremost in its depiction of God as utterly awesome and transcendent.

These verses recount the first half of a prophetic commissioning.[2] God quite literally dominates the scene as Isaiah receives a vision of God as an enthroned king, a thoroughly immense and majestic presence. Winged seraphs shield themselves and Isaiah from directly viewing God, and their shouts praise God as both holy (exalted, sacred, and wholly other) and glorious (magnificent and terrible). We should not consider Isaiah's response to this sight as rehearsed or routine; his expression of fear and danger is utterly appropriate. God's glory elicits from him a clear recognition of his own deficiencies, reflected in his words *woe, lost,* and *unclean.* In God's company Isaiah gains "a fresh sense of himself, his inadequacy, his lack of qualification to be in the holy presence. . . . There is no coziness here, for God's presence is a source of deep jeopardy."[3]

Although the scene culminates in Isaiah's purification and commission for service, proclamation of this passage should resist any temptation to glorify Isaiah as an agreeable volunteer, boldly willing to take up the cause of God's mission. For Isaiah's story is about God. Today it continues to speak a powerful word to a culture that has lost a sense of and a respect for the holy. The point, of course, is not to imagine God enthroned in our midst as if in cold marble, or enthroned in a way that dismisses the tenderness and vulnerability that God also expresses throughout scripture. Instead, when we declare God's unique glory, worshipers confess that the

> PROCLAMATION OF THIS PASSAGE SHOULD RESIST ANY TEMPTATION TO GLORIFY ISAIAH AS AN AGREEABLE VOLUNTEER, BOLDLY WILLING TO TAKE UP THE CAUSE OF GOD'S MISSION.

highest human standards of greatness and achievement can hardly approximate the majesty of God. If such a God be for us, then we can hope.

DEUTERONOMY 4:32–34, 39–40 (RC)

Moses is preaching to the people in the wake of their exodus from Egypt and the revelation at Sinai, proclaiming Israel's deliverance and election as the definitive, incomparable demonstration that the Lord is God and there is no other. Consider the evidence, says Moses. Who else but God could free an entire people? As a preacher, Moses understands the nature of testimony: he identifies and interprets God's presence in the world via the experiences of his audience.

EXODUS 3:1-6 (BCP)

God comes to Moses on Mount Horeb (Sinai) to commission him to lead the Israelites from slavery. The narrative indicates the holiness of God and the danger inherent in a close encounter with God. At the same time, this glorious God attends earnestly to the affairs and struggles of people—the patriarchs in the past, as well as their oppressed descendants currently suffering under the pharaoh.

RESPONSIVE READING
PSALM 29 (RCL)

The psalmist asserts the awesome glory of God. The mention of God over the waters leads some to recall Genesis 1. Likewise, ancient audiences would have recognized references to Canaanite creation mythology in which the god Baal has to conquer the waters of chaos. The psalm therefore exalts the Lord over the supposed powers of other gods, issuing a vibrant call to worship a God much greater than anything in human experience. Psalm 29, writes biblical scholar James Luther Mays, "is a witness to the urgent importance of the doxological experience for the human condition. Existence is subconsciously moved by the need for a kind of ecstasy—not the ecstasy of possession, of being invaded, taken over and used by another, but the ecstasy of the disclosure of another who is what we are not, confrontation by another in the aura of whose power we find possibilities not ours."[4]

> THE PSALM EXALTS THE LORD OVER THE SUPPOSED POWERS OF OTHER GODS, ISSUING A VIBRANT CALL TO WORSHIP A GOD MUCH GREATER THAN ANYTHING IN HUMAN EXPERIENCE.

The representation of "the voice of the LORD" in the various phenomena of a thunderstorm emphasizes that this voice results in effects. We might say that God's word does things.[5]

PSALM 33:4-5, 6, 9, 18-19, 20, 22 (RC)

For a discussion of this psalm, see the comments for the Vigil of Pentecost, above.

PSALM 93 (BCP)

Psalms such as this one, which declares God as king, characterize God's power as greater than any other power in the universe and insist that God's reign encompasses all people, places, and things. This psalm sounds different to many now than it did before the earthquake and tsunamis of December 26, 2004. If, however, God's sovereignty means that God remains greater than the forces of nature and trustworthy despite such massive natural devastation, then we still possess reason to hope.

CANTICLE 2; CANTICLE 13 (BCP ALT.)

For a discussion of these canticles, see the comments for the Vigil of Pentecost, above.

SECOND READING

ROMANS 8:12-17 (RCL, BCP)
ROMANS 8:14-17 (RC)

The comments for the Vigil of Pentecost, above, include a discussion of Rom. 8:14-17 and suggestions for proclaiming it. The immediately preceding verses, Rom. 8:12-13, show Paul commenting about the Spirit as the sign of our adoption as God's children. Believers live in the fray waged between "the flesh" and the Spirit. "The flesh" and "the deeds of the body" are not equivalent to carnal or sensual pursuits, although they may sometimes include them. Instead, Paul's use of these terms indicates any way of life outside of the Spirit's influence, as when one was enslaved to sin and hostile to God (see 8:5-8). The Spirit, not one's own efforts, provides the means by

> PAUL'S ARGUMENT DOES NOT APPEAL TO ETHICAL JUDGMENT OR MORAL PRUDENCE BUT IS ROOTED IN CHRISTIANS' GOD-GIVEN IDENTITY.

which the flesh's influence is disarmed. Paul's argument, then, does not appeal to ethical judgment or moral prudence but is rooted in Christians' God-given identity. The passage reminds believers that they no longer *belong* to the flesh and exhorts them to live according to what the Spirit has already made them: children of God.

A sermon on these verses for Trinity Sunday could highlight the trinitarian relationships suggested in Paul's letter: the Holy Spirit leads us to cry to the Father and testifies that we share in the inheritance of the Son. A didactic lesson on abstract doctrinal tenets, however, will probably elicit only glazed stares from the congregation. While there is a place for theological catechesis, preaching aims to bring people into an encounter with the triune God, not to ensure that they can explain the Trinity. Effective proclamation might instead focus on what this passage says about our place *within* the nature and work of the triune God. A significant thrust of Rom. 8:12-17 concerns the identity of believers as God's own adopted children, now coheirs with Christ of both his glorification and his suffering. The Spirit within and among us bears witness to the truth that we "have been sealed by the Holy Spirit" and "marked as Christ's own forever" (to borrow words from a baptism liturgy).[6] We encounter God not as an aloof or indifferent principle but as a generous parent to whom we graciously belong.

THE GOSPEL
JOHN 3:1-17 (RCL)
JOHN 3:1-16 (BCP)

Designers of the lectionary surely regarded this passage as appropriate for Trinity Sunday because Jesus' words to Nicodemus incorporate the trinitarian titles *Spirit* and *Son.* Moreover, the juxtaposition of "God" and "Son" in vv. 16-17 reveals that Jesus identifies "God" as his Father. Although John 3 suggests the distinct yet related roles of the three divine Persons in accomplishing salvation, the chapter's purpose is not to provide a clear exposition of the Trinity. Rather, Nicodemus's nocturnal visit offers Jesus an opportunity to discuss the ways of God in an irony-laden manner. The discussion proves to accentuate Nicodemus's estrangement from heavenly ideas that would remain utterly inaccessible to everyone were it not for the descending and ascending Son of Man.[7] This is a complex passage, and its proclamation requires a preacher's willingness to explain some of the symbolism at the core of John's Gospel.

Irony and wordplay saturate this passage beginning in v. 3, where Jesus declares that one must be born *anōthen* to see God's kingdom. The word means both "from above" and "again." The word's ambiguity appears to be purposeful, as seen both in Nicodemus's inability to understand it as anything other than "again," as if a new birth by physical means, and in Jesus' subsequent discourse about his descent and ascent (vv. 13-15), which describes a spiritual rebirth accomplished when Jesus is literally raised up on a cross that will result in his return to the Father. A physical birth is not enough, but baptism symbolized by water and the Spirit (v. 5) stands for a new delivery into life made possible by the crucifixion.[8] A significant point is that Nicodemus cannot move himself beyond a certain, limited way of perceiving Jesus' words. His reasonable interpretation of Jesus' speech makes him blind to the meaning that is recognizable to readers who can observe this scene with the whole of John's Gospel in view.

More wordplay follows in v. 8, because the same Greek word, *pneuma,* means both "wind" and "spirit." Like the wind, God's Spirit travels among people while remaining totally beyond our ability to manipulate it. This mirrors humanity's basic ignorance of divine truth. Jesus, the Son of Man who descended from heaven, offers the hope of our gaining access to heavenly things as the source for our spiritual rebirth. Yet again we encounter an ironic dimension to how this will happen. It occurs when Jesus is placed on the cross, as "lifted up" (v. 14) translates a term (*hypsoō*) meaning both to elevate physically and to exalt. In the ugly degradation of a Roman crucifixion, therefore, Jesus will be ironically glorified and will serve as the conduit for new life from God (in an echo of the serpent on a tall stick in Num. 21:8–9).

> JESUS, THE SON OF MAN WHO DESCENDED FROM HEAVEN, OFFERS THE HOPE OF OUR GAINING ACCESS TO HEAVENLY THINGS AS THE SOURCE FOR OUR SPIRITUAL REBIRTH.

Homiletics experts rightly warn against excessive appeals to the biblical languages during the course of a sermon. Detailed word studies and convoluted tangents on Greek syntax can discourage even the most responsive congregations. Proclamation of this passage, however, benefits from preachers' direct and prudent attention to the wordplay that Jesus employs, especially the double meaning of *anōthen* in vv. 3 and 7 (see also 3:31), since the ambiguity of that term provides a basis for most of 3:3–15. Nicodemus might have wished that someone had made the wordplay plainer to him. Many in our churches will have similar wishes and will appreciate hearing the irony clarified.

That darling verse of Christian sloganeering, John 3:16, acquires greater importance when we note that it follows and interprets the first fifteen verses of this narrative. Precisely after so much esoteric and potentially confounding imagery from Jesus, now this verse concretizes the logic of God's salvation as an expression of God's love for the world. While the verse might work as a disembodied summary of the gospel, in the specific context of John 3 it identifies love as the impetus behind the eternal life that eludes any rational explanation. The purpose of the Son's crossing from heaven to earth is, therefore, salvation instead of condemnation (v. 17).

> WHILE JOHN 3:16 MIGHT WORK AS A DISEMBODIED SUMMARY OF THE GOSPEL, IN ITS SPECIFIC CONTEXT IT IDENTIFIES LOVE AS THE IMPETUS BEHIND THE ETERNAL LIFE THAT ELUDES ANY RATIONAL EXPLANATION.

Worship leaders who legitimately chafe at lectionaries' tendencies to truncate narrative segments might elect to extend this reading to the end of the scene, through 3:21. The scene reaches closure in those concluding verses as Jesus lumps Nicodemus, at least at this early stage of John's Gospel, with those who resist the light, since the Pharisee comes to Jesus during the night (v. 2). The light and darkness imagery of vv. 19–21 provides a fitting description of the world's ongoing resistance to the gospel. Jesus' metaphors remind us that a gospel of light cannot help but transform darkness. Even as the body's eyes can adjust so well to dark conditions that any introduction of light seems unnecessary or undesirable, nevertheless a quick infusion of light makes us realize how insufficient the former circumstances were. Yet illumination also entails exposure, and the shining of light into dark places stings the eyes, making it difficult and painful to greet it.

This lection reflects the otherness and centrality of God, an appropriate focus for Trinity Sunday. Jesus' words to Nicodemus portray the works of God for humanity's salvation as inscrutable, but this inscrutability testifies to the larger truth that salvation is something that only God can engineer and accomplish. Groping in darkness we find ourselves entirely dependent upon God to act on our behalf. How can we not sympathize with Nicodemus's inability to comprehend the divide between earthly and heavenly things? It is temptingly easy to read the exchange between Nicodemus and Jesus as Jesus' being deliberately alienating or elusive, nearly delighting in Nicodemus's frustrated inability to get the point. But the goal of Jesus' cryptic discourse is not to torment his questioner. Rather, it illustrates just how ludicrous Jesus' propositions sound to sensible ears, anyone's sensible ears. As the apostle Paul knew, the claims of the cross smack of foolishness (1 Cor. 1:18). The good news, of course, is that God's ways are not our ways. But the God of heaven descends, bridging the separation between Creator and creature in acts of love designed to redeem and give eternal life.

> JESUS' WORDS TO NICODEMUS PORTRAY THE WORKS OF GOD FOR HUMANITY'S SALVATION AS INSCRUTABLE, BUT THIS INSCRUTABILITY TESTIFIES TO THE LARGER TRUTH THAT SALVATION IS SOMETHING THAT ONLY GOD CAN ENGINEER AND ACCOMPLISH.

A recent study of American adolescents' religious beliefs and vocabulary offers the conjecture that the lived religion of most American teenagers is what the author summarizes as "Moralistic Therapeutic Deism."[9] The tenets of this general worldview assume that God created the world but stands apart from it except when called upon to solve someone's problems, and that God's primary concern is that people treat each other well and experience happiness. This God remains accessible to people, but only when selectively summoned. A distant yet therapeutic God "does not offer any challenging comebacks to or arguments about our requests."[10] The God of John 3:1–21 will not conform to this image. The God we meet there utterly invalidates that kind of theology. God knows exactly what we need, dwells beyond our control, and insists on our transformation through a new birth effected by God in the promises of baptism and the mystery of the cross. This God also has our best interests at heart, for "God so loved the world."

The explicit naming of Father, Son, and Holy Spirit in Jesus' commission regarding baptism explains the choice of this text for Trinity Sunday. Jesus' words underscore the sacramental dimensions of discipleship, and these dimensions remind us that Christian worship has been infused with trinitarian symbols and confessions since its early days. Such worship is a response to the God who has been made known to us through three Persons in intimate communion.

Notes

1. Kathleen Norris, *Amazing Grace: A Vocabulary of Faith* (New York: Riverhead, 1998), 109.

2. The disturbing content of Isaiah's commission (6:9-13) has been left out of this assignment, yet lectionary preachers will have the option of addressing those verses on the Fifth Sunday after Epiphany in Year C.

3. Walter Brueggemann, *Isaiah 1–39*, Westminster Bible Companion (Louisville: Westminster John Knox, 1998), 59.

4. James Luther Mays, *Psalms*, Interpretation (Louisville: John Knox, 1994), 137.

5. The expression plays on the title of the philosopher J. L. Austin's book *How to Do Things with Words* (Cambridge: Harvard University Press, 1962). Austin developed theories about the effects of language and communication, contending that speaking something is more than transmitting data; it is also to do something. Certainly the psalmist sees the dramatic effects of God's communication in Ps. 29:3-9.

6. Presbyterian Church (U.S.A.), *Book of Common Worship* (Louisville: Westminster John Knox, 1993), 414.

7. Wayne A. Meeks, "The Man from Heaven in Johannine Sectarianism," *Journal of Biblical Literature* 91 (1972): 57, 60–61, 67.

8. Water serves as a rich symbol throughout the first three chapters of John's Gospel. On the connections among the various contexts, see Craig R. Koester, *Symbolism in the Fourth Gospel: Meaning, Mystery, Community* (2nd ed.; Minneapolis: Fortress Press, 2003), 176–86.

9. Christian Smith, *Soul Searching: The Religious and Spiritual Lives of American Teenagers* (New York: Oxford University Press, 2005), 162–70. Before adults scoff at adolescents for their theological assumptions, we should remember that young people have gleaned most of them from us and in our churches. What Smith sees as pervasive in teenage culture also describes many aspects of twenty-first-century Christianity more generally.

10. Ibid., 165.

SECOND SUNDAY AFTER PENTECOST / BODY AND BLOOD OF CHRIST (CORPUS CHRISTI)

JUNE 18, 2006
ELEVENTH SUNDAY IN ORDINARY TIME / PROPER 6

REVISED COMMON	EPISCOPAL (BCP)	ROMAN CATHOLIC
Ezek. 17:22–24 or	Ezek. 31:1–6, 10–14	Exod. 24:3–8
1 Sam. 15:34—		
16:13	Psalm 92 or	Ps. 116:12–13, 15–
Ps. 92:1–4, 12–15	92:1–4, 11–14	16, 17–18
or Psalm 20	2 Cor. 5:1–10	Heb. 9:11–15
2 Cor. 5:6–10 (11–		
13), 14–17	Mark 4:26–34	Mark 14:12–16,
Mark 4:26–34		22–26

The Bible overflows with assurances that God is committed and able to bring things to their promised fruition. Many of today's lections employ vocabulary and metaphors of confidence, germination, guarantee, and expectation concerning God's care, our future hope, and the emerging reign of God. A persistent confession of the people of God is that God's designs for the whole of creation will yet be fully accomplished. Such a bold claim brings to mind a familiar characterization of faith: "Now faith is the assurance of things hoped for, the conviction of things not seen" (Heb. 11:1).

Beginning with this Sunday the RCL readings include multiple Old Testament and Psalm assignments, reflecting options used by different denominations and traditions. One trajectory of passages allows for semicontinuous reading of an Old Testament narrative over time, in this case the beginning of the story of King David. Preachers who devote several consecutive Sundays to these texts will enjoy leading their congregations into the richness and complexity of God's curious dealings with David and David's uncomfortably human exploits. (This day also brings a good opportunity to launch a short sermon series probing 2 Corinthians, followed by Ephesians.) Different traditions choose to follow the other strand of passages, which selects Old Testament readings guided by the Gospel pericope, usually to introduce language or themes that provide background, analogues, or echoes to the Gospel. Preachers electing this route are encouraged to avoid construing or doctoring the Old Testament texts as if they were merely typologies to prop up the message of the New Testament readings. The comments below will highlight occasions when multiple readings complement one another especially well. For other Sundays (such as this one), where the supposed connections are superficial or even potentially distorting, the comments will suggest that preachers let the Old Testament texts proclaim their particular messages without overdrawing any correspondences to the Gospel lection.

The Roman Catholic readings for today all lend themselves to sustained reflection on the institution and significance of the Holy Eucharist.

FIRST READING
EZEKIEL 17:22-24 (RCL)

These three verses form an encouraging coda to a bleak parable describing Judah's political demise. A sermon should make plain their attachment to the imagery and historical context of all of Ezekiel 17. The key point of attachment is obvious, as God in v. 22 and the first eagle (Nebuchadnezzar) in vv. 3-4 perform similar symbolic acts. In the coda of vv. 22-24, God promises to accomplish a glorious restoration after the current calamities, symbolized by the propagation of a fruitful cedar, a tree whose massive height and longevity make for a dramatic representation of the strength and durability God will foster in a new Israelite society.

It remains unclear whether Ezekiel speaks of Israel's national restoration only in a general sense or if the image of a planted sprig resonates with the promise of a new and particular royal figure in David's lineage, as in Isa. 11:1. More important is the portrait of the cedar itself as a sign of the nation's enjoying stable existence. Ezekiel describes the space encompassed by the tree (we might compare the setting to our modern understanding of a tree as a miniature ecosystem in and of itself) as a community of refuge and sustenance. It

> EZEKIEL DESCRIBES THE SPACE ENCOMPASSED BY THE TREE AS A COMMUNITY OF REFUGE AND SUSTENANCE. IT PROMOTES LIFE.

promotes life. The tree, however, does not create itself or sustain itself. The Lord must accomplish this. The oracle therefore witnesses to God's commitment to the welfare of God's people, then and now.

1 SAMUEL 15:34—16:13 (RCL ALT.)

God has rejected Saul, Israel's first king, for his disobedience. Therefore, the Lord sends the aggrieved prophet Samuel to anoint a successor. As the elders of Bethlehem seem to suspect, Samuel commits a dangerous, subversive act, for King Saul still reigns. But as a theological statement, this act proclaims God's continuing care for the people. God "sees" (v. 7) what Israel needs, and God initiates the solution, choosing and blessing a new leader for Israel's sake. Israel needs a real shepherd! In an ironic scene, the Lord's vision spies a surprising candidate for the royal office, a boy lacking a definitive kingly stature (compare 9:2; 10:23-24). Bible readers should be familiar with God's tendency to challenge and invert accepted expectations and values. Likewise, after Pentecost the church continually reaffirms its convictions that God sees what we cannot and that God works in unexpected ways.

While the anointing signifies a dramatic shift when God commits to David, an almost anticlimactic stillness also accompanies the event. David is an unlikely king, who on this occasion is the object, not subject, of action. Nevertheless, God's spirit comes to him, and Israel will be changed forever.

EXODUS 24:3-8 (RC)

Moses conducts a ritual to symbolize the ratification of the covenant God makes with Israel at Sinai, splashing the blood of oxen on an altar and on the people who have vowed their obedience. The stain and threat of bloodshed binds both God and Israel to the terms of the covenant (compare the interpretation in Heb. 9:18-22). Jesus alludes to this event in his expression "the blood of the covenant" in Mark 14:24.

EZEKIEL 31:1-6, 10-14 (BCP)

The pronouncement compares Egypt to the fallen Assyrian Empire, which once resembled a majestic cedar, beautiful and protecting other nations, yet was struck down by invaders because of its pride and wickedness. The prophet speaks this word as Jerusalem is besieged, thereby extinguishing any hope that Egypt might rush to Judah's defense. Ezekiel insists that history is not random and that political alliances cannot guarantee security. God is the source of nations' greatness, and arrogance precipitates their downfall. The oracle thus aims to stimulate repentance and trust in the Lord.

RESPONSIVE READING

105

SECOND SUNDAY
AFTER PENTECOST

MATTHEW L.
SKINNER

PSALM 92:1-4, 12-15 (RCL)
PSALM 92 or 92:1-4, 11-14 (BCP)

Arboreal images in the psalm, as they do elsewhere in scripture, do not glorify the trees themselves but prompt reflection on the roots and nutrients that sustain a tree just as God nourishes and grows the lives of God's people. The concluding verse's promise, that the persistent fecundity of the righteous proclaims God's own righteousness, means that God is at work in human lives and history. What kinds of human or spiritual flourishing in today's world truly make such a theological statement? Preachers need to answer that question with a thoughtful and perhaps cautious imagination.

PSALM 20 (RCL ALT.)

Scholars often classify Psalm 20 as a prayer to bless the king, God's anointed ruler, perhaps as he prepares for battle. After the monarchy, however, the psalm was transmitted and sung probably because it testifies more generally "to God's continuing ability to save the people," since "the psalm is really more about God than it is about the king."[1] It expresses resolute confidence in God, spurring hearers to pray on behalf of themselves, their leaders, and anyone else.

PSALM 116:12-13, 15-16, 17-18 (RC)

Because God has brought salvation when death appeared imminent (vv. 1-8), the psalmist pledges to sacrifice a drink offering as an expression of thanksgiving. Jews came to employ this psalm in Passover celebrations, and Christians have used it to interpret the Eucharist.

SECOND READING

2 CORINTHIANS 5:6-10 (11-13), 14-17 (RCL)
2 CORINTHIANS 5:1-10 (BCP)

These assigned divisions of verses are peculiar in light of the flow of Paul's rhetoric. Preachers could reduce the potential for confusion by instead reading 4:16—5:10 (on Christian hope in the contrasts between external/internal, transitory/eternal, seen/unseen, away/home) or 5:11–21 (on the cross and reconciliation). Comments below treat these two sections in turn.

Paul likens the believer's life in the body to living in a temporary tent. Decay, affliction, and longing characterize this transient existence, yet the Spirit serves as a down payment of hope in anticipation of God's judgment and the promise of permanent bodies (buildings from God) to replace our current ones. Deliverance from the travails of this world does not mean escape from bodily existence but being clothed with a new, resurrected body. Paul does not use the promise of a future fulfillment as grounds for hating this life and minimizing its pains. Instead, future hope should spur redeemed people toward action that pleases the Lord.

> DELIVERANCE FROM THE TRAVAILS OF THIS WORLD DOES NOT MEAN ESCAPE FROM BODILY EXISTENCE BUT BEING CLOTHED WITH A NEW, RESURRECTED BODY.

"We walk by faith, not by sight" (v. 7). The expression erodes into cliché in some circles, but it nevertheless states a fundamental Christian explanation of why believers "do not lose heart" (4:1, 16) in the face of adversity or disappointment. In a culture that pushes people to grasp and protect their job security, financial security, homeland security, and social security—all good things but none the ultimate thing—Christians stand apart in finding security through faith and the guarantee of the Spirit.

The rich words of 2 Cor. 5:11–21 have given comfort and fortitude to countless Christians through the centuries. They include a number of central Pauline themes concerning the cross of Christ as the critical transformational event that has altered all of existence. Although this section begins with Paul continuing a defense of the ministry he conducts with Timothy (see 2 Cor. 1:1) and others, clearly his words extend to the vocation of all believers: the love of Christ compels all Christians to regard the world through the lens of the cross and to engage in ministries of reconciliation. These few verses place preachers in fertile fields for proclamation.

The crucifixion makes a bold statement about who we are in God's eyes.

> THE CROSS MUST TRANSFORM THE WAY WE THINK ABOUT OTHERS, AND THIS NEW WAY OF THINKING FINDS ITS EXPRESSION THROUGH LOVE ENACTED IN CHRISTIAN COMMUNITIES.

"The most basic fact for Christians is this: People have value because Christ has died for them. People, whoever they are, whether they have responded to Christ or not . . . are treasured by God."[2] The cross, therefore, must transform the way we think about others, and this new way of thinking finds its expression through love enacted in Christian communities.[3]

The startling declaration that God makes through the cross also confirms that God deeply desires to reconcile humanity to God. Although God has every right to punish, shame, or ignore us, nevertheless in love God claims us. The season after Pentecost creates a fitting context for exploring a consequence of God's claiming, emphasized by Paul: the church exists as a community of reconciled reconcilers. As people reconciled to God by God, we now serve as instruments through whom God continues to appeal to the world. Congregations may perform this evangelistic responsibility in a myriad of ways, but doubtlessly few outsiders will pay attention unless reconciliation also characterizes our relationships among ourselves and within our society.

HEBREWS 9:11-15 (RC)

The book of Hebrews contends that Christ in his death functioned as both high priest and sacrifice. This passage reflects the core message of Heb. 8:1—10:18, that the blood of Christ has effected a perfect, superior cleansing of sin, thereby instituting and mediating a new and greater covenant between God and humanity.

THE GOSPEL
MARK 4:26-34 (RCL, BCP)

If the preceding parable of the sower and soils (Mark 4:1-20) depicts Jesus' dissemination of the word as arbitrary and the reign of God as concealed (4:11-12), then the teachings of 4:21-34 create a meaningful counterbalance in their descriptions of God's reign mysteriously but inevitably emerging and maturing. Just as Mark's Gospel portrays Jesus' identity as a mystery to his contemporaries until its clear disclosure in the Passion narrative (14:61-62), likewise these parables insist that the full manifestation of the reign of God will blossom gradually, unavoidably culminating in a state of completion. The lection advocates patience and confidence in the God who will make this happen. These two seed parables may give today's discouraged congregations a shot in the arm and prompt them to think about their place in the work of the emerging reign of God.

> THESE TWO SEED PARABLES MAY GIVE TODAY'S DISCOURAGED CONGREGATIONS A SHOT IN THE ARM AND PROMPT THEM TO THINK ABOUT THEIR PLACE IN THE WORK OF THE EMERGING REIGN OF GOD.

The situations described by the parables are simple and generally familiar. The simplicity and familiarity must not, however, blind us to the rich potential for meaning we discover here. The parable of the seed growing secretly, which is unique to Mark, relates events we all understand. At least three basic aspects of the parable deserve attention. First, people plant seeds and wait for them to grow without needing to know or worry about the science of germination and photosynthesis. Assuming the environmental conditions are right, we can go about our lives and let nature do its job. These details reflect the fact that God is responsible for the growth of the kingdom, not we. Nor must we dissect the mysteries of the kingdom's emergence. But, second, it is also true that seeds do not instantly transform into mature plants. They grow. Jesus knows that part of the joy (and anxiety) of planting involves observing that growth. Any preschoolers who have planted beans in plastic cups can attest to the anticipation reflected in v. 28, as a shoot gradually develops into a plant over time. Jesus' parable includes no discussion of weeds, frost, or pests hindering growth—only relentless, certain progress toward harvest. The kingdom is coming. Third, when the time for harvest arrives, that marks the culminating moment, requiring a sudden response. Farmers understand the need to begin and complete the harvest on time. Patience yields to decisive action, indicated by the familiar Markan word for "at once" or "immediately," *euthus* (v. 29). The Bible often speaks of harvest as a symbol of God's judgment. Such judgment indicates the fullness of the materialization of God's reign.

The parable of the mustard seed highlights the contrast between the smallness of the seed and the magnificence of the shrub it becomes. We can forgive the horticultural overstatement about the mustard seed being the smallest seed. The conventional wisdom of the ancient Mediterranean world assumed it was.[4] Jesus' point is that the reign of God, although it begins in obscurity, limited scope, and apparent insignificance, will reach a majestic fulfillment. It will attract attention and offer refuge, just as a large mustard plant can shelter birds. The final words of the parable, concerning the branches and birds, recalls but does not directly quote language from Ezek. 17:23; 31:6; and Dan. 4:12, 21. There is not enough correspondence between this parable and those texts to suggest that Jesus reinterprets specific prophetic oracles in light of his proclamation of God's reign, or that he understands the birds to represent particular peoples. It is better to conclude that he employs familiar imagery in a general sense to connote an expansive, attractive community that God creates. Various Old Testament passages speak of trees as symbols of fulfillment or societies that God nurtures. That social symbolism likewise infuses Jesus' parable, for the seed's "job" is to become a mature shrub, and the mustard shrub exists not only to attract attention but to provide benefits of life and sanctuary.

JESUS' POINT IS THAT THE REIGN OF GOD, ALTHOUGH IT BEGINS IN OBSCURITY, LIMITED SCOPE, AND APPARENT INSIGNIFICANCE, WILL REACH A MAJESTIC FULFILLMENT.

Jack Nicholson plays obsessive-compulsive author Melvin Udall in the film *As Good as It Gets.* In one bittersweet scene, distressed because his psychiatrist refuses to see him without an appointment, Melvin exits the doctor's office through a crowded waiting room. To the patients there, he blurts out, "What if this is as good as it gets?" Faced with daily news reports of more violence, greed, starvation, racism, and disease, we might despair to the point of posing Melvin's acid question to ourselves. If *this* manner of existence is as good as God's reign gets, then we are all in big trouble. These two parables, however, correct our vision. They offer encouragement to those who would either conclude that God's reign is an impotent one or equate it with pie-in-the-sky idealism.

Both parables orient us to the future through their end-of-days symbolism of a harvest and a mature plant. Underscoring the inexorable emergence of the fullness of God's rule in our lives and our world, the parables instruct us toward patience and hope. The agricultural representation of God's reign reminds us that God alone will bring it to pass.

At the same time, these parables in Mark's Gospel confirm that Christians are not hoping for a future promise that lacks a basis in the past or present. The reign Jesus describes here is the same one he himself inaugurates in his proclamation of the gospel (1:14-15). Seeds have been planted and have germinated. They are growing, even now in our midst. Do we see them? A growing plant might look the same to us on consecutive days, yet it grows. The preaching vocation includes the responsibility of helping a community discern signs of God's fostering such growth in its midst.

Proclamation of this passage should steer clear of two potential pitfalls. The first pitfall assumes that since God is the agent behind the realization of God's reign, believers play no role. The rest of Mark's Gospel rules out such a conclusion, for Jesus calls others to *participate* in the same ministry he conducts (3:13-15; 6:7-13). As Jesus' disciples, we share in Jesus' ministry of proclaiming the reign of God. Biblical scholar Brian Blount accurately characterizes the distinction in this way: "Human performance . . . never *becomes* the consummate kingdom of God. Instead, it tactically *re-presents* the strategic reality of that kingdom, particularly as it is portrayed in Jesus' life and ministry."[5] The fullness of our kingdom hope remains in the future, but we enact it, in part, in the present, through God's power, following the contours of Jesus' ministry as a model. This ministry attends to all aspects of human vitality, as reflected in the lush agricultural visions of the parables. The second pitfall confuses the certain emergence of the reign of God with a doctrine of steadily improving social progress. An understanding of sin derived from the scriptures should make us very suspicious of such a move.

> THE FULLNESS OF OUR KINGDOM HOPE REMAINS IN THE FUTURE, BUT WE ENACT IT, IN PART, IN THE PRESENT, THROUGH GOD'S POWER, FOLLOWING THE CONTOURS OF JESUS' MINISTRY AS A MODEL.

In Mark, Jesus offers little explicit interpretation of the supper and no command to repeat it. His interpretations of the bread and cup nevertheless connect his coming death to Passover themes. The corporate sharing, the expression *for many,* and the recall of Exod. 24:8 indicate the ratification of a new covenant forged in Jesus' own death.

Notes

1. J. Clinton McCann Jr., "The Book of Psalms: Introduction, Commentary, and Reflections," in *The New Interpreter's Bible,* vol. 4 (Nashville: Abingdon, 1996), 755.

2. J. Paul Sampley, "The Second Letter to the Corinthians: Introduction, Commentary, and Reflections," in *The New Interpreter's Bible,* vol. 11 (Nashville: Abingdon, 2000), 11:98.

3. J. Louis Martyn, "Epistemology at the Turn of the Ages," in *Theological Issues in the Letters of Paul* (Nashville: Abingdon, 1997), 89–110.

4. Arland J. Hultgren, *The Parables of Jesus: A Commentary* (Grand Rapids, Mich.: Wm. B. Eerdmans, 2000), 395. Hultgren says the seed measures .075 inch in diameter and can produce a plant up to fifteen feet tall.

5. Brian K. Blount, *Go Preach! Mark's Kingdom Message and the Black Church Today* (Maryknoll, N.Y.: Orbis, 1998), 8 (italics in original).

THIRD SUNDAY AFTER PENTECOST

JUNE 25, 2006
TWELFTH SUNDAY IN ORDINARY TIME / PROPER 7

REVISED COMMON	EPISCOPAL (BCP)	ROMAN CATHOLIC
Job 38:1-11 or 1 Sam. 17:(1a, 4-11, 19-23) 32-49 or 1 Sam. 17:57—18:5, 10-16	Job 38:1-11, 16-18	Job 38:1, 8-11
Ps. 107:1-3, 23-32 or Ps. 9:9-20 or Psalm 133	Ps. 107:1-32 or 107:1-3, 23-32	Ps. 107:23-24, 25-26, 28-29, 30-31
2 Cor. 6:1-13	2 Cor. 5:14-21	2 Cor. 5:14-17
Mark 4:35-41	Mark 4:35-41 (5:1-20)	Mark 4:35-41

No one can encounter God and expect to resume life unchanged. Several of today's readings suggest that God's claim upon our lives brings with it significant discomfort, as God conforms us through Christ and the dynamic activity of the Word of God. To live in this world is to encounter fearful situations, and this fact requires us to cultivate a theological vision that can discern and embrace the assurances God makes to us, as individuals and as communities of faith.

FIRST READING

JOB 38:1-11 (RCL)
JOB 38:1-11, 16-18 (BCP)
JOB 38:1, 8-11 (RC)

After numerous chapters of discussion and speculation interpreting Job's predicament, God speaks. Unfortunately for Job and his friends, God does not offer many answers but does offer lots of questions. The Lord's opening words upbraid Job for his presumptions based on the limitations of human knowledge. The rhetorical questions that follow declare God's privileged access to the mysteries of all creation, because God is quite familiar with the universe's design. Over the next few chapters, God takes Job on a verbal tour of the wonders of the world, but this Sunday's reading fixes our attention on God's relationship to the span and limits of the earth and sea. The symbolism describing God's association to the sea does not depict the waters as frightfully as does other maritime imagery in the Bible (see the discussion of Mark 4:35–41, below). In vv. 8–9 the Lord treats the sea as a nurse treats a newborn. Only God can care for the delicate sea, which appears utterly vulnerable when compared to the surpassing might of God.

It is difficult to do justice to God's words as a particular address to Job in his specific situation of misery and complaint without taking into account the overall sweep of Job 38:1—42:6. The book of Job deals with such complex questions about life and God's intentions that Christian leaders better serve their congregations by finding avenues for devoting sustained attention to the book and its issues. Nevertheless, this individual lection provides an important backdrop to today's Gospel text by offering a firm declaration of God's mastery over a potentially chaotic element in creation.

1 SAMUEL 17:(1a, 4-11, 19-23) 32-49 (RCL ALT.)

The eminently beloved story of David defeating Goliath poses a challenge to preachers because of its length and familiarity. Still, thoughtful proclamation of this passage can give it a much-needed lift out of its captivity to cultural clichés and certain promotions of "muscular Christianity."[1]

David answers the Philistine's challenge while still a boy. His anointing in chapter 16 has functioned only as a pledge of what God yet intends for him. In David's motivation for fighting Goliath, we glimpse something of what God might have earlier seen in his heart (16:7), a resolute conviction about God's involvement in human affairs and a determined trust in God. His theological insight, not his personal courage, sparks his willingness to face the feared warrior. For David cannot survey any challenge without imagining that God plays a role in it.

> THOUGHTFUL PROCLAMATION OF THIS PASSAGE CAN GIVE IT A MUCH-NEEDED LIFT OUT OF ITS CAPTIVITY TO CULTURAL CLICHÉS AND CERTAIN PROMOTIONS OF "MUSCULAR CHRISTIANITY."

Worship leaders should add vv. 24–26 to the reading, for here we observe that none of the other Israelites sees God as part of the equation, but David perceives Goliath's affronts as nothing less than ridiculous in the face of "the living God." Everyone else shortsightedly views the situation in terms of the strategic or physical exigencies, the offense of Goliath's sacrilege, and the warrant for a true national hero to emerge. David, however, understands God as actively involved in this and other affairs. When he tells Saul about killing lions and bears, he does not boast about his own strength or accomplishments; he attributes this to God's care. Likewise, David's claims that *God* will defeat Goliath bracket his taunts in vv. 46-47. The story thereby moves us, when we pore over observable evidence and statistical analyses, to ask, "But what difference does God make for this situation?"

1 SAMUEL 17:57—18:5, 10-16 (RCL ALT.)

After slaying Goliath, David becomes a military commander. In his successes he meets with widespread acclaim and love, but also with growing hostility from King Saul. Saul's story becomes increasingly tragic as he clearly cannot derail what God intends for David, and his anger and envy drive him toward derangement. The evil spirit that intermittently influences him appears to be partly the result of his own behavior.

Others respond quite differently to the one whom God has anointed. The actions of Jonathan, Saul's son, express his deep love and allegiance to David. The gifts Jonathan gives suggest he relinquishes his right to succeed his father as king, and the love he expresses also implies a political commitment.[2] Jonathan's devotion to David entails a significant and risky cost.

RESPONSIVE READING
PSALM 107:1-3, 23-32 (RCL, BCP ALT.)
PSALM 107:23-24, 25-26, 28-29, 30-31 (RC)
PSALM 107:1-32 (BCP)

The psalm begins by confessing that the Lord is good. How does the psalmist know? The balance of the psalm recalls various means by which God has demonstrated such goodness in the past, in specific occasions of divine deliverance and provision, and continues to demonstrate it in the ongoing experiences of God's people. Jesus performs similar acts in the Gospels, giving additional expression of this divine goodness.[3] Verses 23-29 set a key context for today's Gospel text, attesting to God's authority over wind and waves and to God's ability to save those who cry out in distress.

PSALM 9:9-20 (RCL ALT.)

In its attention to "the oppressed" and "the afflicted" and its references to the judgment of nations, this passage declares God's opposition to the tyrannical practices of people and their social systems. We want to identify ourselves with the troubled people in the psalm, those whom God will assist. Sometimes we are like these, but oftentimes we resemble the wicked, the troublemakers. The psalm pushes us to consider our society's collective accountability before God.

PSALM 133 (RCL ALT.)

The selection of this psalm attempts to celebrate the kind of life-giving unity that Jonathan expresses to David in 1 Samuel 18:1-4. The psalm juxtaposes images of family ("kindred") with those of God's people ("Zion"), reflecting the deep intimacy inherent in the Bible's use of familial terminology to describe the community composed of the people of God.

SECOND READING
2 CORINTHIANS 6:1-13 (RCL)

Paul's quotation of Isa. 49:8 directs attention to the urgency of his evangelistic appeals and his intention not to hinder God's work of salvation. In vv. 4-10, continuing the defense of his ministry, Paul gives an interesting résumé of the adversities he has faced as an apostle, the character traits he has exemplified, and the ambivalences of his reputation. The list is not entirely negative or defensive, but Paul's point is that through all circumstances he has faithfully exercised his call as Christ's ambassador (see 5:19-20). This catalogue of difficult circumstances intends to demonstrate Paul's trustworthiness to the Corinthian believers whose relationship with the apostle was strained by recent events (see 1:15—2:11).

Our modern era may condition us to read Paul's history of personal hardships with suspicion or outright cynicism concerning his true motives. We must keep in mind, however, that other ancient writings employ similar rhetorical strategies to distance a teacher from dishonorable or shady figures who seek personal glory or monetary gain from their teachings. Paul notes that the gospel has brought him neither fame nor earthly riches but rather suffering and recrimination. His words go beyond skillful rhetoric. The theological dimension of Paul's argument claims that his own experiences as an apostle have resembled those of Jesus on the cross. In crucifixion Christ embraced suffering and responded with virtue. Authentic Christian ministry, Paul insists, entails the same.

THE THEOLOGICAL DIMENSION OF PAUL'S ARGUMENT CLAIMS THAT HIS OWN EXPERIENCES AS AN APOSTLE HAVE RESEMBLED THOSE OF JESUS ON THE CROSS.

What does authentic Christian ministry look like in today's contexts? If the church is continuing the apostolic work first performed by Paul and others, what should it expect? Many North American believers have no clue that in numerous countries systematic and violent persecution remains a consequence of Christian faith.[4] We might learn from the experiences of beleaguered believers even as we petition for their welfare. Paul's words do not call us to glorify or seek out hardship. They do, however, prompt us to consider whether the message of the cross remains our criterion for life and outreach. Does a congregation's priorities reflect complacency or "cruciformity"?[5] Have Christianity's alliances with civil religion removed the offense of the cross from our contexts?

2 CORINTHIANS 5:14-21 (BCP)
2 CORINTHIANS 5:14-17 (RC)

For a discussion of this passage, see the comments for the Second Sunday after Pentecost (Eleventh Sunday in Ordinary Time/Proper 6), above.

THE GOSPEL
MARK 4:35-41 (RCL, BCP, RC)

Although Jesus' followers enjoy privileged explanations of Jesus' teachings (4:34), this "insider knowledge" does not sustain them in the fury of a storm on the Sea of Galilee. When Jesus resolves the crisis with a miraculous deliverance, he simultaneously makes a statement about his identity. For those in the boat, that statement proves to be even more terrifying than the storm.

Many elements of this story point beyond the immediate context, forging connections with other parts of Mark and the Bible. Before probing those, it is instructive to examine an important dimension of the story's structure. In the midst of the sea crossing, a "great" storm falls upon the travelers. If we assume that the boat includes local fishers (see 1:16-20), then this must be some storm to lead them to conclude that death is near (v. 38). They do not misread the potential of the gale. They fail to grasp the power of the One sleeping in the boat. Next, when the awakened Jesus dispatches the threat, a

> THE TRAVELERS DO NOT MISREAD THE POTENTIAL OF THE GALE. THEY FAIL TO GRASP THE POWER OF THE ONE SLEEPING IN THE BOAT.

"great" stillness emerges ("dead calm" in the NRSV). This indicates a sudden, dramatic turn. The storm does not gradually abate; Jesus stops it, creating deafening silence. Finally, the account concludes with an emphatic mention of people's "great" fear (misleadingly rendered by the NRSV as "great awe"), prompted by the terrifying implications of Jesus' deed.[6] Three times the same adjective "great" (*megas*) dramatizes the intensity of the situation, culminating in the portrait of Jesus' followers possessed by fear instead of faith. We discover reasons behind their fright through a deeper exploration of the story.

The sea hardly makes for a safe environment in the Bible. Just as the creation account in Genesis 1 imagines waters as primordial chaos, other passages (including today's Old Testament lections) claim that only God can contain the seas and its threatening powers (Pss. 65:7; 74:13-15; 89:8-9; 104:1-11; 107:23-32; Job 38:1-11). This testifies to the awesome potential of the seas even as it suggests that the disciples may infer the answer to their own question in v. 41. Moreover, Jesus' response to the storm resembles a contest between opposed powers. Much here resembles the exorcism of Mark 1:23-27, suggesting that Jesus conquers any forces that might marshal themselves against humanity.[7]

Of course, the events preceding this confrontation throw Jesus and the others into dramatic relief. Jesus naps in an area below the helm, a sign of his confidence (see Ps. 4:8) or indifference to the circumstances. His boatmates, however, have concluded that no hope remains. They wake Jesus, not to seek assistance, but to announce that they "are perishing." This is why Jesus can diagnose them as lacking faith, both during *and after* the storm ("Why *are* you afraid?"): they presume to know the outcome and conclude that he could have no effect, then they fear because of what follows. Jesus' miracle comes unexpectedly and as a demonstration of his efficacious authority over wind and sea. Precisely this authority evokes great fear as Jesus' followers find themselves face-to-face with the power of God in their presence, a force utterly beyond their ability to control. They have yet to grasp how this Jesus might exercise his awesome authority on their behalf.

> JESUS' AUTHORITY OVER WIND AND SEA EVOKES GREAT FEAR AS HIS FOLLOWERS FIND THEMSELVES FACE-TO-FACE WITH THE POWER OF GOD IN THEIR PRESENCE, A FORCE UTTERLY BEYOND THEIR ABILITY TO CONTROL.

Sermons that explain this story's resonances with other biblical texts about God's power over the seas will focus hearers' attention on what the Gospel account says about God's presence in the ministry of Jesus Christ. The calming of the storm proclaims that God works on behalf of God's people, to be sure. But this kind of work also frankly declares the claims that God makes upon us. If we cannot sympathize with the disciples' terror in the presence of a man who instantly calms a raging sea, perhaps we have become numb to the discomfort or danger that accompanies the notion of God's visitation. In a 1928 Advent sermon, Dietrich Bonhoeffer suggested that the tenderness of the Incarnation has left people unable to "feel the shiver of fear that God's coming should arouse in us. We are indifferent to the message, taking only the pleasant and agreeable out of it and forgetting the serious aspect, that the God of the world draws near to the people of our little earth and lays claim to us."[8] The fear that afflicts people in Mark derives from the personal risk inherent in God's laying such claims. When Christ quiets the forces that threaten chaos, makes the unclean clean, and restores the unacceptable to wholeness, these acts upend our cherished assumptions about order, security, autonomy, and fairness. When God comes so near, we cannot hide. Nor can we push God away.

The fault with Jesus' followers in Mark 4:35-41 lies in the persistence of their fear, which Jesus juxtaposes with the desired response of faith. Faith denotes a willingness to let God be God. The faith Jesus has in mind is both faith *like* his (enabling him to remain tranquil in the throes of a storm) and faith *in* him (relying upon his ability to save). Such faith cannot leave us unchanged.

> WHEN CHRIST QUIETS THE FORCES THAT THREATEN CHAOS, MAKES THE UNCLEAN CLEAN, AND RESTORES THE UNACCEPTABLE TO WHOLENESS, THESE ACTS UPEND OUR CHERISHED ASSUMPTIONS ABOUT ORDER, SECURITY, AUTONOMY, AND FAIRNESS.

A good deal of Christian interpretation of this story throughout the centuries has identified the boat with the church, tossed to and fro in the world yet dependent on Christ for its stability upon the unpredictable sea. Some occasions surely warrant such a reading, but a more fruitful interpretation might focus on the aims and implications of *crossing over* the Sea of Galilee, a voyage made possible only because Jesus defeats forces seeking to halt him. When the sailing party disembarks the boats on the eastern shore of the sea, it will find itself in predominantly Gentile territory for the first time in Mark's Gospel. Many accompanying Jesus might think that those lands make for an unpleasant, if not scandalous, destination. Nevertheless, this broadening of Jesus' influence across traditional geographic, ethnic, and religious divides, represented in his determination to cross the sea, reflects the inclusive scope of the gospel and the call that God subsequently issues to the church to welcome outsiders as equal members of the body of Christ. This kind of vocation strikes great fear in many, for the journey toward new horizons and the dismantling of former stereotypes entail change that sometimes proves painful. Living in the wake of Pentecost makes for a felicitous context for sermons to consider how the people of God might embrace these kinds of itineraries in faith.

MARK 5:1-20 (BCP ALT.)

Attaching these verses to Mark 4:35-41 allows an opportunity to observe another group of people respond to Jesus' works with fear instead of faith, as the unmistakable sight of the cured demoniac causes fear and rejection (5:15-17). Assimilating the former madman into their society would require the citizens to acknowledge the display of power that healed him and their own inability to "manage" him in his former condition. His newfound health tests their defining assumptions about who does and does not belong, or who deserves restoration. It is easier to fear and send Jesus elsewhere.

Notes

1. On the origins, heyday, and perseverance of "muscular Christianity" and its efforts to promote qualities of manliness and heroic militarism as Christian ideals, see Clifford Putney, *Muscular Christianity: Manhood and Sports in Protestant America, 1880–1920* (Cambridge: Harvard University Press, 2001).

2. Walter Brueggemann, *First and Second Samuel*, Interpretation (Louisville: John Knox, 1990), 136.

3. For a comparison of specific similarities, see J. Clinton McCann Jr., "The Book of Psalms: Introduction, Commentary, and Reflections," in *The New Interpreter's Bible,* vol. 4 (Nashville: Abingdon, 1996), 4:1119.

4. Many Christian organizations document persecution and advocate on behalf of suffering Christians.

5. Michael J. Gorman uses the term *cruciformity* with respect to Paul's writings to describe the apostle's foundational convictions that the cross of Christ most thoroughly reveals God's grace and that the cross shapes all aspects of life and Christian witness. See Gorman's *Cruciformity: Paul's Narrative Spirituality of the Cross* (Grand Rapids, Mich.: Wm. B. Eerdmans, 2001).

6. The emphasis lies in the syntax, which one could translate literally as "They feared a great fear." While the Greek verb and noun used in v. 40 for "fear" *(phobeō and phobos)* can indicate either reverential awe or frightened alarm, similarities to other passages in Mark that depict similar environments (6:50) or that clearly contrast "fear" with either "faith" or another desired response (5:15, 36; 10:32; 16:8) indicate that in this case Jesus' followers are terrified.

7. The similarities are striking. Jesus rebukes *(epitimaō)* both unclean spirit (1:25) and wind (4:39). He silences *(phimoō)* the spirit (1:25) and the sea (4:39). After the exorcism onlookers ask, "What is this?" (1:27), while the calming of the storm elicits the question, "Who is this?" (4:41).

8. Dietrich Bonhoeffer, "The Coming of Jesus in Our Midst," *Living Pulpit* 6/4 (October–December 1997): 39.

FOURTH SUNDAY AFTER PENTECOST

July 2, 2006
Thirteenth Sunday in Ordinary Time / Proper 8

Revised Common	Episcopal (BCP)	Roman Catholic
Lam. 3:22-33 or Wisd. of Sol. 1:13-15; 2:23-24 or 2 Sam. 1:1, 17-27	Deut. 15:7-11	Wisd. of Sol. 1:13-15; 2:23-24
Psalm 30 or 130	Psalm 112	Ps. 30:2, 4, 5-6, 11, 12, 13
2 Cor. 8:7-15	2 Cor. 8:1-9, 13-15	2 Cor. 8:7, 9, 13-15
Mark 5:21-43	Mark 5:22-24, 35b-43	Mark 5:21-43 or 5:21-24, 35-43

What do you do when you reach the end of your rope? How do you respond to suffering? In anguished moments, what language do you use? What do you believe? To whom do you turn? From where can you expect help? Today's readings compose a collage of portraits of people in dire circumstances. The deep hopes and faith of many of these individuals defy what the world would consider to be good sense.

First Reading
LAMENTATIONS 3:22-33 (RCL)

These verses are situated in a larger, complex poem (Lam. 3:1-66) spoken by someone who has suffered God's wrath, experienced perhaps in the Babylonian offensives against Judah or in another large-scale tragedy. Beginning in v. 21, the poet recalls truths that usher hope into contexts of despair: God is loving, merciful, and faithful. Those confessions, mixed with admonitions for patience, express the paradoxical existence of faithful people who embrace adversity with expectant trust. The confidence of this sufferer insists that the salvation and compassion of the Lord must be coming, for the travails of the present hour do not square with the idea of a God of steadfast love and mercy. Assurances like these come easily to comfortable people. But what spawns such hope among those who suffer? In the Bible "hope does not emerge from proper reasoning or new information. It is not optimism or wishful thinking. It is not a simple act of the will, a decision under human control, or a willful determination. It emerges without clear cause like grace, without explanation, in the midst of despair and at the point of least hope. It comes from elsewhere, unbidden, illusive, uncontrollable, and surpassing, given in the pit, the place of no hope."[1]

WISDOM OF SOLOMON 1:13–15; 2:23–24 (RC, RCL ALT.)

The outlook of this deuterocanonical/apocryphal book does not regard death as a natural part of life. Death is contrary to God's intentions for creation (but compare Deut. 32:39). The apostle Paul calls death "the last enemy to be destroyed" (1 Cor. 15:26). In a similar vein, the book of Wisdom also personifies death as an alien power that wreaks havoc in the world, brought about by evilness (compare Rom. 5:12). These verses reflect the human inclination to deny death, our resistant impulse to "rage, rage against the dying of the light."[2] They also speak to the dissonance we experience between our anxiety about mortality and our identity as creatures formed in God's image. They proclaim to us in this tension God's resolute commitment to life and God's opposition to all that degrades life, an apt prelude to today's Gospel reading.

2 SAMUEL 1:1, 17–27 (RCL ALT.)

Between last Sunday and this one, the lectionary skips more than a dozen chapters in 1 Samuel. These chapters recount ongoing strife between Saul and David, and the book concludes with Saul and three of his sons dying during a battle with the Philistines. Even though his mortal adversary Saul has been eliminated, David grieves the passing of Saul and Jonathan, singing a lament that recalls their greatness and the benefits Saul brought to Israel. David's personal anguish over Jonathan's loss is understandable. His praise for King Saul may come as a surprise, given their fierce rivalry. But David has repeatedly shown reverence to Saul as God's anointed (see 1 Sam. 24:1–12; 26:6–11). David's time to lead Israel will come, but in his lament we remember that he has not sought the throne at any cost, and certainly not at the cost of his own earnest hopes for Israel's well-being.

THIS IS A SAD TEXT. A STARK EXPRESSION OF HUMAN PAIN, THE LAMENT CAN MAKE A CONGREGATION UNCOMFORTABLE. ALL THE MORE REASON TO PREACH IT.

This is a sad text. A stark expression of human pain, the lament can make a congregation uncomfortable. All the more reason to preach it.

North American societies have largely lost their capacity for public lament and replaced it with public outrage. Both lament and outrage express one's powerlessness, but while the former opens a person up to authentic interaction with others and God, the latter enforces separation through the politics of blame. Have we lost our capacity for national lament? Have Christians responded to their losses and frustrations by imitating the kinds of proud and outraged rants that fill op-ed pages and political talk shows? David's dirge and other biblical models of lament recommend an alternative, candid dialect for Christians in their struggles.

DEUTERONOMY 15:7–11 (BCP)

So that the mandate to remit debts every seventh year (Deut. 15:1) would not stifle lending, these verses warn against preoccupation with self-interest and commend generous and cheerful giving. The passage implies that one has a specific obligation to assist those who are needy, for they are "neighbors," not strangers.

RESPONSIVE READING
PSALM 30 (RCL)
PSALM 30:2, 4, 5–6, 11, 12, 13 (RC)

The Lord responds to the cries of the needy who face the threat of destruction (symbolized as death, named by Sheol and the Pit). Those who recite the psalm testify to God's ability to deliver and restore, transforming occasions of weeping into joy, mourning into dancing. To respond to life's vicissitudes with praise is to interpret reality through a distinctly theological lens: *God is present in these transformations.*[3]

PSALM 130 (RCL ALT.)

For a discussion of this psalm, see the comments for the Vigil of Pentecost, above.

PSALM 112 (BCP)

Considered alone, Psalm 112 appears to celebrate "those who fear the LORD" more than it celebrates the Lord. The language and structure of this psalm, however, closely mirror what one finds in Psalm 111, which clearly praises the Lord in similar ways.[4] The idea of *fearing* this righteous God yokes Pss. 111:10 and 112:1, making the latter psalm a sequel that describes the qualities that God forges in God's people.

Second Reading
2 CORINTHIANS 8:7-15 (RCL)
2 CORINTHIANS 8:1-9, 13-15 (BCP)
2 CORINTHIANS 8:7, 9, 13-15 (RC)

In 2 Corinthians 8–9 Paul entreats his audience to continue contributing financially to his collection for the impoverished church in Jerusalem (see 1 Cor. 16:1-4; Rom. 15:25-27). In 8:1-6 he extols the believers of Macedonia who gave generously despite their own struggles and poverty, thereby encouraging the Corinthians to follow suit. Next, in this lection, the rhetoric of Paul's appeal calls for a contribution not in response to a command but as a free statement of love, generosity, and fairness.

The incentives for the Corinthians' charity extend beyond keeping up with the Macedonians and following ethical obligations. Giving is a theological issue for Paul, because it stems from and mirrors the grace Christ issued to us (v. 9). In fact the word for grace, *charis,* saturates Paul's appeal, although the term's wide semantic range causes English translations to render it in different ways.[5] Paul asserts that Christ's gracious acts of humiliation and redemption actually create the occasion and motivation for us to share in his grace by expressing charity toward others. Of course, the economic language Paul employs to describe Jesus is symbolic, not indicating any connection between the cross and believers' material prosperity. The point remains, nevertheless, that people experience

PAUL ASSERTS THAT CHRIST'S GRACIOUS ACTS OF HUMILIATION AND REDEMPTION ACTUALLY CREATE THE OCCASION AND MOTIVATION FOR US TO SHARE IN HIS GRACE BY EXPRESSING CHARITY TOWARD OTHERS.

true riches in Christ, who is our exemplar in his willingness to sacrifice his own resources to benefit others (compare Phil. 2:4-8). To give, therefore, is to participate in Christ's demonstration of grace.

The passage concludes with Paul's urging the Corinthians to complete the campaign with the same enthusiasm they showed at the beginning. He cares more about their eagerness than about the amount of the gift. The language of a "fair balance" of wealth that will not overburden the Corinthians finds an analogue in the equal distribution of manna in Exod. 16:18.

Paul's efforts to raise funds for the Jerusalem church instruct us today about the theological rationale for giving our resources to assist others. Probably all preachers understand the need for helping congregations understand "stewardship" as rooted in a broader Christian understanding of God, ourselves, and the world.[6] A sermon on this passage might also focus on the ways God's grace manifests itself in Christians' concrete acts of charity and reciprocity (as discussed above), or the ways in which Paul conceives of believers' connections to one another. Paul's language reflects a strong connectional relationship between the church in Jerusalem and the predominantly Gentile churches in the regions of Macedonia and Achaia (where Corinth was situated). Paul can appeal to a sense of mutual obligation among believers because he understands them as yoked together. Christian freedom entails belonging to one another. The freedom Christ secures for us makes us "slaves to one another" (Gal. 5:13), not autonomous individuals. The institutional church of the twenty-first century provides a structure that approximates the connections we observe among the scattered churches of the first century, but in administrating those relationships it also often renders them invisible to many in our pews who may not perceive how the gospel compels them to assist in the welfare and ministries of their brothers and sisters in Christ in distant lands.

> THE FREEDOM CHRIST SECURES FOR US MAKES US "SLAVES TO ONE ANOTHER," NOT AUTONOMOUS INDIVIDUALS.

THE GOSPEL

MARK 5:21–43 (RCL, RC)
MARK 5:22–24, 35b–43 (BCP)
MARK 5:21-24, 35–43 (RC ALT.)

Preachers who preach on the Gospel text this week cannot omit vv. 25-34, which tell of a hemorrhaging woman touching Jesus' cloak. Her story emphasizes her invisibility in her world, for her condition could result in regular ostracism from community life. To erase her from the reading is to remove her from view once more and to miss crucial elements of the Gospel narrative. The story of Mark 5:21-43 has its strongest effect when an audience gets a sense of the interruption that stalls Jesus and the crowd's excited trek to Jairus's house. In fact, worship leaders might want to arrange for two readers, so that a different voice, situated at a different reading station, reads vv. 25-34, thereby creating a dramatic experience of one story intruding into another.

These are two separate stories, of course, told together. Two unnamed, suffering women receive Jesus' help, and the interspersion of their stories (the technical term for this sandwiching structure, in which one story surrounds another, is *intercalation*) begs us to interpret each one in light of the other. Similar and contrasting details of each part make for a richer whole. Both speak of a "daughter": one given this name by Jesus as an intimate indication of her restoration, one the revivified daughter of Jairus. The narrative notes twelve years of suffering for the former, twelve years of age for the latter. In each story someone falls at Jesus' feet, first a synagogue leader who entreats Jesus in humble desperation, then a fearful woman who has been revealed through the success of her surreptitious attempt to receive healing. Jesus' interactions with the woman and Jairus both mention "faith" despite the threat of "fear." Both stories employ language of deliverance or salvation as people hope to be "made well" (literally "saved," from *sōzō*). In terms of contrasts between the stories, one healing benefits the daughter of a socially influential and named man, while the other cures a poor anonymous woman. Jairus is a religious insider (although nothing suggests that he aligns himself with a group that opposes Jesus); the woman exists in a state of perpetual uncleanness, capable of defiling others according to Lev. 15:19-30. No wonder Jairus meets Jesus face-to-face while the woman creeps up behind him. He is a somebody, perhaps respected. She is a nobody, a victim, and perhaps an outcast.

TWO UNNAMED, SUFFERING WOMEN RECEIVE JESUS' HELP, AND THE INTERSPERSION OF THEIR STORIES BEGS US TO INTERPRET EACH ONE IN LIGHT OF THE OTHER.

The intercalation creates several effects. It intensifies the desperate needs of those who seek immediate help from Jesus, and it magnifies Jesus' power and the many ways he can heal. He exudes salvation in this passage. The contrasts between the stories exemplify the wide spectrum of people and problems that Jesus encounters. Most significant, perhaps, is the interruption created by the hemorrhaging woman's appearance. Imagine the scene: a large crowd bustles along with Jesus, off to see whether he can heal the daughter of a community leader. This makes for a very public and perhaps momentous spectacle. When the woman furtively touches Jesus' clothing, her hemorrhaging ceases at once. Jesus does not *need* to pause and seek her out, for it appears that she receives what she came to get. Yet he does stop, and this has two effects: it summons the healed woman from obscurity, and it creates a delay in which the sick girl crosses the chasm from life to death. The first effect reveals that the woman's healing involves more than removing the hemorrhage. Jesus publicly reveals her cure and deliverance from ritual impurity. This act completes her salvation, visibly demonstrating her transfer from a despised, depleted sufferer to a "daughter" at peace with her world. She belongs. The second effect does not finally prevent Jesus from delivering Jairus's daughter back to health, but no one foresees this when the messengers arrive to announce that she has died. Surely to some onlookers, Jesus' extended attention to the woman seems like a colossal and costly waste of time. But by the end of the story, we discover that the interruption allows these things to come into focus:

Jesus' priorities are guided by his own principles of urgency, and his power can bring life from death.

Sermons on this vivid passage could address numerous important topics. The two stories raise foundational questions about the essence of "faith" and the character of the "salvation" that Jesus provides. The hemorrhaging woman and Jairus make for interesting paradigms of faith. For them expressing faith, or believing, does not mean voicing a correct confession about Jesus' identity. Rather, it is a resolute conviction that he can provide their deepest hope despite the reality of apparently overwhelming obstacles. They express faith as a rugged yet fragile confidence that Jesus will help them, even in the midst of potentially debilitating fear. The salvation that Jesus accomplishes shows him to be the worthy object of such faith, because he defeats death and makes the wounded whole—physically, socially, and spiritually.

Jesus' willingness to resist the electric expectancy of the crowd and to complete the restoration of a faithful yet nameless woman paints him as a person who sees opportunity in interruption. This passage encourages us to consider a theology of interruptions, to understand that God is neither bound to nor limited by human allocations of value and priority. God attends to all and is committed to the salvation of the whole person. In Jesus' delay in order to address a woman wrecked for over a decade by disease and a powerless healthcare system, we witness grace in action. Grace means that God has no task more urgent than to bend to assist those who seek help.

This text raises the question of what Jesus' power over illness and death means for the church's witness today. Too often Christians take passages like this and devise simple interpretations that overstate a kernel of truth so much that they create deleterious consequences. For example, claims that Jesus stands ready and available to heal *all* physical afflictions quickly run aground on the fact that congregations

> THIS PASSAGE ENCOURAGES US TO CONSIDER A THEOLOGY OF INTERRUPTIONS, TO UNDERSTAND THAT GOD IS NEITHER BOUND TO NOR LIMITED BY HUMAN ALLOCATIONS OF VALUE AND PRIORITY.

include many faithful people who suffer from unwanted ailments that God has not healed. Other interpretations diminish Jesus' role as a healer so much as to imply that the healings in the Gospels are merely symbolic of a "true" salvation that is exclusively spiritual. This strategy, however, totally discounts the real benefits and grace that the Bible promises in terms and images of physical and emotional wholeness. The church does better to steer between these errors and explore how its theology, practices, worship, and structures best echo the promises that Jesus makes when he heals people in the Gospels. That is, the church embodies Jesus' ministry of healing when it exists as a community that promotes, facilitates, and prefigures God's intentions for human wholeness and health. Believers proclaim salvation as multifaceted, as God promises to end all sorts of captivity, to right every wrong, and to cleanse various wounds. Congregations can bear this good news in countless ways, even as their members remain scarred and incomplete themselves. We pray for healing, thank God for healing when it happens by any means, and extend the promise of the gospel that "we will be changed" (1 Cor. 15:51-54). At the same time the Spirit compels us earnestly to proclaim all of God's deeds on our behalf and to labor actively to relieve suffering or exclusion wherever it may be found.

Notes

1. Kathleen M. O'Connor, *Lamentations and the Tears of the World* (Maryknoll, N.Y.: Orbis, 2002), 57.

2. Dylan Thomas, "Do not go gentle into that good night," *The Poems of Dylan Thomas*, ed. Daniel Jones (New York: New Directions, 1971), 207–8.

3. See Rolf Jacobson, "The Costly Loss of Praise," *Theology Today* 57 (2000): 377–78.

4. James Luther Mays, *Psalms*, Interpretation (Louisville: John Knox, 1994), 359.

5. *Charis* appears in the following verses (NRSV translations in parentheses): 2 Cor. 8:1 (grace), 4 (privilege), 6 (generous undertaking), 7 (generous undertaking), 9 (generous act), 16 (thanks), 19 (generous undertaking); 9:8 (blessing), 14 (grace), 15 (thanks).

6. Of course, countless resources exist to assist congregations and their leaders in thinking about stewardship and the biblical texts that situate it in a theological framework. For an online database of valuable resources, visit http://www.luthersem.edu/stewardship.

FIFTH SUNDAY AFTER PENTECOST

JULY 9, 2006
FOURTEENTH SUNDAY IN ORDINARY TIME /
PROPER 9

REVISED COMMON	EPISCOPAL (BCP)	ROMAN CATHOLIC
Ezek. 2:1-5	Ezek. 2:1-7	Ezek. 2:2-5
or 2 Sam. 5:1-5, 9-10		
Psalm 123	Psalm 123	Ps. 123:1-2, 2, 3-4
or Psalm 48		
2 Cor. 12:2-10	2 Cor. 12:2-10	2 Cor. 12:7-10
Mark 6:1-13	Mark 6:1-6	Mark 6:1-6

The Holy Spirit empowers Christians for our work, life, and witness on behalf of the gospel. The precise means by which God exercises this power through us eludes explanation, but the Bible presents a diverse collection of snapshots that fuels our imaginations about the potent nature and vast extent of God's influence. One truth remains consistent throughout these diverse expressions: we are sharers in God's work, but only insofar as we exist as God's servants.

FIRST READING

EZEKIEL 2:1-5 (RCL)
EZEKIEL 2:1-7 (BCP)
EZEKIEL 2:2-5 (RC)

After Ezekiel's account of his visions of God in chapter 1, occurring during the period after the first deportation to Babylon in 597 B.C.E. (see 2 Kings 24:10-16), comes his commission to declare the word of the Lord to the exiles of Judah. Ezekiel's difficult message to the exiles will offer a theological interpretation of the affliction Judah suffers under the Babylonians. The story of Ezekiel's call to prophetic ministry extends through 3:15, but the verses at the beginning of chapter 2 announce a critical detail of his vocation: he must face a recalcitrant and dismissive audience, one that probably will choose to ignore him (compare 3:7). In 2:4 the NRSV's "impudent and stubborn" translates Hebrew expressions involving body parts; "headstrong and hard-hearted" also legitimately describe Ezekiel's audience. But God does not hold Ezekiel responsible to soften his hearers or make them respond. The prophet's task is merely to speak.

From one perspective, Ezekiel's commission resembles other call narratives that candidly include struggle and potential for disappointment as part of the prophet's job description (see Isa. 6:9-10; Jer. 1:17-19). Hostility toward prophets is a recognizable biblical motif (2 Chr. 24:19; 36:15-16; Neh. 9:26; Matt. 5:12; Luke 13:33-34; Acts 7:52). Basic notions of humanity's unwillingness to heed prophecy create an important background for the particular action in a section of today's Gospel reading, Mark 6:1-6, where the residents of Nazareth reject Jesus. This Ezekiel lection poses a precedent that illustrates people's refusal to recognize the word of God when it is delivered.

Besides setting the stage for the conflict in Mark 6:1–6, this text also allows preachers to explore the purpose of prophecy and the character of a God who sends prophets to instruct. As we observed on the Day of Pentecost, God continues to feed and correct God's people through prophecy, although we understand the dynamics of prophetic activities differently today than in Ezekiel's era. Always, however, prophecy implies God's fidelity. When God sends Ezekiel to speak, God declares that the Israelites' implacability will not stand as the final word. God has not given up on them. Although Ezekiel's unrelenting oracles of woe and divine judgment can sometimes overshadow the expressions of mercy that dot this biblical book, nevertheless the prophet testifies that the people still belong to God.

> THIS TEXT ALLOWS PREACHERS TO EXPLORE THE PUR-
> POSE OF PROPHECY AND THE CHARACTER OF A GOD
> WHO SENDS PROPHETS TO INSTRUCT.

2 SAMUEL 5:1–5, 9–10 (RCL ALT.)

Although he becomes king over Judah right after Saul dies (2:4), David does not rule over all Israel until this passage. The intervening narrative of 2 Samuel 2–4 details the downfall of other claimants to power and establishes the legitimacy of David's ascent to the throne.[1] Today's lection skips over three troublesome verses that describe the dirty work of David's military achievements, concentrating our attention instead on the consummation of the promise God made when Samuel anointed the shepherd boy back in 1 Samuel 16.

The tribes of Israel do not reward David with kingship as the spoils of his military successes. They consent to David's rule in recognition that God has chosen him and guided him toward this office. As for David, his ascent to the throne calls for a covenant ceremony with the elders of the people in the Lord's presence. This event publicly reinforces his identity as a shepherd-king, accountable to God for the care of the people.

The passage concludes with the taking of Jerusalem and a summary of David's continuing magnification. From the seed of the assertion that David serves as a conduit of God's blessings, a royal theology will flower and subsequently provide raw material for Israel's later hopes and messianic expectations. With regard to the current context, David's grand successes testify to God's power at work in him. Kingship does not render political carte blanche to David (as he will tragically learn in stories that follow). He rules as God's servant, for Israel's sake (see 5:12).

Sermons on this text could explore the foundations of spiritual leadership, perhaps in comparison and contrast to Mark 6:6b–13 and biblical descriptions of servant leaders. An alternative approach might explore this passage as a demonstration of God's fidelity to promises. Significant time must elapse after David's anointing before he is established as Israel's king, but the promise of that anointing holds fast, just like the pledges about our identity and future that God makes in Christian baptism and the giving of the Holy Spirit.

> KINGSHIP DOES NOT RENDER POLITICAL CARTE BLANCHE TO DAVID. HE RULES AS GOD'S SERVANT, FOR ISRAEL'S SAKE.

RESPONSIVE READING

PSALM 123 (RCL, BCP)
PSALM 123:1–2, 2, 3–4 (RC)

This psalm prays for God's mercy. The comparison to servants' watchful and absolute dependence upon their masters intensifies the expectancy in the petition. The contempt and scorn of others, however, exacerbate the difficulty of waiting faithfully when God appears absent or unreliable. In likening God to a mistress, the psalmist reminds us that traditionally female imagery appropriately describes God.

PSALM 48 (RCL ALT.)

This celebration of Jerusalem (Zion) may sound strange to some who inhabit our highly mobile society. Why invest so much significance in a single city? For the psalmist, Jerusalem announces that there is a God in heaven who cares about God's people on earth. In a similar spirit Elie Wiesel calls Jerusalem "a promise" and "the symbol of survival." He says, "No one can enter it and go away unchanged."[2] Which locales in our world alter the way we interpret reality? Which places represent authentic theological truths and hopes to us? What in our world sings a chorus about the certain reign of God?

SECOND READING

2 CORINTHIANS 12:2-10 (RCL, BCP)
2 CORINTHIANS 12:7-10 (RC)

Knowledge of the wider context is critical for understanding Paul's description of his personal revelation. The final four chapters of 2 Corinthians comprise Paul's focused counterattack against a group of people (whom he calls "false apostles" and "super-apostles") who have come to Corinth seeking to discredit him and his teachings among the local believers. Paul goes beyond simply denouncing these outsiders; he also contends for his own qualifications and faithfulness as an apostle of Christ. A portion of his defense (11:1—12:13) involves boasting about such matters as sufferings and revelations he has experienced in his service to the gospel. Although throughout these chapters Paul repeatedly labels boasting as a foolish enterprise, he boasts of what God has demonstrated through and to him, if that will persuade the Corinthians of the truth.

It appears that the Corinthians or those opposing Paul expect their leaders to be spiritual giants who experience and relate otherworldly visions, and so Paul boasts that he can fit that bill, except that his vision has taught him to rely more deeply upon God, not upon the privileged knowledge gained from ecstatic episodes. Paul speaks about himself elliptically, as "a person," to emphasize that his mystical experience of Paradise and its secrets occurred totally beyond his control.[3] He did not generate the experience, and it commends him in no way. The vision, however, left Paul with some kind of affliction, although its precise nature remains tantalizingly unclear from his obscure references to "a thorn in the flesh" and "a messenger of Satan." More important than the precise source or identity of this physical infirmity or spiritual irritant is that it serves as a chronic reminder of the experience and the grace of God that gives Paul strength to persevere. Therefore, it is not the heavenly knowledge taken from the revelation that ultimately sustains Paul in his ministry and hardships; it is the lived conviction that God's grace suffices for those who recognize their weakness before God.

PAUL'S REMEMBRANCE OF HIS REVELATION REMINDS US THAT THE ULTIMATE PURPOSE OF ANY AUTHENTIC SPIRITUAL EXPERIENCE IS INCREASED RELIANCE UPON GOD.

Paul's remembrance of his revelation reminds us that the ultimate purpose of any authentic spiritual experience is increased reliance upon God. Particularly during the season after Pentecost this passage reaffirms that gifts of the Spirit, wisdom and spiritual insight, and theological or biblical studies all must drive us toward greater dependence upon God's grace. Christians rightly pursue deeper knowledge of God through a variety of avenues, but each becomes a dead end if it produces pride or a false sense of self-sufficiency.

The Gospels speak of people demanding miraculous signs from Jesus, the Corinthians were persuaded to expect impressive manifestations of spiritual might, and Christians throughout history have been tempted to rely upon displays of power or hypercharismatic leaders to accomplish the work of the gospel. But if the church is to be an agent of change in the world, its power must come from Christ, and Christians recognize that power paradoxically in glad acknowledgment of their own weaknesses. Congregations' strategic planning should include honest awareness of this truth.

THE GOSPEL
MARK 6:1–13 (RCL)
MARK 6:1–6 (BCP, RC)

In Mark 6:1-13 readers find two discrete episodes that create a sharp contrast between the rejection Jesus encounters from the people who are ostensibly closest to him and the authority he grants to the new society of people he chooses to share in the ministry of the reign of God. Doubts about the source of Jesus' power and authority continue to repel some (see 3:21-35), yet Jesus remains committed to empowering others for his work.

The first scene (vv. 1-6a) describes Jesus' return to his hometown (identified as Nazareth in Mark 1:9, 24). Although the responses of amazement in v. 2 first appear to echo positive statements made earlier (see 1:27; 2:12), the next verse makes it clear that the onlookers are expressing their incredulity. This audience dismisses the possibility that *God* might be supplying Jesus with wisdom and power. Although the previous chapters are replete with accounts of miraculous deeds, these stories carry no credence in Nazareth. No one there appears to have any idea that God has named Jesus "Son" (1:11) and that Jesus has redefined membership in his family (3:33-35). Jesus' former neighbors assess him by their established criteria, and so they presume to know him already all too well. He is Mary's son (the failure to identify him by his father's name may reflect rumors about the legitimacy of his birth). Just who does he think he is? The mention of his occupation stresses his unremarkable reputation and lack of religious credentials.

The naming of his brothers and sisters prompts attentive readers to recall 3:21, 31–32, where Jesus' family, fearing for his sanity, attempts to restrain him.[4] Now members of both his family and his hometown have judged him crazy, or perhaps demon-possessed. The verb that summarizes their rejection at the end of v. 3 *(skandalizō)* elsewhere means to be an apostate. Here, "it is used of outsiders and means to be prevented from becoming a disciple. . . . [The people of Nazareth's] opinions about who Jesus is stand in their way. Jesus' combination of human ordinariness and divine power makes no sense to them."[5] This condition constitutes their "unbelief," or non-faith *(apistia),* in v. 6.

Jesus' response is mixed. Although amazed (v. 6) by the rejection, he borrows a familiar maxim in v. 4 that suggests he should have expected this to happen.[6] While Mark's account of Jesus' inauspicious homecoming reflects the biblical pattern of prophets encountering hostility, its focus is less on Jesus' prophetic role and more on the failure of the people to embrace the possibility that God is the driving authority behind Jesus' words and deeds. The Nazarenes' "unbelief" does not imply that they disagree with Jesus' teaching or discount his miracles as shams. It means that they fail to acknowledge God as the source of the power and authority

> THE NAZARENES' "UNBELIEF" MEANS THAT THEY FAIL TO ACKNOWLEDGE GOD AS THE SOURCE OF THE POWER AND AUTHORITY JESUS DISPLAYS IN WORD AND DEED.

Jesus displays in word and deed. They assume that another kind of power works in him. Their response inhibits but does not entirely forbid Jesus' ability to perform works in Nazareth.

The second scene (vv. 6b–13), where Jesus sends out the Twelve in pairs, is less complicated than the first, yet it illustrates the stark difference between the outsiders of the previous episode and the insiders Jesus has chosen to participate in ministry. The dispatching of the Twelve serves as the first narrated occasion of their living out their vocation of preaching and delivering people from demonic oppression (see 3:13–15). Jesus calls followers to himself for a purpose. He also sends them out to partake in his work. As they call for repentance, cast out spirits, and heal the sick, their ministry explicitly mirrors Jesus', performed with the divine authority he confers upon them.

Jesus' traveling orders make a number of statements about what should characterize this ministry. First, the testimony of the Twelve occurs in twosomes, reflecting a witness's membership in a wider community and confirming the reliability of the message (see Deut. 17:6; 19:15; Matt. 18:16; John 8:17). Second, instructions that limit what one may bring on the journey differentiate these preachers from the familiar sight of Cynic philosophers, who in that time traveled also in austere simplicity but under slightly different regulations. In forsaking all but the barest of necessities, the Twelve tell others (and themselves) that they are fully dependant upon God in their work. They survive on the goodwill of others and profit not at all from their labors. Third, by not staying in more than one house in any given town, Jesus' followers avoid appearances of seeking undue comforts or taking advantage of hospitality. Finally, the requirement of shaking away the dust of a recusant village underscores the seriousness of rejecting what Jesus and his representatives proclaim. By removing from their bodies every speck of a place's residue, they utterly dissociate themselves. In all these instructions Jesus states that their ministry is his ministry.

These two adjoining episodes frame many contrasts that deserve exploration in a sermon. One concerns the Nazarenes' inability to perceive God as the source of Jesus' power (as well as the effects their unbelief has on Jesus' performance of deeds of power) and the potent authority that Jesus grants to the Twelve who go out in mission. Human beings are perhaps universally suspicious of power, yet we crave it for ourselves often to our own demise. It does not matter what the arena is—relationships, politics, religion—power distorts our vision and convinces us that we know best who exercises it most profitably and for the best ends. The Christian gospel, however, continually subverts human standards of power—who really possesses it and how it is exercised. In Mark 6, Jesus' neighbors cannot get past their own prejudices about who deserves power or who can speak for God. By refusing to recognize the manifestation of God's reign among them through the words and deeds of the familiar carpenter, they barricade themselves from the fullness of blessings that God might have poured out in Nazareth. In the subsequent scene, the Twelve's ability to tap into God's authority requires them to relinquish any tokens of personal sufficiency. The packaging of their ministry connotes powerlessness; they are walking examples of the lack of self-sufficiency. Later in Mark's Gospel Jesus will amplify this power paradox by saying, "You know that among the Gentiles those whom they recognize as their rulers lord it over them, and their great ones are tyrants over them. But it is not so among you; but whoever wishes to become great among you must be your servant, and whoever wishes to be first among you must be slave of all. For the Son of Man came not to be served but to serve, and to give his life a ransom for many" (10:42-45).

> THE CHRISTIAN GOSPEL CONTINUALLY SUBVERTS HUMAN STANDARDS OF POWER—WHO REALLY POSSESSES IT AND HOW IT IS EXERCISED.

Once again in the season after Pentecost, a lection beckons us to explore the work to which God calls the church. The sending of the Twelve paints a striking picture of a ministry entirely derived from Christ and totally reliant upon him for its success, variously defined. After Pentecost we recall that God continues to equip Christians for service through the Spirit. This season also reminds us that the call to apostolic—or "sent"—ministry is not exclusive but extends to all believers. Although Jesus sends only the Twelve in this passage, other texts remind us of additional disciples who contribute to Jesus' cause (Mark 15:40-41) and additional people he commissions for ministry (Luke 10:1-12). Finally, the activities of the Twelve in Mark 6:6b-13 define Christian ministry as mirroring the proclamation and deeds of Christ as recorded in the Gospels. Even if many Christians today experience biblical tales of exorcism and miraculous healing as foreign, nevertheless these stories direct us toward concrete service that delivers people from various types of oppression and that promotes wholeness of all kinds. God is the source of our salvation, and all ministries that point to God's salvific activity participate in the persistent manifestation of God's reign in the world.

Notes

1. As nearly all commentators note, propagandistic tones resound in this narrative and other passages recounting David's rise to power. This requires interpreters to assess carefully the almost deterministic theology and opportunistic politics that pepper the story. For a recent discussion, see Marti J. Steussy, "David, God, and the Word," *Word & World* 23 (2003): 365–73.

2. Elie Wiesel, *A Beggar in Jerusalem* (New York: Pocket Books, 1970), 19; quoted in J. Clinton McCann Jr., "The Book of Psalms: Introduction, Commentary, and Reflections," in *The New Interpreter's Bible,* vol. 4 (Nashville: Abingdon, 1996), 4:874.

3. The third was the highest level of heaven, according to some Jewish traditions. On Paradise and various tiers of heaven in Jewish traditions of Paul's time, see Andrew T. Lincoln, *Paradise Now and Not Yet: Studies in the Role of the Heavenly Dimension in Paul's Thought with Special Reference to His Eschatology*, Society for New Testament Studies Manuscript Series 43 (Cambridge: Cambridge University Press, 1981), 77–81.

4. The Greek text of Mark 3:21, while not entirely unambiguous, indicates that it is Jesus' family members who think he has gone "out of his mind." The NIV, NJB, and other translations render this verse more accurately than does the NRSV.

5. Sharyn Dowd, *Reading Mark: A Literary and Theological Commentary on the Second Gospel*, Reading the New Testament (Macon, Ga.: Smyth & Helwys, 2000), 60.

6. Similar proverbs appear in contemporaneous Greco-Roman writings. Compare this from the moral philosopher Plutarch: "The most sensible and wisest people are little cared for in their own hometowns" (*De exilio* 604D; quoted in Joel Marcus, *Mark 1–8*, Anchor Bible 27 [New York: Doubleday, 2000], 27:376).

SIXTH SUNDAY AFTER PENTECOST

JULY 16, 2006
FIFTEENTH SUNDAY IN ORDINARY TIME / PROPER 10

REVISED COMMON	EPISCOPAL (BCP)	ROMAN CATHOLIC
Amos 7:7-15	Amos 7:7-15	Amos 7:12-15
or 2 Sam. 6:1-5, 12b-19		
Ps. 85:8-13	Psalm 85	Ps. 85:9-10, 11-12,
or Psalm 24	or 85:7-13	13-14
Eph. 1:3-14	Eph. 1:1-14	Eph. 1:3-14 or 1:3-10
Mark 6:14-29	Mark 6:7-13	Mark 6:7-13

We should not pretend that we can maintain an absolute separation between religious and political matters. They press upon and influence one another in countless ways. Many of this Sunday's readings reflect the complex and often volatile interplay between the rule of God and humanity's ways of ruling itself. For many Christians, these scriptures pique misgivings about uniting religious and political convictions too closely. More broadly, the texts spark important conversations about the church's role in the landscapes of public discourse and political policy. In those discussions the Bible insists we keep in mind at least one essential truth: people who speak genuinely prophetic words are often judged dangerous by established political and religious institutions. The stories of such modern martyrs as Martin Luther King Jr. and Oscar Romero keep us from mistakenly assuming that this truth no longer applies in our civil societies.

FIRST READING

AMOS 7:7-15 (RCL, BCP)
AMOS 7:12-15 (RC)

Immediately prior to this reading, Amos receives two ominous visions and twice begs successfully for God to relent (7:1-6). Now the vision of the plumb line and God's certain judgment against Israel meets with no argument (vv. 7-9). The unopposed oracle against King Jeroboam II prompts the alarmed priest Amaziah to indict Amos as a conspirator and to attempt to expel the officious prophet back to his home in neighboring Judah. That Amaziah values above all else his security as a parasitic minion to the king is clear from his reference to Bethel (which means "house of God") as "the king's sanctuary."[1] The priest's intimidation tactics earn him a rebuke from Amos (vv. 14-15), followed by a dismal prophecy against Amaziah and his family (vv. 16-17, which the lectionaries exclude).

As it decries systemic injustice perpetuated during an era of widespread prosperity in Israel, the book of Amos presents the prophet as a dangerous man. The plumb line in this vision proclaims the Northern Kingdom to be a precarious structure, out of alignment. People like Amaziah, who benefit from the established political and religious systems, cannot hear Amos's words. They use their power to silence disagreeable prophets. By contrast, Amos understands himself as answerable only to God. He does not claim the authority of a recognized guild of prophets (v. 14), only the authority of God's call. He cannot heed Amaziah and "go" (*lēk*) away (v. 12), for God has told him to "go" (*le⁻k*) and speak prophecy to Israel (v. 15).

The confrontation between Amaziah and Amos reminds us of the ways in which we grow deaf to God because of our desires for strong, stable institutions and our quests to ensure our own national, economic, and religious interests. Are there cherished denominational mechanisms, theological traditions, or political prerogatives that we guard so closely as perhaps to shelter us from a word from God? The truth hurts when it exposes our idolatries and injustices, and we hope that Amos also aches as he delivers the awful truth about Israel's impending collapse. But the truth is sure to sting us even worse if we greet the word and its bearers with contempt. "Do not despise the words of prophets" (1 Thess. 5:20).

> THE TRUTH HURTS WHEN IT EXPOSES OUR IDOLATRIES AND INJUSTICES, AND WE HOPE THAT AMOS ALSO ACHES AS HE DELIVERS THE AWFUL TRUTH ABOUT ISRAEL'S IMPENDING COLLAPSE.

2 SAMUEL 6:1-5, 12b-19 (RCL ALT.)

Anyone who doubts that the Bible presents David as a complex character, capable of provoking mixed reactions in both ancient and modern eras, should examine this passage. The full story of the ark's transfer to Jerusalem, in two stages (including vv. 6-12a), contains many disquieting elements that warrant extended commentary. One nevertheless can easily sense the story's potential for provoking ambivalent responses by reflecting on David's motivations and the symbolic significance of installing the ark in Israel's new royal capital.

The ark of the covenant, that preeminent sign of God's sovereignty and presence among the Israelite tribes as they sought to arrive at and settle into the promised land, has been out of readers' sight for twenty years, since 1 Sam. 7:1–2. Why does David want this storied and potent item brought to his city? Does he co-opt religious symbolism and power to buttress his political ambitions and bless the new vision of a monarchical Israel, or does his move correspond to genuine, revivalist celebration of God's continuing sovereignty over the nation?[2] Whatever the actual combination of reasons, David's action boldly combines political and religious ideologies, providing a great opportunity for preachers to explore the necessary yet risky alliances people forge between articulations of political and religious power, vocabulary, and symbolism. In David's story we discover, not a model for nations to emulate, but an impetus to consider the uneasy relationships between church and state in our world.

The lectionary ducks vv. 6–12a and the seemingly capricious death of Uzzah, but this episode is crucial for reasserting the ark's terrible power (see 1 Samuel 4–6). Uzzah's tragedy so frightens David that he temporarily aborts his plan to bring the ark to Jerusalem. The ark is no one's servant. It will not be manipulated. The ark is not God but a symbol, yet symbols can possess awesome power, capable of overwhelming their handlers. When David chooses to resume the ark's transfer three months later (v. 12), surely he does so as one with a new awareness of the ark's potential.

Whether Michal despises her husband for his revealing outfit, the religious overtones of the procession, his unrestrained and therefore undignified exuberance, or some implied unseemly behavior remains unclear, but her contempt reveals her alienation from David and his ideals while providing him an opportunity to characterize his actions as appropriate and pious self-abasement before God (6:21–22).[3]

RESPONSIVE READING

PSALM 85:8–13 (RCL)
PSALM 85 or 85:7–13 (BCP)
PSALM 85:9–10, 11–12, 13–14 (RC)

The people of God are a covenant people, sojourning in this world in light of God's promises. This psalm captures the appeal of those promises in beautiful language fit for prayerful meditation that leads us to behold God's own qualities.

Salvation, according to the psalmist, is "a dynamic process in which the character of God in all its fullness is at work."[4] Only God has wrought this salvation, and only God can bring it to its completion.

PSALM 24 (RCL ALT.)

Many scholars conclude that this psalm originally belonged to some kind of processional liturgy, and so it might shape an atmosphere for preaching on 2 Samuel 6. A sermon focused on Psalm 24 could also unpack the image of the Lord as king, whose realm and authority encompass all aspects of creation and human experience. Since contemporary North American society has no real, lived understanding of monarchs and their roles, it is profitable for preachers to dwell with and reestablish the potential of this metaphor for God.

SECOND READING
EPHESIANS 1:3-14 (RCL)
EPHESIANS 1:1-14 (BCP)
EPHESIANS 1:3-14 or 1:3-10 (RC)

"Blessed be the Lord" introduces numerous prayers in the Old Testament. The first main section of Ephesians consists of a similar expression of praise, directing an extended prayer of blessing toward God that establishes the tone for the entire epistle. This prayerful preface comprises many weighty theological ideas. A number of these—election, adoption, knowledge, and inheritance—connect to the work of the Holy Spirit and have resounded in other days' lections since Pentecost. The passage holds these ideas together in its announcement that the foundation of all these things is what God does "in Christ."

From the perspective of the blessing in vv. 3-14, it almost seems as if time has collapsed, for the author discusses past, present, and future realities all at once and speaks as if we have the ability to know the eternal thoughts of God. The key to this vantage point across time is Jesus Christ, for through the gospel, through the work of God "in Christ," God's mysterious intentions come into view. We should not read this catalogue of benefits and ask, echoing the children's question repeated in every minivan, "Are we there yet?" or "Have we really *now* received 'every spiritual blessing' in full?" The passage is less concerned with mapping out a formal sequence or timeline than it is with

GOD INTENDS, AS THE GOSPEL REVEALS, TO BRING TOGETHER ALL THINGS IN CHRIST, TO RECLAIM ALL OF CREATION WITHIN THE CANOPY OF GOD'S RIGHTEOUSNESS.

proclaiming that through Christ Christians recognize their place in the overarching sweep of God's eternal purposes. God intends, as the gospel reveals, to bring together all things in Christ (v. 10), to reclaim all of creation within the canopy of God's righteousness. The language of promise and security in vv. 13-14 also indicates that we are a people who still wait for the complete consummation of all this.

Preachers will want to note that the mention of God's will and election does not imply a mechanistic or fatalistic understanding of world history and humanity's redemption. The predominance of the focus "in Christ" and the attention to the Holy Spirit remind us that God is actively and consistently involved in accomplishing our salvation. When Ephesians mentions our redemption as part of "a plan," it emphasizes that salvation and God's love toward humanity are no mere afterthought.[5] Nor does the mention of God's choosing or destining people imply that anyone *deserves* such a gift.[6] The passage insists that God adopts us as an act of free grace, an expression of God's "good pleasure."

THE GOSPEL
MARK 6:14-29 (RCL)

The four Gospels and the book of Acts all include accounts of Jesus and his followers attracting the attention and curiosity of regional political leaders. Within the scope of biblical literature, such events represent nothing new, for the Old Testament prophets frequently participate in conversations with kings, with mixed results. The imperial context of the first century places its own stamp on Jesus' and others' encounters with political power. In this context, the potential for conflict and danger is high, as evidenced by the story of John the Baptizer's gruesome execution at the hands of the Roman puppet Herod Antipas. These stories confirm the public nature of the Christian gospel, and they function to expose corrupt values that stand opposed to the way of God's reign. John's indictment of Herod and the skullduggery that snuffs out John's life also prefigures the kind of deadly opposition that Jesus and his followers should expect as a consequence of their proclamation of the gospel.

To grasp the theological contributions of this scene, which the Gospel of Mark presents as a flashback (vv. 17-29) occasioned by Herod's worried reaction to reports of Jesus' activities (vv. 14-16), it is essential to highlight details of the historical context that the narrative assumes. These details reveal the episode's unambiguously critical tone.[7] The Herod of the story is a son of Herod the Great known as Herod Antipas, who began to rule Galilee as a Roman client after his father's death in 4 B.C.E. His wife, Herodias, had formerly been married to one of his half brothers, who was also called Herod (and whom Mark 6:17 names as Philip). After Herodias divorced this Herod, she married Herod Antipas, creating the situation that John the Baptizer condemns, probably in light of Lev. 18:16; 20:21. Herodias had a daughter named Salome from her first marriage; this girl was both a stepdaughter and a niece to Herod Antipas. It appears that Salome is the one strangely identified as "his daughter Herodias" in 6:22, although Mark could be designating another daughter unknown to us through any other historical writings.[8]

The marriage that John condemns as unlawful is but one element of the story signaling the depravity of this household. A daughter of the aristocracy dancing before a roomful of men violates many cultural mores of the day. Context and vocabulary only hint that the girl's dance is erotic, arousing her stepfather's (or father's) sexual interests, but this is not totally clear.[9] Whatever the specific nature of Herod Antipas's pleasure, his response to the dance results in a foolish pledge that opens him up to manipulation and exposes him as a buffoon. Because Herod Antipas shows off in front of his elite guests, John dies. Finally, the machinations of Herodias and the macabre detail of presenting John's head on a platter portray a gathering of fiends. The whole account therefore suggests that Herod Antipas has no control of himself, his household, and perhaps his political domain. Wickedness runs rampant.

> THE WHOLE ACCOUNT SUGGESTS THAT HEROD ANTIPAS HAS NO CONTROL OF HIMSELF, HIS HOUSEHOLD, AND PERHAPS HIS POLITICAL DOMAIN. WICKEDNESS RUNS RAMPANT.

In short, the passage depicts a political culture in need of repentance. But this culture's self-absorbed corruption and pride render it unable to repent, and so it destroys the prophetic voice that exposes it. In doing so, it reveals the depths of its depravity and its enslavement to fear. The passion of Jesus of course tells a similar tale.

The death of John the Baptizer creates an occasion for the Gospel of Mark to give its readers a brief introduction to the corrosive and destructive powers of sin. The story of Herod Antipas and his lurid birthday party does function as a sort of morality play that reflects how people, even despite their intentions, are done in by their own deeds and the situations they create. But the story also involves more people than Herod Antipas alone. The episode depicts the wages of sin at systemic, familial, cultural, and political levels. Sin infects the worlds we create and the models of kingdom that stand as alternatives to the one Jesus proclaims. Power corrupts all human institutions, and corrupted power will have deadly effects on those prophets and reformers who dare to speak truth to it.

The Gospel of Mark presents Jesus' arrest, trials, and death as a miscarriage of justice so severe that it approaches satire. The beheading of John bears similarities.

In addition, in Mark 13:9–11 Jesus warns that his followers should expect political opposition, precisely because they bear his name. Jesus also promises that these encounters will provide opportunities for his people to give witness concerning him through the power of the Holy Spirit. John's story, although ghastly, is therefore not so unique. Preachers can and should point out that this passage comes between Jesus' sending his followers out to engage in ministry (6:6b–13) and their debriefing upon their return (6:30). The location of John's execution at this point in Mark's narrative therefore underscores the resistance that awaits all those who minister on behalf of the reign of God.

Of course, such a statement about resistance often disorients Christians who live comfortably in twenty-first-century North America. Persecution touches few of us, and sermons about it run the risk of implying that we must seek out opposition, or that altercations are somehow in and of themselves proof of true Christian commitment. A more fruitful approach to this passage might address the claims that Christian prophecy makes to those who occupy positions of power (whether it be political, commercial, or social power). How do the privileges and self-preserving impulses of power prompt all of us to disregard prophetic words that call us to account through their demands for righteousness and justice? Do our desires to hold and wield power, even for benevolent purposes, lead us to presume that we are exempt from certain requirements of living in light of the gospel?

> HOW DO THE PRIVILEGES AND SELF-PRESERVING IMPULSES OF POWER PROMPT ALL OF US TO DISREGARD PROPHETIC WORDS THAT CALL US TO ACCOUNT THROUGH THEIR DEMANDS FOR RIGHTEOUSNESS AND JUSTICE?

MARK 6:7–13 (BCP, RC)

For a discussion of this passage, see the comments for the Fifth Sunday after Pentecost (Fourteenth Sunday in Ordinary Time/Proper 9), above.

Notes

1. J. Clinton McCann, "Amos 7:7–17," in *The Lectionary Commentary: Theological Exegesis for Sunday's Texts,* vol. 1, ed. Roger E. Van Harn (Grand Rapids, Mich.: Wm. B. Eerdmans, 2001), 1:478.

2. See Walter Brueggemann, *First and Second Samuel,* Interpretation (Louisville: John Knox, 1990), 248–51.

3. On the possible reasons behind Michal's disdain, see David J. A. Clines, "Michal Observed: An Introduction to Reading Her Story," in *Telling Queen Michal's Story: An Experiment in Comparative Interpretation*, ed. David J. A. Clines and Tamara C. Eskenazi (Sheffield: Sheffield Academic Press, 1991), 52–61.

4. James Luther Mays, *Psalms*, Interpretation (Louisville: John Knox, 1994), 277.

5. The NRSV renders *oikonomia* as "plan" in Eph. 1:10. The word suggests a particular ordering or arrangement here and in Eph. 3:2, 9.

6. See John Calvin, *Institutes of the Christian Religion,* 3.22.2–3.

7. The Jewish historian Flavius Josephus gives a differing account of John's execution, interpreting Herod Antipas's motives as fear concerning the potential for John's popularity to incite a political uprising (*Antiquities* 18.5.2).

8. For a genealogical chart depicting the intertwined family tree of the Herodians, see David Noel Freedman, ed., *The Anchor Bible Dictionary,* vol. 3 (New York: Doubleday, 1992), 3:175.

9. The possibility of an erotic dance and the scheme of Herodias have led many interpreters to resort to stereotypes and to assign blame to the two female characters to such a degree as practically to exonerate Herod Antipas. This will not do, for the text thoroughly condemns Herod Antipas and his wife. The corruption of the girl is clearly seen in her (willing or unwilling?) participation in delivering John's head to her mother, Herodias, in v. 28. On interpreters' and artists' renditions of the dance as either a sexual or innocent display, see Janice Capel Anderson, "Feminist Criticism: The Dancing Daughter," in *Mark and Method: New Approaches in Biblical Studies*, ed. Janice Capel Anderson and Stephen D. Moore (Minneapolis: Fortress Press, 1992), 121–26.

SEVENTH SUNDAY AFTER PENTECOST

JULY 23, 2006
SIXTEENTH SUNDAY IN ORDINARY TIME / PROPER 11

REVISED COMMON	EPISCOPAL (BCP)	ROMAN CATHOLIC
Jer. 23:1-6	Isa. 57:14b-21	Jer. 23:1-6
or 2 Sam. 7:1-14a		
Psalm 23	Ps. 22:22-30	Ps. 23:1-3, 3-4, 5, 6
or Ps. 89:20-37		
Eph. 2:11-22	Eph. 2:11-22	Eph. 2:13-18
Mark 6:30-34,	Mark 6:30-44	Mark 6:30-34
53-56		

Organizations sometimes host Christmas in July parties to mix up the summer routine. Today's lectionary readings lend themselves well to a celebration of Advent in July. Old Testament prophecies make magnificent promises about what God will accomplish through a descendant of David. An epistle text identifies the gospel as a proclamation of peace to humankind. The reading from Mark's Gospel depicts the care and abundance Jesus offers, illustrated by an impromptu banquet springing up in the wilderness. These passages swell with hope, foretelling new possibilities emerging out of ostensibly hopeless circumstances. "The desert shall rejoice and blossom!" (Isa. 35:1). Such texts remind us that God promises an extravagant consummation of all things, the same kind of promise that gives rise to the observance of Advent and that fuels the perseverance of the church in all seasons.

FIRST READING
JEREMIAH 23:1-6 (RCL, RC)

Through Jeremiah, God castigates kings who have failed in their vocation to shepherd the people. The NRSV employs the verb *attend* in v. 2 to render the multiple meanings of a repeated Hebrew word: because the kings did not show concern *(pāqad)* for the flock, God will call them to account *(pāqad)*.[1] Jeremiah pins blame for the exile on the leaders' failures, but he also promises brighter days to come. First God will perform the work of a shepherd, gathering and prospering the flock. Then God will raise up a new series of kings who are capable leaders. The reading concludes with the promise of a particular king, "a righteous Branch" out of David's lineage. The image of a branch or a shoot symbolizing a new beginning appears elsewhere (see Zech. 3:8; 6:12; Isa. 11:1) and lends itself to a vision of messianic hope.

Jeremiah describes the Branch's name and policies in terms of *righteousness.* When the Old Testament speaks about God's righteousness, it is not speaking about moral perfection or separation. Instead, to talk about the righteousness of God is to indicate God's commitments to deliver and preserve God's people. *Righteousness* summarizes all of God's salvific activity (see Pss. 71:15-19; 98:2 [in this verse the NRSV's "vindication" could also read "righteousness"]) and God's identity as a savior; thus it "characterizes not merely an abstract attribute of God but an aspect of the divine character made manifest in the action of claiming and delivering Israel."[2] Jeremiah's description of the Branch means that the character and deeds of this king find their source in and point people's attention toward the Lord's own righteousness, the Lord's unswerving commitment to ensure the welfare of God's people.

> WHEN THE OLD TESTAMENT SPEAKS ABOUT GOD'S RIGHTEOUSNESS IT IS NOT SPEAKING ABOUT MORAL PERFECTION OR SEPARATION BUT INDICATING GOD'S COMMITMENTS TO DELIVER AND PRESERVE GOD'S PEOPLE.

2 SAMUEL 7:1-14a (RCL ALT.)

David's proposal to build a temple for the Lord and Nathan's oracle together play on the semantic possibilities of the word *bayit,* which can mean "palace," "temple," or "dynasty." Since God cannot be contained, Nathan explains, why localize God in a building? Instead, God freely promises to build a political dynasty from David and his descendants. Not only is Solomon in view throughout vv. 12-15, so too is the entire Davidic lineage. These particular verses, along with the promises of blessings to Israel under its king, became central to many Jews' expectations for a messianic deliverer and to early Christians' understanding of Jesus the Christ.

Nathan's oracle describes a God-given covenant to David, his offspring, and their reign, all cast in the permanence of God's unconditional commitment. Nothing suggests that kings will be perfect, but God will remain steadfast. Nathan describes God's fidelity in dramatic terms also in vv. 15-16, where he contrasts God's commitment to David with God's unstable dedication to David's predecessor, Saul.

The theological scope of this passage centers intensely upon a God who delights in freely dispensing good news. At the same time, the articulation of such divine favor within the mechanics of a national political system carries potential both for good and for exploitation. We should not ignore the possible dangers of a theology that intrudes roughshod into today's world of human politics, but neither should we spirit away the political dimensions of this text and limit our attention to David solely as an individual. Biblical scholar Bruce Birch understands the delicate tension that this passage calls us to embrace, saying, "This text is a summons to stand boldly in the tension created by faith commitment and political engagement— to stand between God's interests and the world's interests. . . . God has taken the risk of engaging with the political interests of kingdom. This text summons the

> THE THEOLOGICAL SCOPE OF THIS PASSAGE CENTERS
> INTENSELY UPON A GOD WHO DELIGHTS IN FREELY
> DISPENSING GOOD NEWS.

church to risk such engagement as well. . . . In David, God risks the dangers of ideological manipulation of faith for the sake of bringing the grace of divine promise into close engagement with public and political realities. The church can do no less."[3]

ISAIAH 57:14b-21 (BCP)

The peace that Christ proclaims to those far and near, as described in Ephesians 2 (see below), finds its roots of course in God's activities in the Old Testament. God does not simply wish or commend peace *(šālôm)* in this oracle (v. 19); God *delivers* it in assurances of putting away anger and providing healing and comfort to the contrite people of Judah. The *šālôm* that God wills encompasses so much more than the peace that humanity tries in vain to establish for itself. Without such divine condescension and compassion, the world can never know true peace.

RESPONSIVE READING
PSALM 23 (RCL)
PSALM 23:1-3, 3-4, 5, 6 (RC)

Theology is never more real or true than when it comes in the suggestive, dynamic language of poetry. Chock-full of metaphor, Psalm 23 offers a matchless articulation of God's goodness toward humanity. This poem moves our hearts because it describes our deepest needs and resonates with the lived experiences of God's people throughout the ages. This kind of traction allows the psalm to transcend—

even to defy—the dry dialect of theological explanations. When we consider this psalm in concert with other lections (namely Jeremiah 23 and Mark 6), God's shepherd-like care manifested precisely in Jesus Christ floods our sights. In Jesus we know a shepherd who tends not the flock from a distance but within our midst—a good shepherd, indeed.

PSALM 89:20-37 (RCL ALT.)

Psalm 89 concerns the Davidic dynasty, reflecting on its establishment in 2 Sam. 7:1-17 (Ps. 89:19-37) and an unknown crisis besetting it (Ps. 89:38-51). Today's lection describes God's covenant to David with much more detail than the 2 Samuel 7 passage, dwelling on the constancy of God's fidelity and echoing the notion of the king as God's son (see also Ps. 2:7).

PSALM 22:22-30 (BCP)

The Lord receives dramatic praise in these verses, as the psalmist declares that God neither abandons the afflicted nor leaves the poor in hunger. God's deeds will elicit praise from all peoples and nations. Today's New Testament lections pick up and amplify these great truths.

SECOND READING
EPHESIANS 2:11-22 (RCL, BCP)
EPHESIANS 2:13-18 (RC)

This passage describes important consequences of salvation by grace through faith (introduced in 2:1-10), namely the reconciliation of Jews and Gentiles that God accomplished through the cross of Christ. Of course, such a reconciliation was a scandalous idea to many in the first century. The epistle characterizes the former state of its readers (who are Gentiles) as one of separation, alienation from the blessings of God's covenants to Israel. Jesus' death and resurrection, however, transformed those circumstances, as signaled by the dramatic words *but now* in v. 13. God has done a surprising new thing. By bringing both Jews and Gentiles from death to life through Christ, God also obliterated the distinctions that had divided the two groups. The "dividing wall" that enforced the partitioning of Gentiles and Jews

> BY BRINGING BOTH JEWS AND GENTILES FROM DEATH TO LIFE THROUGH CHRIST, GOD ALSO OBLITERATED THE DISTINCTIONS THAT HAD DIVIDED THE TWO GROUPS.

is identified in v. 15 as the Law of Moses, for some considered the law to offer a means of salvation that wholly excluded Gentiles, an exclusion amplified by certain practices (including but not restricted to circumcision, dietary regulations, and sabbath observance) that reflected a sense of Jewish prerogative. The startling claim that the law was "abolished" through the cross probably does not mean that Christ entirely abrogated or canceled the whole law (see Rom. 3:31 and compare Matt. 5:17; Luke 16:17). Rather, the law's ability to make qualitative appraisals between different kinds of people becomes trumped by the cross of Christ (see Gal. 3:27-29).[4]

The gospel, therefore, is a message of peace—humanity's peace with God and peace with one another. The Holy Spirit confirms these new reconciliations, since believers are possessed by God's own Spirit and all of us share that same Spirit. By the work of the Holy Spirit, we who are in Christ are being built into a new structure. The wall has been removed; now a temple, a place where God dwells, constructed out of the community of faith, is emerging.

Christians today live in a world full of walls and borders that we construct to keep others out and to create a sense of our own security from those whom we consider harmful, distasteful, sinful, or just different. The varied imagery of this passage from Ephesians celebrates the gospel's power to demolish barriers, to transform aliens into citizens, and to let God be manifested in the presence of communities of believers. Publicized events such as the fall of the Berlin Wall, immigrants taking oaths of citizenship on the Fourth of July, and the dismantling of apartheid in South Africa supply preachers with tangible examples of the joy and power that accompany peacemaking, inclusion, and reconciliation. They help us express God's work in our own lives and inspire us to engage in new ministries of reconciliation (2 Cor. 5:18-20), proclaiming peace with God (Rom. 5:1) and peace with one another (Mark 9:50) wherever such ministries may be needed.

> THE VARIED IMAGERY OF THIS PASSAGE FROM EPHESIANS CELEBRATES THE GOSPEL'S POWER TO DEMOLISH BARRIERS, TO TRANSFORM ALIENS INTO CITIZENS, AND TO LET GOD BE MANIFESTED IN THE PRESENCE OF COMMUNITIES OF BELIEVERS.

THE GOSPEL
MARK 6:30-34, 53-56 (RCL)
MARK 6:30-34 (BCP, RC)

In all three lectionaries, the reading begins with the conclusion of the apostles' preaching and healing mission, a story juxtaposed with the account of John the Baptizer's execution (see the comments for the two immediately preceding Sundays). Next, because Jesus and his followers have achieved such popularity, they find themselves unable to escape the fast-moving crowds. Despite his desire to get to a place where he and his disciples can rest, Jesus is seized by compassion for the crowd, and he takes time to teach them. The Gospel narrator describes the crowd with a familiar expression, "sheep without a shepherd," portraying the people as vulnerable, at risk in a desolate environment and needing sustenance and direction. The passage clearly implies that Jesus functions as this crowd's shepherd, symbolizing the care and leadership he promises, by extension, to the Jewish people.

After v. 34, the lectionaries follow differing paths. That verse concludes the Roman Catholic reading, placing emphasis on the crowd's desperation and Jesus' willingness to forgo repose and address the needs of the people. The RCL skips the stories of Jesus' feeding five thousand men (the text's explicit mention of "men" in v. 44 suggests that the size of the crowd, including women and children, is even greater) and walking on water (6:35-52) and resumes with a summary of Jesus' ministry and people's attraction to him in Gennesaret and beyond. The RCL lection distorts the narrative progression yet places strong emphasis on the portrait of Jesus confronted at every turn by human need. Jesus' effective and consistent response to so many needs evidences the dynamism of his work and the ongoing manifestation of God's reign through acts of preaching and healing. Preachers who use the RCL lection should indicate that a pair of important scenes (6:35-52) are omitted, for the feeding provides a vivid example of Jesus' deeds on behalf of shepherdless people, and the walking on water reveals that fear and confusion continue to afflict his closest followers even as other, anonymous characters continually flock to Jesus for healing. The familiarity of those two beloved Gospel stories allows preachers to summarize them quickly while acknowledging that (as the discussion below shows) they contribute to our understanding of the material in 6:30-34, 53-56. Finally, the BCP includes, then concludes with, the story of Jesus' feeding five thousand men, preserving the narrative flow and recognizing that the scene in the wilderness offers a meaningful expression of what it means for Jesus to act as shepherd to helpless people. Indeed, the image of shepherding is pivotal to this section of the Gospel.

> JESUS' EFFECTIVE AND CONSISTENT RESPONSE TO SO MANY NEEDS EVIDENCES THE DYNAMISM OF HIS WORK AND THE ONGOING MANIFESTATION OF GOD'S REIGN THROUGH ACTS OF PREACHING AND HEALING.

Two other lections assigned for today (Jer. 23:1-6; Psalm 23) describe the need for God's people to have capable, godly shepherds. In the comforting words of Psalm 23, the Lord fills that role (see also Ps. 78:52; Ezek. 34:15). In Jeremiah, as in Ezek. 34:22-23, God promises to appoint human shepherds for the good of the flock. In distinctive ways, each of these prophetic texts ascribes a shepherding role to David, generating messianic tremors that Christians see opened up in Jesus

Christ. (Preachers who have been using the RCL options to explore David's story over the previous five weeks have here an opportunity to compare Jesus' inaugurating the reign of God to the Davidic ideal of a shepherd-king.)

When Mark 6:34 recalls Old Testament passages about shepherds, old scriptures bring a living word to a new context (recall the opening section of Peter's Pentecost sermon in Acts 2). Likening the people to shepherdless sheep criticizes their current political and religious leaders (easy to do, after the events of 6:14–29!). Jesus' visceral compassion betrays his principal motivation in responding to the people's plight: first and foremost he is for the people, not against their leaders. The simile of v. 34 also introduces the idea of Jesus's providing a shepherd's care. The subsequent feeding miracle in "a deserted place" expands this image, first by recalling Ps. 23:2 through the mention of reclining on green grass (v. 39), second in the motif of distributing food until all are satisfied.[5] Understood as part of Jesus' ongoing proclamation of God's reign, this miraculous meal supplied by a teaching shepherd describes that reign as bringing compassionate, abundant care to the needy and downcast.

> JESUS' VISCERAL COMPASSION BETRAYS HIS PRINCIPAL MOTIVATION IN RESPONDING TO THE PEOPLE'S PLIGHT: FIRST AND FOREMOST HE IS FOR THE PEOPLE, NOT AGAINST THEIR LEADERS.

If we choose to extend the shepherd symbol a little further, into the summary given in 6:53–56, we notice an unusual aspect of this shepherd's relationship to the flock he tends. Unlike other shepherds, Jesus does not need to chase his sheep and compel them to remain near. People are attracted to him; sheep seek out this shepherd. Comparisons to another Gospel metaphor of Jesus the Good Shepherd (John 10:3–5, 14–16, 27) add richness to this portrait.

The challenges posed by human brokenness are always staggering. The brief descriptions of people's desperation in 6:31–33, 53–56 indicate a world so in need of God's help that it cannot afford to give Jesus a day off. Jesus' willingness to meet people's needs commends perseverance to the church. Perseverance is essential, for the weight of suffering has not diminished over two thousand years. We easily observe human need on a global scale in reports of the African HIV/AIDS pandemic, acts of genocide, and homelessness. Scratch the surface, and every member of a congregation harbors hidden pains brought on by troubled marriages, mental illness, loneliness, substance abuse, and on we go. Even without taking into account qualitative distinctions among the varieties of human brokenness, we can note that still today humanity's needs besiege Jesus. The Gospel text assures us that he sees these needs and responds with compassion. The overarching gospel message insists that Jesus meets our greatest need by authentically identifying with human brokenness in the flesh and accomplishing a radical, fundamental solution.

150

THE SEASON
OF PENTECOST
―――――――――
MATTHEW L.
SKINNER

The invocation of the shepherd image offers another avenue into this passage, one that helpfully incorporates other assigned lections. Together, these passages proclaim that the flock is the Lord's. The work of biblical shepherds who tend the flock in service to God sheds light on the church's conception of what it means to participate in the in-breaking of God's reign. Jesus teaches, feeds, and heals the crowd in Mark 6, actions consistent with the biblical idea of shepherds' responsibilities (see Ezek. 34:1-23). But Jesus does not do these things by himself. Just as he sends the Twelve to proclaim, exorcise, and heal in 6:6b-13, so also when he feeds five thousand men he involves his followers in the tangible labor of feeding. In v. 37 he commands them to take care of the problem of a hungry throng, then he has them marshal resources, organize the people, and distribute the food. When the meal is complete, perhaps each apostle carries a basket stuffed with leftovers, for there are twelve baskets. Jesus orchestrates and enacts the miracle, but the disciples participate in it. They literally handle every part of it. In the season after Pentecost, this story reminds communities of faith of their vocations. We will be involved in God's work to manifest and grow God's compassionate reign. Although the needs of the world remain overwhelming, God can use what we have at hand to address them. But we dare not restrict our vision only to resources that we perceive as available. Their finitude becomes irrelevant in view of the unlimited compassion of the Shepherd.

Notes

1. Another form of the verb *pāqad* appears in v. 4 bearing an additional meaning: none of the restored remnant will be *missing*.

2. Richard B. Hays, "Justification," in *The Anchor Bible Dictionary,* vol. 3, ed. David Noel Freedman (New York: Doubleday, 1992), 3:1129.

3. Bruce C. Birch, "The First and Second Books of Samuel: Introduction, Commentary, and Reflections," in *The New Interpreter's Bible,* vol. 2 (Nashville: Abingdon, 1998), 2:1258.

4. This interpretation of vv. 14-15 is far from obvious. For a thorough discussion of opinions about the identity of the "wall," see Ernest Best, *A Critical and Exegetical Commentary on Ephesians,* International Crtical Commentary (Edinburgh: T&T Clark, 1998), 253–57. The statement in v. 15 about the law being abolished is notoriously difficult to reconcile with other passages in the New Testament. See Best, pp. 259–60, for an argument that the epistle considers Christ's death to have abolished the whole law.

5. A miraculous increase of food also recalls the deeds of prophets (see 2 Kings 4:42-44; 1 Kings 17:1-16). Additionally, the provision of food in a wilderness setting calls to mind God's supplying manna to the Israelites.

EIGHTH SUNDAY AFTER PENTECOST

JULY 30, 2006
SEVENTEENTH SUNDAY IN ORDINARY TIME /
PROPER 12

REVISED COMMON	EPISCOPAL (BCP)	ROMAN CATHOLIC
2 Kings 4:42-44 or 2 Sam. 11:1-15	2 Kings 2:1-15	2 Kings 4:42-44
Ps. 145:10-18 or Ps. 14	Psalm 114	Ps. 145:10-11, 15-16, 17-18
Eph. 3:14-21	Eph. 4:1-7, 11-16	Eph. 4:1-6
John 6:1-21	Mark 6:45-52	John 6:1-15

At the beginning of this section of Pentecost, the texts are about the power of God revealed in abundance: abundance of food, where there appears to be too little (2 Kings 4 and John 6), and an abundance of God's own presence, first revealed in the healing and feeding miracles of Elisha and then in the presence of Jesus walking on the water, saying, "Do not be afraid; it is I [better put, 'I am']." Psalm 145 further reminds us that God provides all with their "food in due season."

FIRST READING
2 KINGS 4:42-44 (RCL, RC)

Interpreting the Text

Elisha has already received Elijah's mantle and is performing acts that reveal God's power/abundance across the land. The widow of Zaraphath's food lasts beyond the meager amount she has left. Elijah brings her son back to life (2 Kings 4:1ff.). Now, in the latter portion of the fourth chapter, Elisha reveals God's ongoing abundance when a man brings him twenty loaves of barley and fresh ears of corn. Elisha's servant cannot understand how this will be enough to feed one hundred people, but at Elisha's command the servant places it before the people who are gathered. All eat their fill, and there is indeed food left over. Thus is fulfilled the promise of

God, spoken through Elisha: "They shall eat and have some left" (2 Kings 4:43). This text's story of abundance points hearers toward the Gospel text of the feeding of the five thousand; this text's story of power points hearers toward the Gospel text of Jesus' walking on the water.

Reflecting on the Text

It is important to go a step beyond Elisha's power to its source. The source of Elisha's power is the power of God, the overwhelming abundance of God. It is, after all, only through God's generous sharing of God's power to heal, feed, and protect that Elisha has access to such power in the first place.

Explicitly and clearly naming the source of Elisha's power as the power of God is important in any age, but particularly in our age. The overarching narrative of our time is that of individual ability to reach any height, to gain any goal if one is focused, driven, or hardworking enough. Individual drive and skill lie at the heart of success. The power that regularly accompanies such success, at least in the hands of human beings, is not benign.

> EXPLICITLY AND CLEARLY NAMING THE SOURCE OF ELISHA'S POWER AS THE POWER OF GOD IS IMPORTANT IN ANY AGE, BUT PARTICULARLY IN OUR AGE.

Power can be used for life and the commitment to abundance; it can also be used in harmful, life-threatening ways, exerting itself over and against others.[1] A challenge for the preacher is to lift up and name the difference: power that is used to protect oneself and what one has gained for oneself does not generate true abundance and therefore is not life-giving; power that is of God is others-oriented, is life-giving, and generates abundance in areas where the assumption is one of scarcity.

2 KINGS 2:1-15 (BCP)

There are two powerful narratives in the history of Israel that leap to mind when moving through this text in 2 Kings. Both speak of faithfulness and life-giving power. The first part of the dialogue between Elijah and Elisha rings of the words spoken by Ruth to her mother-in-law, Naomi: "Do not press me to leave you or to turn back from following you! Where you go, I will go; where you lodge, I will lodge . . ." (Ruth 1:16-17). Can't you hear these words surrounding Elisha's response to Elijah, "As the LORD lives, and you yourself live, I will not leave you" (2 Kings 2:2)? The faithfulness of both Ruth and Elisha is not theirs alone. Indeed, it is God's own faithfulness. Likewise it is for us: the faithfulness that rises up out of us is not ours alone but is a gift from God and is God's own presence in and through us.

In the second part of the text—the striking of water, first by Elijah and then Elisha—takes us back to Moses' striking the water in the Red Sea. This connection with Moses places Elijah and Elisha in the line of those who are able to loose the power of God for life. We will see Jesus following in this tradition in today's Gospel. And, indeed, we ourselves follow in this tradition when we allow God's power and faithfulness to rise up and move through us.

RESPONSIVE READING
PSALM 145:10-18 (RCL)
PSALM 145:10-11, 15-16, 17-18 (RC)

Psalm 145 expresses the joy and gratitude of Israel for its creator.[2] In the verses that are the focus for the day, this joy and gratitude is expressed in acknowledgment of God's mighty deeds and glorious splendor. This includes the words that many of us grew up praying as the beginning of our table prayer: "The eyes of all look to you, and you give them their food in due season. You open your hand, satisfying the desire of every living thing . . ." (vv. 15-16). God's power is again used on behalf of life, and particularly in this case the life of those who are hungry. This affirmation by the psalmist connects this psalm with the other texts for the day, revealing God's acts to feed the hungry.

PSALM 114 (BCP)

This psalm carries on the affirmation of God's power over water in order to save and fortify life, which is at the center of the Episcopal lectionary's lessons for the day. Elijah and Elisha's striking of the water at the Jordan and Jesus' walking on the water in the Gospel text both attest to God's desire to save and be with us. Here the earth trembles at the presence of the God "who turns rock into a pool of water, and flint into a spring of water" (v. 8).

SECOND READING
EPHESIANS 3:14-21 (RCL)

Interpreting the Text

This text immediately follows Paul's speaking to the Gentiles of his calling to bring the word of the gospel to the Gentiles (Eph. 3:7-8) and precedes a call to unity of purpose for the church, making a claim that there is "one body and one

Spirit" (Eph. 4:4). This placement suggests that the writer of Ephesians wants to affirm the inclusion of Gentile Christians in the emerging church. Paul prays that they may be strengthened internally by the power of the Spirit and that Christ may reside in their hearts through faith (vv. 16-17). He further prays that they may have the power to comprehend God's "plan and purpose." Paul's prayer ends with a doxology, a prayer of praise to the One who works in us what we could not accomplish or even imagine on our own.

Reflecting on the Text

The language of power, particularly God's power and the power of the Spirit, flows through this beautiful prayer and doxology. God's power holds the church together when differences (the addition of Gentile members to a predominantly Jewish Christian community) might otherwise tear it apart. One of the opening verses of the assigned reading in Psalm 145 in the RCL, v. 12, prepares us for such a calling of unity by claiming that the faithful will "make known to *all* people your mighty deeds, and the glorious splendor of your kingdom."

The call to "oneness" is one of the central themes of Paul's ministry,[3] a reality Paul knows is created by the presence and power of God, Jesus, and the Holy Spirit, not a result of a human capacity for oneness. God's power is, again, not a power over God's people but a power that draws together those who otherwise would be estranged. It is through the grace-filled power of God that we are called together and held together when our fault lines on social issues, racial-ethnic identity, and liturgical practices (to name just a few) would keep us apart.

> GOD'S POWER IS NOT A POWER OVER GOD'S PEOPLE BUT A POWER THAT DRAWS TOGETHER THOSE WHO OTHERWISE WOULD BE ESTRANGED.

EPHESIANS 4:1-7, 11-16 (BCP)
EPHESIANS 4:1-6 (RC)

See the comments on the second reading for the Ninth Sunday after Pentecost, below.

THE GOSPEL
JOHN 6:1-21 (RCL)
JOHN 6:1-15 (RC)

The Gospel lesson is the apex toward which the readings for the day have been moving. Here we find moving narratives that show the power of God made known in Jesus' feeding of the five thousand and Jesus' walking on the water. The feeding of the five thousand is the only miracle of Jesus that is found in all four Gospels. As such, it is in a unique position to influence the early church in its understanding of Jesus and the God revealed in Jesus. The story begins with Jesus' withdrawing and being followed by the multitude. John notes that the multitude follows because "they saw the signs that he was doing for the sick" (v. 2). In John, signs are those things that reveal that Jesus is "I am" (*ego eimi*), language common to the Gospel's understanding of Jesus.[4] This language will be used again in reference to Jesus in the miracle of walking on the water (v. 20).

Jesus goes up the mountain, where he sits with his disciples. We are told that Passover is at hand. This may simply be a way of placing this miracle in time.[5] It also may be a way of letting us know that what follows is a connection to the foot-washing and meal that Jesus celebrates with his disciples before being betrayed and taken away (John 13 begins, "Now before the festival of the Passover . . ."). In comparison with the other Gospels, John has Jesus asking the question, "Where are we to buy bread for these people to eat?" and then goes on to say that Jesus said this in order to test Philip. Philip responds that two hundred denarii will not buy enough bread for everyone to receive a little, establishing a mind-set of scarcity.

Bringing us further into the experience of scarcity in the text, Andrew says that there is a lad who has five barley loaves and two fish.[6] At Jesus' direction, the five thousand gathered sit. Then, in language strongly eucharistic in tone, Jesus takes the loaves, gives thanks, and distributes the bread to those who are seated. He does the same with the fish. Everyone eats their fill, and Jesus tells the disciples to gather up the fragments that are left, which fill twelve baskets. When people see the "sign" that Jesus has done, they say, "This is indeed the prophet who is to come into the world." John alone picks up the political reality in this story: because of Jesus' action in feeding the crowd, they see in him the Messiah who is to come. The Messiah they are expecting is one who will overthrow the Romans who occupy their land and set them free. Jesus understands what they are saying, and knowing that they would come and make him the Messiah, their kind of Messiah, by force, he withdraws again to be alone.

> JOHN ALONE PICKS UP THE POLITICAL REALITY IN THIS STORY: BECAUSE OF JESUS' ACTION IN FEEDING THE CROWD, THEY SEE IN HIM THE MESSIAH WHO IS TO COME.

That evening the disciples go down to the Sea of Galilee, get into a boat, and start across the sea to Capernaum. When it becomes dark, the sea rises up because a strong wind is blowing. After they row for several miles, they see Jesus walking toward them on the sea. They are frightened! Jesus says to them, "*ego eimi*," literally, "I am," and tells them not to be afraid. Then they are glad to take him into the boat, and immediately the boat is at the land to which they were going.

In comparison with other Gospel accounts of both of these stories, John more than any develops these stories not as miracle stories alone but as occasions for divine revelation.[7] In both miracle stories, Jesus identifies himself as *ego eimi*, the Greek translation of the words spoken by God to Moses (Exod. 3:13). It is God who is acting in Jesus to bless and multiply the bread and who comes to the disciples on the rough sea and accompanies them to safety.

The preacher may focus on God who is so generous that God makes Godself available in Jesus. Further, this same God in Jesus acts in ways that reveal God's power used on behalf of life, first in the multiplication of the loaves and fish and later in God's own presence on rough seas. It is the power of God that fills people with what they need and sees that there is plenty left over. In a world where we are told repeatedly that there is not enough to go around, God gives face to the lie by feeding a large crowd with what appears to be a meager amount. What would a world grounded in an understanding of abundance look like in comparison with one based on fears of scarcity?

> WHAT WOULD A WORLD GROUNDED IN AN UNDERSTANDING OF ABUNDANCE LOOK LIKE IN COMPARISON WITH ONE BASED ON FEARS OF SCARCITY?

Another way into a sermon is to go again to the most frequent saying of Jesus in the New Testament, "Do not be afraid." Jesus walks over a sea that has risen up because of a strong wind. In John's Gospel, Jesus does not calm these rough seas—instead, he walks over them, accompanying and comforting those who are frightened in the boat. Developing this movement of God through/over those events that frighten us in order to be with us could be a compelling way of reshaping the question, "Why didn't God prevent this?" to the affirmation, "God moves through and over this in order to be with us and comfort us." God's power again is used for life.

MARK 6:45-52 (BCP)

This is Mark's version of Jesus' walking on the water. The 2 Kings text and the psalm assigned for the BCP texts prepare the stage for this text by revealing God's power over water, first through Elijah and Elisha's separating the water of the Jordan, and then by the acclamation of the God who turns rocks and flint into water. Like John's telling of this story, Mark's Gospel lifts up the revelation of Jesus as God, putting the words "*ego eimi*" on the lips of Jesus. Mark, too, has the disciples frightened, this time by what they think is a ghost. In the face of their fear, Jesus identifies himself and then joins them in the boat. Specific to Mark, the disciples do not understand the revelation of God that they have just witnessed.

Notes

1. A well-developed discussion of power and the complexity of the reality of "the powers" are in Charles Campbell's *The Word Before the Powers* (Louisville: Westminster John Knox Press, 2002), chap. 1.

2. Walter Brueggemann, *The Message of the Psalms* (Minneapolis: Augsburg, 1984), 28.

3. See also Rom. 12:5; 1 Cor. 10:17; 12:12 for central references to "oneness."

4. Robert Kysar makes brief note of the variety of Christologies found in the book of John in *Preaching John,* Fortress Resources for Preaching (Minneapolis: Fortress Press, 2002), 47–48. Raymond Brown gives particular attention to Jesus as divine revelation in *The Gospel according to John I–XII,* Anchor Bible (Garden City, N.Y.: Doubleday, 1966), 255.

5. See Raymond Brown's "Notes" in *The Gospel according to John I–XII,* 245ff.

6. The explicit naming of barley loaves in this version of the feeding of the five thousand explicitly links Jesus' action here with that of Elisha's feeding of the one hundred with barley. The other Gospel accounts do not name barley when developing their narratives of feeding the crowd.

7. Brown, *The Gospel according to John I–XII,* 254–55.

THE TRANSFIGURATION OF THE LORD

AUGUST 6, 2006

EPISCOPAL (BCP)	ROMAN CATHOLIC
Exod. 34:29-35	Dan. 7:9-10, 13-14
Psalm 99 or 99:5-9	Ps. 97:1-2, 5-6, 9
2 Peter 1:13-21	2 Peter 1:16-19
Luke 9:28-36	Mark 9:2-10

FIRST READING
DANIEL 7:9-10, 13-14 (RC)

Today's text draws on key elements in the first of four visions received by Daniel, visions that are meant to "hold out a promise of deliverance in the new kingdom of God for those who remain faithful in the face of persecution."[1] There are two key figures that are central to the fulfillment of this promise. In imagery that prepares us for the transfiguration of Jesus, we hear of "an Ancient One" whose clothing is white and whose hair is like "pure wool" (v. 9). The exiled Israelites place their hope in this "Ancient One" because it is through this one that judgment will come. How is judgment good news for the exiles? The implication is that the judged are those who have kept faithful Israelites in captivity and that this judgment is part of a series of events that will bring deliverance to the exiles.[2]

The second key figure in which the exiles place their hope is the "human being coming with the clouds of heaven" (v. 13). This human being comes before the Ancient One and is given "dominion and glory and kingship, that all peoples, nations, and languages should serve him" (v. 14). This dominion will not pass away and will not be destroyed (v. 14). While the writer of Daniel was not prefiguring the

WITHIN CHRISTIAN TRADITION THE PRESENTATION OF THIS HUMAN BEING IS LINKED WITH THE IDENTIFICATION OF JESUS AS THE MESSIAH WHO IS THE ULTIMATE HOPE OF ALL EXILES.

transfiguration of Jesus, within Christian tradition the presentation of this human being is linked with Jesus' presentation on the mountain,[3] and therefore with the identification of Jesus as the Messiah who is the ultimate hope of all exiles. We could include ourselves in that group as well.

159

TRANSFIGURATION
OF THE LORD
────────
ADELE STILES
RESMER

EXODUS 34:29-35 (BCP)

Immediately preceding this text, God renews the covenant with Israel in language distinctive to Exodus. God recites the fullness of this covenant renewal (vv. 10-26), and again it is rich, full, and generous. At the end of this recitation, God asks Moses to write it all down, and Moses writes the Ten Commandments (v. 27).

After Moses' time on the mountain with God, he comes down the mountain with the Ten Commandments on two tablets. He does not realize that his face is shining because he had been talking with God and is about to speak for God. His face continues to shine when he speaks on behalf of God, and each time he is finished speaking, he covers his face. In the person of Moses, who is on the mountain during the transfiguration, and in his descent down the mountain with his face aglow following his encounter with God, our hearts and minds continue to be primed to hear the story of the transfiguration that is soon to follow.

RESPONSIVE READING
PSALM 97:1-2, 5-6, 9 (RC)

This psalm acts like a pivot between the earlier Hebrew scripture text and the Gospel text that is yet ahead. This psalm acknowledges that "clouds and thick darkness are all around [God]" (v. 2) and that "the heavens proclaim his righteousness; and all the peoples behold his glory" (v. 6). Looking back we see Moses' interaction with God and his resulting transfiguration. Looking forward we see Jesus' encounter with God on the mountaintop and his transfiguration.

PSALM 99 or 99:5-9 (BCP)

Psalm 99 shares several key themes of Psalm 97, affirming that God spoke to Moses, Aaron, and Samuel in a pillar of cloud (v. 7) and that they kept God's decrees. Again, we see a pointing back to the Exodus text of Moses' speaking with God on the mountain, and a pointing forward to God's presence with Jesus on the mountain in a pillar of cloud.

SECOND READING

2 PETER 1:13-21 (BCP)
2 PETER 1:16-19 (RC)

Second Peter's telling of the transfiguration of Jesus is clear enough, even if the audience of this story is not.[4] Regardless of the audience, whether it be new hearers of the story of Jesus or those who are challenging what the followers of Jesus are saying, the author of 2 Peter finds it important to affirm that "we" were eyewitnesses of Christ's majesty, and "we" heard God say, "This is my Son, my Beloved, with whom I am well pleased," while we were with him on the holy mountain. This is no secondhand information being offered here, but truth from the mouths of those who were present, followers who saw and heard.

THIS IS NO SECONDHAND INFORMATION BEING OFFERED HERE, BUT TRUTH FROM THE MOUTHS OF THOSE WHO WERE PRESENT, FOLLOWERS WHO SAW AND HEARD.

Further, hearers are reminded that the message affirmed in this telling does not come from anyone's individual interpretation but rather from women and men "moved by the Holy Spirit [who] spoke from God" (v. 21)—a final declaration of the veracity of the declaration made about Jesus.

In all likelihood, this text is included where it is in the day's lessons in order for present-day hearers to have their minds and hearts primed for the fuller telling of the transfiguration of Jesus that is about to be told.

THE GOSPEL

LUKE 9:28-36 (BCP)
MARK 9:2-10 (RC)

Interpreting the Text

The transfiguration of Jesus takes place like this: Jesus invites Peter and James and John to accompany him up the mountain "apart, by themselves" (Mark 9:2), in order "to pray" (Luke 9:28). When they go up the mountain, Jesus is transfigured; that is, his appearance is altered (Luke 9:29), and his garments become radiant and white. While they are there, Elijah and Moses join them. In the Lukan version, Moses and Elijah speak of Jesus' departure (Luke's actual word is *exodon*—exodus—linking Jesus' crucifixion and resurrection with the exodus event of the Israelites). Peter and those with him are heavy with sleep (language that points toward the Garden of Gethsemane) but do stay awake and see Jesus in his transfigured state.

Both Gospel accounts tell of Peter's speaking with Jesus, stating that it is good to be there. Perhaps they can build three booths—one for Jesus, one for Moses, one for Elijah. In other words, let's stay here in the midst of this intense experience. A cloud overshadows them, and a voice from the cloud says, "This is my Son, the Beloved [a Lukan variation uses the same language]; listen to him!" (language connected to Jesus' baptism). When they look around, only Jesus is there with them. Luke's account ends here. It is in Mark's account that as they are coming down the mountain, Jesus charges them to tell no one what they have seen until after he has risen from the dead (Mark 9:9). So they kept it to themselves.

Reflecting on the Text

Just as God transfigured Moses in their conversation together on the mountain, now God transfigures Jesus, changes him, and claims him again as God's own. Often our focus is on the *how* of the transfiguration—how was Jesus transfigured exactly, how did Jesus look, did Jesus look like he will look after the resurrection? The technicalities of the transfiguration can capture our minds. Yet God's final words concerning this event are "Listen to him!" What would it mean for preachers to pick up this focus and have it serve as the centerpoint for preaching on the transfiguration: What does it mean to listen to Jesus, where are we invited to go, what will we leave behind? How will we be changed by listening?

This final question—How might we be changed by listening?—points to another related area for preaching. God transfigures Moses, God transfigures Jesus; what does it mean for God through Christ to transfigure us? Kathryn Spink of the Taizé community offers this picture: "God penetrates those hardened, incredulous, even disquieting regions within us, about which we really do not know what to do. God penetrates them with the Spirit and acts upon those regions and gives them God's own face."[5] The transfiguration of Jesus is not the end of God's transfiguring activity; it continues through Jesus to us.

Notes

1. See introduction to Daniel, in *The HarperCollins Study Bible NRSV* (New York: HarperCollins, 1993), 1303.

2. Ibid.

3. Walter Brueggemann, *Theology of the Old Testament: Testimony, Dispute, Advocacy* (Minneapolis: Fortress Press, 1997), 619.

4. Raymond E. Brown, "Second Epistle of Peter," in *An Introduction to the New Testament* (New York: Doubleday, 1997), 763.

5. Kathryn Spink's quote for "Transfiguration Sunday," in Sharon Iverson Gouwens et al., eds., *Imaging the Word: An Arts and Lectionary Resource, vol. 3* (Cleveland: The United Church Press, 1996), 148.

NINTH SUNDAY AFTER PENTECOST

AUGUST 6, 2006
EIGHTEENTH SUNDAY IN ORDINARY TIME /
PROPER 13

REVISED COMMON
Exod. 16:2-4, 9-15
  or 2 Sam. 11:26—12:13a
Ps. 78:23-29
  or Ps. 51:1-12
Eph. 4:1-16
John 6:24-35

A lengthy discussion that focuses on Jesus as "the bread of life" through the latter part of the sixth chapter of John begins today. The lessons begin with God's saving act in feeding the Israelites in the wilderness. The psalm reiterates in liturgical form God's saving action. The early hearers of John's text will know of these stories and songs as they are told that Jesus is God's saving act, the one who is "the bread of life" that fills human hunger and thirst for all time.

FIRST READING
EXODUS 16:2-4, 9-15

Interpreting the Text

The Israelites are not very far on the other side of the Red Sea when freedom from Egypt begins to feel threatening. First they cry out for drinkable water, and God responds by showing Moses a stick, which he throws into the water, "and the water became sweet" (15:23-25). Now in our text, the thirst-quenched Israelites cry out again, this time for food. They are so distraught over the lack of food that they say to Moses and Aaron, "If only we had died by the hand of the LORD in the land of Egypt, when we sat by the fleshpots and ate our fill of bread" (16:3). Deep-seated fear of starving in the desert makes Egypt look good. God hears this fear and tells Moses, "I am going to rain bread from heaven for you" (v. 4); enough food for each day only, exercising the Israelites' capacity for faith in God.

Moses and Aaron gather before the community of Israelites and tell them that God has heard their complaining and will provide meat in the evening and bread in the morning. That evening quail covered the camp, and in the morning, when the dew had lifted, a fine flaky substance covered the ground. When they ask, "What is it?" (v. 14), Moses tells them it is "the bread that the LORD has given you to eat" (v. 15).

Responding to the Text

This text is true to life in its reflection of the human condition and its revelation of a God of infinite abundance and love for frightened, wandering people. While clearly we live in a very different cultural and historical period than the text, the story told in this text is our story too. The God revealed in this story is the God who meets us in the Jesus of the Gospel text. Preachers would do well to consider this text as they examine the possibilities for preaching. First of all, in comparison with early hearers of the Gospel text, many of our hearers do not know this rich story that lies behind the Gospel affirmation of Jesus as "the bread of life." Whether one chooses to have this text be the primary foundation for the acclamation of the

> THE GOD REVEALED IN THIS STORY IS THE GOD WHO MEETS US IN THE JESUS OF THE GOSPEL TEXT.

Gospel or have it provide a foretaste of the movement to the Gospel text, the text's movement might well provide the movement of a sermon: the cries of people once enslaved, now free, yet still fearful for their lives; and God's corresponding response that meets human need. Our stories weave in and out of this story and into the Gospel story where God provides "the bread of life" that leaves us neither hungry nor thirsty ever again.

RESPONSIVE READING
PSALM 78:23-29

The portion of Psalm 78 assigned for this day reiterates in poetic verse the saving actions of God in the wilderness. As we heard in the Exodus text, we hear again that God "sent them food in abundance" (v. 25), and "they ate and were well filled, for he gave them what they craved" (v. 29). The psalm restates the heart of the Exodus text that came before it and prepares us for the Gospel affirmation in John that is just ahead.

SECOND READING

EPHESIANS 4:1-16

Interpreting the Text

Following the prayer that you "know the love of Christ that surpasses knowledge, so that you may be filled with all the fullness of God" (3:19), the writer of Ephesians continues with a list of attributes that reflect a life lived in the fullness of God: "with all humility and gentleness, with patience, bearing with one another in love, making every effort to maintain the unity of the Spirit in the bond of peace" (4:2).[1] This invitation to a way of life is followed by an affirmation of the oneness that creates the possibility of living in such a way—one body, one Spirit, one hope, one Lord, one faith, one baptism, one God and Father of all, "who is above all and through all and in all" (vv. 4-6).

The one God, revealed in Christ, gives each one grace, gifts for the uplifting of the whole body. "The gifts he gives are that some would be apostles, some prophets, some evangelists, some pastors and teachers . . . for building up the body" (vv. 11-12).

Reflecting on the Text

The oneness to which the early church is called remains an elusive reality for the church in the twenty-first century. We regularly confuse oneness with uniformity, thereby creating the conditions for resentment and alienation within the church and among believers and yet-to-be believers alike. Likewise, the gifts that we receive from Christ are not uniform. A variety of individual gifts are needed for the oneness of the church; a variety of community gifts are needed for the church to be one. We are helpfully reminded here that it is God, revealed in Jesus the Christ, that gives us the gifts we need to be one, to

> A VARIETY OF INDIVIDUAL GIFTS ARE NEEDED FOR THE ONENESS OF THE CHURCH; A VARIETY OF COMMUNITY GIFTS ARE NEEDED FOR THE CHURCH TO BE ONE.

be whole, no longer "tossed to and fro and blown about by every wind" (v. 14). It is the one God, revealed in Jesus the Christ, the bread that fills us with all good things, that strengthens us for the challenging and life-giving work of being one.

JOHN 6:24-35

Interpreting the Text

This text, which is the prologue to the ongoing discussion of the bread of life in chapter 6 of John, moves through several stages.[2] It opens with a dialogue between Jesus and the crowd: When the crowd found Jesus on the other side of the sea, they asked him, "Rabbi, when did you come here?" (v. 25). Jesus' response appears to be the answer to a different question: "I tell you, you are looking for me, not because you saw signs, but because you ate your fill of the loaves" (v. 26). In other words, you have followed me not because you understand that I am of God (the doer of signs) but rather because you were hungry and I gave you food to eat. And so he continues, "Do not work for the food that perishes, but for the food that endures for eternal life, which the Son of Man will give you" (v. 27). In this opening stage of the discussion, Jesus redirects the crowd's question from the surface of things into the heart of the matter—recognizing and responding to God among them.

> JESUS REDIRECTS THE CROWD'S QUESTION FROM THE SURFACE OF THINGS INTO THE HEART OF THE MATTER—RECOGNIZING AND RESPONDING TO GOD AMONG THEM.

The next movement in the conversation draws Jesus and the crowd closer in their conversation. In response to Jesus' invitation to work for the food that endures for eternal life (that which Jesus gives them), members of the crowd respond, "What must we do to perform the works of God?" (v. 28). Jesus responds, "This is the work of God, that you believe in him whom he has sent" (v. 29). In this brief exchange, Jesus corrects any misassumption that a relationship with God is grounded in what they can do. Rather, it is belief, faith in Jesus whom God has sent.[3]

In the next movement of the conversation, the crowd asks Jesus for a sign (despite the sign they have just experienced—the feeding of the five thousand) so that they can see it and believe him. And they continue, in a voice that one can imagine being just a bit haughty, "What work are you performing? Our ancestors ate the manna in the wilderness . . ." (v. 31).

In the final move of this opening discussion, Jesus responds that it was God, not Moses, who fed their ancestors in the wilderness, and that "it is my Father who gives you the true bread from heaven" (v. 32). The crowd asks Jesus to give them that bread. According to Robert Kysar and Raymond Brown, the opening prologue ends here.[4] If indeed the lectionary had the text end here, we would be left with a discussion that ends with a request, unanswered. Lack of resolution, for the crowd and for us, leaves the possibility for varying degrees of discomfort—there is no immediate response to their/our request for the bread from heaven. Those who established the lectionary include the next verse, which ends up bringing closure and, I imagine, a sense of resolution, at least to this opening exchange. Jesus says, "I am the bread of life. Whoever comes to me will never be hungry, and whoever believes in me will never be thirsty" (v. 35).

Reflecting on the Text

One of the first decisions a preacher will need to make when reflecting on this text is where to have the text end. Will you go with the lectionary lead and have the text end with the affirmation of Jesus that he is the bread of life, or will you follow the textual movement that, according to scholars, ends with the previous verse, which is a request by the crowd? Deciding this early on is important because it will influence the movement and tone and affirmation that are preached. For example, if the Gospel reading ends with Jesus' affirmation that he is the bread of life, a sermon that moves, like the text, through a series of questions and answers will conclude with Jesus' words. Certainly, the inability of the crowd to recognize Jesus through the signs he has already done among them moves neatly to our inability to understand the signs that Jesus is doing

> THE CROWD AND WE COME TO JESUS ASKING QUESTIONS THAT SHOW THAT WE DO NOT KNOW WHO HE IS, AND THEREFORE EVEN WHO WE ARE.

among us. The crowd and we come to Jesus asking questions that show that we do not know who he is, and therefore even who we are. But Jesus sticks with the crowd, sticks with us too, until they/we finally hear that it is God who has fed and continues to feed our deepest hungers and thirsts. And then we receive the final affirmation that Jesus himself is the bread of life through whom we are never hungry or thirsty again. With this closing response, we are led to the Lord's Supper, to baptism, to life in community where we who have been fed continue to feed those who still hunger and thirst. And, paradoxically, it is in this going out, having been fed, that we find the One who feeds us waiting for us in those who still hunger and thirst.

In comparison, if the text ends with the crowd requesting, "Sir, give us this bread always," the movement of the text from question to answer will be left with a sense of openness. The final request will not have an answer. What it might do is throw us back into the text itself, where Jesus answers the request through his earlier responses that seem more oblique to the crowd. This fits with the less-than-solid sureness we often feel in the presence of Jesus, who is not responding in the ways we expect or understand. Another approach would be to race through the movement of the questions and responses and end the sermon with the words of the crowd's request and leave the movement flying forward without a solid, wrapped-up answer, more of a sense of anticipation of what is to come. This approach makes sense when engaging listeners who are used to cliff-hangers from one week to the next (or one season to the next) on television. Even if we have been through the "bread of life" series a number of times ourselves, there is still great room for anticipation of what is yet to come for listeners schooled in the dangling story line that gets picked up next week.

Notes

1. See also the language of Col. 3:12-13.

2. What follows draws from Robert Kysar, *Preaching John*, Fortress Resources for Preaching (Minneapolis: Fortress Press, 2002), 187–88. Kysar is subtly adapting material from Raymond E. Brown, *The Gospel according to John I–XII*, Anchor Bible (Garden City, N.Y.: Doubleday, 1966), 287–91.

3. Ibid., 188.

4. Ibid., 187–88.

TENTH SUNDAY AFTER PENTECOST

AUGUST 13, 2006
NINETEENTH SUNDAY IN ORDINARY TIME /
PROPER 14

REVISED COMMON	EPISCOPAL (BCP)	ROMAN CATHOLIC
1 Kings 19:4-8 or 2 Sam. 18:5-9, 15, 31-33	Deut. 8:1-10	1 Kings 19:4-8
Ps. 34:1-8 or Psalm 130	Psalm 34 or 34:1-8	Ps. 34:2-3, 4-5, 6-7, 8-9
Eph. 4:25—5:2	Eph. 4:(25-29) 30— 5:2	Eph. 4:30—5:2
John 6:35, 41-51	John 6:37-51	John 6:41-51

The focus on lifesaving food begun last week continues in today's lessons. Elijah's request that God let him die is responded to with bread and water that fortifies him for the journey ahead (1 Kings 19). The Deuteronomy text draws out a lush picture of the promised land with all its bounty (Deuteronomy 8). The Gospel text is framed with Jesus' affirmations that he is "the living bread"—whoever comes to him will not be hungry or thirsty; whoever eats of this bread will live forever.

FIRST READING
1 KINGS 19:4-8 (RCL, RC)

Interpreting the Text

Elijah is on the run for his life. At the command of the Lord, he has killed the prophets of Baal and incurred the wrath of Jezebel. She sends word to Elijah that if she has anything to do with it, he will suffer the same fate as those prophets. Frightened for his life, he flees to Beer-sheba. He leaves Elisha there and continues on his own (vv. 1-3).

Elijah goes a day's journey into the wilderness. He sits under a solitary broom tree and says to the Lord, "It is enough; now, O LORD, take away my life, for I am no better than my ancestors" (v. 4). Hear the words of a weary, frightened prophet: "It is enough. . . ." Imagine anyone with their head down, hand raised in resistance, "Enough." Then Elijah falls asleep under the tree. An angel awakens Elijah twice and tells him to eat, "otherwise the journey will be too much for you" (v. 7). Elijah eats and drinks; and the nourishment fortifies him for forty days and forty nights until he reaches Horeb, the mountain of God. God's response to Elijah's request to be done with life is to provide what he needs to continue with life.

Reflecting on the Text

The movement of this text from fear, fatigue, and "enough" on the part of Elijah to God's response with food and water that strengthen him for the journey ahead provides a solid movement for a sermon that focuses on this text. A movement that follows the human dilemma and God's response that enables new human responses is to which almost anyone can relate. Even the most faithful, the strongest among us, have times when it all becomes too much, when fear and fatigue overwhelm and death in one form or another appears a better release than carrying on. I remember reading of Martin Luther King Jr.'s fatigue in the last couple years of his life, when there seemed so much to do and he felt like he was accomplishing so little.[1] He talked of death much in those years. He prayed fervently, in weariness, sorrow, and faith. God strengthened him to carry on in his journey, nourishing his spirit for the task of freedom that was set before him. One does not need to be a Martin Luther King to feel that one can no longer do what one has been called to do. It is at this point that God meets us with the bread and water we need for the journey to which God is calling us. It's not that God is unsympathetic to our requests made in weariness and fear; rather, God's response to that fear and weariness is to strengthen us to continue on rather than letting us go.

> GOD'S RESPONSE TO ELIJAH'S REQUEST TO BE DONE WITH LIFE IS TO PROVIDE WHAT HE NEEDS TO CONTINUE WITH LIFE.

DEUTERONOMY 8:1-10 (BCP)

This text has both a backward-looking movement and a forward-moving movement. The Lord begins, "This entire commandment that I command you today you must diligently observe, so that you many live and increase, and go in and occupy the land that the LORD promised . . ." (v. 1). What follows is a retelling of the Israelites' journey through the wilderness and the acts of God to continually strengthen and save them. Central to the focus of today's texts is v. 3: "[The LORD] humbled you by letting you hunger, then by feeding you with manna, with which neither you nor your ancestors were acquainted, in order to make you understand that one does not live by bread alone, but by every word that comes from the mouth of the LORD."

The Lord repeats, "Therefore keep the commandments of the LORD your God, by walking in his ways and fearing him" (v. 6). What follows is a looking-forward to the land where God is leading them: a land of great abundance with flowing streams, a land of wheat and barley and vines and fig trees and more. The theme of the day flows through all the rich abundance of the land, culminating in the statement that this will be "a land where you may eat bread without scarcity, where you will lack nothing. . . . You shall eat your fill and bless the LORD for the good land he has given you" (vv. 9–10). In a culture that quickly forgets its past and is always moving forward quickly, it is helpful to be reminded that our past and our future are gifts from God.

IN A CULTURE THAT QUICKLY FORGETS ITS PAST AND IS ALWAYS MOVING FORWARD QUICKLY, IT IS HELPFUL TO BE REMINDED THAT OUR PAST AND OUR FUTURE ARE GIFTS FROM GOD.

RESPONSIVE READING

PSALM 34:1–8 (RCL, BCP ALT.)
PSALM 34 (BCP)
PSALM 34:2–3, 4–5, 6–7, 8–9 (RC)

This psalm gives a language of praise for events that remind us of Elijah's struggle and the struggle of the Israelites through the wilderness to the edge of the promised land, all of which are seen and responded to by God: those who seek the Lord are answered and delivered from all of their fears (v. 4); the poor who cry out are heard by the Lord and saved from every trouble (v. 6); "O taste and see that the LORD is good; happy are those who take refuge in him" (v. 8).

The remainder of the psalm continues in its affirmations of the Lord's attentiveness to the cries of those in need and of God's swiftness to rescue and save them.

EPHESIANS 4:25—5:2 (RCL)
EPHESIANS 4:(25-29) 30—5:2 (BCP)
EPHESIANS 4:30—5:2 (RC)

Interpreting the Text

Just as the writer of Ephesians calls out for the unity of the church, acknowledging the diversity of gifts that makes up that unity (see the Ninth Sunday of Pentecost), he now lays out rules by which this new community will be able to live their new life in Christ together. These rules are meant to be not a hardship but rather a gift, a way to be community together. What follows might easily be applied to any new community figuring out how to live together. In many ways, they may seem to us self-evident: "Putting away falsehood, let all

> PAUL INTENTIONALLY LET THE EARLY CHURCH KNOW RIGHT UP FRONT, AND IN FRONT OF EVERYONE, WHAT IT TAKES TO BE A HEALTHY COMMUNITY TOGETHER.

of us speak the truth" (v. 25); "Be angry but do not sin; do not let the sun go down on your anger" (v. 26); thieves must give up stealing and work honestly so they have something to share with the needy (v. 28); there is to be no evil talk, only that which builds up the community (v. 29); all bitterness, wrath, anger, wrangling, and slander are to be put away (v. 31); and we are to be kind to one another, tenderhearted, forgiving, as God in Christ forgives us (v. 32). In sum, "Be imitators of God . . . and live in love, as Christ loved us" (5:1-2).

Reflecting on the Text

There are many unspoken rules that exist in congregations: how long one has to be a member before one may speak with authority at an annual meeting; the degree to which children are welcomed and heard during worship; how conflict is acknowledged or not. The list could go on. It is more often than not these unspoken rules that get folks into trouble, because not everyone knows them and owns them. Some people simply by their knowledge of these unspokens have more power than others within the group; those who are not in the know are bound to transgress the rules. The Paul of Ephesians easily could have known such things when he intentionally let the early church know right up front, and in front of everyone, what it takes to be a healthy community together.

Many of us do not like to be given rules right up front, before each other and before God. Yet these are the very guidelines/rules that do allow us to be a healthy, viable community together. Everyone knows them; therefore, everyone is equal. We hold each other accountable, in love. This kind of accountability is truly a gift, even if it doesn't always feel like a gift. Some congregations may already be practiced in this kind of life together. Others may literally be dying for such rules.

THE GOSPEL
JOHN 6:35, 41–51 (RCL)
JOHN 6:37–51 (BCP)
JOHN 6:41–51 (RC)

Interpreting the Text

The RCL text begins with the last verse of the opening section of Jesus' discourse in chapter 6: "I am the bread of life. Whoever comes to me will never be hungry, and whoever believes in me will never be thirsty" (v. 35). If this verse was used to close last week's Gospel text, then its reiteration will provide an explicit connection with the second part of the discourse that is today's text. If, however, this verse was not included last week, then its place at the opening of today's reading provides a landing place, an "aha" to what had been left open. Either way, what follows carries the hearer further along in the discussion of and reaction to Jesus' self-revelation.

In response to this declaration, religious leaders who were present begin to complain (or to "murmur," as the Greek verb suggests[2]). How can Jesus be both bread of life from heaven—suggesting a divine identity—and the Jesus they have known as Joseph and Mary's son—suggesting a very human person? (vv. 41-42). The difficulty is not in getting the leaders to believe that Jesus is human; rather, it is a struggle to get them to believe that he is of God. And so Jesus speaks to his connection to God: "No one can come to me unless drawn by the Father who sent me; and I will raise that person up on the last day" (v. 44); "Everyone who has heard and learned from the Father comes to me" (v. 45); and finally, "Not that anyone has seen the Father except the one who is from God; he has seen the Father" (v. 46).

> THE DIFFICULTY IS NOT IN GETTING THE LEADERS TO BELIEVE THAT JESUS IS HUMAN; RATHER, IT IS A STRUGGLE TO GET THEM TO BELIEVE THAT HE IS OF GOD.

Having laid out more fully his relationship with God, Jesus says again, "I am the bread of life. Your ancestors ate manna in the wilderness, and they died. This is the bread that comes down from heaven so that one may eat of it and not die" (vv. 49-50). With this statement, Jesus moves another step deeper. Back at the beginning of this discussion (v. 35), he says that people who come to him will never be hungry or thirsty. Now he says that he is the "living" bread that comes down from heaven, and whoever eats of this bread will not die. And further, "Whoever eats of this bread will live forever; and the bread that I will give for the life of the world is my flesh" (v. 51). This will surely shake up the leaders who see him as Jesus, son of Joseph and Mary. But Jesus risks this revelation, despite where it will lead him.

Reflecting on the Text

Things are not always as they seem to be. People are not always who they seem to be. The religious leaders cannot get their heads, or their hearts, for that matter, around the truth that the one who is standing in front of them, the one they have known as Jesus, son of Joseph and Mary, is also Jesus, the beloved of God—that this person they recognize as fully human can at the same time be fully divine.

Jesus' claim to be of God is an affront to their belief in the one God who brought their ancestors out of slavery in Egypt. Yet despite their inability to understand, Jesus' claims are true. One completely unexpected among them is indeed of God.

The challenge for the leaders in Jesus' time is not an unknown challenge among us. Even without the help of the media, we easily settle on who we think someone is or, better put, who we *know* someone is. Once we have made up our mind about someone, it is often difficult for us to see that person in a different light, to believe that they are more than we know them to be. Open dialogue that actually adds to or changes a person's mind or opinion is becoming increasingly rare in these early days of the twenty-first century. We come, even to church, with our minds made up not only about those around us but also about God.

This creates quite a challenge for the preacher. We ourselves are part of the culture of the overly sure, completely convinced of opinions and people. So we come to the text with our own degree of locked-in thinking about who God is, how God works, and in whose face we see the living God. This text thus challenges preachers and hearers of the word "to live the questions,"[3] loosen our grip on what is known, make room for the One whom we continue to get to know in new places, in unexpected people, and in new activities. This I believe is one of the huge gifts of this text: challenging our assuredness and opening us to a holy, life-giving picture of God we could never imagine on our own.

> ONE OF THE HUGE GIFTS OF THIS TEXT IS THAT IT CHALLENGES OUR ASSUREDNESS AND OPENS US TO A HOLY, LIFE-GIVING PICTURE OF GOD WE COULD NEVER IMAGINE ON OUR OWN.

Another possibility for preachers is to pick up the thread laid out in the 1 Kings text, where God provides life-giving bread and water for Elijah's journey, and continues in the words of Jesus, in whom God provides the bread and water for our journey through life into eternal life. This eucharistic theme is a strong thread that may run through the whole of a sermon.

Notes

1. See David J. Garrow, *Bearing the Cross: Martin Luther King, Jr., and the Southern Christian Leadership Conference* (New York: Quill/William Morrow, 1986), chap. 11.

2. Robert Kysar, *Preaching John*, Fortress Resources for Preaching (Minneapolis: Fortress Press, 2002), 190.

3. Rainer Maria Rilke, *Letters to a Young Poet* (New York: W. W. Norton & Co., 1934), 35.

ELEVENTH SUNDAY AFTER PENTECOST

AUGUST 20, 2006
TWENTIETH SUNDAY IN ORDINARY TIME /
PROPER 15

REVISED COMMON	EPISCOPAL (BCP)	ROMAN CATHOLIC
Prov. 9:1-6	Prov. 9:1-6	Prov. 9:1-6
or 1 Kings 2:10-		
12, 3:3-14		
Ps. 34:9-14	Psalm 147	Ps. 34:2-3, 4-5, 6-7
or Psalm 111	or Ps. 34:9-14	
Eph. 5:15-20	Eph. 5:15-20	Eph. 5:15-20
John 6:51-58	John 6:53-59	John 6: 51-58

In our ongoing discussion of the saving food that is Jesus, we are invited to a banquet, where there is food and wine at a table surrounded by the simple and the senseless (Proverbs 9), where God promises to fill the hungry with the finest wheat (Psalm 34), and where Jesus invites us to "eat his body and drink his blood" (John 6). These texts work together to create a rich and dramatic environment in which hearers are drawn into an intimate relationship with God in Jesus.

FIRST READING
PROVERBS 9:1-6 (RCL, BCP, RC)

Interpreting the Text

This text falls in the last chapter of the opening section of Proverbs, chapters 1–9, which is made up of instructional poems directed at young people or students.[1] The poem in our text for today has a particular sumptuousness about it, telling of Lady Wisdom's preparation for a feast, both the preparation of the food and the invitation that is sent out on the lips of her servants. First the food preparation: "She has slaughtered her animals, she has mixed her wine, she has also set her table" (v. 2). A luxurious meal is envisioned as we hear of this preparation. And then her servants are sent out with a rich and, at the same time, somewhat surprising invitation on their lips: "You that are simple, turn in here!" (v. 4). "To those without sense she says,

'Come and eat of my bread and drink of the wine I have mixed'" (vv. 4–5). While it is important to resist seeing Jesus hiding in the shadows of Hebrew scripture texts, we can certainly affirm that the language of this text and the meal it invites us to see draw us into Jesus' own offering of a sumptuous meal that is his body and blood, bread and wine for all people, including the simple and those without sense.

Reflecting on the Text

Consider any movie or story that has at its heart the serving of a sumptuous meal, with a gathering of people who would surely fit the description "simple and without sense," and you will capture the heart of this lovely and radical text. *Babette's Feast*, though a little dated now, captures the surprise of this text when strict, unexpressive people gather around a table of food thankfully prepared, wine carefully chosen, and become alive in a new way as they eat and drink together. In the independent movie *Eat, Drink, Man, Woman*, meals that are lovingly prepared by a traditional Chinese father are a counterpoint to the ongoing troubled and confusing relationships with his more "modern" daughters—lack of understanding runs on both sides. This time the surprise is that those who struggle to understand each other continue to eat together, and it is through this regular eating together that healing and renewal come.

> THIS TIME THE SURPRISE IS THAT THOSE WHO STRUGGLE TO UNDERSTAND EACH OTHER CONTINUE TO EAT TOGETHER, AND IT IS THROUGH THIS REGULAR EATING TOGETHER THAT HEALING AND RENEWAL COMES.

RESPONSIVE READING
PSALM 34:9-14 (RCL, BCP ALT.)
PSALM 34:2-3, 4-5, 6-7 (RC)

The psalmist declares that those who seek the Lord will not hunger or want for anything. See further comments on the responsive reading for the Tenth Sunday after Pentecost.

PSALM 147 (BCP)

The psalmist sings praises to the Lord, who "gathers the outcasts of Israel" (v. 2), "heals the brokenhearted and binds up their wounds" (v. 3), "lifts up the downtrodden" (v. 6), and "fills you with the finest of wheat" (v. 14). Among the many attributes of God lifted up and praised in this psalm is the feeding of hungry people, an attribute at the heart of our readings for the day.

EPHESIANS 5:15-20 (RCL, BCP, RC)

Interpreting the Text

The writer of Ephesians continues with guidance for the renewed life in Christ for the early church. Believers are encouraged to be careful how they live. Because the church lives in the world, it must choose to live in a way that reflects its identity in Christ rather than reflecting the common activities of the day. The text is set up, then, in sets of comparisons between a life in Christ and a life according to the world, and it moves quickly from one set to the next, with little extra verbiage: "Be careful then how you live, not as unwise people but as wise" (v. 15); "So do not be foolish, but understand what the will of the Lord is" (v. 17); "Do not get drunk on wine, . . . but be filled with the Spirit" (vv. 18-19). This call for early believers to give "thanks to God . . . at all times" (v. 20) sets them to an activity that will orient them continually to the One in whom they have their life and being.

Reflecting on the Text

There is great clarity in this text about the differences between living a life grounded in faith in Christ and living according to the standards of the world. At first look, this clarity may seem a bit naïve to we moderns who experience life as considerably more complex. For modern believers it is not so much a question of whether we *will be* shaped by the world, but to what degree and in what ways we *are* shaped by the world. This text invites us to ongoing, intentional reflection rather than simple acceptance of the way things are. In its striking clarity regarding life in Christ and life in the world, the text invites us to consider more carefully the question, How do we, as people in the world, live our faith in the world? The invitation to be wise—not simply people with information, but rather people with a par-

> FOR MODERN BELIEVERS IT IS NOT SO MUCH A QUESTION OF WHETHER WE *WILL BE* SHAPED BY THE WORLD, BUT TO WHAT DEGREE AND IN WHAT WAYS WE *ARE* SHAPED BY THE WORLD.

ticular way of being in the world—is the place to begin. If we become people who become practiced at seeing ourselves, the world around us, our activities in the world, and our relationships wisely, we are in a better position to delve into questions of how we give up foolish ways and live according to the will of God. There is no pat answer. The wise person "lives the questions"[2] not as a way to avoid commitments or decisions; rather, living the questions moves our identity from a shadowy corner of our hearts and minds to front and center. We live as people engaged in the questions of what it means to be faithful people in the world. While there are some who might suggest that there is an easy answer to this, we do much better to trust in delving into the questions repeatedly over time. Different times and different places may invite, even require, different faithful responses from us.

THE GOSPEL
JOHN 6:51–58 (RCL, RC)
JOHN 6:53–59 (BCP)

Interpreting the Text

When we first began the discussion of Jesus as the "bread of life" a couple of weeks ago, we began with Jesus' direct statement, "I am the bread of life." Last week, Jesus moves more deeply in his self-disclosure, saying that he is "the bread of life that comes down from heaven." Today's text in the Revised Common and Roman Catholic lectionaries begins with a reiteration of that self-revelation that ended last week's reading: Jesus is "the living bread that came down from heaven. . . .

> JESUS PRESSES ON, IN A WAY THAT TURNS UP THE INTENSITY AND THE CONTROVERSY IN THE ENCOUNTER BETWEEN HIMSELF, CROWD, AND RELIGIOUS LEADERS.

The bread that I will give for the life of the world is my flesh" (v. 51). It is no great surprise that such revelation set the religious leaders debating about how such a thing is possible. How can Jesus give his body to be eaten (v. 52)? Even though the leaders struggle to understand what Jesus is saying, Jesus does not stop there. He presses on, in a way that turns up the intensity and the controversy in the encounter between Jesus, crowd, and religious leaders. He says, "Very truly, I tell you, unless you eat the flesh of the Son of Man and drink his blood, you have no life in you" (v. 53). And he continues, "Those who eat my flesh and drink my blood have eternal life . . . for my flesh is true food and my blood is true drink" (vv. 54–55).

Whether the writer of John believes that what Jesus is saying here holds such potential for offense that it needs to be repeated several times or whether the writer simply wants to drive the point home, he has Jesus repeating again and again in different ways that eating his body and drinking his blood is the only way to be united with Christ and to be fully alive (vv. 56–58). If the text continues to v. 59, as it does in the Episcopal lectionary, we hear that Jesus is saying all of this in the synagogue.

Reflecting on the Text

Frankly, I find this part of Jesus' discussion of his identity as the "bread of life" the most difficult with which to deal. My mind goes back to a discussion with a

classmate in graduate school who professed to be an atheist. We sat across a table
from each other as he said, "Your religion is one based on cannibalism. How can
you believe in a God who you believe is Jesus, who requires that you eat his body
and drink his blood? It's barbaric." The truth is, he probably wasn't too far from
the reaction of the religious leaders of Jesus' time. And if we admit it, not that far
from our own squeamishness when we hear, "Eat my body, drink my blood." The
temptation might well be to use Jesus' self-revelation in allegorical terms, or even
metaphorically: he says this, but what he means is "My body and blood are like. . ."
If we look at the language of the text, however, we see that Jesus uses *sarx*, talking
about his "flesh" rather than his body, and the word he uses for "eating" his body
in vv. 51–53 is *trogo*, which means to gnaw or gobble.[3] The language itself is raw
and probably ought to shock our sensibilities.

Robert Kysar delves into this text and makes a good point about what Jesus
is getting at here. He suggests that Jesus is
telling hearers that they literally need to
take Jesus into themselves, make him "part
of their essence."[4] No arm's-length relation-
ship here, no safe distance between us. As Christians who long for abundant life, we
have no other way to such a life except by taking Jesus in, having him become so
intermingled with our own being that we cannot separate one from the other.

> THE LANGUAGE IN THIS TEXT IS RAW AND PROBABLY
> OUGHT TO SHOCK OUR SENSIBILITIES.

Certainly, the language leads us to think again of the Eucharist, and this is
always a legitimate approach to any of the "bread of life" texts. For many preachers, however, particularly by this time in the "bread of life" cycle, this can be a safe
out with cursory development of what is at stake in Jesus' radical claims of union
with him. While acknowledging that this text does confound us more than the
others, we can still move forward with assurance of Jesus' desire to be intimately
connected with us. So much so that we are literally to be one with him through
his body and blood. In a time when intimacy of a life-giving kind is dramatically
misunderstood—either pushed away, life lived at arm's-length through "reality"
shows, video games, and "virtual reality," or dramatically distorted in domestic
violence and demands for sexual activity in the name of "intimacy"—hearers may
well be ready to hear a word about the kind of intimacy offered by Jesus that leads
to full life, lived in direct encounter with God and with others.

This being said, preachers do need to be careful about talking about intimacy that has no boundaries—Jesus literally in and through us—in a time when
the breaking of boundaries by church professionals in the name of Jesus leads to
violating others, particularly women and children. This text is a bit of a minefield.
Stepping between the mines that lead to misuse of power in the name of intimacy
and landing on the firm ground of full, abundant life in Jesus is a challenge that
each preacher undertakes in engaging this text.

180

THE SEASON
OF PENTECOST
―――――――
ADELE STILES
RESMER

Notes

1. Claudia V. Camp and Carole R. Fontaine, introduction to Proverbs in *The HarperCollins Study Bible NRSV* (New York: HarperCollins, 1993), 939–40.

2. Once again, Rainer Maria Rilke, *Letters to a Young Poet* (New York: W. W. Norton & Co., 1934), 35.

3. Robert Kysar, *Preaching John*, Fortress Resources for Preaching (Minneapolis: Fortress Press, 2002), 191–92.

4. Ibid., 192.

TWELFTH SUNDAY AFTER PENTECOST

AUGUST 27, 2006
TWENTY-FIRST SUNDAY IN ORDINARY TIME / PROPER 16

REVISED COMMON	EPISCOPAL (BCP)	ROMAN CATHOLIC
Josh. 24: 1-2a, 14-18 or 1 Kings 8:(1, 6, 10-11) 22-30, 41-43	Josh. 24:1-2a, 14-25	Josh. 24:1-2a, 15-17, 18b
Ps. 34:15-22 or Psalm 84	Psalm 16 or Ps. 34:15-22	Ps. 34:2-3, 16-17, 18-19, 20-21
Eph. 6:10-20	Eph. 5:21-33	Eph. 5:21-32 or 5:2a, 25-32
John 6:56-69	John 6:60-69	John 6:60-69

What is put before us today is the instruction of Joshua, "Choose this day whom you will serve" (Josh. 24:15). Jesus' question, "Do you also wish to go away?" (John 6:67), is another way of making the same request, this time in question form. Life with and for God, life following the God in Jesus, is affirmed as the life-giving response for followers.

FIRST READING

JOSHUA 24:1-2a, 14-18 (RCL) JOSHUA 24:1-2a, 15-17, 18b (RC) JOSHUA 24:1-2a, 14-25 (BCP)

Interpreting the Text

Chapter 24 of the book of Joshua elaborates a covenanting ceremony between the Israelites (now in the promised land) and Yahweh, their God. Based on God's prior acts, the people are invited to choose whom they will serve. The text begins with Joshua gathering the leaders—"the elders, the heads, the judges, and the officers"—of Israel, and they present themselves before God (v. 1). This gathering sets the stage for God's reminder of God's activities on their behalf, beginning with God's intervention with Abraham and continuing through God's deliverance from Egypt to life in the land promised by God (the unread section of the text, vv. 3–13). This rather extensive prequel cites the faithful activities of God that are the basis for the covenant between God and Israel. It is important that we hear again of the extensive lifesaving activities of God across time, though it is not part of the assigned reading for the day, because it helps us to make sense of the second part of the covenant, which is our assigned reading: What is Israel willing to do in response to God's faithfulness? What is Israel's part in the covenantal relationship?

Joshua lays it out rather clearly: "Now therefore revere the LORD and serve him in sincerity and in faithfulness; put away the gods that your ancestors served beyond the River and in Egypt, and serve the LORD" (v. 14). He continues, "Now if you are unwilling to serve the LORD, choose this day whom you will serve, . . . but as for me and my household, we will serve the LORD" (v. 15). The situation is rather straightforward: either you serve the Lord or you choose some other god to serve. One cannot do both.

> THE SITUATION IS RATHER STRAIGHTFORWARD: EITHER YOU SERVE THE LORD OR YOU CHOOSE SOME OTHER GOD TO SERVE. ONE CANNOT DO BOTH.

The leaders, whose actions in the wilderness showed an ongoing struggle, now respond with great firmness: "Far be it from us that we should forsake the LORD to serve other gods" (v. 16), and they continue with their own recitation of God's saving acts that have brought them from Egypt to the promised place, ending with a reaffirmation: "Therefore, we also will serve the LORD, for he is our God" (vv. 17–18).

The Episcopal lectionary continues with Joshua challenging the statement of trust and faith in God several times and the people responding each time with vigor that they will serve the Lord (vv. 19–24). As a result of the repeated affirmations that they will serve God, Joshua makes a covenant with the people (v. 25).

Reflecting on the Text

A commitment to serve God gets lived out over a lifetime. The trials and challenges that rise up to thwart such a commitment are many: losses, betrayals, promises of success from other gods of wealth and position and power. As the Israelites struggled daily to remain faithful to God, even as God was saving them from slavery, we too live out such struggles. One of the gifts of this text is that it reminds us of the importance of reading scripture in worship and in daily life. It is in the reciting of our history, salvation history, that we are reminded of who God is and who we are in response to God. It is at such times that it is possible to commit again and again to serve God. There is an old saying,

> IT IS IN THE RECITING OF OUR HISTORY, SALVATION HISTORY, THAT WE ARE REMINDED OF WHO GOD IS AND WHO WE ARE IN RESPONSE TO GOD.

"If you want to hear the train, you need to be near the tracks." If you want to be faithful, position yourself in a place where your story is recited again and again so that you can remember who you are in relationship with this God. If you want to invite new members to see themselves as part of this salvation history, tell the story, again and again.

RESPONSIVE READING
PSALM 34:15-22 (RCL; BCP ALT.)
PSALM 34:2-3, 16-17, 18-19, 20-21 (RC)

See the comments on the responsive reading for the Tenth Sunday after Pentecost.

PSALM 16 (BCP)

This psalm gives poetic voice to the covenantal commitments made by the Israelites in front of Joshua at Shechem, stating as Joshua did the difference between those who serve Yahweh and those who serve other gods: "Those who choose another god multiply their sorrows" (v. 4a); those who choose Yahweh can say, "I keep the LORD always before me; because he is at my right hand, I shall not be moved. Therefore my heart is glad . . . ; my body also rests secure. . . . In your presence there is fullness of joy; in your right hand are pleasures forevermore" (vv. 8–11).

SECOND READING
EPHESIANS 6:10-20 (RCL)

Interpreting the Text

A statement to be "strong in the Lord and in the strength of his power" (v. 10) carries forward the invitation to choose God rather than other gods. In this text, the language is not so much that of a recitation of history but rather a development of imagery that shows what is at stake in this choice: nothing short of a battle with the evil and the devil. This text develops with great creativity how one is to be positioned to respond to this battle of followers of God "against the rulers, against the authorities, against the cosmic powers of this present darkness, against the spiritual forces of evil in the heavenly places" (v. 12): one clothes oneself in the whole armor of God. "Stand therefore, and fasten the belt of truth around your waist, and put on the breastplate of righteousness. As shoes for your feet put on whatever will make you ready to proclaim the gospel of peace. With all of these, take the shield of faith. . . . Take the helmet of salvation, and the sword of the Spirit, which is the word of God" (vv. 14–17). Thus clothed, the believer is to "pray in the Spirit at all times in every prayer and supplication" (v. 18). While unstated, the assumption is that dressed as for battle with the gifts of God, one will be able to preserve against the powers that are death dealers.[1]

Responding to the Text

As I write, the Iraq war is raging on, with no end in sight. It makes the reading of this text, with all of the military imagery, difficult. It is certainly difficult to read this text as a paradigm for the fight between God and evil, which is how many religious circles too often interpret this war of the United States in Iraq. Perhaps by the time you read this text, there will be a little more space between such harmful characterizations that now exist and the reality of the world surrounding our congregational settings.

If we are still in the midst of a war in Iraq, the preacher will be challenged to find a way to tease apart the rich metaphorical language for the life of faith and the reality of war that will surround the hearers. Our allegiances are not so neat. Joshua may have said to choose God or another, but our lives reveal that we live as citizens of both—the country and the church of Jesus Christ. Perhaps herein lies a fruitful approach: name the complex reality we live in, name the mistaken clarity with which sides are identified as godly and evil, name the challenges that lie before believers as they struggle to be faithful people in the world. No easy affirmations are necessary to close up this sermon, only an affirmation that the God witnessed to in Joshua, the Psalms, Ephesians, and John is a God passionately committed to God's people. What is asked of us is faithfulness, usually not found in easy false dichotomies but rather struggled with in ongoing deliberation and prayer. The sermon might well be a model of such struggle.

> WHAT IS ASKED OF US IS FAITHFULNESS, USUALLY NOT FOUND IN EASY FALSE DICHOTOMIES BUT RATHER STRUGGLED WITH IN ONGOING DELIBERATION AND PRAYER.

EPHESIANS 5:2a, 21–32 (RC)
EPHESIANS 5:21–33 (BCP)

This text has been at the heart of many difficulties for preachers and hearers of the Word alike. The invitation of wives to be "subject" to their husbands (vv. 22, 24) has, over time, too frequently been used to encourage women to return to or remain with men who are abusive and cruel. Despite this troubled history, there are some who suggest[2] that this text can be redeemed from its troubling history by listening closely to what is being said, which generally goes something like this: the relationship of husbands and wives is parallel to Christ's relationship to the church. Therefore, when the text invites, "Wives, be subject to your husbands as you are to the Lord" (v. 22), its parallel is "just as the church is subject to Christ . . ." (v. 24). No abuse is involved in this subjection, only praise and thanksgiving. Likewise, "Husbands, love your wives," and its parallel, "just as Christ loved the church and gave himself up for her . . ." (v. 25). Husbands are to love their wives as they do their own bodies, and the parallel is "just as Christ does for the church" (v. 29). While this is a more fruitful line of pursuit for the preacher, it is still appropriate to ask the question if any relationship, whether it be between wives and husbands or Christ and the church, can be helpfully understood with the language of "subjection."

The Gospel

JOHN 6:56–69 (RCL)
JOHN 6:60–69 (RC, BCP)

Interpreting the Text

Once again, the RCL text provides an opening restatement of the closing of last week's Gospel text, providing the last link between sections of the ongoing discussion of Jesus as the "bread of life": "Those who eat my flesh and drink my blood abide in me, and I in them. Just as the living Father sent me, and I live because of the Father, so whoever eats me will live because of me" (vv. 56–57). Through this whole discussion we hear only what Jesus has to say and the concerns of the religious leaders who are gathered to hear Jesus. Nowhere so far have we heard from the disciples. Not known to be a silent group, even in the Gospel of John, they have been atypically quiet through this long discussion in which Jesus' self-revelation shocks many.

> NOT KNOWN TO BE A SILENT GROUP, THE DISCIPLES HAVE BEEN ATYPICALLY QUIET THROUGH THIS LONG DISCUSSION IN WHICH JESUS' SELF-REVELATION SHOCKS MANY.

Now, in this closing section, disciples of Jesus speak up, and as we would expect, they say what most everyone else is thinking: "This teaching is difficult; who can accept it?" (v. 60). Jesus' response is direct: "Does this offend you? Then what if you were to see the Son of Man ascending to where he was before?" (vv. 61–62). According to Ray Brown, Jesus' reference to ascension here includes both his crucifixion and resurrection[3] (there is no ascension of Jesus in the book of John). The disciples' confusion now is a foretaste of the fear and confusion that will overwhelm them following the crucifixion of Jesus (John 20:19ff.). Jesus appears to know that the path he is taking as "the bread of life given for the sake of the world" will be more than some of his followers will be able to bear, because he continues, "The words that I have spoken to you are spirit and life. But among you there are some who do not believe" (vv. 63-64). Jesus' words, "There are some of you who do not believe," signal Jesus' knowledge that some will fall away and that one will betray him (v. 64).

And indeed, many of Jesus' followers do leave and no longer follow him (v. 66). Jesus asks the Twelve, "Do you also wish to go away?" (v. 67). In the words of our opening text for the day, "Choose this day whom you will serve." Simon Peter speaks up with an affirmation of faith and commitment: "Lord, to whom can we go? You have the words of eternal life. We have come to believe and to know that you are the Holy One of God" (vv. 68-69).

Reflecting on the Text

Looking at many of the pictures of Jesus found in Sunday school classrooms across the church—Jesus the Good Shepherd, Jesus with his arms open to little children, Jesus with his hands sublimely folded—it is easy to believe that Jesus is, in the words of the children's song, "gentle Jesus, meek and mild." We easily sentimentalize such a Jesus, and the thought of following him comes with little difficulty. Who wouldn't want to follow such a gentle, sweet soul?

In comparison, if we look at the pictures of Jesus that come out of Central and South America and in other parts of the world that have known great suffering, we see a very different kind of Jesus: one broken and bleeding, outstretched on the cross. These pictures, icons, and crucifixes can be difficult to look at for any length of time because they speak of pain, vulnerability, suffering, and death. Following this Jesus is a much riskier proposition. It means walking a path where the vulnerable, the weak, and those in pain walk. Such a path may lead to death.

THE INVITATION, THE QUESTION OF THE TEXT, IS, WILL WE CHOOSE JESUS, THE ONE WHO OFFERS HIS BODY AND BLOOD FOR THE LIFE OF OTHERS?

As in the text, some of us hurry back to the Jesus of our Sunday school classrooms, where gentleness abides. And yet the invitation, the question of the text, is, Will we choose Jesus, the one who offers his body and blood for the life of others? It's a radical posture that Jesus takes—giving himself for others, many of whom will turn away from him before he is finished speaking. Yet this is the heart of who we have been told Jesus is over the last several weeks: one who gives himself as food and drink for all who are hungry and thirsty. We want to be careful that we do not simply spiritualize Jesus' claim. While it is true that Jesus feeds spiritual hunger and quenches spiritual thirst, here Jesus goes further. He will feed with his own body and blood bodily hungers and thirsts. It is this claim, of giving himself for those who hunger and thirst, the poor of our cities and country and countries around the world, that makes the path such a dangerous one and leads finally to the cross. How do we respond to an invitation to follow such a risky path? It is only through Jesus, found in the faces and the stories of those who hunger and thirst, those who are poor among us, that we find the strength and the commitment to stay the course.

Notes

1. Read Charles L. Campbell's explanation of the "rebellious powers" in *The Word Before the Powers* (Louisville: Westminster John Knox Press, 2002), chap. 2.

2. See Carol A. Newsom and Sharon H. Ringe, eds., *Women's Bible Commentary* (Louisville: Westminster John Knox, 1998).

3. Raymond E. Brown, *The Gospel according to John I–XII*, Anchor Bible (Garden City, N.Y.: Doubleday, 1966), 296.

THIRTEENTH SUNDAY AFTER PENTECOST

SEPTEMBER 3, 2006
TWENTY-SECOND SUNDAY IN ORDINARY TIME /
PROPER 17

REVISED COMMON	EPISCOPAL (BCP)	ROMAN CATHOLIC
Deut. 4:1-2, 6-9 or Song of Sol. 2:8-13	Deut. 4:1-9	Deut. 4:1-2, 6-8
Psalm 15 or Ps. 45:1-2, 6-9	Psalm 15	Ps. 15:2-3, 3-4, 4-5
James 1:17-27	Eph. 6:10-20	James 1:17-18, 21b-22, 27
Mark 7:1-8, 14-15, 21-23	Mark 7:1-8, 14-15, 21-23	Mark 7:1-8, 14-15, 21-23

Although we have now returned to Mark for our Gospel readings, and Mark surely has a different theology than John, today's texts do carry on the concern from last week, that of life with and for God, life following the God in Jesus, affirmed in life-giving responses rather than empty practices.

FIRST READING

DEUTERONOMY 4:1-2, 6-9 (RCL)
DEUTERONOMY 4:1-9 (BCP)
DEUTERONOMY 4:1-2, 6-8 (RC)

Interpreting the Text

Moses describes for the people of Israel what it means to function as a people who are defined by their relationship with God, a people who are shaped by their responses to God, a people ready to leave the wilderness and enter the land God promised them. Moses says, "Give heed to the statutes and ordinances that I am teaching you to observe" (v. 1); "You must neither add anything to what I command you nor take away anything from it" (v. 2). The people of Israel have seen how God destroyed those who followed another god (v. 3) and protected the lives of those who "held fast" to God (v. 4).

Moses continues, "See, just as the LORD my God has charged me, I now teach you statutes and ordinances for you to observe in the land that you are about to enter and occupy" (v. 5). God knows, even if the people themselves do not yet recognize it, that in order to live successfully in the place that God has prepared for them, in order to live together as people defined by their relationship with God, certain guides are required. This is a foreign concept to many of us, the Hebraic understanding of "law as gift," but it is at the heart of what Moses is getting at here. If the people are to live together successfully as God's people, they will need to be tutored, as it were, schooled in the kind of behav-

ior that reflects people in relationship with God and with each other in community. God provides the schooling that they will need. What a generous act! "For what other great nation has a god so near to it as the LORD our God is whenever we call to him? And what other great nation has

> IF THE PEOPLE ARE TO LIVE TOGETHER SUCCESSFULLY AS GOD'S PEOPLE, THEY WILL NEED TO BE SCHOOLED IN THE KIND OF BEHAVIOR THAT REFLECTS PEOPLE IN RELATIONSHIP WITH GOD AND WITH EACH OTHER IN COMMUNITY.

statutes and ordinances as just as this entire law that I am setting before you today?" (vv. 7–8). And then Moses commands them to remember what they have seen and to retell all that they have seen to their children and their children's children (v. 9).

Reflecting on the Text

The relationship between God and God's people that is laid out in this text is an intimate one. God has come through with God's promise—they are standing near the promised land. And now, before they ever enter this long-longed-for place, God, through Moses, provides the ordinances and

> THE JOURNEY THROUGH THE WILDERNESS HAS SHOWN THAT THESE ARE NOT A PEOPLE WHO DO WELL WHEN LEFT TO THEIR OWN DEVICES.

statutes that they will need in order to live in this place; ordinances that they will need to live in the promised land as God's people. Certainly, the journey through the wilderness has shown that these are not a people who do well when left to their own devices. And so God offers what is needed—these ordinances are not simply things that the people will do; they are activities that will shape who they will become as they live in the land.

It is very challenging for a preacher to share this story and not have it heard by the modern mind-set as "things one must do" in order to be a Christian believer. What is really set forth for people to wrestle with here is the notion that one doesn't have to do certain things to prove one is a Christian; rather, one who is in a living relationship with God is one who is open to being shaped by that relationship. That shaping is dynamic, continuing across the span of one's life. We are called

189

THIRTEENTH
SUNDAY
AFTER PENTECOST

ADELE STILES
RESMER

to be open to that kind of intimate relationship with God and the commitments and activities that are a result of that relationship.

RESPONSIVE READING
PSALM 15 (RCL, BCP)
PSALM 15:2-3, 3-4, 4-5 (RC)

Psalm 15 does what many of the psalms chosen to be part of the lectionary do: they reiterate in poetic form what has been heard in the Hebrew scripture reading and what may lay ahead in the Gospel reading. So, consistent with the ordinances laid out before the people of Israel as they wait to enter the promised land, this psalm asks, "O LORD, who may abide in your tent? Who may dwell on your holy hill?" (v. 1). What follows is a way of being that is consistent with those who abide with God: "those who walk blamelessly, and do what is right, and speak the truth from their heart; who do not slander with their tongue, and do no evil to their friends, nor take up a reproach against their neighbors" (vv. 2-3). Those who stand by their oath "even to their hurt" (v. 4) will never be moved (v. 5). They will remain with God.

SECOND READING
JAMES 1:17-27 (RCL)
JAMES 1:17-18, 21b-22, 27 (RC)

Interpreting the Text

Martin Luther is famously known to be one who disliked the book of James and wondered about its inclusion in the canon. Yet at least the portion of James we read today fits well within a Reformation understanding of "works": they grow out of God's prior action on our behalf.[1] "Every generous act of giving, with every perfect gift, is from above, coming down from the Father of lights. . . . In fulfillment of his own purpose he gave us birth by the word of truth, so that we would become a kind of first fruits of his creatures" (vv. 17-18). It is God who is the giver of all gifts and the one through whom we become "a kind of first fruits." With barely a pause after acknowledgment of the gifts from God, the writer moves us right into an explanation of what those first fruits look like: "Let everyone be quick to listen, slow to speak, slow to anger, for your anger does not produce God's righteousness" (v. 19); "Rid yourself of all rank growth of wickedness, and welcome with meekness the implanted word that has the power to save your souls" (v. 21).

191

THIRTEENTH
SUNDAY
AFTER PENTECOST
_____

ADELE STILES
RESMER

Following this almost introductory laying out of the theology of James—the gifts of God bear fruits in us in certain ways of being—we hear what is probably one of the best-known verses in the book, a verse I have seen engraved across the back arches of many a sanctuary or narthex: "Be doers of the word, and not hearers only." The verse actually reads, ". . . not merely hearers who deceive themselves. For if any are hearers of the word and not doers, they are like those who look at themselves in a mirror . . . and, on going away, immediately forget what they look like" (vv. 22-24).

Responding to the Text

The relationship between faith and works is one that requires the sort of careful attention with which James attends to the question. Who would argue that everything begins and ends with the actions of God, who reaches out and shares all good gifts with us, that it is only as we receive this generosity that we in a sense "become the kind of people" who cannot do anything

> THE RELATIONSHIP BETWEEN FAITH AND WORKS IS ONE THAT REQUIRES THE SORT OF CAREFUL ATTENTION WITH WHICH JAMES ATTENDS TO THE QUESTION.

but respond in love toward God and our neighbor? What easily happens is the separation of the two, and it is here that we run into trouble. When the actions of God are heralded but appear to have no relationship with who we become and how we live in the world, the claim of a relationship with God itself becomes suspect. On the other hand, if hearers are regaled with all that they are to do in order to be good Christians, any claims about gifts of God seem dishonest. It is the work of the preacher to hold these two realities together: the gifts of God that create the people of God; and the responses of God's people to these wonderful, life-giving gifts that continue to shape them into the people of God.

EPHESIANS 6:10-20 (BCP)

See the comments on the second reading for the Twelfth Sunday after Pentecost.

THE GOSPEL
MARK 7:1-8, 14-15, 21-23 (RCL, BCP, RC)

Interpreting the Text

The opening verses of the Markan text focus on the concerns of the Pharisees with the carrying out of Pharisaic laws. The laws of concern in this particular situation are these: "For the Pharisees, and all the Jews, do not eat unless they

192

THE SEASON
OF PENTECOST
─────────
ADELE STILES
RESMER

thoroughly wash their hands, . . . and they do not eat anything from the market unless they wash it; and there are also many other traditions that they observe, the washing of cups, pots, and bronze kettles" (vv. 3-4). Having already noticed that Jesus' disciples were eating without washing their hands (v. 2), contrary to their law, they ask Jesus, "Why do your disciples not live according to the traditions of the elders, but eat with defiled hands?" (v. 5)

Jesus does not respond to this question on the surface of it, but instead speaks to the broader issue that underlies Pharisaic concerns about the fulfilling of traditional laws. Jesus' response comes from Isaiah[2]: "This people honors me with their lips, but their hearts are far from me; in vain do they worship me, teaching human precepts as doctrines" (vv. 6-7). With the citing of this text, Jesus appears to want to draw a distinction between laws that are drawn up by humans, that is, traditional laws, and the laws that come from God, for he continues, "You abandon the commandment of God and hold to human tradition" (v. 8).

> HUMAN LAW IS THAT WHICH IS OUTSIDE; DIVINE LAW IS THAT WHICH IS INSIDE AND EXPRESSES ITSELF IN THE LIFE OF THE BELIEVER.

As if to reiterate this distinction in another way, Jesus says to the crowd, "There is nothing outside a person that by going in can defile, but the things that come out are what defile" (v. 15). Human law is that which is outside; divine law is that which is inside and expresses itself in the life of the believer. One can't help but remember Moses' admonition to the people of Israel that they not add or take away from the statutes and ordinances that were being given by God for their life together, a law that would shape them as individuals and as a community.

One more time, Jesus drives home the importance of the inner condition of the believer in comparison with the outward condition: "For it is from within, from the human heart, that evil intentions come: fornication, theft, murder, adultery, avarice, wickedness, deceit, licentiousness, envy, slander, pride, folly. All these evil things come from within, and they defile a person" (vv. 21-23).

Responding to the Text

In hearing this text, the words of Amos echo in my mind: "I hate, I despise your festivals, and I take no delight in your solemn assemblies" (5:21); "Take away from me the noise of your songs; I will not listen to the melody of your harps. But let justice roll down like waters, and righteousness like an ever-flowing stream" (5:23-24). Traditions that are carried out for tradition's sake alone are not pleasing to God and represent a focus on external practices, which Jesus challenges. Jesus' constant concern is with the nature of the relationship between believers and God. He appears, here in Mark, to be impatient with laws and rules made up by humans, which present themselves as being about the God-human relationship but in fact are human laws made up to distract people from the heart of the issue.

Who has not heard, "We have always done it that way," as a reason not to change some practice in the life of the congregation? Indeed, change is difficult, and few humans jump to it readily. Yet many of us end up stymied or simply tired out by referrals to the history of some practice as a reason to continue with things the way they are. Surely, what this text helps us to sort out is that we do no better if we simply want to replace one long-term practice with a newer one for the sake of change, or for the sake of popularity. One human practice or another is really of little concern—perhaps we ought to waste less energy and concern over our current-day versions of washing our hands before we eat and washing what we eat before ingesting it. What might some of those be in your engagement with leaders in your congregation?

There likely is no easy way out of this—human traditions grow deep roots into the human spirit, and in all likelihood, the more they corrupt our spirits, the harder it is for them to die. This is the reality the preacher faces. Therefore, we do well to think of preaching, teaching, and being available pastorally over a period of time when it comes to addressing the heart of this Gospel lesson. A preacher may want to do a series about the human practices that lie at the heart of congregational life and what different biblical texts say, including this text, about those practices: a word that may be difficult to hear but one that is offered pastorally and with compassion for people (ourselves included) who get caught up in the externals. Freedom from external trappings is, in fact, a word of grace, but all won't hear it that way. Teaching carries on this focus; likewise, pastoral care is available for those who are pained, even offended by such reorientation.

It is most helpful if the preacher begins to draw hearers' hearts and minds to God's concern for our relationship with the Divine that is reflected in the way we are in worship and in life when there is no major change afoot that the preacher wants done. When it is understood that we are not using the focus of this text as a pretext for what we want, the likelihood of hearers' engaging this invitation of Jesus to open ourselves to God and each other in new ways, leading to new ways of being together as church, may be transforming for individuals and congregation alike.

Notes

1. See Luther's treatise, "The Freedom of the Christian," in *Martin Luther's Basic Theological Writings*, ed. Timothy F. Lull (Minneapolis: Fortress Press, 1989), 585ff.

2. The Isaiah text used by the writer of Mark comes from the Greek text and not the original Hebrew, per Eduard Schweitzer, *The Good News according to Mark* (Atlanta: John Knox Press, 1977), 145.

193

THIRTEENTH
SUNDAY
AFTER PENTECOST

ADELE STILES
RESMER

FOURTEENTH SUNDAY AFTER PENTECOST

<small></small>

SEPTEMBER 10, 2006
TWENTY-THIRD SUNDAY IN ORDINARY TIME /
PROPER 18

REVISED COMMON	EPISCOPAL (BCP)	ROMAN CATHOLIC
Isa. 35:4-7a 　or Prov. 22:1-2, 8- 　9, 22-23	Isa. 35:4-7a	Isa. 35:4-7a
Psalm 146 　or Psalm 125	Psalm 146 　or 146:4-9	Ps. 146:7, 8-9, 9-10
James 2:1-10 (11-13), 　14-17	James 1:17-27	James 2:1-5
Mark 7:24-37	Mark 7:31-37	Mark 7:31-37

The centrality of responding to the poor, those who experience need for healing, and those normally silenced lies at the heart of today's lessons. We hear that God responds in opening the eyes of the blind (Isaiah 35) and setting the prisoners free (Psalm 146). James reminds us of Jesus' commandment, "You shall love your neighbor as yourself" (James 2). And in spectacular fashion, a Syrophoenician woman challenges even Jesus to hear and respond to the needs of one who is normally not heard (Mark 7).

FIRST READING
ISAIAH 35:4-7a (RCL, BCP, RC)

Interpreting the Text

The people of Israel have been so long in exile in Babylon that many have given up hope, hope of returning to their home, hope that their God has even remembered them and will act in a saving way on their behalf. Without a home, and without a God, many have begun to make their home in exile and to worship the gods of their captors. It is into this situation that the words of Isaiah come as a clarion call: even after all these years, God indeed has not forgotten God's people.

195

FOURTEENTH
SUNDAY
AFTER PENTECOST
———————
ADELE STILES
RESMER

And not only that, but God is acting again to bring the exiles home to the long-ago promised land (v. 4).

This saving action of God will surpass every human expectation. It is so stunning it is worth quoting at length here: "Then the eyes of the blind shall be opened, and the ears of the deaf unstopped; then the lame shall leap like a deer, and the tongue of the speechless sing for joy" (vv. 5-6). The saving acts of God include not only the changing of life for the exiles but the transformation of creation itself: "For waters shall break forth in the wilderness, and streams in the desert; the burning sand shall become a pool, and the thirsty ground springs of water" (vv. 6-7).

Reflecting on the Text

When I read this text, I am reminded of a not-infrequent struggle—it goes to the question of the experience of the absence of God in the midst of life's deepest struggles, the apparent abandonment felt at times of deep pain and loss, the silence of God in response to cries for help even in the face of death. What pastor has not thought about, prayed, and struggled with this experience with others and within themselves? The response to such struggles, for the preacher, is not so much to give a right answer to the question of "theodicy," but rather to witness to the ongoing work of God even while the experience may be one of silence and exile. Isaiah 35 gives beautiful, captivating language for the preacher to proclaim "presence" and "healing" and "saving."

Another human response in the face of pain and loss is to ask for too little of God. Our conceptions of what God can and will do for us are defined and shaped by our own experience, and so we regularly ask God for human-sized, bite-sized action, when what God is prepared to do is to respond in God-sized, larger-than-human-life action. While preachers are often cautioned to be careful about suggesting they know the mind of God (a caution not without merit), we can too easily lean in the other direction and say and expect very little of God. Isaiah challenges the preacher to stretch, to allow the language of the prophet to make its way into our hearts and minds and into our words of proclamation to those who are in need—all who come to hear a saving word from the Lord.

> WE REGULARLY ASK GOD FOR HUMAN-SIZED, BITE-SIZED ACTION, WHEN WHAT GOD IS PREPARED TO DO IS TO RESPOND IN GOD-SIZED, LARGER-THAN-HUMAN-LIFE ACTION.

RESPONSIVE READING

PSALM 146 (RCL, BCP)
PSALM 146:7, 8-9, 9-10 (RC)
PSALM 146:4-9 (BCP ALT.)

This hymn of praise begins with an invitation to sing praises to God (vv. 1-4). This beginning in praise moves the psalmist to acknowledge the futility of human abilities and then moves immediately to statements of affirmation of what God will do, can do, chooses to do for all those who are in need. Using similar language to that of Isaiah, we hear that God sets the prisoners free, opens the eyes of the blind, and lifts up those who are bowed down (v. 8). If these words sound familiar, it is likely because they are the words that form Jesus' response to John's question from prison: "Are you the one, or shall we wait for another?" (Matt. 11:5; Luke 7:22).

SECOND READING

JAMES 2:1-10 (11-13), 14-17 (RCL)
JAMES 2:1-5 (RC)

Interpreting the Text

James wants to make clear that before God there is no partiality. Those with wealth and fine clothing have nothing over those who are poor, who wear dirty clothes when they come to worship. No notice is to be made of such differences and no distinctions made when deciding who will sit where in the assembly (vv. 2-4). The gathered church is to reflect God's radical acceptance of all, and particularly God's partiality for the poor (v. 5). Then, as if to give further authority to what he is saying, he repeats the commandment given by Jesus: "You shall love your neighbor as yourself" (v. 8).

THE GATHERED CHURCH IS TO REFLECT GOD'S RADICAL ACCEPTANCE OF ALL, AND PARTICULARLY GOD'S PARTIALITY FOR THE POOR.

God's action on behalf of the poor forms the starting point for James's ongoing concern, which is that faith is intimately connected with works (v. 14). To say that one is concerned about the poor and then to do nothing on their behalf is an oxymoron in James's way of thinking (vv. 15-16). He words it this way: "Faith by itself, if it has no works, is dead" (v. 17). In the words of James's antagonist, Luther, "I will therefore give myself as Christ to my neighbor, just as Christ offered himself for me; I will do nothing in this life except that which is salutary to my neighbor, since through faith I have an abundance of all good things in Christ."[1] Faith is inseparable from acts that serve our neighbor in need.

While much of the theological argumentation that takes place about the relationship between faith and works is linear in approach, ensuring that faith comes before works, the actual living of faith and works is less linear and more cyclical. By this I mean that faith feeds works to which Jesus invites us, particularly, in James's context, loving our neighbor and caring for the poor. At the same time, when we love our neighbor and care for the poor, we meet Christ ("For I was hungry and you gave me food, I was thirsty and you gave me something to drink, I was a stranger and you welcomed me" [Matt. 25:35ff.]). This meeting of Christ renews and strengthens faith, out of which a desire to respond is deepened. And so it continues. The preacher of this text is invited to step into this ongoing relationship between faith and works and highlight for hearers how this relationship unfolds in examples from their lives and those of others in the communities in which they live and work.

> FAITH FEEDS WORKS TO WHICH JESUS INVITES US, PARTICULARLY LOVING OUR NEIGHBOR AND CARING FOR THE POOR.

JAMES 1:17-27 (BCP)

See the comments on the second reading for the Thirteenth Sunday after Pentecost.

THE GOSPEL
MARK 7:24-37 (RCL)
MARK 7:31-37 (BCP, RC)

Interpreting the Text

The opening section of this text stands out among the many others that portray Jesus' encounter with someone in need. Generally speaking, the pattern goes something like this: a person expresses a need, or someone expresses a need on behalf of another, and Jesus responds by feeding, healing, and/or raising the dead. In this encounter between Jesus and the Syrophoenician woman, the dynamics are strikingly different. It begins routinely enough. Jesus is traveling to Tyre when a "Greek" woman, of Syrophoenician origin (the literal word is *Greek* rather than *Gentile*), hears of Jesus and comes to him immediately (vv. 24-26). Her daughter is ill with a demon, and she begs Jesus to heal her daughter. This act on her part takes a great deal of courage, because she, if anyone, knows and has likely experienced the hatred of the Jews. Yet she comes to Jesus anyway. Her love for her daughter emboldens her. So far so good.

And then Jesus opens his mouth, and what we hear is not in line with his usual responses to such shows of trust and need. He replies, "Let the children be fed first, for it is not fair to take the children's food and throw it to the dogs" (v. 27). We shake our heads and say, "What?" Words of dismissal and prejudice coming out of Jesus' mouth? While this is shocking to our ears, it does remind us that Jesus was, as we proclaim, truly human as well as truly divine. His response to this woman comes out of the mouth of a first-century Jew. Not an easy thing to hear, not an easy thing to believe about Jesus. But to rob him of his response by explaining it away is to rob him of his humanness. And to explain it away is to rob us of the opportunity to see that Jesus the first-century Jew grew and changed—thanks to the repugnant Greek Syrophoenician woman.

> WHEN JESUS OPENS HIS MOUTH, WHAT WE HEAR IS NOT IN LINE WITH HIS USUAL RESPONSES TO SUCH SHOWS OF TRUST AND NEED.

We cannot know if she half-expected such a response or if she was surprised, given what she had heard about Jesus. Whatever the case, this nameless woman is not put off: "Sir, even the dogs under the table eat the children's crumbs" (v. 28). In her response, she acknowledges the reality of their ethnic differences and challenges Jesus to move beyond them. And we know that her words touched Jesus and changed him, because this time he replies in quite a different manner: "For saying that, you may go—the demon has left your daughter" (v. 29).

The second section of this text shows a very different relationship between Jesus and one who is brought to him in need of healing. This encounter proceeds as we have come to expect. The man is deaf and has an impediment in his speech—his friends beg Jesus to lay his hand on him and heal him (v. 32). Now, instead of attempting to distance himself from the man in need, as he did with the Greek woman, Jesus takes him aside, puts his fingers in his ears, spits, and touches his tongue (v. 33). Close contact, this! Jesus then looks up to heaven and cries out, "*Ephphatha*," which means, "Be opened." And the man's ears are opened and his tongue "released" (v. 35). People are astounded, telling what they have seen despite Jesus' admonition to tell no one. They say, "He even makes the deaf to hear and the mute to speak" (v. 37).[2]

Reflecting on the Text

This text offers interesting opportunities for the preacher. Falling between the two feeding miracles, first the feeding of the five thousand and later the feeding of the four thousand, such healing events could go unnoticed, feel even anticlimactic compared to the feeding of so many. Yet the writer of Mark does not seem to want these stories to get lost in the shuffle. Why else place this wonderful dialogue

199

FOURTEENTH
SUNDAY
AFTER PENTECOST
_____
ADELE STILES
RESMER

between Jesus and the Syrophoenician woman right in the middle? Hearing that Jesus responded in a very human way to this woman in need may be very unsettling for hearers who want Jesus to be divine only—interacting with and responding to the woman, and by connection to us, in the way that God can be counted on to respond. Jesus' humanness is many times a tough pill to swallow, as is our own for that matter. Surely we do spend a good deal of time covering for our human foibles, mistakes in judgment, and downright failures. A preacher assists hearers to deepen their knowledge and experience of Jesus and each other by showing Jesus' recognition of ethnic tensions and how even he is changed when confronted by a woman who will not let go of her belief that he can heal her daughter. Stretching out Jesus' humanness and his response to the challenge to grow and change provides

> HEARING THAT JESUS RESPONDED IN A VERY HUMAN WAY TO THIS WOMAN IN NEED MAY BE VERY UNSETTLING FOR HEARERS WHO WANT JESUS TO BE DIVINE ONLY.

an opening to imagine Jesus' invitation to hearers to open themselves to who they truly are, in their entirety, and to hear the invitation to be changed by the One who has been changed himself.

Another approach by the preacher might be to focus on the tenaciousness of the woman, who is initially dismissed by Jesus. She does not let go; she does not go away. She stays and engages Jesus until he agrees to heal her daughter. What might such tenaciousness look like in the lives of the hearers of this text? What might prayer, work, leisure, worship, and care of self and others look like if wrapped in this tenaciousness?

Surely tenaciousness is a part of the second section of this Gospel lesson. A man who cannot hear or speak is brought by friends to Jesus. He may not be able to get there on his own, but his friends diligently bring him and speak of his need for him. Remember, here the friends lowered their companion on a mat through the roof of a house so that he might receive healing (Mark 2:4). The preacher finds fruitful ground for a sermon that explores the many faces of faithfulness. One side is that which propels people to Jesus when they are in need, knowing that he is the true source of healing. Another side is that

> WE BECOME THE CARRIERS OF THE MAT, THE SPEAKERS FOR THOSE WHO HAVE NO VOICE, AND THE ONES WHO SPREAD THE NEWS OF WHAT WE HAVE SEEN.

which propels us to be rigorous, tireless, and committed in our actions for our friends and neighbors who on their own cannot get to the One who is the healer "of our every ill."[3] We not only go to Jesus for ourselves; we become the carriers of the mat, the speakers for those who have no voice, and the ones who spread the news of what we have seen.

Notes

1. Martin Luther, "The Freedom of the Christian," in *Martin Luther's Basic Theological Writings,* ed. Timothy F. Lull (Minneapolis: Fortress Press, 1989), 619.

2. These words echo the words from the first lesson of the day, Isaiah 35.

3. See Marty Haugen, "Healer of Our Every Ill," in *With One Voice* (Minneapolis: Augsburg Fortress, 1995), #738.

FIFTEENTH SUNDAY AFTER PENTECOST

SEPTEMBER 17, 2006
TWENTY-FOURTH SUNDAY IN ORDINARY TIME /
PROPER 19

REVISED COMMON	EPISCOPAL (BCP)	ROMAN CATHOLIC
Isa. 50:4-9a	Isa. 50:4-9	Isa. 50:4c-9a
or Prov. 1:20-33		
Ps. 116:1-9	Psalm 116	Ps. 116:1-2, 3-4,
or Psalm 19	or 116:1-8	5-6, 8-9
or Wisd. of Sol.		
7:26—8:1		
James 3:1-12	James 2:1-5, 8-10,	James 2:14-18
	14-18	
Mark 8:27-38	Mark 8:27-38	Mark 8:27-35
	or 9:14-29	

God's saving action on behalf of those who are exiled (Isaiah 50), those caught in the snares of death (Psalm 116), and those possessed by spirits (Mark 9) is affirmed, first through the words of the "servant," and later in the person of Jesus, whose messiahship is one of persecution, suffering, death, and rising (Mark 8). This kind of self-giving Messiah invites discipleship that is shaped by the cross and resurrection, discipleship that is self-giving.

FIRST READING

ISAIAH 50:4-9a (RCL)
ISAIAH 50:4-9 (BCP)
ISAIAH 50:4c-9a (RC)

Interpreting the Text

This text in Isaiah is the third of what are named "the servant songs." While there is some disagreement about the identity of the servant referred to in these texts,[1] a solid consensus suggests that the servant is Israel. And the one speaking in today's text is the Israel of the exile, on the cusp of returning home. The "servant song" of Israel develops like this: as one who has received much from the Lord God, the tongue of a teacher and an ear to listen to what is taught (vv. 4–5), the servant turns his back on those who mock and spit on him for his relationship with God (v. 6). The servant is able to take such mistreatment among his peers because God is the one who will come and "vindicate" him (v. 8). The servant challenges those who have rebuked him and ends with a resounding affirmation of his assurance of God's help.

The recitation of this relationship between the servant and the God of Israel serves to remind the whole community of Israel of their relationship with God and to assure them that God not only has not forgotten them in exile but is the One who will come and deliver them.

Reflecting on the Text

On this side of the exile event, it is easy to hear the words of assurance that God is helping and will come and vindicate those who have been away from home for so long that many have no memory of home. Well, of course, God helps and God vindicates and God returns the scattered to their homes. Yet on the other side of the exile event, while the Israelites were still living in Babylon, I wonder how difficult it was to keep clinging to such assurances, how much energy it took to turn a back to those who would taunt and strike. We know that some were not able to hold on, converting to the life and beliefs of their exiled home. The ones who were able to hold on, to cling to belief and trust in their God, did so, in part, because of the assurances that rose up in the midst of the community, even when evidence seemed to the contrary. Faith grows in just such situations.

Of course, preachers and hearers live on this side of that historic exile, but we find that we too live in experiences and times of exile, both individually and collectively. Lost employment, estranged relationships, lack of access to opportunities. How do we hold on and trust that we will be brought home? What are the words of assurance and trust that rise up in the midst of our experiences of exile that enable us to hold on, to cling to God? What else can we preachers say but "God is with us. God is coming to gather us up and to return us to the places from where we have been lost"?

WHAT ELSE CAN WE PREACHERS SAY BUT "GOD IS WITH US. GOD IS COMING TO GATHER US UP AND TO RETURN US TO THE PLACES FROM WHERE WE HAVE BEEN LOST"?

PSALM 116:1-9 (RCL)
PSALM 116 (BCP)
PSALM 116:1-2, 3-4, 5-6, 8-9 (RC)

In Jewish tradition, this psalm is one of the "Egyptian Hallel" psalms, a praise song that is sung before and after the Passover meal.[2] The psalm opens with words of gratitude for God, who has delivered the psalmist from distress (vv. 1-2). This is followed by the psalmist's affirmation that though he was caught in the snares of death, God responded and saved him (vv. 3-8). As a result of God's saving action, the psalmist now walks before God as one who is living (v. 9). The heart of the remainder of the psalm is known to many as the words of a sung offertory, found in the weekly liturgy (vv. 12-19)—an appropriate use for such words of thanksgiving, given their roots around the Passover meal.

SECOND READING
JAMES 3:1-12 (RCL)

Interpreting the Text

For the last couple of weeks, James has expressed particular concerns for the relationship of faith and works. He hammers home the point that faith without works is dead and that works without faith are folly. Today, in the end of that discussion, James makes a move to delineate more clearly exactly what one who has faith and does works looks and sounds like. He draws on wisdom literature, which is concerned in good part with right behavior and focuses on the nature of right speech. He begins by acknowledging that everyone makes mistakes in speech (vv. 1-2). Yet if we find a way to keep our speech in check, we are able to keep our whole bodies in check (vv. 2-5). As James suggests, "So also the tongue is a small member, yet it boasts of great exploits" (v. 5).

> WE ARE LEFT WITH THIS CONUNDRUM: WITH OUR TONGUES, WE BLESS GOD, AND WITH THEM WE CURSE THOSE MADE IN THE LIKENESS OF GOD.

Quick on the heels of affirming the positive nature of speech and a tongue that is held in check, James explains what happens when the tongue is let go—it is a "fire" (v. 6). It destroys all that is in its path. And so we are left with this conundrum: with our tongues, we bless God, and with them we curse those made in the likeness of God. Blessing and cursing come from the same tongue, and this ought not be so (vv. 9-10). One cannot help but think of *simul justis et peccator* (simultaneously justified and sinner). The only remedy for our inability to live in the way that we "ought," as v. 10 puts it, is the gracious mercy of God.

Reflecting on the Text

If we had not had the previous weeks' discussion of faith and works, this text could easily become an ethical directive for which we do not have the capacity to respond. Talk about a wall of frustration! You ought to contain your speech, but you can't do it. We could continue on with a whole other list of "oughts." And we might even want to do them but ultimately find out that we are incapable. Here is where ethical mandates without a prior understanding of a relationship with God are of little help. It is indeed through a living relationship with God, who accepts us, unbridled tongue and held, that we are able to be the kind of people for whom right speech becomes important. James is right: sometimes we are able, and sometime we are not successful. But we are always God's children who care about what we say and how we say it. It's not clear from the text that James would make this turn of placing attention to correct speech in the arms of God. I do believe that his linking of faith with works allows us to go there theologically and pastorally.

JAMES 2:1-5, 8-10, 14-18 (BCP)
JAMES 2:14-18 (RC)

See the comments on the second reading for the Fourteenth Sunday after Pentecost.

THE GOSPEL
MARK 8:27-38 (RCL, BCP)
MARK 8:27-35 (RC)

Interpreting the Text

This Gospel text begins with Mark's telling of Peter's confession of faith and moves immediately into one of Jesus' predictions of suffering and death. We would be wise to see that the two are deeply connected, particularly in the understanding of Mark. When Peter answers Jesus' question of who Jesus is with the response, "You are the Messiah" (v. 29), little did he know what he was saying. Misunderstanding by the disciples, even Peter, is also a hallmark of Mark's Gospel. As soon as Peter

IT IS THROUGH A LIVING RELATIONSHIP WITH GOD, WHO ACCEPTS US, UNBRIDLED TONGUE AND HELD, THAT WE ARE ABLE TO BE THE KIND OF PEOPLE FOR WHOM RIGHT SPEECH BECOMES IMPORTANT.

makes his great declaration, Jesus launches into a teaching moment, where he tells them that he going to be rejected, suffer, die, and be raised (v. 31). Indeed, Peter had not had this kind of Messiah in mind when he spoke up so quickly (something more along the line of a political deliverer would have served Peter's image), and now he rebels at what Jesus is saying will be his way of being Messiah. His fright must have been deep, because we are told that he takes Jesus aside and "rebukes" him (v. 32). How often do we hear of disciples rebuking Jesus?

But Jesus does not allow himself to be swayed by the force of Peter's response. Rather, he looks at the other disciples and says to Peter, "Get behind me, Satan! For you are setting your mind not on divine things but on human things" (v. 33). Here we have Peter who, with great commitment, has proclaimed Jesus to be "Messiah" while the others are stopped cold. They can only reiterate what they have heard others say and recite their way through a roster of prophets. This same Peter who spoke "Messiah" is now being rebuked by Jesus. The turn-around is quick and stunning. But Jesus immediately identifies the direction of Peter's thinking, a focus on human things—his friendship and loyalty to Jesus, his desire to have Jesus with him always—not thinking that his friend is going to suffer and die and be raised. No one wants that for a friend and teacher. But Jesus tells them now, and will tell them again, that it is necessary for him go along the path of suffering, death, and resurrection.

Jesus' clarity about the kind of Messiah that he is lends itself to a certain kind of discipleship—not the blind discipleship with which the text began but rather a discipleship informed by the cross and resurrection: "If any want to become my followers, let them deny themselves and take up their cross and follow me. For those who want to save their life will lose it, and those who lose their life for my sake, and for the sake of the gospel, will save it" (vv. 34–35). A life-giving Messiah who will live again draws disciples who, by giving their lives for the sake of the gospel (the news that in Jesus, God has come to save us), will gain life. It is a paradox that challenges not only the first-century hearers but hearers today as well.

> A LIFE-GIVING MESSIAH WHO WILL LIVE AGAIN DRAWS DISCIPLES WHO, BY GIVING THEIR LIVES FOR THE SAKE OF THE GOSPEL, WILL GAIN LIFE.

Reflecting on the Text

It likely will not be the last time that someone thinks he or she has it—that is, knowledge of who Jesus is and what the nature of his life and ministry is all about. Particularly for those who are well schooled in theology, whether clergy or lay—we like to believe we know who this One is. If we know, then we will not be caught in any shocking, embarrassing, powerless circumstances like Peter. Why else would we fight so hard against other faiths and traditions that understand Jesus in a

205

FIFTEENTH
SUNDAY AFTER
PENTECOST

ADELE STILES
RESMER

different way than we do? Why is it so important for us to be right if not to contain the presence and the power of Jesus in such a way that we can understand and handle? Likewise, it will not be the last time that someone who thinks he knows better finds out that he has missed the boat altogether—that is, Jesus will rebuke us for being overly concerned with human things (our getting it right—issues of power) and will tell us again the piece that really matters to Jesus: that he will be rejected, suffer, die, and be raised. About anything else, Jesus seems to exhibit little interest in this lesson, or even in this entire Gospel. He will be rejected, suffer, die, and be raised. And if this is true, then like it or not, we can only be the kind of disciples who pick up our crosses (our crosses of denial, suffering, and death, not Jesus' cross) and follow him. To do so is to embrace one of the great paradoxes of the faith: we commit our cause to One we know and understand only in part along a path that is life threatening yet ultimately life giving. And if our experience is anything like Peter's, likely as not, Jesus' identity will unfold in our lives in a way that we do not expect or necessarily even want, at least initially. In an age when religious dogmatism is having more than its day, a preacher who proclaims this One who comes to save us is likely in for a time of it. Yet it is the path in which anyone who is eager to come to know whatever one can about Jesus, and the God who comes near to us in him, will walk.

> WE COMMIT OUR CAUSE TO ONE WE KNOW AND UNDERSTAND ONLY IN PART ALONG A PATH THAT IS LIFE THREATENING YET ULTIMATELY LIFE GIVING.

MARK 9:14-29 (BCP ALT.)

Jesus' ability to heal and to free is highlighted again, this time in juxtaposition with the abilities and the faith of the disciples. While the disciples are not able to free the man's son of the spirit that has possessed him from youth, Jesus casts out the spirit that has plagued this young man after the spirit recognizes him (even the spirits know who Jesus is—this in comparison with the unknowing disciples as presented in Mark) and the boy's father makes a pronouncement of belief: "I believe; help my unbelief!" (v. 24). A challenge for the preacher is examining the relationship between faith and healing. In Mark especially the two are brought into relationship in a way that implies a direct relationship between belief and healing—this in comparison with other Gospel writers' interpretation of healing and belief.[3] The relationship of faith and healing has been misused and harmed faithful people; at the same time we do have to wrestle with what Mark wants to share about the gospel through his understanding of faith and healing.

Notes

207

FIFTEENTH
SUNDAY AFTER
PENTECOST

ADELE STILES
RESMER

1. See the text notes for 42:1-9, which discuss the identity of the servant in the servant songs in Isaiah in *The HarperCollins Study Bible NRSV* (New York: HarperCollins, 1993), 1071; and discussion of the servant songs in "The Servant of the Lord" in *The Interpreter's Dictionary of the Bible* (Nashville: Abingdon Press, 1990), 4:292–93.

2. See text notes for Psalms 113 and 116 in *The HarperCollins Study Bible NRSV*, 908–9.

3. In comparison with Mark, see Luke 5:17ff.; 7:11ff.; 9:37ff.; John 9; 11.

SIXTEENTH SUNDAY AFTER PENTECOST

SEPTEMBER 24, 2006
TWENTY-FIFTH SUNDAY IN ORDINARY TIME /
PROPER 20

REVISED COMMON	EPISCOPAL (BCP)	ROMAN CATHOLIC
Wisd. of Sol. 1:16— 2:1, 12-22 or Jer. 11:18-20 or Prov. 31:10-31	Wisd. of Sol. 1:16— 2:1 (6-11), 12-22	Wisd. of Sol. 2:12, 17-20
Psalm 54 or Psalm 1	Psalm 54 James 3:16—4:6	Ps. 54:3-4, 5, 6, 8 James 3:16—4:3
James 3:13—4:3, 7-8a		
Mark 9:30-37	Mark 9:30-37	Mark 9:30-37

God's presence and protection show up all over the place in today's lessons. God protects the righteous one in the face of the mocking and death threats of the wicked (Wisdom of Solomon 2); God protects the psalmist in the face of ruthless threats (Psalm 54); God draws near to us as we turn to God in the midst of the conflicts of our lives (James 3); and God in Jesus is present with us, continuing, time and again, to tell us who God is (Mark 9). We know that with God is the only place to be.

FIRST READING

WISDOM OF SOLOMON 1:16—2:1, 12-22 (RCL)
WISDOM OF SOLOMON 1:16—2:1 (6-11), 12-22 (BCP)
WISDOM OF SOLOMON 2:12, 17-20 (RC)

Interpreting the Text

This text develops much in the way a traditional lament evolves, although in this case it is not the faithful who are crying out but the wicked. They lament the state of their lives: "Short and sorrowful is our life, and there is no remedy when

209

SIXTEENTH
SUNDAY AFTER
PENTECOST

ADELE STILES
RESMER

a life comes to its end" (2:1). In the intervening verses, the wicked continue with declarations of invitation to use the fullness of life to their own ends, partying and drinking fine wine, as well as oppressing the righteous man and not sparing the widow (vv. 6-11). An angry lot they are! One gets the sense that even their partying and merrymaking do not bring them joy.

The wicked remain angry and vindictive. This becomes even clearer as we hear that they are lying in wait for the righteous one and plan to harm him. The description of the suffering that is to come to the righteous one is based on the fourth "servant song" in Isaiah 52 and follows a development similar the other servant songs: a picture of the mocking, oppression, and suffering the servant will receive at the hands of those who despise him, followed by a statement of the servant's vindication by God. The wicked say, "He professes to have knowledge of God, and calls himself a child [servant] of the Lord. He became to us a reproof of our thoughts; the very sight of him is a burden to us" (vv. 13-15). Further, they mock the servant's claim that God is his Father and plan to test him. After all, if indeed God is the servant's father, then God will come and save him (vv. 17-18). They insult and torture him and finally condemn him to death. This is the reasoning of the wicked, but they are blinded by their own wickedness and do not know "the

> THIS TEXT'S ADAPTATION OF A SERVANT SONG, AS WELL AS SERVANT SONGS IN GENERAL, PROVIDES THE TEMPLATE FOR THE PASSION OF JESUS.

secret purposes of God" (vv. 21-22). If this progression in the treatment of the servant and the language to describe what is done to the servant sounds very familiar, it ought to be no surprise. This text's adaptation of a servant song, as well as servant songs in general, provides the template for the passion of Jesus. While the writer of Wisdom would have had no such thought, the writers of the Gospels would have known the servant songs well, and it would not have been difficult to see Jesus as the ultimate righteous man and the servant of God who is spoken of here.

Reflecting on the Text

If we were simply to pay attention to the weight of this text, we would have to say that it is heavy with the activities of the wicked. Almost the entire text gives voice to their dissatisfaction, anger, and rebuke of anyone in their wake who seems vulnerable. They seek out the "righteous one," and we hear in great detail of their destructive plan for him.

One almost gets the picture of a roving gang, eating and drinking whatever they can find, using whatever they find to their own benefit, and belittling and beating up on those who cross their path—a dark, frightening picture. Some of our parishioners live in exactly these kinds of circumstances, where the streets are not safe and they are targets when they go outside their doors. Drug dealers and gang members shoot up neighborhoods, hitting and sometimes killing innocent bystanders. For many in the country and some in our pews, the picture painted by Wisdom is a familiar one. The preacher in such circumstances knows not to diminish the weight and darkness of a text that reflects the reality in which these people live. And the preacher knows well the importance of not ending in that darkness, because indeed, that is not the final word—just as the servant knows that God will protect him, so too the hearers of this text are held up, reaffirmed in their faith that God will protect them. Protection comes for all from God through the now-living Christ who conquered the death that lay in wait for him. Death has no power over those who trust God. Hearers can live their lives without fear and live their faith ferociously, as ones whose lives have been reclaimed.

> PROTECTION COMES FOR ALL FROM GOD THROUGH THE NOW-LIVING CHRIST WHO CONQUERED THE DEATH THAT LAY IN WAIT FOR HIM.

JEREMIAH 11:18-20 (RCL ALT.)

Jeremiah's life is threatened, and this brief text encapsulates a brief lament that he submits to the Lord, whom he challenges to protect him. It is through the Lord, in fact, that Jeremiah even finds out that his life is threatened. He did not know that "they devised schemes, saying, 'Let us destroy the tree with its fruit, let us cut him off from the land of the living, so that his name will no longer be remembered!'" (v. 19). Once aware of these life-threatening schemes, Jeremiah invites God to bring "retribution" upon them—bring them what they are due—because Jeremiah has committed his cause to God (v. 20). In this text, as well in the Wisdom text, it appears clear that to commit one's cause to God is to invite a certain amount of hostility and even to have one's life threatened. It is only because one is committed to God that facing such hardship, suffering, and pain is tenable.

RESPONSIVE READING

PSALM 54 (RCL, BCP)
PSALM 54:3-4, 5, 6, 8 (RC)

This prayer for vindication fits well within the emphases of the day's texts. Its movement is rather straightforward, allowing it to contain deeply riveting dialogue. In vv. 1 and 2, the psalmist cries out to God to hear and to vindicate; v. 3 provides the reason for the cries for help—"The insolent have risen against me, the ruthless seek my life"; vv. 4-5 affirm the psalmist's belief that God can and will provide help; and the remaining verses give thanks to God who has heard and responded to this prayer. Deep cries for help in the face of threat are wed to confidence in God's ability to protect and thanksgiving that indeed God has already done so.

211

SIXTEENTH
SUNDAY AFTER
PENTECOST

ADELE STILES
RESMER

SECOND READING

JAMES 3:13—4:3, 7-8a (RCL)
JAMES 3:16—4:6 (BCP)
JAMES 3:16—4:3 (RC)

Interpreting the Text

James contrasts two kinds of wisdom: a wisdom that is from above and therefore is "full of mercy and good fruits" (v. 17), and a wisdom that is "earthly, unspiritual, [and] devilish" (v. 15). As if providing us with another angle from which to view the actions of the wicked, in comparison with the wise, James puts forth his argument clearly. Those who have bitter envy and selfish ambition are lacking in wisdom from above, and their lives will be full of "disorder and wickedness of every kind" (v. 16). This does not appear to be a threat on James's part; rather, it is a descriptive statement of what likely is already the case. Imagine the wicked protagonists in our opening lesson for the day and you'll get the picture. One need not threaten disorder; the wicked are already living it.

In comparison, wisdom from above exhibits itself in different attributes. It is "peaceable, gentle, willing to yield, full of mercy and good fruits, without a trace of partiality or hypocrisy" (v. 17). We might argue that such fine attributes do not stand a chance in the face of the wicked, and we would likely be right. The wicked turn even good to their distorted benefit.

James now turns his concerns to conflict in the community and what lies at its heart. He says, "You want something and do not have it; so you commit murder" (v. 2). Further, "you covet something and cannot obtain it; so you engage in disputes and conflicts" (v. 3). We ask for the wrong things and therefore do not receive. We are too wed to the things of this world, when it is God to whom we are to turn (vv. 3-5). Finally, all—the wicked, the wise, and those who are wed to the things of this world—are thrown back into the arms of God. We are told, "Draw near to God; and [God] will draw near to you" (v. 8).

Reflecting on the Text

James continues to express his concern for right living, making a case for "wisdom from above" in comparison with the turmoil of earthly wisdom and conflict in community. Those preachers who know themselves and their people will find that this is an easy sell. That is, we know what our lives are like when wrapped up in bitter envy and selfish ambition. We're a mess. We become bitter, lonely people. Ditto when it comes to conflict with others due to their having things we want—and so we go after them, dust flying, conflict raging, both in the church and in our lives outside church doors. There's no use in pretending that we are above such things. It's just too common among us for anyone to play naïve. Thanks be to God that we are reminded at the same time that drawing near to God is the only place to be as we struggle in the face of these human realities. Being within arm's length of God transforms and heals us and the messes we create. We will hear a similar recognition in the Gospel when the disciples know, in the midst of everything else they don't know, that Jesus is the only place to be.

> BEING WITHIN ARM'S LENGTH OF GOD TRANSFORMS AND HEALS US AND THE MESSES WE CREATE.

THE GOSPEL
MARK 9:30-37 (RCL, BCP, RC)

Interpreting the Text

Jesus tells the disciple a second time of his coming death and resurrection, saying, "The Son of Man is to be betrayed into human hands, and they will kill him, and three days after being killed, he will rise again" (vv. 30-31). It goes without saying that the disciples do not understand what Jesus is saying any better than the first time he told them. As if to drive home the reality of the disciples' lack of understanding, Mark follows Jesus' prediction with a brief story in travelogue form.

Jesus and the disciples go to Capernaum. Along the road there has been some heated discussion that Jesus has overheard. Indeed, when asked, they admit that they have been arguing about who is the greatest among them (vv. 33-34). After just having heard of Jesus' pending betrayal, death, and resurrection, one might think that such jostling for position would seem a rather moot point. Mark's point is clear: they are indeed in the dark. So Jesus tries again: "Whoever wants to be first must be last of all and servant of all" (v. 35). And then as if to show them, he takes a little child in his arms and tells the disciples that whoever welcomes one little one like this child (no positional power has this one), welcomes Jesus, and not only welcomes Jesus but welcomes the God who sent him. We are not told how the disciples respond to this further attempt both in words and in action to explain the kind of Messiah Jesus is. Perhaps the lack of any response by the disciples on Mark's part tells us what he wants us to know.

We are a stubborn lot. Once we get an idea into our heads, we have a hard time getting it out. I'm not quite sure why this is, except that once we have made a commitment to an idea, it rapidly becomes ours and we easily wrap our identity up with that idea—right or wrong or in between. I say this to remind us, just in case we are about to forget, that we can be a bunch of slow learners when it comes to accepting a new idea or an idea that challenges our view of things. We hang on to what we believe for dear life, even if it may lead to our dear death. Therefore, we ought not get too disgusted with the disciples just yet. They are still struggling mightily and apparently losing in their attempts to grasp what Jesus is trying to tell them. You have to give them this: they're still with Jesus and they're still listening, even though they cannot hear. An interesting approach for a preacher of this text might well be to give up beating up on the disciples and lift up their tenacious presence with Jesus when they really don't have a clue what he is talking about. They must know that there is something about this Jesus, even if they don't have it all clear in their heads, that makes it impossible to do anything but stay and listen to him. They keep talking with him, even when they get it wrong.

Now that is no small thing. We normally don't like to hang around places where we repeatedly are told we're not getting it or we're getting it wrong, where our confusion or lack of understanding is brought up to us repeatedly. As someone said to me one time, "I do what I'm good at," in response to my question asking what he liked to do. In comparison, it appears that the disciples liked to stay with One they did not understand, and they stayed even when they were reminded that they weren't very good at getting what Jesus was trying to tell them. Regardless of what will come down the road, the fact is that they stay at this time when it might have been easier to leave. Might there be gospel in this for preachers and hearers alike? We don't have to get it right; we don't have to understand in order to stay. We stay as the disciples stayed, because we know that Jesus is the only place worth being.

> IT APPEARS THAT THE DISCIPLES LIKED TO STAY WITH ONE THEY DID NOT UNDERSTAND, AND THEY STAYED EVEN WHEN THEY WERE REMINDED THAT THEY WEREN'T VERY GOOD AT GETTING WHAT JESUS WAS TRYING TO TELL THEM.

SEVENTEENTH SUNDAY
AFTER PENTECOST

OCTOBER 1, 2006
TWENTY-SIXTH SUNDAY IN ORDINARY TIME /
PROPER 21

REVISED COMMON	EPISCOPAL (BCP)	ROMAN CATHOLIC
Num. 11:4-6, 10-16, 24-29	Num. 11:4-6, 10-16, 24-29	Num. 11:25-29
or Esth. 7:1-6, 9-10; 9:20-22		
Ps. 19:7-14	Psalm 19 or 19:7-14	Ps. 19:8, 10, 12-13, 14
or Psalm 124		
James 5:13-20	James 4:7-12 (13—5:6)	James 5:1-6
Mark 9:38-50	Mark 9:38-43, 45, 47-48	Mark 9:38-43, 45, 47-48

God's abundance, which was with us as we began this section of Pentecost, remains with us to the end. God provides seventy members of the community to assist Moses and then goes on to feed the people (Numbers 11). God's bounty in the created order and in the gift of the Law is celebrated in Psalm 19. God in Jesus invites us into and enables us to join in a discipleship that is inclusive, attentive to the vulnerable, insightful, and capable of sacrifice (Mark 9).

FIRST READING
NUMBERS 11:4-6, 10-16, 24-29 (RCL, BCP)
NUMBERS 11:25-29 (RC)

Interpreting the Text

While the stories of the people of Israel complaining (or "murmuring") in the wilderness are well known, especially within the book of Exodus,[1] they are perhaps less well remembered in the book of Numbers. Chapter 11 tells of the people's unhappiness during their journey from Sinai to the Jordan, coupled with God's ongoing, faithful response. Our narrative today takes that standard development of people complaining, Moses interceding, and God responding, and gives

215

SEVENTEENTH
SUNDAY
AFTER PENTECOST
——————
ADELE STILES
RESMER

it a bit of a twist. It begins with the "rabble" (a group within the community) craving and the people weeping because their hungry stomachs remember the fish and the meat they ate in Egypt; now they have "only" manna on which to feed (vv. 4-6). The Lord hears their weeping and becomes "very angry." In comparison with other times, when Moses takes the people's cause to the Lord, this time Moses sounds frustrated and angry himself. He lashes out at God, decrying the day he ever became the leader of these people. "Why have I not found favor in your sight, that you lay the burden of all this people on me?" (v. 11). After all, he hasn't given birth to these people (is he intentionally reminding God that it is God who gave birth to "the people of Israel" through his act of liberation from Egypt?), and he has no way to provide for them on his own. It's too much.

God listens to and hears Moses—perhaps God is persuaded by Moses' reminder of the parentage of the whole people of Israel—and tells him to gather seventy leaders from within the community around the tent (the place outside the community where God comes and speaks to those gathered). God then comes down in a cloud and takes some of the spirit that is in Moses and puts it on the seventy who are gathered (vv. 21-25). When the spirit rests on them, they prophesy. At the same time, the spirit rests on two who are not part of the gathering at the tent, and they begin to prophesy as well. The people ask Moses to stop them, but Moses responds, "Would that all the LORD's people were prophets, and that the LORD would put his spirit on them!" (vv. 26-29). Moses recognizes that the prophesying of these two, along with those who were gathered at the tent of meeting, is God's response to Moses' cry for assistance in carrying the burden of the people.

Reflecting on the Text

It is not uncommon for clergy and lay leaders in the church to feel like the whole weight of leadership falls to them. We know what it's like to feel overwhelmed by demands. We know laypeople whom we cannot imagine being without. Their commitment and ministry on behalf of the whole community seem to be what holds the ministry of the church together. We know, too, of the complaints of many such people who, after a time, feel like they are burning out, like they no longer have the energy to continue to provide the leadership that they have been giving. Some become angry because others will not step up to the plate and relieve them of some of their responsibility. Sometimes we are those angry leaders.

When we and other leaders in the church become angry and weighed down and keep it to ourselves, we become bitter and cynical. Ministry turns to dust over time. However, there is another way: like our ancestor in the faith, Moses, we are invited to move outside of ourselves and call on God, lay our case before God, and then behave as though God has heard us. God does provide. New leaders do arise where none have been seen before. Some ministries go and other ones begin as new people are invited and empowered both by our invitation and by the power of the Spirit of God. There is no need for us to go it alone. God provides what we need.

RESPONSIVE READING

PSALM 19:7-14 (RCL, BCP ALT.)
PSALM 19 (BCP)
PSALM 19:8, 10, 12-13, 14 (RC)

The first part of Psalm 19 proclaims the "glory of God" (v. 1) in all of the creation. "The firmament proclaims his handiwork"; "There is no speech, nor are there words; . . . yet their voice goes out through all the earth"; and, "In the heavens he has set a tent for the sun, which comes out like a bridegroom from his wedding canopy" (vv. 1-5). The second portion of the psalm proclaims the blessings of the Law. Within the Hebraic mind-set, Law (Torah) is a gift that is given by God and is known in creation and in the living in community in the midst of creation. Therefore, while these two portions of the psalm address distinct aspects of God's activity, they function as a whole when we recognize how the glory of God becomes known: through creation and through God's law. Hear the words extolling the Law through the lens of God's glory: "The law of the LORD is perfect, reviving the soul; the decrees of the LORD are sure, making wise the simple" (v. 7); "The ordinances of the LORD are true and righteous altogether. More to be desired are they than gold, even much fine gold; sweeter also than honey, and drippings of the honeycomb" (vv. 9-10). Even when the Law provides warning, it is a gift (vv. 11-13). After acknowledging God's gift in creation and the Law, the psalmist closes with a prayer that is well known as one often offered by preachers before they begin to preach: "Let the words of my mouth and the meditation of my heart be acceptable to you, O LORD, my rock and my redeemer" (v. 14).

> LIKE OUR ANCESTOR IN THE FAITH, MOSES, WE ARE INVITED TO MOVE OUTSIDE OF OURSELVES AND CALL ON GOD, LAY OUR CASE BEFORE GOD, AND THEN BEHAVE AS THOUGH GOD HAS HEARD US.

JAMES 5:13-20 (RCL)
JAMES 4:7-12 (13—5:6) (BCP)
JAMES 5:1-6 (RC)

Interpretation of the Text

In the string of texts in James, we hear his ongoing concern for life in community, addressing that which lifts up life and that which breaks it down. The opening of James's claims begins with a restatement from last week of the foundation of his instruction: "Submit yourselves therefore to God. . . . Draw near to God, and [God] will draw near to you" (4:7-8); "Resist the devil, and he will flee from you" (v. 7). Once individuals and the community resist the devil and draw near to God, and God draws near to them, they are able to hear the instruction that follows: "Humble yourselves before the Lord, and he will exalt you" (v. 10); "Do not speak evil against one another" (v. 11); for "there is one lawgiver and judge who is able to save and to destroy. So who, then, are you to judge your neighbor?" (v. 12).

James's instruction now focuses on what breaks down life in community. He addresses those in the community with riches. He boldly tells the rich that their riches will rot and their clothes will be moth-eaten. Gold and silver will rust and eat their flesh like fire (5:1-3). The harvesters who have worked for them and have been cheated by them cry out to God and are heard (v. 4). The rich have lived in luxury and have condemned and murdered the righteous one who does not resist them (vv. 5-6). While James does not say how the wealthy are to live in community, it is safe to

> JAMES'S PASSION FOR COMMUNITY, LIVED IN THE BELIEF IN GOD AND LIVING OUT THAT BELIEF THROUGH WORKS ON BEHALF OF OTHERS, FIRES BRIGHTLY FROM THE BEGINNING OF JAMES TO THE END.

assume that the opposite of what he has just laid out is something like how he sees wealth working to uplift the community: fair and equitable treatment of workers, distribution of their wealth rather than the hoarding of it for themselves.

Finally, James turns to that which builds up community. "Are any among you suffering? They should pray" (v. 13). Those who are cheerful should sing songs of praise; the sick should call the elders of the church and have them pray over them (v. 14). Prayer will save the sick and forgive sins. Therefore, believers are to confess to one another and pray for one another, because the prayers of the righteous are "powerful and effective" (vv. 15-16). When they bring back a member of the community who has wandered off, they save them (v. 17).

James's passion for community, lived in the belief in God and living out that belief through works on behalf of others, fires brightly from the beginning of James to the end. In a time when so much emphasis is placed on singling out individuals for condemnation or lauding their behavior based on subjective and inconsistent grounds, when we hold ourselves and our self-worth to criteria such as "achievement, affluence, and appearance,"[2] we would do well to learn about the nature of community, grounded in belief in a loving and merciful God and defined by loving acts for our neighbors. In such a community we lift each other up for the sake of the community, and we admonish each other for the sake of community. Such a change of emphasis comes only with a reschooling of sorts: blessed by God to see ourselves as people created with the desire for community in our very bones (Genesis 2); and with the help of God, committing ourselves to the activities that build up life in community.

The Gospel
MARK 9:38-50 (RCL)
MARK 9:38-43, 45, 47-48 (BCP, RC)

Interpreting the Text

We don't know if it's because of the disciples' lack of understanding or in spite of it that Jesus follows his predictions of suffering and death with a brief series of "sayings" that are invitations to ongoing discipleship. The sayings run together like pearls on a string, each having its own integrity but the whole creating a fuller picture of a life of discipleship. First, John expresses concern that someone else is casting out demons in Jesus' name and tells Jesus that they tried to stop him because he was not one of them. Jesus in turn encourages the disciples to think less protectively and more inclusively: "Whoever is not against us is for us" (v. 40).

> JESUS CHALLENGES DISCIPLES TO AVOID ACTIVITIES THAT WILL CAUSE THEM TO STUMBLE, TO OFFEND.

Jesus continues by saying that if anyone causes a little one[3] who believes in him to stumble,[4] it would be better if that one had a millstone tied around his or her neck and was "thrown into the sea" (v. 42). Jesus invites the disciples to be attentive to the vulnerable among them.

Jesus challenges disciples to avoid activities that will cause them to stumble, to offend. In quick succession, he says, "If your hand causes you to stumble, cut it off"; "And if your foot causes you to stumble, cut it off"; "And if your eye causes you to stumble, tear it out" (vv. 43–47). It is better, says Jesus, that one enter the kingdom of God without an offending part than to end up in hell because of participating in offending behavior.

219

SEVENTEENTH
SUNDAY
AFTER PENTECOST
———
ADELE STILES
RESMER

He closes these sayings about discipleship with a final word. In v. 49, some ancient manuscripts say, "And every sacrifice will be salted with salt."[5] The naming of sacrifice as part of the life of a disciple of Jesus picks up an emphasis that Jesus has made earlier (following his first prediction of suffering and death in 8:31), that discipleship of Jesus includes sacrifice. It is only through the power of Jesus' resurrection and the giving of the Spirit that disciples and those who come after are able to follow such a path of discipleship.

Reflecting on the Text

Jesus' description of discipleship that is inclusive, attentive to the vulnerable, and diligent in recognizing those things that will lead one "to stumble" or "to offend" requires a certain degree of self-awareness and self-honesty and remains a good clarion call for us today. This is said in full awareness of the false dichotomies that are presented to believers: either one focuses on individual behavior and goes about rooting out anything that offends the group in the name of Jesus, or anything goes. Neither

> THE PREACHER'S INVITATION IS TO A DISCIPLESHIP THAT IS INCLUSIVE, THAT ATTENDS TO THE VULNERABLE, AND IS SELF-AWARE NOT FOR ITS OWN SAKE BUT FOR THE SAKE OF DISCIPLESHIP ITSELF.

picks up the nuance that in which Jesus is inviting us to participate. Preachers have the wonderful task of offering an invitation to discipleship that is neither parochial nor irrelevant, followed by a promise. The invitation is to a discipleship that is inclusive, that attends to the vulnerable, and that is self-aware not for its own sake but for the sake of discipleship itself. The invitation also acknowledges that this discipleship brings "sacrifice" with it; we do not come away unscathed.

The promise is this: this kind of discipleship is possible, even desirable, because Jesus makes it possible. Jesus himself carries out a ministry that is inclusive, attentive to the vulnerable, free of activities that would cause him to stumble, embodying sacrifice throughout his ministry and in his death, finally rising to new life in God. Augustine had it right: "Our hearts are restless 'til they rest in thee." It is Jesus, through living example and living invitation, who creates both the longing and the possibility for this kind of discipleship that brings us to rest with God.

Notes

1. See also Exod. 15:22—16:36.

2. Marcus Borg uses these three "A's" to describe current cultural norms in *Meeting Jesus Again for the First Time* (New York: HarperCollins, 1994), 87.

3. Since Jesus is speaking to the disciples about the nature of discipleship, he may be speaking about other believers or of "little ones" just as he says. Neither interpretation alters the sense of the saying, which focuses on ones who are vulnerable.

4. In all the uses of the word "stumble" that follow in this passage, the Greek word is *skandalizo*, which carries with it the connotation of "causing offense." Jesus is directing the disciples not to do anything that will lead others or themselves into activities that will be offensive to their identities as disciples of Jesus.

5. See text notes for Mark 9:49 in *The HarperCollins Study Bible NRSV* (New York: HarperCollins, 1993), 1936.

EIGHTEENTH SUNDAY AFTER PENTECOST

OCTOBER 8, 2006
TWENTY-SEVENTH SUNDAY IN ORDINARY TIME /
PROPER 22

REVISED COMMON	EPISCOPAL (BCP)	ROMAN CATHOLIC
Gen. 2:18-24	Gen. 2:18-24	Gen. 2:18-24
or Job 1:1; 2:1-10	Psalm 8	Ps. 128:1-2, 3, 4-5, 6
Psalm 8 or Psalm 26	or Psalm 128	
Heb. 1:1-4; 2:5-12	Heb. 2:(1-8) 9-18	Heb. 2:9-11
Mark 10:2-16	Mark 10:2-9	Mark 10:2-16
		or 10:2-12

FIRST READING
GENESIS 2:18-24 (RCL, BCP, RC)

Interpreting the Text

As the text opens, only one human being exists—whom we typically call Adam but whose meaning in Hebrew is something like "earth creature" (one made from the earth) and does not necessarily imply male gender. When the text says, "It is not good that [the earth creature] should be alone," the text means that relationship is essential to human identity (Gen. 2:18). The term "helper" does not imply subordination, for the Hebrew *ezer* ("helper") carries no hierarchical status but implies that the earth creature needs others to carry out God's purposes. Indeed, the term *ezer* sometimes refers to God helping people (as in Ps. 121:1-2). The NRSV captures the spirit of the Hebrew by speaking of the helper as the earth creature's "partner" (Gen. 2:18, 20).

The partnership of the earth creature with the animals is insufficient (Gen. 2:19-20). God causes the earth creature to sleep, thus reminding the reader that the earthling had no role in shaping this partner; the partner is God's gracious gift. Commentators today almost universally point out that the making of the second human being from the rib does not imply secondary status. Rather, it indicates that this new person is made not from the dust but from the same stuff as the first (2:21-22). Only when there are two human beings created for partnership does gender identity appear explicitly in the text (2:23), and even then mutuality between them is indicated in the interrelatedness of their names *ishshah* (woman) and *ish* (man). Indeed, so responsive are they to one another that they are called "one flesh," a designation not only of sexual intimacy but of the fact that each is affected by what happens to the other (2:24).

Responding to the Text

Genesis 2:4—3:24 moves from the shaping of the world (Gen. 2:4-25), through disobedience (3:1-7), to the curse of human beings and the earth (3:14-21), with the result that human beings are expelled from Eden (3:22-24). Genesis 2:18-24 pictures the relationship of woman and man as God intended it and before it was damaged by disobedience and curse. This motif is key to Mark 10:2-16 (discussed below).

A sermon focused on Gen. 2:18-24 might explore the nature of the relationship between women and men in Christian community. Such a sermon should emphasize that equality for women is not simply an assertion of political correctness but is theologically warranted.

The contemporary stir around "creationism" in school curricula suggests that this might be an opportune moment for the preacher to take up how Christians can interpret the creation of the world. Still another sermon could take its cue from the fact that the animals were created initially not as food for human beings but as helpers (though not fully partners in the sense of human beings). Only in Gen. 9:2-5 were human beings authorized to eat animals; until that time we were vegetarian. A preacher might explore the implications for diet, clothing, and the use of the environment that result from thinking of animals as partners with the human family.

> A PREACHER MIGHT EXPLORE THE IMPLICATIONS FOR DIET, CLOTHING, AND THE USE OF THE ENVIRONMENT THAT RESULT FROM THINKING OF ANIMALS AS PARTNERS WITH THE HUMAN FAMILY.

JOB 1:1; 2:1-10 (RCL ALT.)

Interpreting the Text

The book of Job is one of the most difficult to interpret in the whole Bible; indeed, there are almost as many interpretations of Job as interpreters.[1] Moreover, the story of Job is one interpretive unit. To preach from any single text, one must deal with the whole story. A minister should regard a single pericope as an entry into the whole.

One reason the book of Job is interpreted so many ways is that we do not know the circumstances that prompted its writing. For these next four weeks, I focus on one aspect of the book: as a response to deuteronomic theology. To over-simplify, a central tenet of deuteronomism is that obedience to the instructions (laws) of the covenant brings about blessing, while disobedience results in curse (for instance, Deut. 27:1—28:68). In the deuteronomic worldview, blessing and curse often involve (but are not exhausted by) material dimensions such as family, land, and animals. The book of Job objects to this way of thinking, prompting biblical scholar Jon L. Berquist to call Job "literature of dissent."[2]

As the book begins, Job's affluence leads us to assume that Job is obedient and blessed. The hearers know that the collapse of Job's life is not divine curse resulting from Job's sin but the outcome of God's allowing Satan (who in the book of Job is viewed as a member of God's court) to experiment with whether Job would honor God even if material prosperity disappeared. In 1:13-19, Satan destroys Job's livestock, servants, and children. In today's reading, Satan inflicts "loathsome sores" on Job (2:7-8).

Responding to the Text

Given the fact that today's text only raises the question that is the focus of the speeches of chapters 3:1—42:6, it is hard to imagine preaching a sermon on today's reading alone. It may be enough for this sermon—as the beginning of a four-week series on Job—to raise the issue and for subsequent sermons to deal with the substance of the responses in the book of Job, as well as the preacher's own theological response. If so, a preacher might help the congregation recall circumstances in today's world that raise questions similar to those of Job's world. The preacher could ask, "How is God related to such occurrences?"

If such an approach does not fit a congregation, a preacher might use the lection for today as a jumping-off point into the whole narrative of Job. The preacher could then summarize the story of Job and the issues raised by the book and offer a perspective regarding God's relationship to obedience and disobedience, blessing and curse, and the suffering of the innocent.

The book of Job brings a voice into a contemporary theological conversation that many preachers will welcome. For this volume rejects the notion that suffering is necessarily the result of sin and that material success necessarily points to faithfulness. The truth is that sometimes innocent people suffer. Of course, a preacher needs to be honest. Sometimes sinners prosper, and sometimes sin does bring about suffering. For example, abusing one's body with alcohol causes the body to deteriorate.

> THE BOOK OF JOB REJECTS THE NOTION THAT SUFFERING IS NECESSARILY THE RESULT OF SIN AND THAT MATERIAL SUCCESS NECESSARILY POINTS TO FAITHFULNESS.

The book of Job occasions haunting questions. Does God really have the absolute power depicted in this text such that God either directly causes or allows

223

EIGHTEENTH
SUNDAY
AFTER PENTECOST

RONALD J.
ALLEN

everything that happens? Does God really allow other beings (such as Satan) to experiment with people? Does God cause (or allow) bad things to happen to people without reason? In the end, I think we need a fuller and more positive theological interpretation of these matters than we find in the book of Job, but such questions are a great place to start.

RESPONSIVE READING

PSALM 8 (RCL, BCP)
PSALM 128 (BCP ALT.)
PSALM 128:1-2, 3, 4-5, 6 (RC)

The exuberant Psalm 8 celebrates God as the living creator and sovereign of all things and highlights the human being as a little lower than the divine being(s) or the angels, but still as the crown of creation to whom God has given dominion over the world. The preacher would want to remind the congregation that dominion does not mean freedom to exploit the world but, according to Gen. 1:26-27, responsibility to help the various elements of creation live together in covenantal relationship so that all are blessed. This psalm appears today because Heb. 2:6-7 quotes vv. 4-6. However, Hebrews interprets the psalm in a different direction.

Psalm 128 emphasizes that those who live according to God's purposes will be "happy," that is, blessed. The text itself focuses largely upon males as blessed (and women as instruments to blessing). The psalm lures its hearers into living covenantally with God and with one another to share in a life of blessing. A sermon could transcend the male bias in the text and invite women and men into covenantal life aiming toward blessing.

PSALM 26 (RCL ALT.)

This psalmist has evidently been falsely charged of wrongdoing in a specific (though unnamed) instance by people who are wicked. The psalm pleas for God to vindicate the psalmist because the psalmist has "walked with integrity," that is, has been faithful to God's purposes. Indeed, without such vindication, the speaker fears being condemned and "swept away with the sinners and bloodthirsty." The psalm thus struggles with one of the underlying questions of the book of Job: the undeserved suffering of the innocent.

HEBREWS 1:1-4; 2:5-12 (RCL)
HEBREWS 2:(1-8) 9-18 (BCP)
HEBREWS 2:9-11 (RC)

Interpreting the Text

Hebrews is likely a sermon employing sophisticated first-century rhetorical ele-ments.[3] In Hebrews, we hear a preacher pleading a case with a congregation. The makeup and circumstances of the congregation are debated.[4] I follow L. K. K. Dey in thinking that Hebrews was written to a congregation who shared the same world of thought found in the Alexandrian Jewish author Philo (15 B.C.E.–50 C.E.).[5]

In Philo, religious existence is divided into two spheres. The realm of perfec-tion (much like Plato's world of forms) is the arena wherein people have unmedi-ated access to God and full participation in the gifts of God. In the lower realm, where human beings live, we have inferior copies. The unperfected have knowl-edge of perfection only through intermediaries who perform similar functions but go by different names. In this use of language, the designation "intermediary" does not have the positive function that it often does in later Christian theology, but refers to beings who are second class and practices that cannot lead to perfection. The goal of the religious life is to leave imperfect existence where incomplete religious knowledge comes only through intermediaries and to enter the sphere of perfection. Philo uses figures from Jewish history, such as Abraham, Isaac, Moses, and the high priest, as representatives of the religious journey toward perfection. These figures function as "traits of the soul" or "types" or "virtues" that believers should imitate and inculcate.[6]

According to Dey, the congregation to which Hebrews is addressed was in danger of turning away from the religion of Jesus (which, Hebrews claims, leads to perfection) toward a Philonic form of Hellenistic Judaism that also promised perfection. Some people in the world of Philonic Judaism may have claimed that the religion of Jesus could not lead to perfection because the death of Jesus showed that he himself was only an intermediary. The author of Hebrews seeks to discredit this mode of Judaism by showing that the latter is itself an inferior religion that offers only revelation that comes through intermediaries and cannot eventuate in perfection. The content of Hebrews is a series of comparisons between Jesus (who leads many others to perfection) and the intermediaries: the angels, Moses, Melchizedek, Levi, Aaron, and the old covenant and temple, which are but "cop-ies" of the perfect ones in heaven.[7]

Hebrews 1:1-4 begins the letter by using a series of designations that indi-cates that Jesus is perfected and, therefore, is superior to the angels (and other intermediaries). In Philo's thought the designation "Son" refers to an exalted being who originated from God, had a role in creation, and is perfected. Philo associates the other terms for the Son in 1:3a-b with this being. Philo, however, also claims that Isaac, Moses, and others share these qualities. The author connects these notions with making purification for sin. The implicit proposition of Heb. 1:1-4 is that God has given these epithets (and the power to lead others to perfection) only to Jesus.[8] Others are only intermediaries.

In Heb. 2:1-4, the author appeals to the congregation not to settle for a religious path that has come through intermediaries such as angels (Heb. 1:5-14) but to "pay greater attention" to the Son. Opponents of the author of Hebrews might argue that the suffering and death of Jesus make him no better than an intermediary. However, in 2:5-18, the author contends that the suffering of Jesus does not discredit his role as Son but is the means whereby Jesus is able to help human beings leave the imperfect world and journey toward perfection. This book thus seeks to help people bear suffering by interpreting suffering as a part of the path that leads to perfection.[9]

Responding to the Text

On the one hand, a preacher could use this text to remind today's congregation that some religious views do not reveal the fullness of divine purpose (as represented in the text by the notion of perfection). A preacher could compare and contrast Jesus as a source of religious insight with other sources on the meaning of life.

On the other hand, Hebrews presents the preacher with a major theological problem. This document dismisses Philonic Judaism as a second-rate religion and implies that its adherents will not be perfected. If God is truly unconditional love and is truly faithful to the promises God made to Israel (and to others), then the preacher needs to point out that Judaism has not been superseded by Christianity but is still a religion whose adherents have full standing before God. Indeed, today's preacher should help the congregation recognize that synagogue and church today should discover points we have in common in service to the one God and at which we can engage in mutual witness.[10]

> THE PREACHER SHOULD HELP THE CONGREGATION RECOGNIZE THAT SYNAGOGUE AND CHURCH TODAY SHOULD DISCOVER POINTS WE HAVE IN COMMON IN SERVICE TO THE ONE GOD AND AT WHICH WE CAN ENGAGE IN MUTUAL WITNESS.

MARK 10:2-16 (RCL)
MARK 10:2-9 (BCP)
MARK 10:2-26 or 10:2-12 (RC)

Interpreting the Text

Many scholars think that the Gospel of Mark was written about the time of the fall of the temple in Jerusalem in 70 C.E. As becomes clear on the Twenty-fourth Sunday after Pentecost and the discussion there of Mark 13:1-14, Mark thought the present age was in its last days and that an apocalypse would soon return Jesus from heaven to destroy evil and establish the realm (NRSV "kingdom") of God as a new cosmic world in which all persons, communities, and events manifest God's purposes fully.

Mark sets today's reading in this apocalyptic context by saying that the Pharisees came to "test" Jesus. The term "test" (*peiradzō*) occurs in Mark 1:13 (where it is translated "tempted") and refers to the fact of a time of suffering that will immediately precede the apocalypse. During that time, Satan will "test" people's faithfulness. By using this term, Mark pictures Pharisees as agents of Satan in the last days. Jesus' reply describes an approach to life that prepares one for life in the eschatological realm of God.

Behind the question of 10:2 was a discussion in the first-century Jewish community on the subject of the grounds necessary for divorce. The Jewish community took a negative view of divorce (Exod. 20:14; Deut. 5:18) and prescribed the death penalty for adultery (Lev. 20:10; Deut. 22:22). However, Judaism recognized that under some circumstances a woman and a man could not learn to live together, and so provided for the husband to dissolve the marriage (for instance, Deut. 24:1-14). By the time of Mark, the death penalty was seldom invoked, and the Jewish community debated the grounds for dissolution. For example, Shammai took the limited view that divorce was possible only in the case of sexual infidelity, while Hillel allowed for divorce for a range of reasons.

In 10:3-5, the Markan Jesus explains that Moses allowed for divorce because of "hardness of heart," that is, inability or unwillingness to learn to live together. In 10:6-9, Jesus cites Gen. 1:27 and 2:24 as basis for rejecting the possibility of divorce altogether. The impossibility of divorce is reinforced in 10:10-12.

Mark's prohibition against divorce is not a wooden legalism. By turning to the passages from Genesis, Mark evokes an important apocalyptic theme: the end times (the coming realm of God) will be like the beginning times (the world as it was at creation). For Mark, people living in the force field of the divine realm should relate with one another as God intended in Genesis. Under such conditions divorce will not be necessary.

Mark 10:13-16 continues the theme of the divine realm remaking perspectives of the present age. In the highly stratified social world of antiquity, children were not quite "nobodies," but they were near the bottom of the social pyramid. Nevertheless, rabbis often blessed children. While Mark does not directly state why the disciples discouraged parents from bringing children for blessing, we may presume (based particularly on Mark 10:35-45, Twentieth Sunday after Pentecost) that the disciples regarded the children as too socially insignificant for Jesus' attention. A sobering thought: the disciples, while not in league with Satan, are no more perceptive than the Pharisees of 10:2-12.

Mark, however, corrects the disciples by pointing out that the realm of God belongs to people who are similar to the children. The divine realm welcomes people at the bottom of the social ladder and provides a place of full standing in community. When Mark has Jesus say that those

> THE DIVINE REALM WELCOMES PEOPLE AT THE BOTTOM OF THE SOCIAL LADDER AND PROVIDES A PLACE OF FULL STANDING IN COMMUNITY.

who do not receive the divine realm like children will not enter it, Mark has reference to children's awareness that they have little social power to determine their own worlds. People who want to be a part of the divine realm must recognize that they cannot create or manipulate this world. It comes from God as a gift.

Responding to the Text

Divorce as such continues to trouble many people and congregations. Mark 10:2-12 presents both a problem and an opportunity. The problem is Mark's absolute prohibition against divorce. Matthew 5:32 introduces a qualification indicating that almost immediately the second generation of Jesus-followers needed to adapt Mark's stance. Mark's position is predicated on the expectation of an imminent apocalypse so that Mark did not expect marriages to last long. We are in a different situation. While a preacher does not want to take a casual attitude toward marriage and divorce, the world today is beset by so many tensions that even under the best conditions, some good relationships and good intentions go sour. Some people in some relationships seem unable or unwilling to learn to live together and are better freed for fulfilling God's purposes by ending a marriage. At the same time, the preacher can invite the congregation to consider how to encourage marriages to embody qualities of the beginning and ending times.

Single people lament the lionization of the married couple (with children) by the church. The preacher could use Mark 10:2-12 as a jumping-off point for exploring how other interactions with relatives, friends, and comrades in workplace and recreation can move toward qualities that God purposed in human relationships at the beginning and that God seeks to renew in the eschatological world.

Many people in today's congregations bring to Mark 10:13-16 the contemporary idealization of children as beings full of wonder, curiosity, spontaneity, and trust. A preacher likely needs to contrast this perception of children with the more typical one of antiquity described above. This awareness might invite a sermon that compares and contrasts attitudes and behaviors toward children in antiquity and today. What is gained and lost in each perspective? A sermon might explore the degree to which the congregation itself is a realm-like environment for young people, and the degree to which the congregation is working in the larger culture to call for realm-like conditions for children. A minister might also identify people today who are on the bottom of the social pyramid in a way similar to children in antiquity but whose welcome of the realm is a paradigm of the way people of more social power and self-determination might receive it.

229

EIGHTEENTH
SUNDAY
AFTER PENTECOST

RONALD J.
ALLEN

Notes

1. For a concise overview of interpretations, see Mayer Gruber, "Job," in *The Jewish Study Bible,* ed. Adele Berlin and Marc Zvi Brettler (New York: Oxford University Press, 2004), 1555. I am grateful for the careful work of my colleague J. Gerald Janzen, *Job,* Interpretation: A Bible Commentary for Preaching and Teaching (Louisville: John Knox Press, 1985), and to John C. Holbert, *Preaching Job,* Preaching Classic Texts (St. Louis: Chalice Press, 1999). Where I depart from their readings, I do so at interpretive peril.

2. Jon L. Berquist, *Judaism in Persia's Shadow: A Social and Historical Approach* (Minneapolis: Fortress Press, 1995), 207–15.

3. For a compact analysis, see Judith Hoch Wray, "An Exhortation to Faithfulness: Hebrews," in Dennis E. Smith, ed., *Chalice Introduction to the New Testament* (St. Louis: Chalice Press, 2004), 281–305.

4. For a survey, see Harold W. Attridge, *Hebrews,* Hermeneia (Philadelphia: Fortress Press, 1989), 9–14.

5. Lala Kalyan Kumar Dey, *The Intermediary Worlds and Patterns of Perfection in Philo and Hebrews,* SBL Dissertation Series 25 (Missoula, Mont.: Scholars Press, 1975).

6. Ibid., 48.

7. Ibid., 126, passim.

8. Ibid., 40–42, 134–45.

9. Ibid., 222–25.

10. E.g., Clark M. Williamson, ed., *A Mutual Witness: Towards Critical Solidarity between Christians and Jews* (St. Louis: Chalice Press, 1992).

NINETEENTH SUNDAY AFTER PENTECOST

OCTOBER 15, 2006
TWENTY-EIGHTH SUNDAY IN ORDINARY TIME /
PROPER 23

REVISED COMMON	EPISCOPAL (BCP)	ROMAN CATHOLIC
Amos 5:6-7, 10-15	Amos 5:6-7,10-15	Wisd. of Sol. 7:7-11
or Job 23:1-9, 16-17		
Ps. 90:12-17	Psalm 90	Ps. 90:12-13, 14-15,
or Ps. 22:1-15	or 90:1-8, 12	16-17
Heb. 4:12-16	Heb. 3:1-6	Heb. 4:12-13
Mark 10:17-31	Mark 10:17-27	Mark 10:17-30
	(28-31)	or 10:17-27

FIRST READING

AMOS 5:6-7, 10-15 (RCL, BCP)

Interpreting the Text

In the background of the book of Amos is the notion of covenant that presumes that God intends a life of blessing for all people, that is, circumstances in which all people have access to resources that support life (social relationships, food, clothing, housing, means of production, and so forth). The prescriptions of Torah describe values, attitudes, and behavior by which covenantal people share resources for life with one another. Obedience brings about blessing in community, while disobedience brings about curse.

Amos (preaching about 750 B.C.E.) interprets many people of Israel as disobeying the covenant not only by neglecting to share resources but also by actively and mercilessly exploiting others (especially the poor). The prophet describes their behavior in 5:7 as turning "justice to wormwood" and bringing "righteousness to the ground." Amos 5:10-13 cites specific examples of such disobedience. The wealthy not only ignore the justices who sit in the gate and render verdicts on behalf of the poor (5:10), but even bribe these elders (5:12). The privileged class has built lavish houses while economically exploiting the poor (5:11).

The phrase "seek the Lord" that begins today's text means to intend to live according to God's covenant.[1] When the people do not live covenantally, God will destroy the community (Amos 5:6b, 11d, f).

Responding to the Text

The preacher may need to bring forward specific contemporary examples to help middle- and upper-class congregations in North American feel the sting of this text. Even when individuals attempt to be personally covenantal in our everyday settings, we often have investments or are caught up in broader networks of association that effectively turn "justice to wormwood" and "trample the poor" and "push aside the needy in the gate" while we live in "houses built of hewn stone." Such behaviors deny our covenantal relationship not only with the poor and otherwise disadvantaged in our own neighborhoods and cities, but also with people in other parts of the world.

Although our personal lives and the life of our culture may not be threatened with immediate destruction, such attitudes and behavior set in motion forces that will cause communities and, indeed, our whole culture to collapse. In the meantime, people are so interconnected that when the life of one person is diminished, the lives of all are diminished, and the quality of life in the community as a whole is less than God desires.

Commentators struggle with whether 5:5a and 5:14-15 imply that the people can still repent, avoid destruction, and live in blessing, or whether the community has so perverted justice that collapse is inevitable. The preacher does not need to settle this exegetical issue. Regardless of what Amos intended, the congregation *today* still has an opportunity to live covenantally and to call the wider culture to do so. The vocation of the preacher is to call the congregation to seek God so that all can live in blessing.

> REGARDLESS OF WHAT AMOS INTENDED, THE CONGREGATION *TODAY* STILL HAS AN OPPORTUNITY TO LIVE COVENANTALLY AND TO CALL THE WIDER CULTURE TO DO SO.

231

NINETEENTH
SUNDAY
AFTER PENTECOST

RONALD J.
ALLEN

JOB 23:1-9, 16-17 (RCL ALT.)

Interpreting the Text

To preach from any single text in the book of Job, the preacher needs to bring that text into dialogue with the overall story and themes of the whole volume. The congregation needs to hear today's passage in the context of the collapse of Job's life (described in Job 1:1—2:10, Eighteenth Sunday after Pentecost) and the theological questions raised by the friends who come to help Job interpret his situation and to encourage him to make what they think is an appropriate response.

With great oversimplification, we can say that Eliphaz (Job 4:1—5:27) voices the conventional assumption that righteous people prosper while evil ones suffer (for instance, 4:6-7) and that suffering is a form of divine discipline (5:17). According to Bildad (8:1-22), God is just and punishes those who sin. Job's suffering, therefore, indicates that Job has sinned. Job should turn to God for forgiveness. Zophar (11:1-20) reiterates that God is just and punishes sin and that God knows more than Job about who has sinned and who has not. These themes (and others) are nuanced and expanded in a second round of remarks from the friends (Eliphaz: 15:1-35; Bildad: 18:1-21; Zophar: 20:1-29). Eliphaz speaks a third time in Job 22:1-30 to reiterate that Job's destitution indicates that Job has done something wicked (22:5-9). If Job will cease disobeying, then God will accept Job's repentance and restore Job's fortunes (22:15-30).

Job replies to each speech (raising too many issues to report here but all maintaining that he is innocent and refusing to say otherwise because to do so would violate his integrity) in Job 6:1—7:20; 9:1—10:22; 12:1—14:22; 16:1—17:16; 19:1-29; 21:1-34. Today's lesson, which should really be Job 23:1—24:25, enlarges the theme that God allows injustice. In fact, God sometimes hides, thus allowing the unjust to prosper at the expense of the just. Indeed, the innocent do sometimes suffer (23:1-17). Job gives several illustrations of wicked people whose prosperity comes at the suffering of others. Such wicked folk should be punished (24:1-25).

Responding to the Text

If this is the preacher's second sermon in a series on Job (following the suggestion made on the Eighteenth Sunday after Pentecost regarding preaching on Job), then this is the preacher's major opportunity to deal with the specific arguments raised in the book regarding the various ways of understanding the relationship among obedience, disobedience, sin, suffering, and prosperity. A sermon might summarize the speeches of the friends and Job's replies in 3:1—22:30 by shaping the sermon as a dialogue between the characters and Job in which the preacher slips from one character to another—Eliphaz/Job/Bildad/Job/Zophar/Job. The preacher could briefly consider Job's speech for today with its complaint that the wicked prosper while the just suffer. The sermon, like the text (and indeed, like the whole of 3:1—37:24) could end in a theological standoff between Job and the friends with the invitation to return the next two weeks to see how the standoff ends.

To take another approach, Job complains that God hides so that Job cannot confront God (Job 23:1-9, esp. 8-9). Some Christians think that God does, in fact, hide from human beings from time to time. Other Christians believe that God is omnipresent, and does not or even cannot hide. Preachers need to think about where they fall on this issue, as it makes a difference in the direction the sermon takes. From the latter point of view, Job does not *perceive* the divine presence, but that is not the same as God actually hiding. A preacher could help the congregation consider ways we might become cognizant of the divine presence, even when we are in the midst of circumstances such as Job's. Still another message is suggested by Job's being "terrified at [God's] presence" and "in dread" because of what God has done to him (23:15-17). To be sure, a congregation should respect the otherness of God, but we should not be terrified of a God who often in the First Testament is described as "full of com-

passion and steadfast love." Some interpreters believe that at this point in the narrative Job *misconceives* God by thinking that God directly visits (or allows) evil upon people; such people think that God acts only in

> A PREACHER COULD HELP THE CONGREGATION CONSIDER WAYS WE MIGHT BECOME COGNIZANT OF THE DIVINE PRESENCE, EVEN WHEN WE ARE IN THE MIDST OF CIRCUMSTANCES SUCH AS JOB'S.

ways that are loving and supportive and kind. From this point of view, a sermon might listen to Job's view of God as one voice in a conversation about the character of God, and then invite the congregation to consider other ways of thinking about the divine presence, purpose, and power.

WISDOM OF SOLOMON 7:7-11 (RC)

Interpreting the Text

The unknown author of the Wisdom of Solomon probably wrote in Alexandria near the end of the last century B.C.E. or in the first half of the first century C.E. In this book, "wisdom" is a feminine personification, as in Prov. 8:22-31 and other places, who reveals the meaning of life and how to live faithfully toward blessing (and how to avoid folly that leads to torment (Wisd. 3:1-13; 4:20—5:23). The book reinforces Jewish identity by celebrating the benefits of wisdom and by showing that Jewish wisdom shines through select other philosophical and religious systems. This book rejects idolatry and warns that idolatry leads to condemnation.

Solomon functions as a model for readers who are implicitly invited to learn as Solomon did. Though himself a royal figure, Solomon needed to pray for wisdom (Wisd. 7:7). The monarch came to prefer her to the trappings of power (7:8). Gold and silver are as sand and clay in comparison (7:9). Indeed, having wisdom is better than health, beauty, and light, because her radiance never ceases (even in the night) (7:10). Though Solomon did not initially know that wisdom was the mother of "all good things" (even those that come to expression in philosophical

is omnipresent, and does not or even cannot hide. Preachers need to think about where they fall on this issue, as it makes a difference in the direction the sermon takes. From the latter point of view, Job does not *perceive* the divine presence, but that is not the same as God actually hiding. A preacher could help the congregation consider ways we might become cognizant of the divine presence, even when we are in the midst of circumstances such as Job's. Still another message is suggested by Job's being "terrified at [God's] presence" and "in dread" because of what God has done to him (23:15-17). To be sure, a congregation should respect the otherness of God, but we should not be terrified of a God who often in the First Testament is described as "full of com-

passion and steadfast love." Some interpreters believe that at this point in the narrative Job *misconceives* God by thinking that God directly visits (or allows) evil upon people; such people think that God acts only in

> A PREACHER COULD HELP THE CONGREGATION CONSIDER WAYS WE MIGHT BECOME COGNIZANT OF THE DIVINE PRESENCE, EVEN WHEN WE ARE IN THE MIDST OF CIRCUMSTANCES SUCH AS JOB'S.

ways that are loving and supportive and kind. From this point of view, a sermon might listen to Job's view of God as one voice in a conversation about the character of God, and then invite the congregation to consider other ways of thinking about the divine presence, purpose, and power.

is omnipresent, and does not or even cannot hide.

and religious traditions other than Judaism), the royal grew into this awareness. Wisdom so fills Solomon that the ruler imparts her without grudging, knowing that all who receive her "obtain friendship with God" (7:11-14).

Responding to the Text

The preacher can lift up wisdom as a feminine window into the divine and come into today asking how women's experiences reveal God's purposes. A preacher can also use this text as an invitation for the congregation to join the journey to wisdom. Where does the congregation encounter such wisdom today, and what difference does it make? On the one hand, the text encourages people on both the upper and under sides of life to recognize deeper values than such things as possession of material resources and social standing. On the other hand, the sermon should not reinforce quietude in the face of poverty or injustice. True wisdom should lead to community in which people use all resources for the good of all.

> TRUE WISDOM SHOULD LEAD TO COMMUNITY IN WHICH PEOPLE USE ALL RESOURCES FOR THE GOOD OF ALL.

RESPONSIVE READING

PSALM 90:12-17 (RCL)
PSALM 90 or 90:1-8, 12 (BCP)
PSALM 90:12-13, 14-15, 16-17 (RC)

On the one hand, this psalm declares that from the birth of the world, God has been an unfailing dwelling place or refuge (90:1-2). The preacher can certainly turn to this aspect of the text, especially when the congregation experiences disruption and chaos, as at the time of death. On the other hand, the text assumes that God angrily sweeps people away, that is, causes them to die (vv. 3-12), and pleads for God to have compassion and to turn from that course (vv. 13-17). These latter themes raise questions for preacher and people: To what degree or under what conditions can the congregation truly count upon God as a refuge if God also sweeps people away? Do we really believe that God actively "afflicts" us, or do we suffer the natural consequences of our own sin and of living in a broken world?

PSALM 22:1-15 (RCL ALT.)

Because we hear Ps. 22:1 in Matt. 27:46 and Mark 15:34, the congregation may automatically associate this psalm with Jesus. The preacher thus has an important teaching opportunity to remind the congregation that this text (as well as other psalms and the whole First Testament) has its own life prior to Jesus and the church and that the earlier testament can instruct us without reference to Jesus. The part of the psalm assigned for today coheres with the reading from Job as a lament that God seems absent in the face of suffering. When do members of the congregation feel similarly? The limits of the reading, however, violate the literary and theological integrity of the psalm, which moves from distress (vv. 1-18) to a statement of trust in God (vv. 19-31).

235

NINETEENTH
SUNDAY
AFTER PENTECOST

RONALD J.
ALLEN

Second Reading
HEBREWS 3:1-6 (BCP)

Interpreting the Text

This passage begins by assuring the congregation that they are "holy partners in a heavenly calling"; that is, they are on the path to perfection. The text continues the contrast (announced in Heb. 1:1-4) between Jesus and figures in Judaism to show the superiority of Jesus. Although Moses and Jesus are both faithful, this passage presents Moses as merely a servant of God, whereas Jesus is the Son who is also the agent through whom the house was created (Heb. 1:2).[2] In Philo's Judaism, a servant is an intermediary who cannot give people the full knowledge of God that leads to perfection, whereas Jesus is the Son who is an exemplar of that path. Through Jesus the congregation becomes "God's house" as long as they "hold firm" (Heb. 3:6). In Hebrews, the term "God's house" refers not to the church but to the realm of perfection.[3]

Responding to the Text

On Pentecost 18, I explained the ongoing theological problems with preaching from Hebrews, namely unfortunate negative and unwarranted caricature of Judaism as well as supersessionism (as in today's text). Nevertheless, without casting aspersion on Judaism, the preacher could take a cue from the end this passage to encourage the congregation to hold firm in following the call of Jesus to the heavenly world and to turn away from the many other voices that offer as ultimate things that are only penultimate.

HEBREWS 4:12–16 (RCL)
HEBREWS 4:12–13 (RC)

Interpreting the Text

Hebrews 4:1–11 uses the language of "rest" to speak of the realm of perfection and exhorts the congregation to continue on the path that leads to rest. Hebrews 4:12–13 continues 4:1–11 by assuring the congregation of the trustworthiness of the promise of rest. This promise is guaranteed by the word of God. In Philo the "word of God" is not the Bible but is the agency through whom God created, sustains, and judges; in Philo, the word is often synonymous with other agents of perfection. For Hebrews, Jesus is the Word who can lead people to rest because he is able to separate with swordlike penetration and precision the imperfect from the perfect.

Hebrews 4:14–16 explains that the congregation can have confidence that they can reach the rest because Jesus is the great and sympathetic high priest who has passed through the heavens.[4] In Philo, the high priest is an exemplar of perfection. Jesus is a superior high priest, for (a) Jesus is already in heaven, that is, the realm of perfection, and (b) Jesus can help human beings because he has experienced every temptation that we have yet did not drift into sin (that is, behaviors that hold one captive to the realm of imperfection).[5]

> THE IMAGE OF JESUS AS SYMPATHETIC HIGH PRIEST IS A REMINDER THAT AT THE CENTER OF LIFE IS A PRESENCE WHO EMPATHIZES WITH OUR EVERY FEELING AND TEMPTATION.

Responding to the Text

In today's world, many people (perhaps like the recipients of Hebrews) feel that life is uncertain, hard, even brutal. The image of Jesus as sympathetic high priest is a reminder that at the center of life is a presence who empathizes with our every feeling and temptation. Even more, this priest, like the ones of old, imparts mercy and grace that not only allow us to hold firm in life but empower us to follow a path that, even through suffering, is marked by meaning and hope.

MARK 10:17–31 (RCL)
MARK 10:17–27 (28–31) (BCP)
MARK 10:17–30 or 10:17–27 (RC)

Interpreting the Text

The apocalyptic motifs sketched for the Gospel of Mark on the Eighteenth Sunday after Pentecost are the backdrop of today's passage. The rich person's question, "What must I do to inherit eternal life?" is a question about what this person needs to do to be a part of the coming realm of God with its unending blessing. The Markan Jesus dissuades the rich person from calling Jesus "good" by implicitly invoking the memory from Genesis 1 that *God* is the source of good (Gen. 1:4, 10, 12, 18, 21, 25, 31) in the world and that God created the elements of the world to live in covenant.

The rich person has followed the commandments. From apocalyptic perspective, the commandments are necessary to guide people in the way of the covenantal life, a quality of life that will persist in the new age. While apocalyptic theologians recognize that material resources are necessary for life, they also recognize that people in the present can seek security through trust in their possessions rather than in covenantal living, that accumulation of wealth and resources in the present can become an end in itself and can even become idolatrous. Members of

> THE COMPARISON OF A RICH PERSON ENTERING THE DIVINE REALM WITH A CAMEL TRYING TO GO THROUGH THE EYE OF A NEEDLE IS STUNNING IN ITS EFFECT ON THE LISTENER.

some apocalyptically oriented groups, such as at Qumran, put their possessions in a common fund and lived communally. This approach provided for the material needs of all while relieving community members of the distractions that sometimes come with wealth. Mark implies that members of the Markan community have done something of the same. They have removed themselves from many social relationships from the old age and adopted the Markan community as family (Mark 3:31-35) and have pooled their economic resources (Mark 10:29-30).

In Mark 10:21, Jesus invites the rich person to lessen the suffering and anxiety of the poor by putting his wealth in their service. For his part, the rich person is to become a part of the community of Jesus' followers who expect the present age to end soon with the apocalypse. The rich person need not fear, because the community itself would provide food, shelter, and a network of eschatological relationships. The reader knows further that Jesus provides abundantly (Mark 6:30-42; 8:1-9). However, the rich person is unwilling to trust the community for day-to-day sustenance and support.

238

THE SEASON
OF PENTECOST
─────────
RONALD J.
ALLEN

In 10:23-27, Mark explains that many wealthy people have a difficult time embracing the realm of God with its turn away from basing one's security and identity in material possessions. The comparison of a rich person entering the divine realm with a camel trying to go through the eye of a needle is stunning in its effect on the listener. However, v. 27 affirms that the possession of wealth does not inherently keep one out of the realm of God, for all things are possible in the sphere of God's activity. Some rich people will respond positively to God's invitation.

Mark 10:28-31 describes the coming realm of God as unbelievably abundant in material resources. Indeed, those who are a part of it receive "a hundredfold" in the present and in the age to come, eternal life. Divesting oneself of one's present resources and putting them at the service of the community is a small price for such a gain.

Responding to the Text

This text puts the preacher eyeball to eyeball with one of the most entrenched values in North American society: the accumulation of material resources. This text makes North American Christians exceedingly uncomfortable. On the one hand, the preacher can ameliorate some such discomfort by pointing out that the perspective on time was very different in Mark's community than it is today. The

> HOW CAN A CONGREGATION MAINTAIN RESOURCES NECESSARY FOR VITAL MISSION OVER THE LONG HAUL WHILE NOT LETTING THE ACCUMULATION OF RESOURCES BECOME AN IDOL?

ancient followers of Jesus did not think that they needed to plan for a long-term future, whereas most congregations today anticipate a protracted future. How can a congregation maintain resources necessary for vital mission over the long haul while not letting the accumulation of resources become an idol?

On the other hand, many individual Christians and even many congregations are contemporary examples of the rich person's attitude toward resources. The text confronts us with the claim that material resources are (a) to be used for the blessing of all in the community and (b) not to become ends. The preacher can encourage such folk to use their resources in joining God in increasing blessing for all (especially the poor) while recognizing that an increase in blessing for the poor enhances the security of the whole community. A sermon could help the wealthy realize that they can be liberated from self-preoccupation and anxiety by joining their resources with God in mission.

Beyond such relatively comfortable considerations, the text challenges the congregation toward more communal ways of envisioning and using its resources. Indeed, it pushes the church toward communal living. In North America, such a move would demonstrate that with God all things are possible.

Notes

1. Patrick D. Miller, *Interpreting the Psalms* (Philadelphia: Fortress Press, 1986), 94–96.

2. Lala Kalyan Kumar Dey, *The Intermediary Worlds and Patterns of Perfection in Philo and Hebrews*, SBL Dissertation Series 25 (Missoula, Mont.: Scholars Press, 1975), 153.

3. Ibid., 63–68, 155–79.

4. Ibid., 225–27.

5. Ibid., 58–63.

RONALD J.
ALLEN

TWENTIETH SUNDAY AFTER PENTECOST

OCTOBER 22, 2006
TWENTY-NINTH SUNDAY IN ORDINARY TIME /
PROPER 24

REVISED COMMON	EPISCOPAL (BCP)	ROMAN CATHOLIC
Isa. 53:4–12 or Job 38:1–7 (34–41)	Isa. 53:4–12	Isa. 53:10–11
Ps. 91:9–16 or Ps. 104:1–9, 24, 35c	Psalm 91 or 91:9–16	Ps. 33:4–5, 18–19, 20, 22
Heb. 5:1–10	Heb. 4:12–16	Heb. 4:14–16
Mark 10:35–45	Mark 10:35–45	Mark 10:35–45 or 10:42–45

FIRST READING

ISAIAH 53:4-12 (RCL, BCP)
ISAIAH 53:10-11 (RC)

Interpreting the Text

The identity of the "servant" in this passage is approached from many different exegetical angles.[1] However, in view of the obvious identification of "the servant" earlier in Deutero-Isaiah with the community of Israel, it makes sense to see the servant in this passage as the community. The vocation of the servant community is to witness to the covenantal life that God seeks among all peoples. Indeed, the servant community is to be a "light to the Gentiles" (Isa. 42:6).

Isaiah 52:13—53:9 remembers that the community in exile and "marred" is the epitome of weakness and defeat. It appears that God rejected the servant. Consequently, the "nations" (Gentiles) are surprised that God is now prospering the servant. Indeed, the servant community silently suffered the kind of affliction that should befall the nations even though the servant was not as guilty as they (the Babylonians who put them into exile). According to 53:10-12, God deliberately crushed the servant "with pain" and considered the situation of the community as a sin offering that releases many from the curse of sin and frees them for the life of blessing.

When preaching on this text by itself (without reference to a reading from the Second Testament), a preacher could focus on how the suffering and restoration of the Jewish community should alert Gentiles to obedience to God as the pathway to blessing. Since the prophet uses the motif of sacrifice metaphorically, the preacher need not press that language too woodenly but could underscore the underlying point that through the experience of the servant God makes restoration of community possible for all. Furthermore, the preacher's theology may be loath to think that God *willed* to "crush [the servant] with pain" (Isa. 53:10). In my view, God does not actively inflict suffering on people (even for redemptive purposes). However, God can work with the suffering caused by others (such as the Babylonians) for redemptive purposes.

This passage from Isaiah is part of the pattern of thought presupposed in Mark 10:35-45, especially v. 45. The preacher who turns this direction should clarify that Isaiah did not have Jesus in mind when the prophet wrote. Rather, Mark (in company with many other early followers of Jesus) interprets Jesus' death as functioning similarly to that of the suffering servant of Isaiah 53. From this perspective, the suffering of Jesus as redemptive is not something altogether new but is a continuation of a historic Jewish motif. The element that is new for Mark (and others) is interpreting Jesus' suffering as part of the tribulation sufferings immediately prior to the apocalypse.

> A PREACHER COULD FOCUS ON HOW THE SUFFERING AND RESTORATION OF THE JEWISH COMMUNITY SHOULD ALERT GENTILES TO OBEDIENCE TO GOD AS THE PATHWAY TO BLESSING.

JOB 38:1-7 (34-41) (RCL ALT.)

Interpreting the Text

Prior to today's lection, God has not spoken directly with Job. The reading for today represents the whole of God's responses to Job in 38:1—40:1 and 40:6—41:34. These speeches largely consist of God's putting questions to Job. When reading these materials the preacher engages in what Charles R. Blaisdell calls "tone of voice exegesis," that is, giving an interpretation to the text through the tone and inflection with which one voices it.[2] God's words can be read in moods as diverse as angry, impatient, disdainful, imperial, compassionate, or with a touch of humor.

> GOD'S WORDS CAN BE READ IN MOODS AS DIVERSE AS ANGRY, IMPATIENT, DISDAINFUL, IMPERIAL, WITH A TOUCH OF HUMOR, OR COMPASSION.

In the divine speeches, God's questions push Job and the reader to recognize that they (and we) neither created nor sustain the world and do not have omniscience. God does not directly address Job's questions and does not offer a direct interpretation of what happened to Job. Most interpreters think that God declares that Job's previous understanding is not adequate regarding God and the relationship of obedience and disobedience, blessing and curse, and the suffering of the innocent. Unfortunately, God does not offer an alternative understanding of issues of obedience and disobedience, blessing and curse.

Responding to the Text

Despite the fact that it comes from the mouth of God, the text for today does not resolve the major theological question raised by the book of Job. Nevertheless, two interpreters note points at which the divine speeches imply positive dimensions that are fruitful for preaching. J. Gerald Janzen hears irony.[3] Instead of putting Job down, God provokes Job to recognize that God approves of Job's challenges and wants Job to continue the human vocation of "ruling" creation in the mode of Psalm 8 and Gen. 1:26-27. The fact that God came to Job reveals continuity of relationship between them.

Biblical scholar Carol Newsom notes that the divine speeches do imply a certain moral order in the universe through the language "of place, limit, and nonencroachment." Thus, "if one realizes that each thing, each person, has place, purpose, and limit, then there are places where I must not tread, places where the energy and vitality, indeed, the violence of my being must meet its limit."[4] Job and we must respect the limits of our own understanding and learn to live constructively within them.

A PREACHER MIGHT HELP A CONGREGATION TO RECOGNIZE THAT A KEY ELEMENT IN EXERCISING DIVINE VOCATION IS TO HELP THE VARIOUS ELEMENTS OF CREATION RELATE WITH ONE ANOTHER IN THE RESPECTFUL PATTERNS GOD INTENDS.

A preacher could encourage a congregation to respect the boundaries of other human beings and the elements of creation as created by God. A preacher might further help a congregation to recognize that a key element in exercising divine vocation is to help the various elements of creation relate with one another in the respectful patterns God intends. The continuing relationship between God and Job is itself enough for Job to live into the vocation of the human being (which includes raising questions) in a world that does not always conform to simple moral rules.

Responsive Reading

243

Twentieth
Sunday
After Pentecost

Ronald J.
Allen

PSALM 91:9–16 (RCL)
PSALM 91 or 91:9–16 (BCP)

Parts of Psalm 91 have been set to music in a popular arrangement, "On Eagle's Wings," by Michael Joncas. This psalm uses a dramatic montage of images to affirm that God protects from harm people who trust in God. The preacher who focuses on this psalm needs to deal forthrightly with the fact that many people who trust in God do experience difficulty and that, at least for now, evil forces are not scattered (as the psalm promises). The preacher has a further opportunity to lead the congregation in canonical criticism by noting that the devil uses Ps. 91:11–12 to tempt Jesus to demonstrate in a public, spectacular, and pain-free way that Jesus is the apocalyptic redeemer by jumping from the pinnacle of the temple in the confidence that the angels will catch him (Matt. 4:5–6; Luke 4:10–11). Jesus replies by citing Deut. 6:16, which, in its context, means,

> GOD WILL INDEED PROVIDE FOR JESUS, BUT BY STRENGTHENING THE SAVIOR ON THE PATH THAT LEADS THROUGH SUFFERING AND DEATH.

"You should not question God's ability to do what God has promised in the way that God has promised [that is, to bring the children of Israel safely through the wilderness]." In the same way, Jesus and the church can trust God to provide for them as they move toward the cross and the suffering of the tribulation prior to the apocalypse. Jesus does not dispute the promise of Ps. 91:11–12. According to Jesus, the devil misunderstands this psalm. God will indeed provide for Jesus, but by strengthening the Savior on the path that leads through suffering and death (Matt. 4:5–7; Luke 4:9–12).

PSALM 33:4–5, 18–19, 20, 22 (RC)

Psalm 33 assumes that God created the world as a sphere of blessing for all (vv. 1–7) and that God seeks to protect and provide for the peoples of the earth while frustrating the plans of those who would go against the divine design for blessing for all (vv. 8–15). For a nation engaged in a war that is designed to end the threat of terrorism, vv. 16–17 are sobering. This psalm implies that living in covenant with one another as God ordains is the path to peace (vv. 18–22).

PSALM 104:1–9, 24, 35c (RCL ALT.)

Psalm 104 interprets God as creator and sovereign of all things, with the excerpt for today stressing that God has limited the power of chaos (represented here by the waters), which makes stability possible. A preacher might suggest that while the congregation continues to experience chaos, God seeks to limit the chaos so that it does not overwhelm the congregation or the world, and can even turn chaotic forces (such as water) into means of blessing (104:10-18). Certainly that was true for Job, whose life was reduced to chaos but who survived by virtue of God. Indeed, the main themes of Psalm 104 resonate with Job 38.

SECOND READING
HEBREWS 5:1-10 (RCL)

Interpreting the Text

Today's reading continues the theme of Jesus as sympathetic high priest introduced last week (see Nineteenth Sunday after Pentecost). In keeping with the motif of comparing Jesus with the exemplars of perfection in Hellenistic Judaism, this passage compares the mortal high priest with the immortal Jesus whose priesthood is forever. In Philo, the high priest is an exemplar. However, according to Hebrews, while the mortal high priest does have value (Heb. 5:1-3), his works bring people relief only within the imperfect sphere of existence, whereas Jesus leads to perfection.[5]

Commentators often puzzle over why the author of Hebrews would declare that Jesus is "a priest forever after the order of Melchizedek," since the First Testament mentions this figure only in Gen. 14:17-24 and Ps. 110:4 (cited here). In Philo, Melchizedek is of a higher order of priesthood than the mortal line of Aaron (and other priests) since God appointed Melchizedek a priest forever and from the very beginning made him immortal. Jesus is of this higher order (see further Heb. 7:1-23).[6]

THE PRIMARY EMPHASIS IN HEBREWS IS THAT THE SUFFERING IS NOT MEANINGLESS BUT IS A PART OF THE BELIEVER'S PATH TO PERFECTION, JUST AS IT WAS FOR JESUS.

Hebrews 5:7-10 notes that Jesus was perfected through suffering. Hebrews specifically has in mind suffering that results from obedience (see comment below).

Responding to the Text

Although the supersessionistic comparison between Jesus and figures in Judaism (such as the mortal high priest) is invidious, a preacher could identify people and ideas about the meaning of life that function in the same way as the mortal high priest in this passage. Who in our world is like the mortal high priest—offering perspectives that are helpful but limited? How do perspectives deriving from the transcendent Jesus enlarge our awareness and deepen our living?

On the Nineteenth Sunday after Pentecost, we noted that the emphasis on Jesus' suffering as part of the path to perfection in Hebrews is a point of identification between Jesus and people who suffer today. However, a preacher does not want to use this recurrence to encourage neurotic attitudes toward suffering. The suffering that Hebrews has in mind is not generic suffering (such as sickness) but is directly because of one's faithfulness. The primary emphasis in Hebrews is that the suffering is not meaningless but is a part of the believer's path to perfection, just as it was for Jesus. A preacher can thus encourage the congregation to remain faithful in such suffering because Jesus has gone ahead and prepared the way and ever functions in their behalf as sympathetic high priest.

245

TWENTIETH
SUNDAY
AFTER PENTECOST

RONALD J.
ALLEN

HEBREWS 4:12-16 (BCP)
HEBREWS 4:14-16 (RC)

For discussion of these readings, please see the Nineteenth Sunday after Pentecost.

THE GOSPEL
MARK 10:35-45 (RCL, BCP, RC)
MARK 10:42-45 (RC ALT.)

Interpreting the Text

As is well known, Mark presents the disciples as imperceptive. Today's Gospel lesson immediately follows Mark 10:32-34, the third prediction of the passion, and calls to mind Mark 8:31—9:1 with its emphasis on the way of discipleship as the way of the cross. For Mark, the cross is the result of the resistance of the entrenched powers of the present world to the coming of the divine realm. The reader is not surprised when the disciples completely miss this point with their questions in 10:35-37. When James and John ask for seats on Jesus' right and left hands in glory, they are asking for places of power and authority in the post-apocalypse realm of God.

The reader remembers that the disciples' question in 10:35 is eerily reminiscent of that of Herod in 6:22. The disciples want to function in the eschatological world with the same force and power that Herod has in the present age.

In 10:38a, the Markan Jesus stresses that the disciples do not have an adequate grasp of the new world. In 10:38b-39, the Markan Jesus uses the imagery of cup and baptism to restate the point of 8:31—9:1. Noted scholar Jon L. Berquist points out that the motif of the cup echoes passages in the Hebrew Bible that describe God's pouring out a cup that purifies the earth by eradicating evil.[7] The pouring of the cup creates suffering as evil is destroyed. The death of Jesus functions in this way, and the disciples will share in the suffering. We learn from Mark 13:1-14 (Twenty-fourth Sunday after Pentecost) that such pain indicates that the apocalyptic transformation is near. The reference to baptism functions similarly here. The act of immersion represents the death of the old world as preparation for the emergence of the new (as in Rom. 6:3-4).

In 10:42-45, Mark explains that leaders in the Gentile world "lord it over" and act as "tyrants" over the population. Such leaders use their positions to reinforce their own social power at the expense of the suffering of the people. For a definitive Jewish impression of "tyrants," see the story told in 4 Maccabees, especially how the tyrant puts to death the mother and her sons because of their refusal to compromise their faith.

In the realm of God, leadership is expressed through service to one another. Mark here echoes Deutero-Isaiah's notion of Israel as servant of God (discussed above). To serve, in this sense, is to live in covenantal relationship in community. The responsibility of the leader is to urge community members to keep covenant so that the life of the community embodies how God wants all people to live so that all may be blessed. According to 10:45, Jesus came not to be served but to serve, that is, not to accumulate social control for himself but to continue the vocation of the servant of Deutero-Isaiah. Jesus' followers are to do the same.

> THE RESPONSIBILITY OF THE LEADER IS TO URGE COMMUNITY MEMBERS TO KEEP COVENANT SO THAT THE LIFE OF THE COMMUNITY EMBODIES HOW GOD WANTS ALL PEOPLE TO LIVE SO THAT ALL MAY BE BLESSED.

Preachers sometimes develop complicated theories of atonement from Mark 10:45 with its mention of "ransom." The simplicity of the actual reference, however, suggests that Mark uses the term figuratively to refer to the *effect* of the death of Jesus. His death sets in motion the final stages of history that will culminate in the apocalypse, which will mean the liberation of the world.

Responding to the Text

This text raises difficult questions for preacher and congregation. In 10:35-37, James and John assume that community in the realm of God will be structured much like communities of the old age. To what degree does the congregation think similarly? Furthermore, the preacher might ask, "Does the congregation view leadership in ways that are similar to James and John in 10:35-37?" Do people in the congregation "lord it over" one another or tyrannize one another?

If particular people do not do so directly, do congregational policies, values, or mores function in these destructive, old-age ways?

Even more poignantly, preachers might inventory ways we think of our own ministerial roles as means to "glory." Does the minister sometimes "lord it over" the congregation and manifest tyrannical attitudes or behaviors?

Apropos of 10:43-45, the preacher can hold out the image of the servant community as a vision for today's congregation. The values and structures of congregational life should model relationships in the realm of God after the manner of the vocation of servant community in Deutero-Isaiah. The preacher can indicate how this vision already comes to expression in the church's life and also can indicate points at which it can reshape current attitudes and practice.

While these remarks have thus far concentrated on leadership and community in the congregation, the same questions and criteria can be posed to leaders and bodies beyond the congregation. The preacher can catalogue where we find leaders functioning in government and civic institutions in self-serving ways and "lording it over" other people. How can the congregation call for better styles and ends in leadership in public life?

247

TWENTIETH
SUNDAY
AFTER PENTECOST

RONALD J.
ALLEN

> THE VALUES AND STRUCTURES OF CONGREGATIONAL LIFE SHOULD MODEL RELATIONSHIPS IN THE REALM OF GOD AFTER THE MANNER OF THE VOCATION OF SERVANT COMMUNITY IN DEUTERO-ISAIAH.

Notes

1. For a succinct review of interpretations (including in rabbinic sources), see Benjamin D. Sommer, "Isaiah," in *The Jewish Study Bible*, ed. Adele Berlin and Marc Zvi Brettler (New York: Oxford University Press, 2004), 890–92.

2. Charles R. Blaisdell, cited by Clark M. Williamson and Ronald J. Allen, *A Credible and Timely Word: Process Theology and Preaching* (St. Louis: Chalice Press, 1991), 89 n. 34.

3. J. Gerald Janzen, *Job*, Interpretation: A Bible Commentary for Preaching and Teaching (Louisville: John Knox Press, 1985), 225–27.

4. Carol A. Newsom, "Job," in *The New Interpreter's Bible,* ed. Leander Keck et. al. (Nashville: Abingdon Press, 1996), vol. 4, 626.

5. Lala Kalyan Kumar Dey, *The Intermediary Worlds and Patterns of Perfection in Philo and Hebrews*, SBL Dissertation Series 25 (Missoula, Mont.: Scholars Press, 1975), 58–63, 70–71, 185–87.

6. Ibid., 61–62; 199–202.

7. Jon L. Berquist, *Ancient Wine, New Wineskins: The Lord's Supper in Old Testament Perspective* (St. Louis: Chalice Press, 1991), 54–59.

REFORMATION SUNDAY

OCTOBER 29, 2006

LUTHERAN
Jer. 31:31–34
Psalm 46
Rom. 3:19–28
John 8:31–36

FIRST READING
JEREMIAH 31:31–34

Interpreting the Text

Jeremiah's preaching spanned the years leading up to the exile of 587 B.C.E. and the exile itself. The prophet interpreted the national collapse by saying that the nation fell and its leaders were exiled because they had been disobedient to the covenant. While Jeremiah wanted the people to understand why their world had collapsed, today's text, an oracle of salvation, is one of hope. Although the exile was divine punishment for disobedience, God did not abandon the community. Jeremiah 31:31–34 declares that God will make a new covenant. The difference between the new covenant and the old is that the new is written on the heart of the community, a hope shared by other Jewish leaders of much the same time (for instance, Deut. 10:16; 30:6; Ezek. 36:26-27). The community will thus be empowered to live obediently to Torah in the regenerated community.

Responding to the Text

Many Christians think God replaced the so-called old covenant that God made with the Jewish people at Sinai with a brand-new covenant made through Jesus Christ. Such people believe that in order to be part of the new covenant, people must become a part of the Christian community. Jeremiah, however, envisioned the "new covenant" as one with Israel; indeed, according to Jer. 31:35-37, the Jewish people will exist as long as the creation itself. Furthermore, those who think that a new covenant through Christ superseded the old must recognize that such a break with Judaism would mean that God is not faithful to the covenant God made with Israel. If so, why should Christians believe that God will remain faithful to the promises God has made to us? Furthermore, such Christians must reckon with the fact that the church is hardly a community of new heart in which people no longer need to teach one another because all "know the LORD" and live accordingly.

To be sure, some early Christian writers used the language of "new covenant" to interpret the event of Jesus Christ (for instance, Luke 22:20; 1 Cor. 11:25; 2 Cor. 3:5-14). A closer look at most of these sources reveals that they think of the Christ event not as canceling the prior covenant but as extending it, especially for Gentiles in preparation for the apocalypse. Only in the eschatological realm of God does the vision of Jer. 31:33-34 become an every-day-all-the-time social world.

> CHRISTIANS MUST RECKON WITH THE FACT THAT THE CHURCH IS HARDLY A COMMUNITY OF NEW HEART IN WHICH PEOPLE NO LONGER NEED TO TEACH ONE ANOTHER BECAUSE ALL "KNOW THE LORD" AND LIVE ACCORDINGLY.

RESPONSIVE READING
PSALM 46

The psalm uses traditional ancient symbols to speak both literally and figuratively of changes such as natural disaster and social chaos. This hymn has particular power to strengthen leaders and communities (such as the reformers and their churches) who find themselves in the midst of turmoil. This passage affirms that God will carry the community through various forms of change and chaos. The preacher might ask, "Who in the congregation identifies with forces of renewal today but, as in the time of the Reformation, is finding that the impetus for renewal calls forth negative reaction that makes life a chaos for the renewers?"

SECOND READING
ROMANS 3:19-28

Interpreting the Text

According to a popular interpretation of Romans, Paul claims that obedience to the law is a work that Jewish people perform to be saved. Paul shows the impotence of Judaism (and especially the law) to save. Only the grace of Jesus Christ can save both Jews and Gentiles. In the last forty years, however, a small but growing group of scholars has come to believe that Paul affirms Judaism as a religion of grace whose adherents are saved without Jesus Christ and that the law functions for them as positive guidance in the covenantal way of salvation. This group thinks that Romans was written to Gentile followers of Jesus who have adopted an attitude of superiority toward Judaism and who misunderstand its practices. Paul intends for the letter to call Gentiles to respect Judaism and to live in community with Jewish people.[1]

The latter school has discovered that the phrase "deeds prescribed by the law," sometimes translated "works of the law" (*ergōn nomou*), refers to actions that first-century Gentiles performed in the hope that such acts would save them (Rom. 3:19-20).[2] The Gentiles, in other words, are guilty of works-righteousness. Romans 3:21-26 reminds Gentiles that the grace of God through Jesus Christ frees them from trying to save themselves through such misguided and even harmful efforts. Indeed, God's grace through Christ is a "sacrifice of atonement"; that is, it functions for Gentiles in the same way that the sacrifices in the Temple function for Jewish people by assuring them of God's forgiveness.

In Rom. 3:27-31, some interpreters in the revisionary group see the term "faith" (*pistis*) referring not to human faith but to God's faithfulness. In the diatribe (question and answer format) of this last part of the passage, the apostle confirms that God through Christ is gracious toward Gentiles as God has also been gracious for centuries to the Jewish community. Gentiles, therefore, have no ground for boasting (seeing themselves as superior to Jewish people).

Responding to the Text

In one sense, the revised interpretation is radical, at least in its implications for Christian perception of Judaism and the law. The revisionary school calls Christians to repent of the centuries-old negative caricature of Judaism and the law that fuels anti-Judaism and anti-Semitism. Gentile Christians must respect Judaism and its adherents as already standing fully in divine grace. In another sense, however, the sermon should have a familiar tone. For the preacher in a Gentile Christian congregation still needs to help Gentiles recognize the works that *we Gentiles* perform in misguided attempts to save ourselves. As this passage so beautifully says, we are saved only by grace. Indeed, we rejoice as fellow-heirs with our Jewish counterparts.

> GENTILE CHRISTIANS MUST RESPECT JUDAISM AND ITS ADHERENTS AS ALREADY STANDING FULLY IN DIVINE GRACE.

JOHN 8:31-36

Interpreting the Text

The Fourth Gospel presupposes two spheres of existence: below and above. The "world" below is existence apart from God and is marked by such qualities as hatred, falsehood, darkness, slavery, and death, whereas "heaven" is existence shaped by the divine and is marked by such things as love, truth, light, freedom, and life. Of importance to today's reading is the Johannine notion that "the Jews" are of the realm "below," while Jesus and his followers belong "above." (In the Fourth Gospel "the Jews" do not include all Jews but represent a group of Jewish authorities and followers who reject Jesus as revelation of God). The mission of Jesus in the Fourth Gospel is to reveal the upper sphere in the midst of the world so that people below can partake of the life from above. On All Saints Day/Sunday, we use this reconstruction of the worldview of the Fourth Gospel as a framework for interpreting the resurrection of Lazarus (John 11:1-44).

In John 7:1—8:32, Jesus engages in protracted conflict with some Jewish authorities regarding the validity of his teaching and purpose. Today's text begins an extended teaching designed to bring about two effects in the Johannine community (8:31-59). The first is to assure the community that the revelation that comes from Jesus is the truth and that knowing the truth brings freedom (8:31-32).[3] Indeed, Jesus receives the revelation from God and transmits it to the community (8:38). Those who accept the revelation are free from restrictions of life in the realm of existence "below" and are empowered to live from "above."

The second purpose of the passage is to prompt believers to consider that their Jewish heritage is incomplete and even untrustworthy unless they embrace Jesus. For the Fourth Gospel, the Jewish leaders who oppose Jesus operate from "below." Although descendents of Abraham, they are still enslaved by sin (8:33-36). Some Jewish people have indeed sinned by seeking to kill Jesus (8:37; cf. 7:1, 25, 30, 44; 8:20). As chapter 8 unfolds, John seeks more directly to devalue the teaching of "the Jews," because as the Johannine Jesus soon says, "You are from your father, the devil" (John 8:44).

Responding to the Text

The appeal of this text for preaching on Reformation Sunday is easy to see. It promises that Jesus frees us from enslaving powers. Half a millennium ago, the reforming church heard in this passage freedom from a repressive and legalistic ecclesiastical structure. Although most people in the churches that came from the Reformation have a much more positive attitude about today's Roman Catholic

Church, there are still pockets of anti-Romanism in some churches. Indeed, for such people anti-Romanism itself may now be a form of slavery.

Similarly, a fair number of Christians (including many in the churches descended from the Reformation) are enslaved by a caricature of Judaism like the one found in the Fourth Gospel: as a religion of works whose rigid adherents are concerned only with obedience as empty ceremony. The preacher may need to help some people discover how Jesus frees them from such attitudes toward the Roman Catholic Church and Judaism.

Beyond that, a sermon can name other contemporary forms of slavery that take place in the churches that came from the Reformation, as well as in modes of existence outside the church. Like the characters in John 8:33, many such people may not even be aware that they are living in slavery. A sermon should indicate how the sphere of Jesus' authority can transform them into freedom.

> THE PREACHER MAY NEED TO HELP SOME PEOPLE DISCOVER HOW JESUS FREES THEM FROM CARICATURED ATTITUDES TOWARD THE ROMAN CATHOLIC CHURCH AND JUDAISM.

Notes

1. For representative scholars who share this perspective, see the bibliography in John G. Gager, *Reinventing Paul* (New York: Oxford University Press, 2000).

2. Markus Barth, *Ephesians 1–3*, Anchor Bible (Garden City, N.Y.: Doubleday, 1974), 244–48.

3. Jesus' words in this passage are more like those he customarily addresses to "the Jews" than to "the Jews who had believed in him" (John 8:31). Gail R. O'Day reviews this problem and offers a resolution in her "John," in *The New Interpreter's Bible*, ed. Leander Keck et al. (Nashville: Abingdon Press, 1995), 9:637.

TWENTY-FIRST SUNDAY AFTER PENTECOST

REVISED COMMON	EPISCOPAL (BCP)	ROMAN CATHOLIC
Jer. 31:7-9 or Job 42:1-6, 10-17	Isa. 59:(1-4) 9-19	Jer. 31:7-9
Psalm 126 or Ps. 34:1-8 (19-22)	Psalm 13	Ps. 126:1-2, 2-3, 4-5, 6
Heb. 7:23-28	Heb. 5:12—6:1, 9-12	Heb. 5:1-6
Mark 10:46-52	Mark 10:46-52	Mark 10:46-52

FIRST READING
JEREMIAH 31:7-9 (RCL, RC)

Jeremiah preached at the time of the exile of 587 B.C.E. Elsewhere Jeremiah announced that God caused the nation to collapse because it had not lived covenantally, but that a remnant of the community had persisted in faithfulness. Today's passage is an oracle of salvation intended to encourage the remnant in its practice of faithfulness by promising that God will use the remnant as the foundation for restoring Israel. Unfortunately, the lectionary misses the opportunity to recognize the experience of women by not assigning Jer. 31:1-7, for vv. 2-6 not only draw on general exodus imagery to bespeak the restoration but turn specifically to the memory of Miriam leading Israel through the exodus with dance and tambourine.

The minister who preaches this passage to today's congregation as nothing more than a promise of salvation runs the risk of giving cheap (and possibly false) comfort. The text presumes that the nation as a whole is collapsing because of its unfaithfulness. While the social world of the contemporary West is not in danger of becoming an immediate chaos, deeply entrenched patterns of nationalism, ethnocentrism, self-interest, and injustice point to disintegration. Even so, the preacher can assure the congregation that God has not abandoned the community. In the midst of social tension, God is working with a faithful remnant to use the life of that group as basis for eventually rebuilding the larger social world. A crucial question is how the congregation can live as a faithful remnant demonstrating the practices of justice and mutuality that are necessary to rebuild the fragmented and unjust social world of North America.

ISAIAH 59:1-4 (9-19) (BCP)

Isaiah 40–55 was spoken when the leaders of Israel were in exile in Babylon. The authors of these chapters anticipated that God would return the people to the land of Israel. Isaiah 56–66 was spoken after the return, but the restoration of the community was much slower than expected. Some members of the community may have doubted that God had the power to regenerate. Today's passage explains why the renewal was taking longer than expected. God is powerful enough to renew the community (Isa. 59:1), but many of the people have returned to unjust behavior (59:2-4, 9-15a). Indeed, the community admits its sin (52:12-13). Because "no one" is concerned for covenantal faithfulness, God has dressed for battle and is coming to inflict judgment (59:15b-21).

> IN THE MIDST OF SOCIAL TENSION, GOD IS WORKING WITH A FAITHFUL REMNANT TO USE THE LIFE OF THAT GROUP AS BASIS FOR EVENTUALLY REBUILDING THE LARGER SOCIAL WORLD.

This circumstance is disturbingly contemporary—disturbing because we today have learned so little from Isaiah. The preacher can point out that God is ever-ready to work with communities to restore them to become arenas of blessing for all. Yet, at least in North America, we continue to practice injustice in ways that subvert the possibility of renewal. Even if the preacher does not believe that God is literally coming for battle, Isaiah's sober prediction is that such societies set in motion patterns of destructive behavior that will bring about their own collapse.

> THE PREACHER CAN POINT OUT THAT GOD IS EVER-READY TO WORK WITH COMMUNITIES TO RESTORE THEM TO BECOME ARENAS OF BLESSING FOR ALL.

JOB 42:1-6, 10-17 (RCL ALT.)

Interpreting the Text

In 42:1-6, Job affirms the divine speeches in chapters 38–41. Job believes that God can, indeed, do all things (42:2). In 42:3 Job cites God's words as Job's own. In 42:4-5, Job indicates that he agrees that he cannot understand all things as God understands them.

The key verse of Job's statement (v. 6) is notoriously difficult.[1] Some recent interpreters notice that Job does not simply abase himself but acknowledges the inadequacy of both the deuteronomic perception of the relationship between blessing and curse (voiced by his friends) and Job's earlier demands for another (but equally clear) framework of meaning. Having encountered God face-to-face, Job embraces the notion that chaos is inherently a part of life while recognizing that neither it nor abundance can always be easily explained in simple terms of divine cause and effect. Job learned further in chapters 38–41 that while chaos is potent, it will not finally overwhelm the structures that God made to support creation.

In a brilliant interpretive move, J. Gerald Janzen takes the expression "dust and ashes" to refer to the divine image.[2] To "repent in dust and ashes" is to accept the human vocation of living in the divine image, which is to rule or to have dominion—that is, to help the many elements of creation live toward as much blessing as is possible in a world in which chaos occurs, which, consequently, means that suffering will be inevitable.

In 42:10-17, God restores Job's life twofold. Interpretations of 42:10-17 are as diverse as those of 42:6.[3] Nevertheless, several commentators provocatively observe that in Israelite law, someone who deprived another through theft or mismanagement was required to pay the injured party double the loss (Exod. 22:4). The purpose of such restitution is to allow people to go forward. God's twofold restoration of Job, then, could be God's admitting guilt by causing Job undeserved suffering; God makes restitution. In my view, this part of the story is a narrative statement to the effect that God provides the resources for us to make our way through the chaos and ambiguity of life. However, in at least one respect, the twofold restoration is regrettable. For on the surface, a listener could take it to mean that God will similarly restore all who suffer unjustly. That is seldom the immediate way things work out in our world. At a deeper level, however, we repeatedly encounter individuals and communities who could be overwhelmed by chaos but who continue to do what they can to fulfill the vocation of 42:6.

> GOD'S TWOFOLD RESTORATION OF JOB COULD BE GOD'S ADMITTING GUILT BY CAUSING JOB UNDESERVED SUFFERING; GOD MAKES RESTITUTION.

The difference in Job's life between 1:1 and 42:6 is not a change of external circumstances but a change in Job's perspective within similar circumstances. An underlying message is that how we view God's relationship to (and role in) circumstances is more important than the circumstances themselves in determining whether they beat us down or whether we can live purposefully (if sometimes painfully) through them.

Responding to the Text

Many readers will find the end of the book of Job theologically satisfying. Certainly it offers a credible theological alternative to a wooden deuteronomic interpretation

255

TWENTY-FIRST
SUNDAY
AFTER PENTECOST

RONALD J.
ALLEN

of existence in terms of obedience resulting in prosperity and disobedience in curse. As suggested in the preceding paragraph, the book of Job regards circumstances themselves as more ambiguous but offers a perspective within which to live through all circumstances. A preacher can certainly commend this point of view.

Moreover, the book of Job is an important voice in a Jewish tradition that authorizes honest wrestling with God. The preacher could help the congregation name ways that we can honor God by raising questions about the divine will and purposes in our setting that are as honest as Job was in his setting.

The book of Job contributes to another contemporary theological discussion: what sources do we use (and how do we use them) when interpreting the divine presence and purposes? The four friends largely repeat inherited tradition and apply it to Job's circumstances. Job's experience, by contrast, causes him to question the theological adequacy of the tradition. A preacher might help the congregation reflect on how the congregation does (and should) bring tradition and experience into conversation in search of adequate understandings of the divine purposes.

However, with regard to understanding the extent of divine power, some Christians find another perspective on divine power more persuasive than the one found in the book of Job.[4] The preacher can help the congregation decide where they land on this issue. On the one hand, if God is completely powerful (as the book of Job presumes), then God is responsible for all things either by directly initiating them or by permitting them. God, then, is not only directly or indirectly responsible for all suffering but also has the power to end it in single stroke. Indeed, at 42:10-11, God restored Job's life by fiat. On the other hand, some revisionary believers reason that if God is all-powerful and does not act in love to end suffering, then God is neither altogether loving nor altogether just. These latter theologians conclude that God is not all-powerful. To be sure, the not-all-powerful God has more power than any other entity, but this God cannot simply change circumstances by single divine interventions. God exercises power by attempting to lure others into thoughts and relationships that promise blessing.

> GOD EXERCISES POWER BY ATTEMPTING TO LURE OTHERS INTO THOUGHTS AND RELATIONSHIPS THAT PROMISE BLESSING.

From the revisionary point of view, a part of what it means to live as "dust and ashes" (see above) is to name God's presence helping us make our way through chaos, injustice, and suffering. Even when circumstances do not (or cannot) get better, the awareness of God's presence can make a difference between giving in to chaos and living bitterly, and living through such circumstances on the basis of God's sustaining presence.

Some readers will say that the revisionary viewpoint seeks a level of certainty with regard to understanding God to which the book of Job objects. However, Christians who subscribe to the revisionary viewpoint choose to live with that difficulty rather than to believe that God authorizes evil in any way. Such Christians believe that if God authorizes evil, then God is finally untrustworthy.

257

TWENTY-FIRST
SUNDAY
AFTER PENTECOST

RONALD J.
ALLEN

Responsive Reading

PSALM 126 (RCL)
PSALM 126:1-2, 2-3, 4-5, 6 (RC)

The homecoming from exile revealed God's great power to deliver and was joyous in the mood of 126:1-3. However, after the initial euphoria of return, the fortunes of the community waned, and in this psalm, the people now beseech God to flood them with blessing in the same way that water fills the watercourses (streambeds that are dry most of year) in the desert during the rainy season (vv. 4-6). Confidence in God's regenerative power is palpable in vv. 5-6: what God did, God will do again. On the one hand, the preacher can affirm that God does all that God can do to help revitalize individuals and communities. On the other hand, restoration does not always live up to what we anticipate. A preacher may need to help a congregation adjust its hopes and learn to recognize the opportunities in reduced circumstances. The brute fact is that sometimes we must learn to find the divine providence as we live in a dry watercourse.

> THE BRUTE FACT IS THAT SOMETIMES WE MUST LEARN TO FIND THE DIVINE PROVIDENCE AS WE LIVE IN A DRY WATERCOURSE.

PSALM 13 (BCP)

This psalm is an individual's agonizing cry for deliverance from enemies. Today's reader can feel the pain of the psalmist in vv. 1-2. The singer declares that without the conscious knowledge of God's presence, the singer would die, which would only complete the enemy's victory (vv. 3-4). A preacher might use this psalm as a source of encouragement for individuals in the congregation who feel overwhelmed by racism, disease, poverty, abuse, gender discrimination, and other enemies: the conscious awareness of God's presence may not mean that our circumstances immediately change, but such awareness does help us survive them so that we can witness on another day.

PSALM 34:1-8 (19-22) (RCL ALT.)

Psalm 34 is a song of thanksgiving for deliverance from an unspecified circumstance that caused the psalmist to be afraid (vv. 1-10). The author then turns the psalm in an instructional direction and invites readers to think that if they, too, follow the commandments, God will deliver them should they fall into trouble (vv. 11-22). While a preacher can certainly lead the congregation in rejoicing when individuals and communities are delivered from their fears, the hard fact of life is that the righteous are not always spared or delivered. The preacher needs to help the congregation recognize that God feels their pain (as in v. 15) and that the angel of the Lord (so to speak; v. 7) camping with them helps them survive difficulty. Psalm 34 contains several famous lines (for instance, vv. 5, 6, esp. 8, 22).

SECOND READING
HEBREWS 7:23-28 (RCL)

Interpreting the Text

This reading presupposes Heb. 7:1-22, which uses the eternal high priesthood of Melchizedek as a paradigm for interpreting the high priesthood of Jesus.[5] As pointed out on the Twentieth Sunday after Pentecost, for Philo, Melchizedek was of a different "order" of priesthood than Moses, Aaron, Levi, and others. According to Heb. 7:23, the latter are mortals who are subject to weakness and death, and we learn in 7:27 that they must sacrifice for their own sins before they can function as priests for the people. Consequently, they are only intermediaries and cannot lead believers to perfection.

According to Heb. 7:24-25, Jesus (like Melchizedek) is immortal and, consequently, is even now at work to help believers who seek to approach God (that is, who are on the path to perfection). In Heb. 7:27, Jesus (again like Melchizedek) need not sacrifice for himself nor continue sacrificing for others, for he has offered himself. (On sacrifice in Hebrews, see the Twenty-third Sunday after Pentecost).

Responding to the Text

On the Twentieth and Twenty-first Sundays after Pentecost, we have called attention to themes of assurance and suppression that recur in this reading. A preacher could take a different tack today and use Hebrews 7 as a case study in interpretation of the Bible and other sacred texts. Melchizedek is a minor figure in the First Testament, mentioned only at Gen. 14:17-24 and Ps. 110:4 (cited in Heb. 5:6 and

7:17). However, later authors (such as Philo) expanded their interpretations of Melchizedek to address questions and issues in their times.

On the one hand, a preacher can help the congregation recognize that each generation makes similar interpretive moves with regard to other biblical passages. On the other hand, a congregation needs to consider the limits of such moves. When is it legitimate to expand on a text or tradition, and when does an interpretive community drift into the morass of eisegesis (that is, preachers reading their own meanings into the text rather than carefully determining how people in the ancient world would have understood the text)?

259

TWENTY-FIRST
SUNDAY
AFTER PENTECOST

RONALD J.
ALLEN

HEBREWS 5:12—6:1, 9-12 (BCP)

Interpreting the Text

This passage arises from the Hellenistic idea of *paideia* or education: a person grows by stages into the mature form of life. The particular form of *paideia* invoked here involves conforming one's life to a prototype or exemplar. In the type of Hellenistic Judaism found in Philo, the mature life is "perfection," that is, leaving the lower and imperfect realm of existence and journeying to the perfect realm by means of educatively patterning one's life after exemplars. In this text, the author states that the congregation has not moved far enough on the educational path (Heb. 5:12-13). They need to "go on toward perfection." This means leaving behind the introductory stages of growth (the teachings and practices mention in Heb. 6:1-2). Indeed, these teachings and actions take place in the imperfect sphere and therefore do not advance the believer toward perfection.[6] Believers need to submit to God, recognizing that submission involves suffering but that suffering (as we can see from the model of Jesus) is itself a part of the education to perfection.

> WHEN IS IT LEGITIMATE TO EXPAND ON A TEXT OR TRADITION, AND WHEN DOES AN INTERPRETIVE COMMUNITY DRIFT INTO THE MORASS OF EISEGESIS?

The text contains a hard edge. Hebrews 6:4-6 suggests that backsliders are lost when they turn back from the path led by Jesus. They cannot reach perfection.

Responding to the Text

This text places the preacher in an odd situation. To be sure, a preacher can commend the general notion of *paideia* or continuous growth toward Christian maturity. At the same time, the religion of Jesus as interpreted through the lens of Philo's Judaism is quite different from what became conventional mainstream Christianity. Although the author of Hebrews may have regarded repentance, baptism, and teaching about the resurrection of the dead as elementary things the congregation should leave behind, they are hardly elementary today. Indeed, theological illiteracy in many congregations calls for the preacher to help the membership rediscover such notions and practices.

Most theological movements today disagree with the "hard edge" in this passage discussed above. Whereas Hebrews may suggest that backsliders are lost, the theology of most preachers today pushes them to believe that backsliders can, indeed, return to full participation in Christian community and, in the language of Hebrews, rejoin the journey to perfection.

HEBREWS 5:1-6 (RC)

For discussion of this reading, please see the Twentieth Sunday after Pentecost.

THE GOSPEL
MARK 10:46-52 (RCL, BCP, RC)

Interpreting the Text

At one level, this story authenticates Jesus as agent of the divine realm because he can work its signs (miracles). The miracle itself reveals the social character of that realm as one in which the poor, isolated, and disabled (represented in the blind person) are restored to community and ability. Even more, in Jewish literature, while references to eyes and sight are often physically literal, they sometimes also refer figuratively to theological understanding (for instance, Isa. 43:8; 59:9-10). The healing of this person thus figuratively promises that in the realm of God, people will come to see and understand. The text thus confirms that those who come into the sphere of Jesus will experience social and perceptual restoration.

At another level, as the last miracle story in the Gospel of Mark, this passage plays a more distinctive role. From 1:1 through 8:21, the Gospel writer establishes that the realm of God is proleptically manifest through the ministry of Jesus. The miracle stories, the teaching, the confrontations with Jewish leaders—all demonstrate the presence of the realm. The disciples fail to understand fully the character of these interactions.

As we reach Mark 8:22, the reader (like the disciples) is still blind to an element of this realm. The story of the healing of the blind person in 8:22-26 (who is healed in two stages) functions as a model of what needs to happen to the disciples and to the reader. Like the blind person who has received the first touch and who can see people who look like trees, the listener possesses partial knowledge of the coming of the realm but still needs a second touch (more knowledge) to understand it fully. In 8:27—9:1, Mark reveals the second touch as the news that Jesus will die (and the disciples will suffer) as part of the transition from the present to the future world. In Mark 9:2—10:45, Jesus continues to predict the passion, but the disciples continue to fail to perceive it fully.

In this development, 10:36 and 10:51 are keys. In the former, the Markan Jesus asks the disciples, "What is it you want me to do for you?" They reply that they want seats on Jesus' right and left hands in glory, thus indicating that despite repeated instruction they do not understand. In 10:51, Jesus asks essentially the same question to the blind person. The latter requests the ability to see and is a model for the reader.

Mark thus admonishes the reader to avoid the mistake of the disciples (who continue to operate according to old-age values and who refuse to recognize that they will suffer as a part of the apocalyptic transformation of the world) and to adopt the perspective of the formerly blind person. Mark 11:1 through 16:7 completes the second touch by narrating the death of Jesus and assuring the reader of the coming apocalypse (16:7), at which time they will see fully in the divine realm.

Responding to the Text

The pastor could simply preach the story of blind Bartimaeus as a miracle story (per the discussion at the beginning of the preceding section) that is a paradigm of what can happen to people who come into the sphere of Jesus as agent of the realm of God.[7] Such a sermon might invite the congregation to identify with Bartimaeus and explore ways that people are in situations like the blind beggar. The message could function on either the social or the figurative level (per above). If social, the preacher would indicate ways that impoverished, lonely, or disabled people are restored. If figurative, the sermon would indicate how participation in the realm of God opens us to perceive the meaning and fullness of life from the perspective of the realm of God in regenerative ways.

> THE CHURCH ITSELF SOMETIMES FOSTERS LIMITATION AND MISPERCEPTION, SO THE PREACHER MAY NEED TO LOOK FOR PLACES OUTSIDE THE CHRISTIAN COMMUNITY WHERE THE HEALING POWER OF THE REALM IS AT WORK.

In the cases of both sermons, a crucial question is, where and how do people today come into contact with Jesus in ways similar to the picture in the text? The preacher might point to the Christian community as an arena where such things occur. However, the church itself sometimes fosters limitation and misperception, so the preacher may need to look for places outside the Christian community where the healing power of the realm is at work.

A more complicated sermon could come from the role that Mark 10:46-52 plays in the Gospel of Mark. The preacher might note how the disciples persistently

261

TWENTY-FIRST
SUNDAY
AFTER PENTECOST

RONALD J.
ALLEN

are blind to the ministry of Jesus and the realm of God in the first chapters of the book. Many of us, like them, do not welcome the possibility of suffering for the sake of witness to the divine realm. However, the way Mark portrays the disciples in the Gospel is a warning to the reader; they are missing the blessing of the realm (albeit a blessing that comes with suffering). The story of Bartimaeus promises that those who embrace the realm as a regeneration of the world (accompanied by suffering) will follow Jesus into the new world where they finally and fully will see him and all things.

Notes

1. For a concise overview of possibilities in interpretation, see Carol Newsom, "The Book of Job," in *The New Interpreter's Bible,* ed. Leander Keck et al. (Nashville: Abingdon Press, 1996), 4:628–29.

2. J. Gerald Janzen, *Job,* Interpretation: A Bible Commentary for Preaching and Teaching (Louisville: John Knox Press, 1985), 255–57.

3. E.g., Newsom, "Job," 636. For a dramatically different reading, see Janzen, *Job,* 267–69.

4. For an exceptional discussion of the alternative view—found most fully in process theology—see Clark M. Williamson, *Way of Blessing, Way of Life: A Christian Theology* (St. Louis: Chalice Press, 1999), 131–56.

5. Lala Kalyan Kumar Dey, *The Intermediary Worlds and Patterns of Perfection in Philo and Hebrews*, SBL Dissertation Series 25 (Missoula, Mont.: Scholars Press, 1975), 48, 89–93, 227–35.

6. Ibid., 123–24.

7. For guidance in preaching on this story, see Kathy Black, *A Healing Homiletic: Preaching and Disability* (Nashville: Abingdon Press, 1996), 57–87, esp. 78–87. Professor Black discourages using blindness in a figurative way.

ALL SAINTS DAY /
ALL SAINTS SUNDAY

NOVEMBER 1 OR NOVEMBER 5, 2006*

REVISED COMMON	EPISCOPAL (BCP)	ROMAN CATHOLIC
Isa. 25:6-9 or Wisd. of Sol. 3:1-9	Sir. 44:1-10, 13-14 or Sir. 2:(1-6) 7-11	Rev. 7:2-4, 9-14
Psalm 24	Psalm 149	Ps. 24:1-2, 3-4, 5-6
Rev. 21:1-6a	Rev. 7:2-4, 9-17 or Eph. 1:(11-14) 15-23	1 John 3:1-3
John 11:32-44	Matt. 5:1-12 or Luke 6:20-26 (27-36)	Matt. 5:1-12a

FIRST READING
ISAIAH 25:6-9 (RCL)

Interpreting the Text

Many scholars refer to Isaiah 24–27 as a "little apocalypse" and date this material at about the same time as Third Isaiah (Isaiah 56–66) and the return of the exiles from Babylonia to the Holy Land. Although the exiles had anticipated a joyous return leading to an immediately prosperous life, they found the land and people debilitated and the regeneration much more difficult and fractious than anticipated. Prophets such as those who spoke Isaiah 24–27 (as well as 34–35 and 56–66) planted the seeds of what became the apocalyptic movement by envisioning a time when God would end the present age and begin a new one (later called "the realm [NRSV "kingdom"] of God"). Today's text anticipates a festal meal (sometimes called the eschatological banquet) that God will serve to celebrate the

*Due to space considerations, I have chosen to comment only on the texts offered by the Revised Common Lectionary, which change with each year in the lectionary cycle. The texts for All Saints are consistent from year to year in the BCP and Roman Catholic lectionaries; for comments on those texts, I commend to you earlier editions of *New Proclamation*, particularly those by Robert Kysar (Year A, 2005) and Lucy Lind Hogan (Year C, 2004).

inauguration of the new world. The Canaanites believed that death (whom they regarded as a deity) would "swallow" everything. In a reversal of that image, the God of Israel swallows death itself and removes the shroud that has obscured the peoples' understanding of the divine purposes.

Responding to the Text

A preacher might use this text as the beginning point for a sermon that traces when and how the notion of a full and robust life beyond death entered into Jewish and Christian communities. A preacher might also point out that this text, and others like it, respond to a question that is as important to people today as it was to the people disillusioned by their return from exile. When and how will God finally and fully manifest the divine purposes and keep the divine promises?

TODAY'S TEXT ANTICIPATES A FESTAL MEAL THAT GOD WILL SERVE TO CELEBRATE THE INAUGURATION OF THE NEW WORLD.

While the author of Isa. 25:6-9 did not envision the meal that Christians call the Lord's Supper, the church sees the Supper as an experience that prefigures the eschatological banquet. The preacher might point to other meals that also embody qualities of the eschatological age and invite the congregation to draw encouragement from these moments to continue living faithfully.

WISDOM OF SOLOMON 3:1-9 (RCL ALT.)

Interpreting the Text

For general background on the Wisdom of Solomon, see the Nineteenth Sunday after Pentecost. To that discussion we note that the author of this book incorporates into Jewish thinking about the afterlife a modest (and not always thoroughgoing) Platonic understanding of the self composed as body and soul in which, at death, the nonmaterial soul leaves the material body to become immortal and to dwell with God in the afterlife.

In today's passage, the souls of the righteous (that is, those who have lived according to wisdom) are already in the hands of God (present with God) (Wisd. 3:1). These souls of the righteous have made "departure" and are "going from us," but they are now "at peace" and their hope is "full of immortality" (3:2-4). The suffering that came upon them on earth was a "test" in the same way that gold ore is "tested," that is, purified by being plunged into a fire that burns away the slag (3:5-6). These souls will make an unspecified "visitation" in which they shine and exercise rule over nations and peoples even as God reigns over them and watches over them (3:7-9).

A main purpose of this text suggests a similar purpose for the sermon: to assure the congregation of the well-being of those who have died. Strictly speaking, we do not have empirical evidence about an afterlife, so the preacher is advised not to go into detail. However, the passage gives the preacher an opportunity to explain why the afterlife is something in which we can trust.

When discussing John 11:32-44 below, I propose a sermon to deal with different conceptions of eternal life in the Bible and Christian tradition.[1] In such a message, Wisd. 3:1-9 could be an example of the belief in immortality of the soul.

The text implicitly answers the question of whether death, affliction, and suffering are divine punishment by interpreting such circumstances as divine "discipline" and "test" that lead to immortality with God. The preacher who is theologically uncomfortable with such an idea of God's activity can still commend the underlying theme that those who trust in God through difficult circumstances discover God's grace and mercy watching over them now and in the world to come.

> THE PASSAGE GIVES THE PREACHER AN OPPORTUNITY TO EXPLAIN WHY THE AFTERLIFE IS SOMETHING IN WHICH WE CAN TRUST.

RESPONSIVE READING
PSALM 24 (RCL)

This psalm is well chosen for All Saints as it is from a liturgy for entering the temple at Jerusalem. The psalm begins with a focus on God as creator of all (24:1-2). The people who enter the temple are those who live according to God's design and purposes (24:3-6). The "saints" of today's festival include such folk. Verses 7-9 depict the procession bearing the Ark of the Covenant, representing the divine presence, into the temple: the living God is fully present among people during the liturgy. Further, the temple represents the world; hence, the coming of the Ark portrays God powerfully present in the world. The saints live in companionship with that presence. Liberation theologians point out that v. 1 contains a principle with economic implications: the earth belongs not to private individuals or corporations (to use for personal gain) but to God, who intends that people use its resources to provide blessing for all.

SECOND READING

REVELATION 21:1-6a (RCL)

Interpreting the Text

The book of Revelation was written in the early to mid-90s C.E. in response to either active persecution of Jesus' followers by Rome in Asia Minor (modern-day Turkey) or in fear of such persecution. John the Revelator writes to encourage the church to remain faithful during this season of difficulty when the present world gives the impression that Rome is truly imperial. The author, however, interprets idolatrous, pretentious, oppressive, and violent Rome as an instrument of Satan that God will soon destroy. For God is about to intervene in history with a massive apocalypse that will destroy Rome and replace the present created world with a new one in which all things are made new.

> THE FINAL CHAPTERS OF THE REVELATION ARE DESIGNED TO LURE THE COMMUNITY TO AVOID COMPLICITY WITH ROME SO THAT THEY CAN PARTAKE IN THE UNENDING BLESSING OF THE NEW AGE.

Revelation 18–20 urges the community of the apocalypse to believe that the social disintegration and violence of their world is actually the beginning of the collapse of Rome. Revelation 21–22 climaxes the book with a contrasting vision of the world that is to come. The final chapters of the Revelation are designed to lure the community to avoid complicity with Rome so that they can partake in the unending blessing of the new age.

The eschatological world is marked by an end to chaos (the sea is no more; Rev. 21:1) and by the kind of covenantal relationship between God and the community that is associated with bride and bridegroom (21:2). All relationships and circumstances will take place according to God's design for justice, abundance, joy, and love for all (21:3-4, 6b-7), and the community will have direct and full access to God with no need of mediation (21:3-4). The new world will be altogether reconstituted (21:5) and all evil forces will be eliminated that could violate God's purposes for blessing for all (21:8).

Responding to the Text

The book of Revelation was written to give hope to people in a marginalized situation in the ancient world. From this point of view, the text offers the hope that God is in the world seeking to shape all lives and circumstances according to God's purposes of justice, abundance, and love. This message is particularly relevant to all who suffer social oppression and can be extended to those ravaged by such life-interrupting phenomena as addiction, divorce, and illness.

However, many of the churches in current North America with memberships of non-Hispanic European origin are typically in the mainstream of culture. A minister should not use the hope of this passage to comfort people who inflict cruelty (even inadvertently) on other people through politics, financial investment strategies, and social values. The preacher is obligated to point such folk to Revelation 18–20 as a warning, and to use Revelation 21–22 as a lure to change their ways (repent) and join the movement toward the just, abundant, and loving world a-coming.

For the Revelator, the saints are those who endure. The most characteristic word for the mission of the church in the time of conflict between Rome and God is "endure." By this, John means not only to survive but to engage in active confession of the sovereignty of God and the vision of the coming world in the face of challenges to it. The sermon could lift up persons and communities who have endured (and who continue to do so) and fortify the congregation for witnessing to the vision of Revelation 21–22 in a world that is so often more like Revelation 18–20.

> BY "ENDURE," JOHN MEANS NOT ONLY TO SURVIVE BUT TO ENGAGE IN ACTIVE CONFESSION OF THE SOVEREIGNTY OF GOD AND THE VISION OF THE COMING WORLD IN THE FACE OF CHALLENGES TO IT.

THE GOSPEL
JOHN 11:32-44 (RCL)

Interpreting the Text

The reading for today presupposes the Johannine worldview described on Reformation Sunday. John 11:1-44 is a "sign" and is the climax of the first part of the Fourth Gospel. While the signs are similar in content to the miracle stories of the Synoptic tradition, they differ in function. The first eleven chapters of the Fourth Gospel establish that Jesus reveals the realm above. The signs demonstrate the truth of this revelation and embody its character.

In the Fourth Gospel, the term "death" refers not simply to the end of biological function but also to existence taking place apart from the purposes of God. From this perspective, existence below is itself a form of death (even when biological systems continue). "Life" in the Fourth Gospel is existence permeated by qualities of life above. In 11:25-27, John indicates that when one believes in Jesus, eternal life begins now and continues after the cessation of biological operations: "I am the resurrection and the life." The raising of Lazarus is the definitive sign of the power

> IN THE FOURTH GOSPEL, THE TERM "DEATH" REFERS NOT SIMPLY TO THE END OF BIOLOGICAL FUNCTION BUT ALSO TO EXISTENCE TAKING PLACE APART FROM THE PURPOSES OF GOD.

of God's revelation through Jesus to transform all that is below into the quality of life above. The Fourth Gospel wants the listener to realize that what Jesus did for Lazarus, Jesus does for all believers.

Responding to the Text

One approach to preaching this text is to ask, "Where is God raising Lazarus [in the Johannine sense] today?" That is, what events and relationships and ideas function as signs in the church and in the world today that reveal God's life-giving power in the way that the raising of Lazarus does in the Fourth Gospel? All Saints provides a natural reservoir for responding to such questions, as the preacher could lift up "saints" from the broader church or from the local community whose lives were signs of Johannine "life."

Another approach gives the preacher an opportunity to consider in a thoughtful way an issue on the hearts of many laypeople but that preachers typically mention only in passing: life after death. Many preachers are attracted to the Johannine view of present existence manifesting the Fourth Gospel's quality of "eternal life." However, other voices in the Bible and Christian tradition think of life beyond death in such ways as shady existence in Sheol, apocalyptic resurrection from the dead, and migration of the nonmaterial soul from the body to heaven. What can Christians believe?

Note

1. For an approach to developing such a doctrinal sermon, see Ronald J. Allen, *Preaching as Believing: The Sermon as Theological Reflection* (Louisville: Westminster John Knox Press, 2002).

TWENTY-SECOND SUNDAY AFTER PENTECOST

NOVEMBER 5, 2006
THIRTY-FIRST SUNDAY IN ORDINARY TIME /
PROPER 26

REVISED COMMON	EPISCOPAL (BCP)	ROMAN CATHOLIC
Deut. 6:1–9	Deut. 6:1–9	Deut. 6:2–6
or Ruth 1:1–18		
Ps. 119:1–8	Ps. 119:1–16	Ps. 18:2–3, 3–4, 47,
or Psalm 146	or 119:1–8	51
Heb. 9:11–14	Heb. 7:23–28	Heb. 7:23–28
Mark 12:28–34	Mark 12:28–34	Mark 12:28b–34

FIRST READING

DEUTERONOMY 6:1-9 (RCL, BCP)
DEUTERONOMY 6:2-6 (RC)

Interpreting the Text

Although cast as a report from the time of Moses, the narrative in Deuteronomy was shaped by writers in the period 721 B.C.E. through 535 B.C.E. when the nation was overrun, its leaders exiled to Babylonian, and then returned. The deuteronomists seek to help the community understand why these sad events took place, but more important, to help the community take actions to avoid similar tragedies in the future. According to the deuteronomists, God established the covenant with Israel as an act of grace and instructed the community through Torah in how to live so that all would be blessed. The community, however, had violated Torah and consequently fell under curse (social collapse and exile). The deuteronomic perspective on the joy of Torah is similar to that of Psalm 119 (below).

Today's text prescribes how the people can live in the future to partake of blessing and to avoid curse. They are to live in covenantal community with God and one another as described by Torah (Deut. 6:1–3). Indeed, in every moment of every day the community is to be a teaching community constantly reminding itself of Torah (6:7–9). Torah is to be internalized "in your heart" (6:6). The reason for this all-pervasive focus is given in 6:4-5: God alone is the sovereign of Israel. The community is to love God alone (and no other deity) with heart, soul, and might. Though not stated directly here, the reader would realize the alternative that comes from trafficking with other deities: a return to the chaos of the previous centuries.

Responding to the Text

Many congregations are theologically illiterate and anemic in faith and witness. This text suggests a direct agenda: to urge the congregation to become a teaching community—that is, a community that reminds people of all ages of the graciousness of God in making covenant with us, of the qualities (and requirements) of the

> THE COMMUNITY IS TO LOVE GOD ALONE (AND NO OTHER DEITY) WITH HEART, SOUL, AND MIGHT.

covenantal life, and of the blessing of living in covenant and the destructive consequences of not doing so.[1]

RUTH 1:1-18 (RCL ALT.)

Interpreting the Text

Although the story of the book of Ruth is set in the time of the judges (Ruth 1:1), most scholars think it was dated much later. I follow those who think it was written in the postexilic period when the authors of Ezra-Nehemiah prescribed that Jewish males divorce their non-Jewish spouses to maintain the Jewish identity of the struggling community. The book of Ruth demonstrates that a non-Judean (Ruth) can faithfully follow Torah by keeping covenant with others in community. The community, therefore, can welcome people like her.[2]

The book of Ruth is a complete story so that the preacher cannot simply preach from an isolated passage in the book but needs to set the passage in the story as a whole. Ruth 1:1-18 sets the stage for the story by explaining how the Jewish woman Naomi and her Moabite daughter-in-law Ruth became widows. Naomi has no male to whom she can go for resources but now lives on the very margins of existence, depending upon the community to follow the prescriptions of Torah in behalf of such widows for food and survival (for instance, Deut. 24:19). To spare Ruth such a life, Naomi wants to send the daughter-in-law to live with the Moabites and her dead husband's family.

Ruth, however, does not go to the security of her own family but demonstrates covenantal loyalty to Naomi by staying with Naomi even though that means returning to Israel where they will be alone. The famous words, often used at weddings, "Whither thou goest, I will go" (Ruth 1:16-17 KJV) are actually spoken by a Moabite daughter-in-law to her Jewish mother-in-law. Biblical scholar Phyllis Trible points out that by not seeking refuge with her own people and by committing herself to Naomi, Ruth makes a decision as radical as that of Abram and Sara to leave Ur, but then, that couple "had a call from God."[3]

271

TWENTY-SECOND
SUNDAY
AFTER PENTECOST

RONALD J.
ALLEN

Responding to the Text

Two themes immediately come to mind for homilies. One, of course, is the commitment of Ruth to Naomi as a model for covenantal commitment for today. In contemporary North American culture in which people walk away from relationships as easily as they put used paper cups in the trash, such commitment is a powerful witness to living for the good of another.

Another motif is the relationship between boundary and inclusiveness in community, a theme that is especially important in view of the fractiousness and exclusiveness between people today from different ethnicities, social classes, religious views, and other orientations. Indeed, genocide is taking place in the early twenty-first century. The book of Ruth reminds people not to draw lines of separation in arbitrary

> RUTH REMINDS PEOPLE NOT TO DRAW LINES OF SEPARATION IN ARBITRARY WAYS BUT TO WELCOME OTHERS WHOSE LIVES DEMONSTRATE HUMAN CARE THAT IS COVENANTAL IN CHARACTER.

ways (such as along ethnic lines) but to welcome others whose lives demonstrate human care that is covenantal in character. The sermon might consider how the congregation can testify to God's desire for supportive and inclusive community to those who continue arbitrary and hurtful exclusivity.

RESPONSIVE READING
PSALM 119:1-8 (RCL, BCP, ALT.)
PSALM 119:1-16 (BCP)

Christians have often characterized Torah (the Law) as rigid legalism and Judaism as a religion of people sourly working to obey Torah to earn God's favor (works-righteousness). Psalm 119 exposes this viewpoint as a caricature diametrically opposite the character of Judaism and Torah. This psalm presents Torah as God's gracious gift that people receive with bone-deep joy because of the guidance it provides toward blessing. The old caricature is especially ironic in that Psalm 119 is the longest psalm and, indeed, the longest chapter in the Bible. Given the joy with which the psalmist refers to Torah, we should not be surprised when the Markan Jesus summarizes the core of the life of his followers in today's Gospel reading by turning to a summary of Torah!

PSALM 146 (RCL ALT.)

This hymn of praise contrasts two sources of help during seasons of affliction. The community cannot count on "princes" (probably a reference to foreigners who ruled Israel when this psalm was written), whose reigns were often exploitative and, consequently, "of no help." In contrast, the community can turn to the eternal God whose rule is characterized by upholding justice for the oppressed, giving food to the hungry, returning the exiles from Babylon, and providing for the orphan and the widow—that is, by working toward a community in which all experience blessing. These aspects of God's rule, of course, take place through the actions of the community that lives in covenant. The preacher might help a congregation consider the degree to which its life is more closely aligned with the "princes" or "those whose help is the God of Jacob."

PSALM 18:2-3, 3-4, 47, 51 (RC)

This reading voices the thanks of the monarch of Israel to God for deliverance from enemies when the monarch cried for help. On the one hand, the preacher could use aspects of the psalm as a paradigm for the congregation's opening themselves to God's help in difficulty. On the other hand, biblical scholar Marti Stuessy notes a significant theological issue deriving from the fact that the monarch claims that enemies cried for help but God did not answer them (18:41): "Apparently the promise of help for those who seek refuge does not apply to the [monarch's] enemies, even if they (like Saul, Absalom, Ahithophel, Shimei, and Sheba) are as Israelite as [the monarch] is."[4] I must say that I do not believe that God simply turns away from people. Of course, God may seek to help people reorient their desires from running against the grain of divine purposes to those that are more congruent with divine hopes for the world.

> GOD MAY SEEK TO HELP PEOPLE REORIENT THEIR DESIRES FROM RUNNING AGAINST THE GRAIN OF DIVINE PURPOSES TO THOSE THAT ARE MORE CONGRUENT WITH DIVINE HOPES FOR THE WORLD.

SECOND READING
HEBREWS 9:11-14 (RCL)

Interpreting the Text

In this passage, the author of Hebrews uses the image of the sacrifice of goats and calves in the earthly sanctuary and that of Jesus in the heavenly sanctuary to argue that the latter is superior to the former. Preachers often go to great lengths to explain the mind-set that empowered blood sacrifice in the ancient world. In the worldview of Philo, however, the term "sacrifice" does not refer to the actual practices of sacrifice in the temple, but uses sacrifice as a symbol. The "earthly sanctuary" and the "perfect tent" are not local geographical sites but are symbolic ways of speaking of the lower and upper spheres of existence (see the Eighteenth Sunday after Pentecost).

Those who sacrifice have access to God, whereas those who do not sacrifice have limited or no access. From the point of view of Hebrews, the problem with the sacrifice of goats and calves (the sacrifices of the priesthood of Moses, Aaron, the Levites, and others) is that it takes place in the earthly tent, which represents the sphere of weakness and imperfection and, therefore, cannot open immediate access to God (perfection). On the other hand, the sacrifice of Jesus takes place in the "perfect tent" that is not made with hands and "is not of this creation" (Heb. 9:11b). The work of the intermediary sacrificial and priestly system purifies the flesh, whereas the sacrifice of Jesus brings about eternal redemption by purifying the conscience (which is of a higher order than the flesh) and enables unmediated worship of "the living God" (Heb. 9:12, 14).[5]

Responding to the Text

A preacher can point out that in the world of thought of Hebrews and Philo, the notion of sacrifice is not tied in with a complicated theory whereby the sacrifice of an animal or a human being changes God's disposition. The function of the image of sacrifice in this literature is to assure believers that they have access to God. A preacher might explain this function and also use images from our world to communicate such assurance with a depth analogous to that of sacrifice in antiquity.

Preachers might also take a cue from theology emerging from Christian-Jewish dialogue of the past thirty years that asserts that the promises God made to Israel are still in force. Although the Jewish community no longer sacrifices, they have other practices that assure them that they have access to God. Instead of following the text and regarding the sacrificial system of Israel (and the practices that have emerged in its absence) as second class, ministers could interpret the sacrifice of Jesus as assuring the church of our access to God in the same way that the practices of Judaism assure that community. The sacrifice of Jesus does not replace the assurances given to Israel but is a means whereby God provides for the church in ways similar to God's provision for Judaism.

> THE SACRIFICE OF JESUS DOES NOT REPLACE THE ASSURANCES GIVEN TO ISRAEL BUT IS A MEANS WHEREBY GOD PROVIDES FOR THE CHURCH IN WAYS SIMILAR TO GOD'S PROVISION FOR JUDAISM.

273

TWENTY-SECOND
SUNDAY
AFTER PENTECOST

RONALD J.
ALLEN

For comments on this passage, see the Twenty-first Sunday after Pentecost.

THE GOSPEL

MARK 12:28-34 (RCL, BCP)
MARK 12:28b-34 (RC)

Interpreting the Text

Christians today often think of first-century Judaism and the community to which Mark wrote as two separate religions—Judaism and Christianity. Recent scholarship, however, thinks that such a dramatic distinction did not exit in the first century. Interpreters today tend to think that the Markan community (and likely the groups to whom the other Gospels were written) still saw itself as Jewish, indeed, was even thought of as a Jewish sect. However, as we surmise from the many stories of conflict between Jesus and the Pharisees and other Jewish leaders in the Gospel of Mark, the Markan congregation was almost certainly in tension with other expressions of Judaism, perhaps over the issues of whether Jesus was God's agent to bring about the apocalyptic transformation and the inclusion of Gentiles in the community.

From the perspective of that ancient tension, today's text is an attempt, on Mark's part, to show that the Markan congregation is, in fact, an authentic Jewish community. Indeed, its core values are (from Mark's perspective) the same as those of Judaism. In addition to being fundamental matters of identity for Mark's own group, this passage would help the Markan community defend itself in the face of conflict with other Jewish groups (as implied in Mark 13:9-13).

The question of which "commandment is first of all" is typical of issues that rabbis of the period would discuss. Jesus answers by citing two commandments in such a way as to suggest they are inseparable. The assertion that God is one and that the community is to love God with heart, soul, strength, and mind is from Deut. 6:4-5 (see above), while "You shall love your neighbor as yourself" is from Lev. 19:18. The implication is clear: Love of God issues in love of neighbor, and, of course, to love the neighbor is to demonstrate love for God. The two are inseparably joined. For Mark, this is the heart of Judaism. Some other Jewish theologians of about the same time put these two commandments together similarly—for instance, Testament of Dan 5:3.

> LOVE OF GOD ISSUES IN LOVE OF NEIGHBOR, AND, OF COURSE, TO LOVE THE NEIGHBOR IS TO DEMONSTRATE LOVE FOR GOD. THE TWO ARE INSEPARABLY JOINED. FOR MARK, THIS IS THE HEART OF JUDAISM.

275

TWENTY-SECOND
SUNDAY
AFTER PENTECOST

RONALD J.
ALLEN

Mark 12:32 with its assertion that these commandments are "much more important than all the burnt offerings" has contextual edges. The temple was destroyed in 70 C.E., about the time Mark wrote. This text asserts that community could maintain its essential Jewish identity by practicing love of God and neighbor without going to the temple. Of course, Mark elsewhere polemicizes against some Jewish people whom Mark describes as failing to carry out the best of their own traditions (for instance, Mark 2:23—3:1; 3:19b-30; 7:1-23; 12:38-44). In doing so, Mark envisions speaking in the tradition of Hosea 6:6 and 1 Sam. 15:22 (echoed in Mark 12:33) as a member of the Jewish community engaging in prophetic self-criticism of other members of the community. On this phenomenon, see the remarks on the Gospel reading for the Twenty-third Sunday after Pentecost.

Jesus' final comment is, "You are not far from the [realm] of God," thus indicating that the apocalypse is soon to come and the scribe will be included in the new age.

Responding to the Text

A preacher could certainly use this text as the basis for thinking about the core identity of the Christian community expressed in Mark 12:29-31. A sermon can deepen the congregation's understanding of how to love God, especially by loving the neighbor, and vice versa. While this statement is compelling, it is also so general that the preacher needs to help the congregation envision concretely how to love God and neighbor.

This lection is also an ideal way for the homilist to help the congregation consider continuities between Judaism and Christianity as symbolized by the fact that both communities honor Deut. 6:4-5 and Lev. 19:18 as central to their common life. Toward this end, my colleague Clark M. Williamson suggests that the church cease speaking of a mission to the Jewish people and think instead of mutual witness that church and synagogue might make together.[6]

The passage also illustrates the fact that communities can adapt religious traditions in view of changing circumstances. Many Jewish people in the first century regarded going to the temple as necessary for Jewish life. This text shows how the Markan community reimagined what was necessary for Jewish life in view of the destruction of the temple. The preacher might help the congregation recollect aspects of Christian faith and practice that earlier generations (and perhaps some people in our own time) considered essential but that are now being reconsidered.

> THE PREACHER MIGHT HELP THE CONGREGATION RECOLLECT ASPECTS OF CHRISTIAN FAITH AND PRACTICE THAT EARLIER GENERATIONS CONSIDERED ESSENTIAL BUT THAT ARE NOW BEING RECONSIDERED.

Notes

1. For a recovery of the Jewish and Reformation conceptions of leadership in the community as essentially teaching, see Clark M. Williamson and Ronald J. Allen, *The Teaching Minister* (Louisville: Westminster John Knox Press, 1992). On the sermon as a teaching event, see Ronald J. Allen, *The Teaching Sermon* (Nashville: Abingdon Press, 1995).

2. For a superb sermon on these themes, see Joseph R. Jeter Jr., "Ruth People in an Esther World," in *Patterns of Preaching: A Sermon Sampler*, ed. Ronald J. Allen (St. Louis: Chalice Press, 1998), 51–56.

3. Phyllis Trible, *God and the Rhetoric of Sexuality*, Overtures to Biblical Theology (Philadelphia: Fortress Press, 1978), 173.

4. Marti Steussy, *Psalms*, Chalice Commentaries for Today (St. Louis: Chalice Press, 2004), 21-22.

5. On the notion of tent, see Lala Kalyan Kumar Dey, *The Intermediary Worlds and Patterns of Perfection in Philo and Hebrews*, SBL Dissertation Series 25 (Missoula, Mont.: Scholars Press, 1975), 159–60; 175–77.

6. Clark M. Williamson, ed., *A Mutual Witness: Toward Critical Solidarity between Jews and Christians* (St. Louis: Chalice Press, 1992).

TWENTY-THIRD SUNDAY AFTER PENTECOST

NOVEMBER 12, 2006
THIRTY-SECOND SUNDAY IN ORDINARY TIME /
PROPER 27

REVISED COMMON	EPISCOPAL (BCP)	ROMAN CATHOLIC
1 Kings 17:8-16	1 Kings 17:8-16	1 Kings 17:10-16
or Ruth 3:1-5;		
4:13-17		
Psalm 146	Psalm 146	Ps. 146:7, 8-9, 9-10
or Psalm 127	or 146:4-9	
Heb. 9:24-28	Heb. 9:24-28	Heb. 9:24-28
Mark 12:38-44	Mark 12:38-44	Mark 12:38-44
		or 12:41-44

FIRST READING
1 KINGS 17:8-16 (RCL, BCP)
1 KINGS 17:10-16 (RC)

Interpreting the Text

The books of the Kings were given their present form around the time of the exile (or shortly thereafter) under the impetus of the deuteronomic theology. The editors tell the story to make the point that when the leaders of Israel engage in idolatry and injustice, the nation as a whole falls under the divine curse and suffers. By contrast, the prophets in these books (especially Elijah and Elisha) call the leaders of Israel (and, by implication, the reader) to repent of complicity with the false gods and with injustice and to turn to living in covenant with God and with the members of the community so that all experience blessing.

In 1 Kings 17:1-7, Elijah invokes the curse of drought on the land because the leaders of the land worshiped Baal. The passage for today shows that the God of Israel will take dramatic means to preserve the witness of the prophet. When Elijah is faced with dehydration (1 Kings 17:7), God sends the prophet for survival to Zarephath and to a widow who is apparently without males responsible for her, and who is herself on the verge of starvation. God sends the prophet to a Gentile living on the very margin of society. The reader, of course, thinks of the contrast with the leaders of Israel who are living in the lap of misbegotten luxury and idolatry. Yet God keeps the oil in the jug and meal in the jar. The national regimes will collapse, but God preserves the prophetic witness.

Responding to the Text

A preacher could use this story much as it functioned in antiquity, namely to encourage faithful people who live in unfaithful times to continue in their covenantal witness. Where, today, does God supply faithful witnesses with resources that are as surprising and unexpected as the Gentile widow on the verge of starvation? In the background a preacher might invoke a prophetic warning to the leaders in today's societies who worship false deities and live in luxury while poverty, exploitation, and other forms of injustice abound. Unfaithful leadership (and the people who benefit from it) beget false community that will eventually turn to chaos. Who are the Elijahs (both as individuals and as groups and movements) who point the way toward repentance, living in covenant, and blessing?

> Unfaithful leadership (and the people who benefit from it) beget false community that will eventually turn to chaos.

RUTH 3:1-5; 4:13-17 (RCL ALT.)

Interpreting the Text

Background on the book of Ruth is given for the Twenty-second Sunday after Pentecost. Because the book of Ruth is a unified narrative, the preacher needs to set today's vignettes in the context of the whole narrative. In Ruth 1:17-18, Ruth commits herself to Naomi. In today's reading, Naomi demonstrates mutuality in commitment by creating a circumstance that will lead to blessing for Ruth after the mother-in-law is dead.

Boaz was related to Naomi's husband and therefore could serve as family agent (a redeeming kinsperson or next of kin) to preserve property and to prolong the family. Although Naomi is a powerless widow struggling for survival, the text presents her as a clever woman who is able to entice the powerful Boaz to act in ways that provide a secure future for Ruth and Naomi and that also secure land and lineage. Jewish literature frequently honors clever people who can turn dire circumstances to those of blessing. When Ruth "uncovers the feet" of Boaz, the action may or may not involve sexual encounter but sets the stage as a marriage proposal from Ruth to Boaz (Ruth 3:9).

Although early twenty-first-century listeners often envision romantic magnetism between Ruth and Boaz, such consideration was far less important to ancient people than familial loyalty. Boaz, in fact, singles out such loyalty (*hesed*) as reason for turning to Ruth (3:10).

279

TWENTY-THIRD
SUNDAY
AFTER PENTECOST

RONALD J.
ALLEN

Responding to the Text

The preacher should not miss the opportunity to point to the fact that Ruth and Naomi are *women* who seize the initiative in a difficult situation in a social world in which such initiative was unusual. Can the preacher point to situations in church and world today in which the text authorizes *women* to create more secure worlds for themselves and others and, by so doing, to create greater security in the larger community?

> THE PREACHER SHOULD NOT MISS THE OPPORTUNITY TO POINT TO THE FACT THAT RUTH AND NAOMI ARE WOMEN WHO SEIZE THE INITIATIVE IN A DIFFICULT SITUATION IN A SOCIAL WORLD IN WHICH SUCH INITIATIVE WAS UNUSUAL.

Along this line, the preacher could encourage the congregation to be as clever in our time and setting as Naomi was in hers. What clever actions can the congregation take to persuade instrumentalities of power to act for blessing for the good of the community as a whole?

Ruth committed herself to Naomi in the context of a community whose Torah provided prescriptions for support for widows. To what degree does the congregation provide support for people such as Ruth and Naomi today?

RESPONSIVE READING

PSALM 146 (RCL, BCP)
PSALM 146:4-9 (BCP ALT.)
PSALM 146:7, 8-9, 9-10 (RC)

On Psalm 146, please see the discussion on the Twenty-second Sunday after Pentecost, November 5, 2006.

PSALM 127 (RCL ALT.)

This psalm articulates viewpoints that are simultaneously instructive and problematic for today's church. The psalm rightly indicates that a lasting and secure community—a family ("house"), city, or individual life—is possible only in covenant with God and in a setting in which people live covenantally (vv. 1-2). Given the current conversation about "family values" in our culture, the preacher would find it worth noting that "family values" in antiquity were defined by Torah and that the family was not today's isolated nuclear household but was often an extended, multigenerational family who lived together. Psalm 127:3-5 interprets "sons" as a gift from God because they help provide economic security for the household, especially for parents in their old age. The contemporary preacher should criticize the androcentrism in this text and note that daughters must be equally valued and encouraged to make their distinctive contributions to the household and world in ways that are not gender-limited. Furthermore, the preacher needs to make it clear that childless people (whether as a couple or in the single life) can completely fulfill God's purposes for human life.

Second Reading
HEBREWS 9:24-28 (RCL, BCP, RC)

Interpreting the Text

The reading for today opens one of the most revealing windows into the world of thought behind the letter to the Hebrews when it describes the "sanctuary made by human hands" as a "copy of the true one." We hear echoes of Platonism in the use of "copy" in Hebrews' language context of describing the true sanctuary that exists with God and of which the earthly sanctuary made with hands is a copy. In Philo's Jewish interpretation of such notions, the heavenly sanctuary is the realm of perfection where God dwells and where perfected people have immediate access to God. The copy is the present realm of imperfection.

In this tradition, which uses many different terms for the same reality, sin is the realm of the flesh and weakness and all that prevents complete access to God.[1] Similarly, experiencing physical death in the realm of imperfection and subsequently falling under divine judgment further prevents access to God. The stunning affirmation of the text is that Christ has entered into the realm of perfection and appears "in the [very] presence of God on our behalf" (v. 24). The statement that Christ has appeared "once for all at the end of the age" (v. 26) uses traditional language to indicate that the pathway to God that Christ made continues to be open.

Responding to the Text

According to the line of interpretation of Hebrews we have followed for the past several weeks, themes of all passages from Hebrews are remarkably similar. A major challenge for preaching from this material is for sermons to maintain continuity while developing fresh points of application (and not simply drifting into numbing repetition). The homiletical comments have not hitherto focused on the notion of "sin." What manifestations of sin (as defined above) in the imperfect state inhibit our awareness of God and diminish our receipt of the benefits of God? The preacher can show how the ongoing presence of Christ removes these interferences and makes it possible for us to know God as fully as we can in this present world and to receive God's empowering presence and blessing.

281

TWENTY-THIRD
SUNDAY
AFTER PENTECOST

RONALD J.
ALLEN

The Gospel

MARK 12:38–44 (RCL, BCP, RC)
MARK 12:41–44 (RC ALT.)

Interpreting the Text

On the Twenty-second Sunday after Pentecost, we describe the situation of the Markan community not as a distinctly Christian group (Mark's congregation) against other distinctly Jewish bodies (as if Christianity and Judaism were separate religions) but as a situation of Mark's Jewish group in tension with other Jewish groups. Jewish sources from the first century outside the Second Testament (such as Josephus) depict the Pharisees and others as faithful and even as reform-minded. Some scholars (I among them) regard criticism of

> WHAT MANIFESTATIONS OF SIN IN THE IMPERFECT STATE INHIBIT OUR AWARENESS OF GOD AND DIMINISH OUR RECEIPT OF THE BENEFITS OF GOD?

other Jewish people by Mark not as accurately representing other Jewish groups but as regrettable caricature for the purpose of justifying the tension and growing separation between those groups and Mark's own community.

The scribes were teachers and interpreters of Jewish tradition. However, today's text contributes to Mark's discrediting of them (Mark 1:22; 2:6; 3:22; 7:1, 5; 8:31; 9:14; 10:33; 11:18; 14:1, 43, 53; 15:1, 31) and, by extension, of other Jewish authorities with whom the Markan community engaged in dispute.

The text assumes the social hierarchy of the ancient world in which people on the lower echelons of the social ladder visibly made gestures of respect to people in the upper rungs when encountering them. Mark portrays the scribes as exploiting this hierarchy to reinforce their own repressive social power. In those days most males typically wore short robes for everyday and saved longer garments for worship or other special occasions. The scribes in this text, however, wear them every day. The phrase "the best seats in the synagogue and places of honor at banquets" (v. 39) refers to where the socially elite sat. Other people deferred to them in those places. Mark has already indicated that the present hierarchical social

> MARK HAS INDICATED THAT THE PRESENT HIERARCHICAL SOCIAL ORDER BELONGS TO THE CORRUPT PRESENT AGE AND WILL BE REPLACED BY A SOCIAL WORLD IN WHICH LEADERSHIP TAKES THE FORM OF SERVANTHOOD.

order belongs to the corrupt present age and will be replaced by a social world in which leadership takes the form of servanthood (Mark 10:35-45, Twentieth Sunday after Pentecost). The expression "They devour widows' houses" connects vv. 38-40 to vv. 41-44.

Especially during the season when the congregation is raising support for the budget, preachers have often taken the story of the widow's offering in Mark 12:41-44 as a positive model for the congregation to emulate. Some recent scholarship, however, sees the story as an example of the scribes, in league with the temple, "devouring widows' houses."[2] Mark repeatedly pictures the temple leadership as corrupt (Mark 11:15-16; 14:1-2; 14:49; 15:38). From this point of view, the temple authorities charged exorbitant temple taxes to support the lavish, upper-class life of the priestly families. In order to pay the tax (and to maintain her social standing), the widow bankrupts herself.

The reader knows that Judaism at its best provides support for widows (for instance, Deut. 10:18; Ps. 68:5; Jer. 49:11). Mark thus depicts the scribes and temple leadership as violating a fundamental prescription of covenantal community. This implication not only justifies the Markan community's separating itself from such people but also helps explain why God allowed the temple to be destroyed and the Holy Land to be devastated in 70 C.E.

Responding to the Text

A preacher could make analogies between the negative attitudes and behaviors of the scribes and the temple in these texts and similar attitudes and behaviors in the congregation. Such a probe could help members of the congregation, and even some ministers, face painful aspects of themselves that they need to change. The preacher who adopts such a route, however, must work over time to make it clear that Mark does not report historically accurate information about the scribes and temple but presents them in caricature for the reasons cited above. To make an analogy without such a clarification leaves the impression that Mark has given a historically reliable report of scribes and temple leaders and thereby reinforces the anti-Judaism and even anti-Semitism that linger in many Christian churches. The preacher needs to help the congregation understand and repudiate polemics such as we find in these readings.

> THE PREACHER IS CALLED TO TELL THE TRUTH AND TO HELP THE CONGREGATION EMBRACE THE TRUTH. THE TRUTH COULD OPEN THE WAY FOR A FUTURE THAT IS MORE SOCIALLY CONSTRUCTIVE.

The appearance of the woman in Mark 12:41-44 suggests a sermon that ponders how the church has exploited women.

A pastor might use the occurrence of these passages as occasion to help the congregation reflect on (and repent of) ways that they misrepresent people for

283

TWENTY-THIRD
SUNDAY
AFTER PENTECOST
——————
RONALD J.
ALLEN

their own purposes in ways similar to Mark. The sermon could use the centuries of antagonism between Christians and Jews as a case study in the destructive personal and social effects of such polemic. The focus could extend to worlds outside the congregation. Where do we find such caricatures in public life today? What are the chaotic results of such distortion? Looming over this discussion is the commandment, "You shall not bear false witness against your neighbor" (Exod. 20:16; Deut. 5:20). The preacher is called to tell the truth and to help the congregation embrace the truth. The truth could open the way for a future that is more socially constructive.

Notes

1. Lala Kalyan Kumar Dey, *The Intermediary Worlds and Patterns of Perfection in Philo and Hebrews*, SBL Dissertation Series 25 (Missoula, Mont.: Scholars Press, 1975), 192.

2. Addison Wright, "The Widow's Mite: Praise or Lament? A Matter of Context," *Catholic Biblical Quarterly* 44 (1982): 256–65.

TWENTY-FOURTH SUNDAY AFTER PENTECOST

NOVEMBER 19, 2006
THIRTY-THIRD SUNDAY IN ORDINARY TIME / PROPER 28

REVISED COMMON	EPISCOPAL (BCP)	ROMAN CATHOLIC
Dan. 12:1-3	Dan. 12:1-4a (5-13)	Dan. 12:1-3
or 1 Sam. 1:4-20		
Psalm 16	Psalm 16 or 16:5-11	Ps. 16:5, 8, 9-10, 11
or 1 Sam. 2:1-10		
Heb. 10:11-14	Heb. 10:31-39	Heb. 10:11-14, 18
(15-18), 19-25		
Mark 13:1-8	Mark 13:14-23	Mark 13:24-32

FIRST READING
DANIEL 12:1-3 (RCL, RC)
DANIEL 12:1-4a (5-13) (BCP)

Interpreting the Text

Daniel 7–12 is the last piece of the First Testament to be written (about the time of the Maccabean revolt in 168–165 B.C.E.) and is the most fully developed piece of apocalyptic literature in that Testament. Apocalyptic theology recognizes that evil is pervasive and savage and causes the righteous to suffer. These theologians answer the question of when and how God will be faithful and just, especially to the righteous, by positing that God will end the current evil age with a historical interruption, and apocalypse, and will replace this age with a new one that is sometimes called the realm (NRSV "kingdom") of God.

RESURRECTION IS NOT PIE IN THE SKY BUT, FOR THE APOCALYPTIC THEOLOGIAN, IS NECESSARY FOR GOD TO MAKE RIGHT THE WRONGS THAT PEOPLE HAVE SUFFERED.

Daniel 12:1-13 contributes to this theme in three ways. First, it affirms that God will raise from the dead those who died before the new age and (along with the faithful who are alive at the time of the apocalypse) will give them all resurrection bodies for life in the new world (vv. 1-3). Resurrection is thus not pie in the sky but, for the apocalyptic theologian, is necessary for God to make right the wrongs that people have suffered. Second, the passage indicates that God has chosen the time when this event will occur but that God has not yet revealed the precise time (though, presumably, it will be soon) (vv. 5-13). Third, apropos of the Gospel lection for today, Dan. 12:4 points to an intensification of suffering prior to the apocalypse as the forces of evil entrench themselves to resist the coming of the new world.

285

TWENTY-FOURTH
SUNDAY
AFTER PENTECOST
―――――――
RONALD J.
ALLEN

Responding to the Text

Introducing this passage, one of my teachers, J. Louis Martyn, invited us to imagine hearing it in a cave with the fury of the Maccabean revolt all around, including the killing of the faithful. Such an approach might be an imaginative way to help the congregation consider belief in resurrection of the dead as means whereby God acts to rectify wrongs perpetrated unjustly. Resurrection of the dead, of course, is part and parcel of the apocalyptic worldview shared by relatively few preachers in the historic churches today. How would today's preacher—likely operating out of a postmodern worldview—say God rectifies the injustices that have befallen the righteous?

1 SAMUEL 1:4-20 (RCL ALT.)

Interpreting the Text

Although the books of Samuel and Kings tell stories from the days of Samuel, Saul, David, Solomon, the divided monarchy, and the beginning of the exile, these books were given their present form by deuteronomic theologians about the time of the exile. The latter authors were ruminating on the cause of the nation's fall and sought to offer perspectives for the community to move toward a more hopeful future. As the book of Judges ends, the community is in disarray and suggests that

TODAY'S TEXTS BUILD THE READER'S CONFIDENCE IN SAMUEL AS PROPHET AND JUDGE, FOR THE PASSAGE SHOWS THAT GOD WAS GUIDING SAMUEL'S LIFE EVEN BEFORE HIS CONCEPTION.

this condition results from not having a monarch (Judg. 21:25). Hebrew Bible scholars Lisa Davison and Marti Steussy point out that these books view the monarchy ambiguously: the texts contain materials that both lament and affirm the rise of monarchy.[1] As this saga makes clear, adopting a monarch (and thereby becoming similar to the other nations) did not solve the Israel's troubles. Through the character of Samuel, the deuteronomic writers unmistakably imply that faithfulness or unfaithfulness—not the presence or absence of a monarch—determines the quality of Israel's life (1 Sam. 8:4-22).

Today's texts build the reader's confidence in Samuel as prophet and judge, for the passage shows that God was guiding Samuel's life even before his conception. As the passage opens, Hannah is barren, a stock motif in the First Testament. The reader immediately remembers other women who were barren but through whom God brought leaders to birth for Israel (for instance, Gen. 21:1-8; 25:19-26; 30:1-24; Judg. 13:2-24). In addition to validating God's presence with Samuel, the transition from barren to fertile reveals the character and purposes of God: to transform *all* from barren to generative.

The text highlights the active agency of Hannah in the transformation. She does all that she can do to cooperate with God. She does not seek to become pregnant for her own satisfaction (she volunteers, after all, to give up the child to divine service) but as a means whereby the divine voice can have an expression in Israel through the prophet. She does all that she can to increase blessing in Israel. Later people in Israel's story would, unfortunately, cooperate with idols and injustice and bring about curse (exile).

Responding to the Text

The Israelites want a monarch because other peoples in the earth have one. This notion invites the preacher to explore ways that today's congregation wants to ape organizational patterns and other practices from the larger culture. Who are the Samuels in our world cautioning the church against uncritical adaptation of our life and witness to the zeitgeist?

WHO ARE THE SAMUELS IN OUR WORLD CAUTIONING THE CHURCH AGAINST UNCRITICAL ADAPTATION OF OUR LIFE AND WITNESS TO THE ZEITGEIST?

The motif of barrenness, especially when used figuratively, touches many people in North America. Where do we encounter situations that are barren today? How can people in such situations cooperate with God to help them become generative?

A listener could take from this text the notion that a woman who does not bear a child is incomplete. A minister should avoid giving this impression, even inadvertently. Giving birth is simply the particular way that Hannah participates with God in seeking to bring order to the chaos of Israel's life. In what ways do women today join with God toward similar ends?

PSALM 16 (RCL, BCP)
PSALM 16:5-11 (BCP ALT.)
PSALM 16:5, 8, 9-10, 11 (RC)

This psalm of trust was likely voiced by a Levite. Unlike the other tribes, the Levites (priestly families) did not receive a portion of the land; their livelihood and security came from their work at the temple. From this perspective, vv. 1 and 5 are especially meaningful: this singer trusts that God will provide for the singer's household through the community that participates in the temple and not through ownership of land and animals. In the world of today, who similarly lives day to day on the basis of community provision? The preacher can encourage the community to be generous in making provision.

Although vv. 3-4 are hard to understand in Hebrew, the NRSV renders them in a way that is theologically provocative. Those who "choose another god"— that is, who regard finite values as having ultimate importance—"multiply their sorrows." The preacher can urge the congregation to minimize its sorrow and optimize its gladness by following "the path of life"

> THE PREACHER CAN URGE THE CONGREGATION TO MINIMIZE ITS SORROW AND OPTIMIZE ITS GLADNESS BY FOLLOWING "THE PATH OF LIFE."

(v. 11). The tribulation of Mark 13 is a season in which people are tempted to turn from trust in God's plan for the renewal of the world, and the suffering that accompanies it, and to ease their pain by embracing lesser possibilities. To such folk, this psalm affirms that continued trust will ultimately bring "fullness of joy."

1 SAMUEL 2:1-10 (RCL ALT.)

The RCL substitutes this psalm-like prayer from the book of 1 Samuel for a typical responsive psalm to good effect. For this text continues the story told in one of the first readings for today, 1 Sam. 1:1-20, which announces the birth of Samuel. In response, Hannah prays in 1 Sam. 2:1-10. Although the prayer is probably much later than the folktale in which it is inserted, its narrative function is to interpret theologically the significance of the divine activity surrounding the birth of Samuel and to help the hearer recognize that God's actions in bringing Samuel into the world are paradigmatic of God's intent to create conditions of blessing in Israel. According to this hymnlike text, God has the power to do what is right by all people (to bless and to curse), and God is faithful to work in behalf of people, like Hannah and Eli, who are less than fully blessed. These motifs are consistent with the Gospel reading for today, as that reading, given its current form by a writer whose community was on the social margins of antiquity, anticipates the great day of blessing that will come after the apocalypse.

SECOND READING

HEBREWS 10:11–14 (15–18), 19–25 (RCL)
HEBREWS 10:11–14, 18 (RC)
HEBREWS 10:31–39 (BCP)

Interpreting the Text

Hebrews 10:11–18 reprises themes from the previous chapters by summarizing the ineffectuality of Judaism to perfect believers (Heb. 10:11) and assuring the readers that the sacrifice of Jesus effects forgiveness of sin, that is, that Jesus has effected perfection for believers (10:14). In Heb. 10:15–18 the author adapts Jer. 31:33 and 31:34b to reinforce the idea that the religion of Jesus offers perfection (unmediated access to God), something that Judaism as represented by Philo (a religion of intermediaries) cannot do.

Hebrews 10:19–25 exhorts readers to have the confidence necessary to continue in the path that leads to perfection.[2] The importance of continuing on the path is underscored in 10:26–31: Those who turn back "fall into the hands of the living God"; that is, they receive a terrible and everlasting punishment (Heb. 6:4–8).

The community needs such forceful exhortation because they experience "hard struggle with suffering" by being "publicly exposed to abuse and persecution" and having their goods plundered (Heb. 10:32–34). While we do not know for certain the exact circumstances of these sufferings, it seems clear that outsiders persecute the community because of their religious convictions. When faced by severe challenges to their faith and practice, they are to "endure"—meaning, remain on the path—so they may "receive what is promised," that is, perfection (10:36). By enduring, believers "look at Jesus as he runs the race of life" and form their own "existence on the model exemplified in Jesus' own endurance of the cross in view of the joy of "sitting on the right hand of God."[3]

> WHEN FACED BY SEVERE CHALLENGES TO THEIR FAITH AND PRACTICE, BELIEVERS ARE TO "ENDURE" SO THEY MAY "RECEIVE WHAT IS PROMISED," THAT IS, PERFECTION.

Responding to the Text

The postmodern world puts in the face of the congregation a dizzying diversity of religious (and areligious) viewpoints, many of which are diametrically opposite one another in values. For a congregation beset by questions and doubts concerning the Christian path in the face of such challenges, Heb. 10:19-25 provides an entrée to offer confidence, even boldness. For a congregation that has chosen to make a witness that goes against the grain of current mores and assumptions, Heb. 10:32-39 offers the preacher a platform from which to encourage endurance even in the face of harassment. While immediate suffering is hard to bear, endurance "brings a great reward" (v. 35), that is, unfettered communion with the One who transcends all.

289

TWENTY-FOURTH
SUNDAY
AFTER PENTECOST

RONALD J.
ALLEN

The Gospel

MARK 13:1-8 (RCL)
MARK 13:14-23 (BCP)
MARK 13:24-32 (RC)

Interpreting the Text

Chapter 13 explains more clearly than any other passage in the Second Gospel how Mark understands the final steps in history that lead to the apocalypse and the final and complete manifestation of the divine realm. Mark 13:1-3 interprets the destruction of the temple in 70 C.E. as a key sign that the present evil age of history is in its last stages. Mark 13:4-23 explains that as the apocalypse nears, suffering in the world intensifies as the rulers of the present age (who will be displaced in the new world) entrench themselves to resist the great transformation. Satan, the demons, and the personal and social forces who collude with them particularly cause the faithful to suffer. Believers are tempted, then, to turn away from faithful life. Indeed,

> MARK 13:24-27 LOOKS FORWARD TO THE RETURN OF JESUS IN A DRAMATIC APOCALYPSE WHEN THE STRUCTURES THAT SUPPORT THE PRESENT OLD AGE END AND THE REALM OF GOD IS FINALLY PUT IN PLACE.

according to Mark 13:19-20, the suffering is so intense that if God had not shortened the time of the tribulation, few believers would have been able to survive. Mark 13:24-27 looks forward to the return of Jesus in a dramatic apocalypse when the structures that support the present old age end and the realm of God is finally put in place.

While Mark obviously uses stock apocalyptic imagery in 13:4-23 to suggest that the chaos of Mark's world was the tribulation, many scholars think that this material reveals something of what was happening in and around the community to which Mark wrote. Verses 5-6 and 22-23 suggest that the people are confronted with acclamations that figures other than Jesus are the agents of the coming realm. Hence, some members of the community may be confused as to who is a trustworthy authority. Verses 9-11 suggest that some members of the Markan congregation have been disciplined in the synagogue (v. 9a) and have appeared before Roman authorities (vv. 9b, 11). Verse 12 implies that some families are coming apart as family members disagree with one another on the question of whether Jesus is the agent of the apocalyptic renewal.

In view of the Roman desecration of the temple (to which Mark makes direct reference in 13:14), the community is to "flee to the mountains." The reader will recognize in 16:7 that this means to go to Galilee, where they will be gathered into the apocalypse itself. From vv. 15–20, we learn that the time between the destruction of the temple and the apocalypse will be a chaos.

This passage has two obvious purposes. One is to encourage the community to remain faithful in the midst of intense suffering. The other is to carry out the mission of 13:10. The community is to preach the gospel to Gentiles ("the nations"). In other words, they are to let other people (including Gentiles) know about the immediacy of the apocalypse and invite them to repent and become a part of the community of the new age.

Responding to the Text

The popular interest around the Left Behind books and movies forms a natural point of entry into this sermon. A preacher could use this text as a point of reference for comparing and contrasting the apocalypticism of Charles Darby enshrined in "Left Behindism" with that of Mark and other Jewish and Christian writers in antiquity.

The text confronts the congregation with a problem. Mark expected Jesus to return in a relatively short time. That has not happened. The preacher might help the congregation sort through what they really believe concerning these eschatological matters. Some Christians say that the delay has been longer than expected while they continue to look for an apocalypse. Others simply say that such things are mysterious beyond our understanding. Still others think that the apocalyptic expectation was part of a worldview that we no longer share and that we need to formulate an eschatological hope in language and expectation that are appropriate to postmodernity. The process theologians, for example, do not anticipate a singular interruption in history but believe that God is perpetually active to lure each moment toward its highest possibilities for manifesting the divine purposes.

> A MINISTER CAN HELP THE CONGREGATION REALIZE THAT PERIODS OF TRANSITION FROM OLD WAYS OF LIVING TO MORE FAITHFUL ONES ARE OFTEN DIFFICULT AND EVEN CHAOTIC.

A minister can help the congregation realize that periods of transition from old ways of living to more faithful ones are often difficult and even chaotic. Indeed, some such transformations involve the death of old worlds before a new one can emerge. Mark 13 reminds readers that many people and forces in the old world will profoundly and even violently resist such movements toward change.

Nevertheless, the purpose of a sermon could mirror Mark's purpose in the text to encourage the congregation not only to remain faithful in the midst of social chaos but also to engage in mission. Even congregations who are not directly apocalyptic in theology can appreciate the underlying assurance of apocalyptic theology: God is not content with the injustices and sorrows of the present world and always works for every person, group, and circumstance to manifest as much as possible of God's unconditional love.

291

TWENTY-FOURTH
SUNDAY
AFTER PENTECOST

RONALD J.
ALLEN

Notes

1. Lisa W. Davison and Marti J. Steussy, "Samuel and Kings," in *Chalice Introduction to the Old Testament*, ed. Marti J. Steussy (St. Louis: Chalice Press, 2003), 105.

2. Lala Kalyan Kumar Dey, *The Intermediary Worlds and Patterns of Perfection in Philo and Hebrews*, SBL Dissertation Series 25 (Missoula, Mont.: Scholars Press, 1975), 227–33.

3. Ibid., 228.

THANKSGIVING DAY

NOVEMBER 23, 2006*

REVISED COMMON	EPISCOPAL (BCP)	ROMAN CATHOLIC
Joel 2:21-27	Deut. 8:1-3, 6-10 (17-20)	Deut. 8:7-18 or 1 Kings 8:55-61
Psalm 126	Psalm 65 or 65:9-14	Ps. 113:1-2, 3-4, 5-6, 7-8 or Ps. 138:1-2, 2-3, 4-5
1 Tim. 2:1-7	James 1:17-18, 21-27	Col. 3:12-17 or 1 Tim. 6:6-11, 17-19
Matt. 6:25-33	Matt. 6:25-33	Mark 5:18-20 or Luke 12:15-21 or Luke 17:11-19

FIRST READING

JOEL 2:21-27 (RCL)

Interpreting the Text

Although the book of Joel is difficult to date, most scholars place it in the postexilic period. The prophet wrestles theologically not only with the fact that the return from exile failed to bring the dramatic restoration expected but with the fact that the returnees faced a depleted land and a poor, lethargic, contentious, and even unfaithful people. Joel 1:1—2:11 interprets an invasion of locusts as divine judgment that is prelude to the day of the Lord—a day when God will intervene in history to punish evildoers.

*Due to space considerations, I have restricted my comments to the Revised Common Lectionary texts and to the Gospel in the Roman Catholic lectionary. The BCP lectionary uses the same texts each year; for further commentary on those lections, I commend to you the comments by Lucy Lind Hogan in *New Proclamation, Year C, 2004.*

Nevertheless, Joel's listeners have an opportunity to repent (Joel 2:12-18). Indeed, Joel 2:21-27 announces that God will revive the community by repaying "you the years that the swarming locusts have eaten." Military threat will diminish (2:20), while agriculture and husbandry will thrive (2:19, 21-26). Such signs will be proof that God is in the midst of the community (2:27).

Responding to the Text

On Thanksgiving Day, a preacher would naturally turn to 2:26b with its statement that the people will praise God for the plenty that God wondrously pours on the community. However, the lection in the context of the whole book of Joel reminds the congregation not to give "cheap thanks" (to make a play on Bonhoeffer's "cheap grace"), that is, simply to be grateful for the creature comforts of the middle-class world. The preacher could follow Joel in calling the congregation to gives thanks because God offers the opportunity to repent of the aspects of our lives that move our world toward destruction and to take up attitudes and behavior that fulfill covenant with God and one another. God's offer of repentance to save us from the consequences of our own cheap thanks is one of the most profound reasons for giving thanks.

> GOD'S OFFER OF REPENTANCE TO SAVE US FROM THE CONSEQUENCES OF OUR OWN CHEAP THANKS IS ONE OF THE MOST PROFOUND REASONS FOR GIVING THANKS.

RESPONSIVE READING
PSALM 126 (RCL)

On Psalm 126, see the discussion on the Twenty-first Sunday after Pentecost, October 29, 2006.

SECOND READING
1 TIMOTHY 2:1-7 (RCL)

Interpreting the Text

Many scholars think that this letter was written toward the end of the first century or beginning of the second century C.E. when the congregation(s) to whom it was addressed experienced external and internal tension.[1] Some authorities of the Roman state and some leaders of Roman society viewed the church with disdain and even suspicion. Members of the community of 1 Timothy may have faced the threat of social ostracism. The congregation also had to deal with internal tension regarding what is (and is not) faithful teaching and practice.

Today's passage uses what the author regards as "right and acceptable" teaching to help the church manifest behavior that the Roman state and society would find acceptable. The church is to pray for "everyone" and especially for monarchs and "all who are in high positions." The author hopes that such officials will thereby perceive the church to be nonthreatening and leave it alone so that the community can lead a "quiet and peaceable life in all godliness and dignity." The latter language is drawn from popular Hellenistic philosophy, and its use is a subtle attempt on the part of the writer to show that the pastoral community fits into the wider Hellenistic world. The theological warrant for the practice of praying for the leaders of the society, and indeed for acting in ways that are socially respectable, is that "there is one God" who has acted for all by sending Christ Jesus to mediate between God and humankind and to give his life as a ransom for all.

MEMBERS OF THE COMMUNITY OF 1 TIMOTHY MAY HAVE FACED THE THREAT OF SOCIAL OSTRACISM AND HAD TO DEAL WITH INTERNAL TENSION REGARDING WHAT IS (AND IS NOT) FAITHFUL TEACHING AND PRACTICE.

Responding to the Text

Given the hostility toward the church in the world of 1 Timothy, an early twenty-first-century congregation can understand the desire for social respectability underlying this passage. However, in North America the church is part and parcel of the social world. While this society has many blessings for many people, it is also painfully shot through with exploitation, injustice, and violence—much of which is simply assumed and some of which is actively authorized by governmental bodies. The faithful preacher should not take this text as a blithe stamp of approval on North America and its leaders. In the deepest sense a pastor should encourage the congregation to pray for *all* to enjoy a "quiet and peaceable life" in which all people, relationships, and circumstances take place in justice and love. To call for such a life, a preacher may need to encourage the congregation to stand against popular values and policies.

While the text is not clear whether God's "desire to save all" is a clear statement that God will save all or whether God invites all people to be saved (and will save those who respond) (1 Tim. 2:4-6), the preacher might still use these motifs as a beginning point for a theological reflection on universalism. Many people in today's postmodern world with its emphasis on pluralism and relativity have serious ques-

MANY PEOPLE IN TODAY'S POSTMODERN WORLD WITH ITS EMPHASIS ON PLURALISM AND RELATIVITY HAVE SERIOUS QUESTIONS REGARDING WHO MIGHT AND MIGHT NOT BE SAVED.

tions regarding who might and might not be saved. Of course, this discussion also invites the preacher to clarify what is meant by salvation. Thanksgiving is truly the mood of those who believe they are saved.

THE GOSPEL

MATTHEW 6:25-33 (RCL, BCP)

Interpreting the Text

The historical and literary contexts are important for understanding this text. After the destruction of the temple in 70 C.E., many people in Palestine experienced deprivation, immediate social stress, and anxiety regarding the future. Added to tension for Matthew's congregation (which we might think of as a synagogue that believed that Jesus was the agent of the apocalyptic transformation) was conflict with other synagogues that did not share the Matthean view of Jesus and the imminence of the apocalypse.

The literary context, beginning in Matt. 6:19-21, cautions against storing up treasure on earth but commends storing up treasure in heaven. We learn from other Jewish sources that one "stores up treasure in heaven" by almsgiving and good works that benefit the community (Sir. 29:8-13; cf. 2 Esd. 6:5; 7:77; 8:33; 2 Bar. 14:12; Ps. Sol. 9:5; 1 Enoch 38:12). In other words, one exemplifies the positive Jewish ideals of caring for one another in covenantal community. Matthew 6:22-23 uses the imagery of eyesight and light to underscore the importance of perceiving how to store up treasure in heaven and of facing the choice in Matt. 6:24 of serving either wealth or God. In the literary context, to serve God is to use one's material resources in the service of almsgiving, that is, by providing for the needs of others. In post-70 C.E. Palestine, in which many were economically deprived, such acts could mean survival.

Matthew 6:25-34 addresses the anxiety in the Matthean community generated by giving away material resources as acts of provision for others. The passage uses images from the everyday world that illustrate how God—and an argument from the lesser to the greater to awaken the congregation to the fact that God—will provide for them in the same way. The birds—fragile creatures—do not reap or gather, yet God feeds them. By worry, the readers cannot add an hour to their lives, yet they live. The lilies—delicate plants—do not toil or spin, but God clothes them in glory (Matt. 6:25-30a). If God cares for these lesser things (the smaller), how much more God will care for human beings (the greater).

Consequently, the congregation need not be anxious about such things as long as they are striving for the divine realm, that is, faithfully witnessing to their confidence that Jesus is the avenue into the coming realm of God (Matt. 6:31-34).

God will provide for the community in the immediate setting and in the world to come. Occasional scholars think that Matthew envisioned, as means of preservation, that the congregation would engage in the kind of communal living found at Qumran in which community members put all their material resources in a common pot and lived out of it.

Responding to the Text

The preacher might help the congregation name both ways that they can engage in "storing up treasure for heaven" and the anxieties that get in the way of their doing so. What are practical means whereby the congregation can "strive first for the realm of God" by giving alms, that is, by sharing resources with persons and communities in need? What issues and questions cause the congregation to be anxious and reticent to put their resources into meeting human need?

WHAT ARE PRACTICAL MEANS WHEREBY THE CONGRE-
GATION CAN "STRIVE FIRST FOR THE REALM OF GOD"
BY GIVING ALMS, THAT IS, BY SHARING RESOURCES
WITH PERSONS AND COMMUNITIES IN NEED?

As a strategy for the sermon, the preacher might take a cue from the text. While the text begins with an imperative, "Do not worry . . . ," the text does not simply exhort listeners not to be anxious but provides images of birds and lilies that experience God's care. The sermon could similarly provide stories and other materials that function as imaginative portrayals of the congregation experiencing divine providence in a way that allays anxiety.

MARK 5:18-20 or LUKE 12:15-21 OR LUKE 17:11-19 (RC)

Interpreting the Text

Mark 5:1-20 takes place in Gentile territory (the Decapolis), where Jesus exorcises the Gerasene demoniac. In vv. 18-20, Jesus instructs the exorcised person not to become a part of Jesus' traveling entourage but to remain in the Decapolis and tell other Gentiles "how much [God] has done for you and what mercy [God] has show you." These statements are typically Jewish ways of speaking about God's redeeming work and indicate that the God of Israel will do the same restoring things among the Gentiles that God has done in the Jewish community.

In the background of Luke 12:15-21 (and the larger understanding of poverty, resources, abundance, and keeping covenant with one another that pervades Luke-Acts) is the Jewish idea that material resources are to be used so that all in the community may be free of survival anxiety and can experience blessing. The barn builder violates the community covenant by hoarding resources and denying them to others and, at the great apocalyptic judgment, is condemned. The final line, with its reference to storing up treasures, evokes the Jewish idea that one stores up treasures in heaven (that is, one participates in the realm of God now and in the future) by almsgiving, that is, by providing material resources for the needs of others (for instance, Sir. 29:8-13).

Leprosy, the disease at the center of Luke 17:11-19, was not only a personal health matter but, in the context of antiquity, resulted in social isolation and religious uncleanliness. The healing of the ten lepers thus restores not only their bodies but their social and religious relationships. Jesus tells the ten to show themselves to the priests, where, according to Leviticus 13 and 14, they not only will be examined but will give thanks to God. The Samaritan, of course, had no reason to go to the Jewish temple, and so returned to thank Jesus. Samaritans were first cousins of the Jewish people. While preachers often describe relations between Jews and Samaritans as acrimonious, that was only true occasionally. In our text, a Samaritan leper lived in community with Jewish ones. In any event, the preacher needs to point out that Luke wrongly accuses the nine Jewish lepers of not giving praise to God (vv. 17-18). Likely Luke makes this accusation as a part of the negative caricature of many Jewish people in Luke-Acts that Luke uses to justify the separation between the wider communities of Judaism and Luke's sect of Jesus-followers. The Samaritan is, for Luke, a paradigm of outsiders coming to the God of Israel through provisions made by Jesus Christ. Luke wants the community to welcome such folk.

> THE SAMARITAN IS, FOR LUKE, A PARADIGM OF OUTSIDERS COMING TO THE GOD OF ISRAEL THROUGH PROVISIONS MADE BY JESUS CHRIST. LUKE WANTS THE COMMUNITY TO WELCOME SUCH FOLK.

Responding to the Text

A sermon on Mark 5:18-20 could note that God's gracious actions that lead to thanksgiving create, at the same time, commission for mission. How do members of the congregation experience release from demonic oppression? How can they witness to that release—and invite others to experience it—in their everyday worlds? Gentiles who embrace this witness would surely give thanks to the God of Israel.

The preacher could use Luke 12:15-21 as both a warning and a lure. The passage warns the congregation that those who engage in hoarding and greed face condemnation. While some in the congregation may not believe that a single apocalyptic day of judgment is coming, the preacher could still point to another means of judgment: greed sets in motion patterns of behavior that corrupt and that eventually bring about collapse. Where does the preacher see such greed in the congregation and in the larger world, and how can people repent? Beyond judgment, however, Luke-Acts attempts to lure the congregation into sharing their resources so that all in the community may enjoy the quality of life depicted in Acts 2:41-46 and 4:32-37. What are some practical strategies by which the congregation can engage in such covenantal sharing?

A sermon on Luke 17:11-19 could ask the congregation to identify with the Samaritan. How do we feel like the Samaritan leper—diseased, isolated, religiously unclean? Where do we encounter the restoring power of Jesus and, in consequence, want to give thanks? The preacher might also raise the question, who are Samaritans in our world? How can the congregations today welcome such folk?

Note

1. See Bonnie Bowman Thurston, "The Domestication of Paul," in *Chalice Introduction to the New Testament,* ed. Dennis E. Smith (St. Louis: Chalice Press, 2004), 243–44.

LAST SUNDAY AFTER PENTECOST / REIGN OF CHRIST OR CHRIST THE KING [OR, THE SOVEREIGN RULER]

NOVEMBER 26, 2006
THIRTY-FOURTH SUNDAY IN ORDINARY TIME /
PROPER 29

REVISED COMMON	EPISCOPAL (BCP)	ROMAN CATHOLIC
Dan. 7:9-10, 13-14 or 2 Sam. 23:1-7	Dan. 7:9-14	Dan. 7:13-14
Psalm 93 or Ps. 132:1-12 (13-18)	Psalm 93	Ps. 93:1, 1-2, 5
Rev. 1:4b-8	Rev. 1:1-8	Rev. 1:5-8
John 18:33-37	John 18:33-37 or Mark 11:1-11	John 18:33b-37

FIRST READING

DANIEL 7:9-10, 13-14 (RCL)
DANIEL 7:9-14 (BCP)
DANIEL 7:13-14 (RC)

Interpreting the Text

The discussion of the background of Daniel 7–12 on the Twenty-fourth Sunday after Pentecost stresses that this passage is an apocalypse. Today's passage demonstrates a characteristic element of that literature. The prophet is given a vision in highly figurative language of things that happen in the heavenly world that are prototypes of what will happen on the earth. The vision is intended to encourage a community living in social upheaval, like the one to whom Daniel spoke, to continue in faithful witness even when they are anxious and fearful. The community can live in the present as if the events described in heaven have already come into effect.

Daniel 7:9-14 pictures the transcendent God appointing a heavenly figure described as "like a human being" (or "one like a son of man," as the older versions have it) as ruler, judge, and redeemer of the cosmos. In the larger setting of Daniel 7–12, we learn that while this figure is already sovereign of the cosmos by virtue of being appointed in heaven, the one like a human being will descend to earth in a future apocalypse to put into place the sovereignty that is revealed in heaven. From this perspective, Christians sometimes mistakenly think the phrase "one like a human being" refers to the humanity of this figure, when in fact the figure is of heavenly origin.

Responding to the Text

Christians sometimes think that Dan. 7:13-14 predicted Jesus as an apocalyptic "one like a human being." The preacher could help the congregation recognize that while Daniel did not have Jesus in mind, early followers of Jesus came to believe that Jesus would fulfill the function of the "one like a human being" (for instance, Mark 13:24-27). In any event, the earth still awaits the final apocalyptic manifestation of judgment and redemption.

A sermon could build on the motif of seeing the future of God's sovereign rule, and judgment and redemption, already active in the present (even if not completely fulfilled). Where does the congregation see the sovereignty of God expressed as vividly in world situations today as in Dan. 7:9-14?

The sermon might honestly admit that many people today do not believe a single apocalyptic moment of transformation is ahead. But the vision of Dan. 7:9-14 reminds the congregation that God is relentlessly dissatisfied with the world as it is. Although many Christians today do not expect God to act in a singular apocalyptic moment to end evil and set things right, many of those Christians still believe with ongoing distortions of the divine purposes that God is ever-active to do all that God can do to help the world become more like the realm of God. Where does the preacher see such phenomena in the world today?

> THE SERMON MIGHT HONESTLY ADMIT THAT MANY PEOPLE TODAY DO NOT BELIEVE A SINGLE APOCALYPTIC MOMENT OF TRANSFORMATION IS AHEAD.

2 SAMUEL 23:1-7 (RCL ALT.)

Interpreting the Text

The background of the books of Samuel and Kings given on the Twenty-fourth Sunday after Pentecost is pertinent for understanding this text. In the background is the deuteronomic theology insisting that obedience yields blessing and disobedience brings about curse. The listener, then, is confronted with an oddity in the last words of David. On the one hand, the text indicates that a ruler is to lead the community in the ways of justice. In the deuteronomic theology, the just community is the one that embodies Torah in all its relationships. On the other hand, the reader knows that David himself is deeply flawed and has engaged in profound injustice (for instance, 2 Sam. 11:1—12:14).

The reader knows further that David is mistaken in saying, "Is not my house like this?" (that is, "Are not the members of my family who have ruled Israel just rulers?"). The reader hears this question in the knowledge of the dissipation of the monarchy and the two sovereignties and the fact of the exile, and thinks, "Well, no, David. Neither your family nor our other rulers have fulfilled the deuteronomic ideal, and that is part of the reason we have suffered so much."

Given these facts, one can hear irony in David's insistence that "God has made with me an everlasting covenant" (compare 2 Sam. 7:1-16). Some in the Jewish community may have thought that the everlasting covenant included Davidic rule, but the subsequent events proved otherwise. The disobedience of key rulers contributed to the curse of defeat and exile. That fate should warn readers to be more faithful in leadership and in all aspects of covenantal community.

Responding to the Text

A preacher can certainly hold out David's last words as vision and norm for a leader in the congregation or in the wider world. The primary calling of leaders is to "rule justly," that is, to see that all things that take place in their sphere of influence are truly just. The sermon could examine different arenas of leadership in the church and in other areas of life in North America to ascertain the degree to which such leadership is truly just. The preacher is obliged to help the congregation remember that after David, leaders who practiced idolatry and injustice contributed to the fall first of the Northern territory and then of the Southern.

> THE PRIMARY CALLING OF LEADERS IS TO "RULE JUSTLY," THAT IS, TO SEE THAT ALL THINGS THAT TAKE PLACE IN THEIR SPHERE OF INFLUENCE ARE TRULY JUST.

A minister might also use the story of David in 2 Samuel as a paradigm of assurance to leaders and others in the congregation. The narrators do not flinch in presenting David as deeply flawed. Yet God worked with and through David. Similarly, God can work with and through us, even in our flawed conditions.

David (as described in the text) believed that the Davidic line would rule everlastingly. Today's reader recognizes that David was mistaken, since the monarch's heirs ceased to rule the whole country in only one more generation. However, the preacher might suggest that at a deeper level, the notion of God's everlasting covenant means that God never stops seeking justice, order, and prosperity for all.

RESPONSIVE READING
PSALM 93 (RCL, BCP)
PSALM 93:1, 1-2, 5 (RC)

This enthronement psalm honoring God as absolute sovereign of the universe is especially appropriate for the Reign of Christ. For Christ, according to Christian interpretation, is God's agent in bringing about the final and full apocalyptic manifestation of the divine realm. Although Psalm 93 is not apocalyptic, it reminds the singing community that God created the world by defeating the powers of chaos (represented by the floods in vv. 3-4) and continues as its sovereign. In a sense unanticipated by the psalmist, the psalm proves true. Psalm 93 was likely used at an annual service in the temple at Jerusalem in which the community ritually reenacted God's enthronement, thus rekindling in the community confidence in the divine sovereignty, promises, and commandments in the midst of a world that was often insecure and even malevolent. The choir that sang Psalm 93 evidently believed that the temple would forever be God's house (v. 5b). Yet, while the temple no longer exists, God's purposes continue to reassert themselves in every generation. While the divine aims may not be finally and fully established, they cannot be finally and fully extinguished. The latter theme is especially provocative in view of the Gospel reading for today that presents the crucifixion of Jesus as, in part, an enthronement.

> WHILE THE DIVINE AIMS MAY NOT BE FINALLY AND FULLY ESTABLISHED, THEY CANNOT BE FINALLY AND FULLY EXTINGUISHED.

PSALM 132:1-12 (13-18) (RCL ALT.)

A casual reading could leave the impression that the text simply confirms Zion as the center of Jewish community life and the descendents of David as those who lead the community. However, the language and roles often assigned to the Davidic line are here associated with the priests.[1] Note similar associations in other Second Temple documents such as Zech. 3:6; 6:11-13; and 1 Chron. 17:14; God's clothing the priests with salvation (a designation otherwise used of the monarch) in Ps. 132:16; and the fact that the psalm never explicitly identifies the monarch as "the anointed one." This suggests that the priestly community, who were central figures in the leadership of Israel in the Second Temple period, adapted Davidic traditions to interpret themselves as the legitimate heirs of David. The preacher could lead the congregation in a fascinating exploration of the circumstances in which a community can legitimately reinterpret sacred tradition, especially when the reinterpretation reinforces the social power of the reinterpreters.

REVELATION 1:4b-8 (RCL)
REVELATION 1:1-8 (BCP)
REVELATION 1:5-8 (RC)

Interpreting the Text

On All Saints Day/Sunday, I sketch the historical context to which the book of Revelation was written. The lection for today partakes of the form and function of letters in antiquity by mentioning the sender and recipients (Rev. 1:4a-b), by wishing the recipients grace (1:4c), and by indicating the main theme of the letter, which is expressed as an apocalyptic vision (1:4d-8). In the background of the book of Revelation is contrast between the rule of Caesar over repressive, unjust, imperial Rome and the benevolent rule of God through Christ.

As we see clearly in Rev. 1:4b and 8, the book of Revelation is theocentric. The description of God in vv. 4b and 8 plays on a popular Hellenistic expression for deity, "who is and was and shall be." The substitution of "to come" for "shall be" points to God's actively intervening in history to remake the world into a sphere of blessing. God's agent is Jesus Christ, whose resurrection shows that the apocalyptic transformation is underway. Note that Christ is "the ruler of the [monarchs] of the earth" (1:5).

Christ has already made the community a "sovereign realm" (NRSV "kingdom"); that is, Christ releases aspects of the coming eschatological world into the present. Indeed, the congregations are a priestly presence in the world that mediates the presence of the coming world (Rev. 1:5-6). Beyond present dimensions of eschatological experience, the final apocalypse is ahead: a massive public interruption of history when Jesus appears and when opponents of the divine rule will wail, that is, cry out in fear because they know their condemnation to eternal fire is at hand (1:7; see Rev. 20:7-14).

Responding to the Text

People in the world today are buffeted by leaders and movements of all stripes and from all directions claiming to offer the good life. This passage presents the preacher with an opportunity to help the congregation compare and contrast the rule of God through Christ with other rulers and value systems. Where practices and values outside the church cohere with those of the rule of God, a congregation might make common cause. But when practices and values undermine the rule of God, the preacher needs to help the congregation recognize the difficulty and reject such possibilities.

The preacher can use the text as a powerful encouragement to people who are in situations of limitation and diminution by asserting the sovereignty of Christ over the latter-day Caesars who seek to rule and exploit. These Caesars can assume such forms as human leaders, social ideologies or movements, economic policies, and the like. With only a little reflection, a preacher may recognize people in the church who have a Caesar mentality. Over all who suffer under such self-servants, this text asserts that God through Christ will have the last word, and it is redemptive. The passage (esp. Rev. 1:7) is a warning to all who exploit and otherwise deviate from God's purposes. All are ultimately called to account for the degree to which we participate with (or deny) the divine aims.

Members of congregations frequently come into contact with the popular Left Behind books and movie and with other expressions of popular contemporary apocalypticism. Many members have questions regarding what to believe (and not to believe) concerning eschatology, the end of this world, and divine purposes. The preacher could use the appearance of this passage as an entrée into a comparison and contrast of the Left Behind mentality and the one that is found in the book of Revelation.

WHEN PRACTICES AND VALUES UNDERMINE THE RULE OF GOD, THE PREACHER NEEDS TO HELP THE CONGREGATION RECOGNIZE THE DIFFICULTY AND REJECT SUCH POSSIBILITIES.

THE GOSPEL

JOHN 18:33-37 (RCL, BCP)
JOHN 18:33b-37 (RC)

Interpreting the Text

Commentators identify irony as a major theme of the Fourth Gospel and today's text as one of the places where irony comes to its most vivid expression. Pilate is a representative of the seemingly omnipresent and omnipotent Roman imperial empire and appears to be in charge of the proceedings. Jesus is a prisoner betrayed by one member of his own circle and denied by another, but God is actually in charge. Whereas Pilate demonstrates his limited power (which for John is "of this world") by flexing his muscles, Jesus maintains his position as a prisoner to set the stage so the resurrection can demonstrate that the power behind Jesus is "not of this world" but, indeed, is "from above." The resurrection reveals the difference between Pilate's limited and perverse power and the unrelenting and life-giving power of God.

Irony is already evident in John 18:33-34 when Pilate asks Jesus a question but instead finds that he is being questioned by Jesus. In the first-century context, the term "sovereign of the Jews" was politically loaded; a person could rule over the Jews only by Rome's permission, whereas Jesus had no such authorization. Pilate, therefore, interprets the charge against Jesus as political sedition. Jesus clarifies that the arena of his sovereign rule (NRSV "kingdom") is "not of this world" and that immediate sedition is not Jesus' intent. In 18:37-38, Jesus does not directly answer Pilate's question, "So are you a monarch?" This question and Jesus' response in 18:37b push the reader to ponder the nature of Jesus' sovereignty and the contrast between the rule of Rome and the rule of God; one is false and the other true. Pilate reveals a fatal misunderstanding when the procurator asks, "What is truth?" (18:38a). The reader knows (14:6-7).

One expression deserves special comment: Jesus' declaration that his sovereign rule is "not of this world." Christians often interpret this phrase to refer to a nonmaterial and even nonsocial rule that takes place in the heart of the believer. In the Fourth Gospel, however, it means that Jesus' sovereignty derives not from a power-base in the present world but from God "above." The words "the world" in this Gospel have a negative overtone as they refer to a sphere in which existence takes place without being shaped by God's love and purposes. Jesus comes from God (that is, "not of this world") to reveal God's love and God's provision for abundant life. This sovereign rule—this abundant life—does have a material dimension as we can

> THE WORDS "THE WORLD" IN JOHN'S GOSPEL HAVE A NEGATIVE OVERTONE AS THEY REFER TO A SPHERE IN WHICH EXISTENCE TAKES PLACE WITHOUT BEING SHAPED BY GOD'S LOVE AND PURPOSES.

see from Jesus' signs (such as the raising of Lazarus from the dead—see All Saints Day/Sunday). It is also social in character as we learn from the fact that Jesus' followers form a community that lives according to God's love.

Responding to the Text

The congregation that has been following the readings from Mark with their apocalyptic orientation (especially Mark 13 on the Twenty-fourth Sunday after Pentecost) may expect the text for the Reign of Christ to focus apocalyptically on the Second Coming and may be surprised to hear a scene from trial of Jesus from the Fourth Gospel (with its impulse toward realized eschatology).

Pilate, representing conventional notions of power such as one finds in the mind-set of many government, corporate, military, and other social expressions (including some ecclesiastical ones), thinks that he is in control of existence, whereas, ironically, the prisoner Jesus represents the force that makes abundant life possible. In only a few years (relatively speaking), the Eternal City will be a waste, whereas the way to life eternal will still be open. How can the congregation shape its life so that it embodies the kind of power-through-weakness that is honored today? Where can the preacher point the congregation toward circumstances beyond the congregation where the ironic mode of divine power is offering way, truth, and life abundant to the world today? Those who live under the aegis of the ruling Christ do not strut the streets flexing their muscles and intimidating others but rather give themselves as God gave Christ.

MARK 11:1–11 (BCP ALT.)

Interpreting the Text

This passage plays a significant role in the apocalyptic timeline of the Gospel of Mark (see the Twenty-fourth Sunday after Pentecost). According to Zech. 14:4, the Mount of Olives is the site where the climactic battle will begin between God and the nations that ends the present age, changes the structure of the cosmos, and fully establishes the divine realm. Jesus' entry into Jerusalem from that site reinforces the notion that Jesus is the apocalyptic agent and that the apocalypse is near. Zechariah 9:9-10 depicts a victorious ruler riding into the city on a colt and who, having destroyed the chariots of evil, will now establish an age of peace.

Jesus instructs the disciples to secure a colt in a most unusual way (Mark 11:2-7). When the circumstances unfold just as Jesus said, the reader's confidence in Jesus' authority to predict the future is enhanced. Just as Jesus accurately predicted this event, as well as his death and resurrection, so (the reader reasons) Jesus must be able to predict the events of Mark 13:1-27.

The entry itself invokes the sense of an arriving victor as the spreading of the cloaks is a gesture of welcoming a new ruler (2 Kings 9:13). The waving of the leafy branches recalls the Maccabean revolt of 168–165 B.C.E. when the Jewish people achieved political independence by defeating the forces of Antiochus Epiphanes IV, ruler of the Gentiles who occupied the land (1 Macc. 13:51; 2 Macc. 10:7). The cry "Hosanna" means "Save now." The chant "Blessed is one who comes . . ." is from Ps. 118:25-26. The theme of this psalm, which was used when pilgrims entered the gates of the temple, is thanksgiving for God's delivering an individual when that person cried in distress to God.

The crowd, however, does not fully understand the ministry of Jesus. According to Mark 11:10, the crowd thinks that Jesus is coming to establish Israel as an independent nation as in the days of David. The reader, however, knows that Jesus is superior to David (Mark 12:35-37) and that the "coming realm" is not a repeat of the Maccabean and Davidic achievements but moves through the death and resurrection of Jesus to the apocalyptic end of the old world and the coming of the new.

Responding to the Passage

Because the congregation is accustomed to hearing this passage on Palm/Passion Sunday, the preacher may need to explain why it occurs on the Last Sunday after

Pentecost. Beyond that, the passage invites the congregation to consider ways that we are similar to the crowd in the story by underestimating God's hopes for the world and by not recognizing the means whereby God works. How do we settle for hopes that (like the longing for the independence of Israel in antiquity) are good but that are comparatively parochial when set alongside God's aim to renew every people and the cosmos itself?

The crowd cheers in Mark 11:1-11, but in a few days they turn against Jesus (Mark 15:6-15). They do not recognize that the road to renewal passes through suffering and death, so they reject that road. The reader remembers that faithful disciples, too, will pass through suffering on the way to the apocalypse (Mark 8:34—9:1). The preacher could use the picture of the crowd in Mark as an opportunity to meditate on their willingness to suffer as the powers of present age resist the coming of the realm.

> THE PASSAGE INVITES THE CONGREGATION TO CONSIDER WAYS THAT WE ARE SIMILAR TO THE CROWD IN THE STORY BY UNDERESTIMATING GOD'S HOPES FOR THE WORLD AND BY NOT RECOGNIZING THE MEANS WHEREBY GOD WORKS.

Note

1. Marti Steussy, *Psalms,* Chalice Commentaries for Today (St. Louis: Chalice Press, 2004), 45–56.

APRIL 2006

Sunday	Monday	Tuesday	Wednesday	Thursday	Friday	Saturday
2 5 Lent	3	4	5	6	7	1/8
9 Palm Sunday Passion Sunday	10	11	12	13 Holy Thursday	14 Good Friday	15 Holy Saturday
16 Easter Day	17	18	19	20	21	22
23 2 Easter	24	25	26	27	28	29
30 3 Easter						

MAY 2006

Sunday	Monday	Tuesday	Wednesday	Thursday	Friday	Saturday
	1	2	3	4	5	6
7 4 Easter	8	9	10	11	12	13
14 Mother's Day 5 Easter	15	16	17	18	19	20
21 6 Easter	22	23	24	25 The Ascension of Our Lord	26	27
28 7 Easter	29 Memorial Day	30	31			

JUNE 2006

Sunday	Monday	Tuesday	Wednesday	Thursday	Friday	Saturday
				1	2	3 Vigil of Pentecost
4 Day of Pentecost	5	6	7	8	9	10
11 Trinity Sunday 1 Pentecost	12	13	14	15	16	17
18 Father's Day 2 Pentecost	19	20	21	22	23	24
25 3 Pentecost	26	27	28	29	30	

JULY 2006

Sunday	Monday	Tuesday	Wednesday	Thursday	Friday	Saturday
						1
2 4 Pentecost	3	4 Independence Day	5	6	7	8
9 5 Pentecost	10	11	12	13	14	15
16 6 Pentecost	17	18	19	20	21	22
23 7 Pentecost	24	25	25	27	28	29
30 8 Pentecost	31					

AUGUST 2006

Sunday	Monday	Tuesday	Wednesday	Thursday	Friday	Saturday
		1	2	3	4	5
6	7	8	9	10	11	12
13 9 Pentecost Transfiguration	14	15	16	17	18	19
20 10 Pentecost	21	22	23	24	25	26
27 11 Pentecost	28	29	30	31		
12 Pentecost						

314

SEPTEMBER 2006

Sunday	Monday	Tuesday	Wednesday	Thursday	Friday	Saturday
					1	2
3 13 Pentecost	4 Labor Day	5	6	7	8	9
10 14 Pentecost	11	12	13	14	15	16
17 15 Pentecost	18	19	20	21	22	23
24 16 Pentecost	25	26	27	28	29	30

OCTOBER 2006

Sunday	Monday	Tuesday	Wednesday	Thursday	Friday	Saturday
1 17 Pentecost	2	3	4	5	6	7
8 18 Pentecost	9 Thanksgiving Day (Canada)	10	11	12	13	14
15 19 Pentecost	16	17	18	19	20	21
22 20 Pentecost	23	24	25	26	27	28
29 21 Pentecost Reformation Sunday	30	31				

NOVEMBER 2006

Sunday	Monday	Tuesday	Wednesday	Thursday	Friday	Saturday
			1 All Saints Day	2	3	4
5 22 Pentecost All Saints Sunday	6	7	8	9 Veterans Day	10	11
12 23 Pentecost	13	14	15	16	17	18
19 24 Pentecost	20	21	22	23 Thanksgiving Day	24	25
26 Last Pentecost Christ the King	27	28	29	30